10 0183571 9

D0494466

International Organization in the Modern World

International Organization in the Modern World

The Regional and the Global Process

Paul Taylor

NOTTINGHAM
UNIVERSITY LIBRARY
WITHDRAWN

PINTER
London and New York

PINTER
A Cassell Imprint
Wellington House, 125 Strand, London WC2R 0BB
215 Park Avenue South, New York, New York 10003, USA

First published 1993
Paperback edition first published 1995

© Paul Taylor 1993

Apart from any fair dealing for the purposes of research or private study, or criticism or
review, as permitted under the Copyright, Designs and Patents Act 1988, this publication
may not be reproduced, stored or transmitted, in any form or by any means or process,
without the prior permission in writing of the copyright holders or their agents. Except for
reproduction in accordance with the terms of licences issued by the Copyright Licensing
Agency, photocopying of whole or part of this publication without the prior written
permission of the copyright holders or their agents in single or multiple copies whether for
gain or not is illegal and expressly forbidden. Please direct all enquiries concerning copyright
to the publishers at the address above.

Paul Taylor is hereby identified as the author of this work as provided under Section 77 of
the Copyright, Designs and Patents Act 1988.

British Library Cataloguing-in-Publication Data
A catalogue record for this book is available from the British Library

ISBN 0 86187 111 1 (hardback)
ISBN 1 85567 329 0 (paperback)

1001835719

Typeset by Mayhew Typesetting, Rhayador, Powys
Printed and bound in Great Britain by Biddles Ltd, Guildford and King's Lynn

Contents

Preface   vii

Section 1 – Regionalism and Globalism   1

  1   The concept of regionalism   7

  2   The practice of regionalism   24

Section 2 – The Lessons of the European Community   47

  3   Integration in the European Community in the 1980s and the early 1990s: the new dynamics   49

  4   The limits of European integration: the concepts of consociation and symbiosis   80

Section 3 – The Development of Global Organization   113

  5   The process of reform in the United Nations system: adaptation for efficiency   119

  6   Reforming the system: getting the money to talk in the central system   142

  7   The United Nations system under stress: financial pressures and their consequences   159

Section 4 – Global Organization and the New Agenda   179

  8   Working for global population control   181

  9   The role of the United Nations in global security in the early 1990s: how far forwards?   205

10   Conclusions   250

Index   256

For Frances,
my daughter

Preface

Some years ago a critical reviewer of an article which I had submitted to the journal *International Organization* claimed that there was no general theory of international organization, but only a collection of partial theories. This book is my response to that criticism.

Whatever its achievement it cannot be accused of pursuing modest goals. These are two-fold. First, it sets out to discuss on a comparative basis both regional and global international organization. Normally attention is focused at one or other level, and the other is shunted into a siding to be looked at *en passant*. Second, it attempts to put regional and global international organization into a single, internally consistent theoretical framework. It contains a view of the world which has a place for both regionalism and globalism, and explains them both with reference to an overarching theory.

It is argued that at both levels states remain the primary units in international society. Regional integration, even in the advanced case of the European Community, can be seen as a way of strengthening existing states, not destroying them. But the conditions of their interaction have altered significantly: sovereignty survives as the fundamental principle, but its implications are the result of changing conventions and culture. The book is about the character of that interaction, and the related conventions of international behaviour and the culture which sustains it.

Such are the aims: the achievement will inevitably be less. But theorizing is in any case a dialectical process, and it will be sufficient if this particular product is weighty enough to react against.

It goes without saying that the study is itself a product of innumerable dialectical interactions with the ideas of students and colleagues at the School, and at a large number of conferences throughout the world. Some sections of the book are updated versions of earlier publications. Unless otherwise acknowledged their origins may be traced to chapters in books edited with A.J.R. Groom as follows: *Global Issues in the United Nations Framework*, Macmillan, 1989 (Chapters 5 and 8); *Frameworks for International Cooperation*, Frances Pinter, 1990 (Chapters 1 and 2), and *International Institutions at Work*, Frances Pinter, 1988 (Chapter 6).

Paul Taylor, London School of Economics
May 1992

Section 1
Regionalism and Globalism

Introduction

In this book the development of international organization at two levels is considered – the regional and the global. The conclusion is drawn that regional organization is continuing to develop whilst global arrangements reached a plateau, from which there may well be a further ascent, in the early 1980s.

This pattern of development is described and explained and its implications for international society analysed. In Section 1 the growth of regional integration in the global context is discussed, the factors which support it analysed, and the data concerning its development presented. In Section 2 close attention is given to one example of regional integration, the European Community, in order to deduce lessons from regionalization which may be more widely relevant. In Section 3 specific patterns in the growth of global organizations are discussed and compared with those at the regional level. And in Section 4 the work of global international organizations in two important contexts is considered in order to highlight its impact upon the state compared with that at the regional level.

Throughout the book attention is focused on a fundamental question: how far has the appearance of international organization challenged the sovereignty of the state? Are states under threat or can they adapt to changes in their habitat? The conclusion is that, despite the appearance of schemes for advanced federalism in the European Community, the sovereignty of states has not been challenged fundamentally, and that this has important implications for the progress of regionalization elsewhere. This is not to deny that there have not been changes in the conditions of sovereignty, but these are also detectable, as is shown in Sections 3 and 4, at the global level.

International organization has implications for states and for the pattern of their relations in international society. With a growing regionalism it becomes even more apparent that to generalize about the essential character of international society is a complicated and risky endeavour. Regionalization highlights the problem of deciding how far statements about that character should be qualified in the light of short term exceptions to the rule in the behaviour of states: are such exceptions to be dismissed as anomalies or do they reveal the futility of generalization?

Various key theoretical questions arise when discussing regionalism, particularly if an attempt is made to work within a consistent theoretical framework at the regional and the global level.

For instance, is a process of regional integration among groups of sovereign states capable of fundamentally altering the character of their relations so that they are disposed to peace with each other rather than to war? There have always been alliances and friendships between states, but the traditional reasoning was that these were contingent, and potentially transmutable. The underlying conflictual essence would out! But could things be different?

Where such groupings of states are in relatively durable zones of convergence, integration and common management, it seems perverse to define the general character of their relationship in terms of the unfalsifiable proposition that they might at some future undefined date go to war with each other. Why should a *potential* for war with each other, rather than a long period of *actual* peace and cooperation, be seen as indicative of the essential character of their relations?

Such arguments are about the implications of paradigms for the study of international society, which have been much discussed in the academic literature, and which will not be considered at any length in this study. But applying the paradigms to a comparative study of developments at both the regional and global levels in a single study, which is an unusual enterprise, produces special problems. The liberal-pluralist paradigm appears to lead to a more ambitious view about the potential of regional integration, but transcending the state at that level falls straight into a realist trap: all that happens is that new and larger states emerge.

At the regional level it leads to concern with one or other of the many dimensions of state-building – bringing institutions together or creating an identitive community; but considered at the global level it implies interdependence or transnationalism, which are forms of state dissolution. Indeed interdependence theory has contradictory implications at the regional and the global level: at the regional level it implies a concentration of power, and the placing of functions within common frameworks; whilst at the global level it is concerned with the way in which powers might be disaggregated, and administrations and national interests fragmented by transgovernmental or transnational coalitions.

In other words it is hard to apply liberal pluralism consistently at both the regional and global levels. In fact a more radical view about the way in which regionalism can transform international society is contained within realism itself, and, as this is implicit throughout the following arguments, it needs to be briefly explained here.

What if existing states survive in their regional groupings but become so tied up together that their behaviour is subject to what might be called regional regimes? In this volume it is argued that this is the case in the most prominent example of regional integration – the European Community – and that regionalization in general could be like this. States' policy would be shaped by injunctions upon their behaviour at the regional level – there would be constraints within the region – without allowing the accumulation and direction of a central power in pursuit of goals in foreign policy with regards to outsiders.

But as regime theory implies – which is why it is attractive to those who consider themselves neorealists – states do not cease to be states because they are members of a regime, and their mutual relations stay under the heading of foreign policy. The possibilty of this duality of relationship – long term cooperation as a rational action between entities which retain a potential for separation and conflict – is the major intellectual insight of the theory, and is a position accepted in this book.

This kind of world is, however, capable of being viewed from another kind of realist perspective. The writings of Thomas Hobbes sustain a vision of international society which is arguably quite different from that to which they are usually thought to lead: that there is a perpetual tendency to conflict. An alternative account, developed briefly below, has the great merit that it explains the development of regionalism and the survival of international society in the context of a single internally consistent theory – which seems to be excluded by liberal pluralism and is beyond the reach of the other alternative paradigm, structuralism. In particular, concepts such as consociationalism and symbiosis are more accessible from such a modified realist perspective. These concepts are central to the argument developed in this book, and the reader may wish to turn at an early stage to Chapter 4 where they are discussed.

But from a realist viewpoint the integration process can never lead to a spilling over into a new state. It is true that realism does not *have* to be concerned with states as the basic irreducible political entities, but what necessarily follows from its assumptions is the overwhelming concern of elites to promote the survival of the dominant existing actors, and states are what we have. They may be intensely motivated towards cooperation by realist considerations, but the limits of that must always be short of abandoning their right to a separate existence, a position usually summed up with regard to states by the concept of sovereignty. In other words a federal Europe could not be built on the basis of realist assumptions.

For Hobbes the Leviathan is overwhelmingly concerned with the attainment of internal goals, namely the security of the citizens. What follows from this is not, however, necessarily the result which Hobbes proposed. It is hard to see, in this situation – and given these motives in the sovereign – why there should have to be a tendency towards conflict and war in the international realm. Rather the opposite is the more likely outcome; that there would be a persistent tendency to peace.

Why? To the extent that the sovereigns in the various states succeeded in their task of achieving internal security the opportunities and incentives for war would be reduced for all the others. This is partly a practical matter in that the management of common interests within sovereign states would be bound to be enormously time consuming, and partly because any undue aggression externally would be illogical in Hobbes's own terms, in that it would risk the security of the state which the sovereign was commissioned to defend above all else, and which it would be endangering in other states.

If the other sovereigns succeed in providing security for their people, and the logic of Hobbes's thesis is that they will, then it follows that opportunities for obtaining any advantage from attacking another state will be at a minimum, and risks of damaging the instigator in the process are created with no certainty of gain. To attack other states is irrational in Hobbes's own terms, if the Leviathans are as he says they are.

One of the central assumptions of traditional realism is that states are motivated by the relentless search for power in their mutual relations in order to protect their security. But it is not at all clear that this assumption is an appropriate implication of Hobbes's ideas. The key question is whether there are any limits on this search for power, or whether it is relentless and unlimited.

The answer is in the negative. The sovereign is concerned with the security of its particular state: that is its primary motive. In a company of sovereigns it is reasonable for each to assume that this is the motive of other sovereigns. Within the states individuals come to different conclusions about the others' motives – that they are indeed in mutual conflict – also understanding each other. But each sovereign would be correct, in Hobbes's logic, in assuming that the others would not wish to pursue the relentless increase of power, knowing that such a pursuit would increase the chances of a preemptive strike from other states, thereby challenging the internal security of its own state. The behaviour of the sovereign in the company of sovereigns is the reverse of the behaviour of individuals in society within the state, precisely because of the function of the sovereign, as that is defined by Hobbes.

From these realist assumptions another surprising conclusion follows: the security dilemma, a traditional derivation of allegedly Hobbesian reasoning, turns out to be a *non sequitur*. It holds that states will tend to increase insecurity in international society in attempting to create security for themselves: they will try to establish a preponderance of power, and thus set in train an arms race. But it is illogical in Hobbes's terms to assume that the security dilemma will lead to instability in the balance of power. The opposite is the case.

The sovereign needs to be concerned with power to the extent necessary to defend its own security in the event of another sovereign's failing to preserve the security of its own state, thereby failing as a sovereign, and justifying a rebellion of its subjects. In other words there may be risks which make it prudent to maintain an adequate power. But – again, to stress the logical implications – states would be prudent to maintain power *only* to the extent that they need to protect themselves against a threat arising from *parts* of other states, and to avoid creating that amount of power which would set in train a competitive escalation of power capability.

This indicates the need for an adequate defensive capacity, but does not indicate the relentless and unrestrained pursuit of power, as a threat from the parts is inevitably less than a threat from the whole. Once more the implication is that in the Hobbesian world there will be a tendency towards a stable, and inflexible balance of power, with no need for an overarching sovereign to guarantee contracts.

Another important conclusion follows from this, which again differs from that usually proposed. It is that commerce would be facilitated by the Hobbesian security arrangements, rather than being impeded by them; they would provide a framework of order within which exchange between nations could take place rather than, as is implied, getting in its way.

Why should it be otherwise? If there is peace, even one reinforced by an inflexible balance of power, the aggressive instincts of sovereigns are suitably constrained and there is international order not disorder. The usual realist argument is turned upside down: normal relations between governments in a Hobbesian world support international commerce rather than get in its way. These propositions have the merit that they are more consistent with what Hobbes actually says about arrangements within the state, which is his main achievement, than with what he says about international relations, which is very little.

They also have the merit that they can be applied at the state, the regional and the global levels without any of the inconsistencies in theorizing at the various levels which follow from a liberal-pluralist view of regionalism. The common involvement of a group of highly interconnected states in the outside world, for instance through the European Political Cooperation (EPC) arrangements of the European Community, is also seen as reflecting self-concern, having a certain introspective quality, and tending to be reactive rather than proactive.

Within the regional groupings the greater the involvement of governments in satisfying the wide range of needs for individuals and groups the stronger is the disincentive to pursue high profile foreign policies. Effort is primarily focused upon making the internal regional arrangements work rather than "glorying" externally. The key Hobbesian motive may be given a regional context: the protection of regional security becomes a condition of the protection of the security of the separate member states, a view which fits nicely with the consociation theory developed later in this volume. It is an inner-directed concern, not an outer-directed one.

This stresses that a primary motive for integration is a fear of fragmentation which may encourage a potential threat from outside. Such a purpose is not likely to be conducive towards a "superpower in the making", but it is characteristic of one of the participating states as seen through the reinterpretation of Hobbes attempted here. What is lost is a theory of the absorption of the state within the region; what is gained is a much more radical image of the relationship between regions and international society.

A particular vision of the development of international society can obviously be extracted from the above. It is one of emerging regional groupings of states, of which one, the European Community, is very much ahead of the others, and provides the model of global regionalism. And it is argued that member states lack federal arrangements between themselves, and retain a capacity for defining and pursuing their own foreign policies in relations with other members of the regional group and with non-members. There will, however, be a propensity to act together externally, and to pursue policies lacking in coercive, especially military, threats, in their mutual relations, frequently in the context of arrangements for joint management. There is no assumption of a natural harmony of interests

between states, or between individuals, nor is there any assumption that the
state will disappear. In fact in a world of new states, and emerging regional
organization, the evidence that this has not happened in the most advanced
case, the European Community, is of great importance as a condition of
further regionalization.

Theorizing in the social sciences usually contains prescriptive, as well as
explanatory and predictive elements. Theorizing about European integration
as a form of realism makes it easier for the European model to be emulated
elsewhere. In new states, or even reformed ones, as in the southern tier of
Western Europe, a new sovereignty is not to be absorbed easily in the larger
sovereignty of a regional federation. State-building, in Africa, Asia and
elsewhere, must also be reconciled with regionalization. But advanced
regional integration is compatible with the survival of the existing sovereign
states, and this is an encouragement to states elsewhere to regionalize
without risk. It is a point which has considerable political importance.

These arguments help to clarify the structure of the book, which may
now be restated. As a first step it is necessary to examine the factors that
push towards the strengthening of regional arrangements, and in the rest of
this section the general arguments in favour of this are considered. In the
next chapter the evidence about emerging regional arrangements is
considered. In Section 2 the pressures towards integration in the most
advanced example of regional integration to date, the European
Community, are first considered, and then the limits of regional integration
are examined. In Sections 3 and 4 parallel arguments at the global level are
explored. But in Section 4 it is also shown that the pursuit of the global
agenda, which may appear logically to require a supranational approach,
also needs in practice to be reconciled with state-building among new states.

The theoretical implications of regional developments for global organization are further considered in the second half of Chapter 2 and in the
Introductions to Sections 3 and 4. Consociationalism, which, as stated
earlier, is a key concept in the development of the argument, is discussed
in Chapter 4. The reader who wishes to acquire a sense of the overall argument of the book, without reading the more detailed empirical chapters at
this stage, should move directly to these later accounts. Indeed the introductions to each of the four sections, and the conclusions in Chapter 10, could
be read in succession to discover the bones of the overall argument.

1 The concept of regionalism

There are, of course, a large number of views about the definition of regionalism.[1] A selection has to be made. One recurrent theme, however, is a concern with that particular scale of geographical area which is best fitted to the performance of tasks judged crucial for the welfare of individuals, or for the advantage of governments. That area may extend beyond the boundaries of existing states, or be a part of their territory, or even be coterminous with their frontiers. But what is stressed in this definition of regionalism is a concern with finding that area in which a function might be most efficiently performed and because of this it is a utilitarian concept. Regionalism may, therefore, be seen as part of a strategy for the focusing of popular loyalties upon the institutions, symbols or even, what have been called, the icons of the larger area, but it does not necessarily do so. The territory is also seen as not necessarily being the best for the performance of individual tasks, but rather it reflects a compromise: it is that single space which has been judged suitable for the attainment of a range of tasks, and it may be more or less appropriate for any one of them. In some sense, therefore, there is a general competence within the region as a whole. This means that regionalism is seen as being necessarily multi-dimensional.

This definition of regionalism may be sharpened by considering those concepts with which it may usefully be contrasted. First, there are forms of nationalism which insist that the criterion of utility should always come second to the criterion of demarcating and strengthening the nation.[2] In a nation state which had such an ideology transnational arrangements within regions would be rejected even at considerable cost in terms of the welfare of individuals. This is not to deny that there are occasions when the region can be reasonably judged to coincide with the boundaries of the state, or that nation states with different ideologies might not find regional arrangements congenial. Second, certain forms of "one-world" doctrine stand in opposition to regionalism. These are those which involve a view of the organic unity of space-ship earth which in their implications are an equivalent at the global level of exclusive nationalism at the level of the state: to allow any intermediate level of competence is seen as permitting an unacceptable compromise with the integrity of the essential whole.[3]

A third alternative to regionalism is a group of approaches which can be put under the general heading of sectoralism. These are concerned with individual problems and hold that they can be solved in their own terms. In its more explicit forms, as with Mitrany's functionalism, the idea that problems can be isolated or contained in some way is fundamental.[4] It is the individual problem, in this case identified as a function, which suggests the manner of its solution and the geographical area within which this is to be attempted. As Groom, Burton and others have pointed out the geographical areas of responsibility of the various institutions in the functionalist world are not seen as being coextensive, though they overlap in the manner of a cobweb, and the approach rejects the idea that they should be adjusted so that they might be tackled together by a single institution with a general competence in a single territory.[5] Regionalism and functionalism are, therefore, opposing doctrines, which was one of the reasons for Mitrany's opposition to the emergence of the EEC, in contrast to the ECSC.

But sectoralism may be revealed in other approaches. Whenever problem-solving assumes the primacy of the solution of the particular problem above attainment of satisfactory solutions to the range of interrelated problems in a particular territory it may be judged as being sectoralist. Hence there is a case for saying that in the United Nations system the Specialized Agencies have sometimes taken a sectoral approach in that they have concentrated upon problems in their individual fields of competence at the expense of coordinated programmes (see Chapter 5 below). As Robert Cox argued, the academic approach known as problem-solving (sometimes called puzzle-solving) has also shown a tendency to be concerned with narrowly defined specific issues at the expense of a concern with the validity of the whole.[6] At one extreme, therefore, are those who seemed to be concerned only with the global "whole" seen in the longer term – the short term concerns of the lesser "wholes" could be sacrificed to this;[7] whilst, at the other extreme, it has sometimes been implied that even the unique individual was better seen, not as a single, but as several actors, which could have varied and inconsistent characters, depending upon the needs or interests being pursued. Even the individual personality could be sectoralized![8] Sectoralism may, therefore, be found in approaches other than functionalism which is, however, one where it is particularly stressed.

Each of these alternatives to regionalism has an extreme form – the exclusive nation state or the organic globe – which are hard to reconcile with the regional approach. Each has, however, a more moderate expression which allows compromise. After all, involvement in regional arrangements has frequently served the interests of the nation state; and the global community can be interpreted as relying upon a regional substructure. There is a considerable literature upon these themes.[9] Sectoralism has, however, emerged as the major theoretical and practical alternative to regionalism. It follows that if the sectoral approach could be shown to be flawed then this would have major implications for regionalism. Any defence of the one must also involve an attack on the other.

A reconsideration of regionalism must begin with a discussion of the reasons for the decline in the frequency of writings on that subject since the mid-1970s. What seems to have happened is that the consideration of regionalism as a general phenomenon or as a political doctrine became unfashionable and regionalism in this sense was replaced with studies of the operation of particular policies in the various areas of the world. In other words at the local level there were area studies, and policy studies, but little or no regionalism.

It is, however, essential to realize that the literature on regionalism covers a very wide range. At least five categories may be detected. First is writing which focuses upon the development and application of various indicators of regionalism. These may be seen as measures of the consequences of the practice of regionalism as defined earlier in this chapter. The question is asked of the sense in which international regions exist: how far do economic, social, cultural and political dimensions coincide? The classic book which discussed questions of this type was that by Bruce Russett first published in 1967, and reissued in 1976.[10] He was concerned to discover the degree to which regions showed "social and cultural homogeneity . . . with respect to several kinds of internal attributes"; how far regions shared political attitudes or external behaviour, for instance, in voting in the United Nations; the degree of political interdependence as revealed by joint membership in supranational or intergovernmental political institutions; and the extent of economic interdependence, "as identified by intraregional trade as a proportion of the national income".[11]

Unfortunately this work, which used a highly sophisticated quantitative methodology, was also one of the reasons for the decline of interest in the subject. Russett concluded that he had been largely correct in his expectation that "the degree of congruence among the clusters produced inductively by the various criteria would be relatively low: that is, the socio-cultural groupings would not closely resemble the political groupings, nor the trade groupings etc." He added that "there is no region or aggregate of national units that can in the very strict sense of boundary congruence be identified as a subsystem of the international system . . . such a subsystem must be identified empirically by the agreement of several different criteria."[12] In other words regional groupings showed no particular signs of acting together in the international system. From the point of view of the study of regionalism it was all pretty depressing.

A second type of writing on regionalism was concerned with describing the dynamics of integration. In the terms of the definition of regionalism suggested here the question was put of what factors would tend to increase a propensity to tackle problems at the regional level. Whereas Russett sought to apply measures at particular points, other writers, particulary those who came to be called the Neofunctionalists, sought to explain how the measures of regional integration were altered.[13] Hence they developed dynamic variables such as "spill over". It is not necessary to discuss this very considerable literature in this chapter, but it should be pointed out that it also became unfashionable in the 1970s. The main reason for this was probably that it appeared to have failed to predict successfully the development of regional integration in Western Europe. The leading neofunctionalist, Ernst B. Haas, somewhat self-consciously signalled the "obsolescence of regional integration theory" in 1976, though there were many who thought that in this he was somewhat premature.[14] Indeed, after the mid-1980s, as is shown in Chapter 3, it acquired a new relevance.

A third style sought to explain regionalism primarily in terms of the motives of the political elites who participated in the process. What in their view were the costs and benefits of regional organization? Involvement could be the result of growing popular support for regional integration. Alternatively it could represent attempts to bring about specific improvements, such as a better economy, or the leaders' concern with milieu goals, such as improving the channels of communication with other governments in the region or speaking more directly to the peoples of neighbouring countries; or leaders might seek to develop regional institutions because they were a way of enhancing status as a regional power. Such arguments were to be found in a study published in 1972 by Joseph Nye who noted that, despite the ambiguity of Russett's conclusions about the indicators of regionalism, it had been clear from his evidence that regional intergovernmental organizations had continued to increase in number, and nongovernmental organizations had increased even faster.[15] Between 1957 and 1963 international nongovernmental organizations of the regional type had increased some five times as rapidly as other nongovernmental organizations. These developments needed to be explained.

He agreed that "there will continue to be strong incentives for elites to create and use regional organizations". Moreover,

if the demand for indentity should lead to widespread dissatisfaction with existing nation-states and the development of strong regional attitudes, the technological changes that are reducing – but not eliminating – the importance of proximity could lead statesmen to support more effective regional institutions. If identitive demands are not intense at the regional level, it seems more likely that technological changes will lead in the direction of functional type organizations.[16]

On balance, however, the conclusions were that it was unlikely that the level of regional integration would continue to increase, in the sense that there would be a transfer of powers to the regional centre, and that it was more probable that an equilibrium would be found at which the regional attainment would be fairly modest. The main reason for this was that there were costs as well as advantages in further regional involvement: most leaders would not want the limitations on freedom of action which would begin to increase with the strengthening of regional institutions. Hence

. . . under the current structure of international incentives most political decision-makers will find some point of equilibrium at which they would rather tolerate the inconvenience of the existing level of process forces (i.e. instability producing pressures in the more open international system) than incur the greater political costs of full integration or disintegration. . . . a rapid transformation as the result of existing integration processes is unlikely.[17]

Despite his recognition of an increase in the quantity of regional organization the balance of Nye's argument was, therefore, that it was unlikely that new political actors were in the making. There were good reasons for the ambiguity of Russett's evidence about the increased importance of regional systems. Rather states would balance involvement within the region with continuing high levels of autonomous contact outside it, and the net effect would be to preserve the existing character of the international system. These judgements reinforced arguments developed in 1968 in an article by Oran Young on "Political Discontinuities in the International System". He pointed to an emerging pattern of linkages between the various regions of the world which would focus leaders' attention upon extra-regional interests and activities.[18] But the point should also be stressed that Nye seemed to interpret regional organization as suggesting the conditional involvement by governments in a series of local arrangements with one or more contiguous states. This amounts to local sectoralism rather than regionalism in the sense in which this is understood in this chapter, of englobing most dimensions. His image was not of a world in which there were specific territories in which contiguous states increasingly acted together – a question mark in this regard was even put against the European Community: the question of whether or not states were prepared to accept an increase in the powers of common institutions was addressed – and answered in the negative. The conclusion could be drawn from both of these studies that all in all there was now not much in the evidence on regionalism to interest students of international society.

A fourth style of writing about regionalism was concerned with prediction and prescription and may be differentiated according to the weight given to each. What should, and what would happen to the level of cooperation? The literature in which the element of prescription predominated was frequently derived from the view that globalism inevitably involved exploitative relations between North and South and that, therefore, the various regions in the South should be encouraged to develop stronger relations economically and politically among themselves.[19] Dependency theory was of course one of the main sources of such recommendations. It may also be found, however, in the work of those who were not so self-consciously structuralist, such as Rajni Kothari. The flavour of the product may be indicated in his recommendation that

there is need for much greater regional cooperation among the various small and weak countries of the world, pooling their economic political and military resources, entering the world power structure on that basis, and ultimately upsetting the system through which a handful of states are able to dominate the world.[20]

The stress here was upon what ought to motivate regional leaders in their own interest and that of their subjects rather than upon what had in fact motivated them.

A somewhat different kind of prescription and a greater concern with prediction was to be found in the 1985 Bertrand Report, which is one exception to the earlier observation that no significant writing about regionalism as a general phenomenon had been produced since the mid-1970s.[21] Being himself a scholarly insider – a member of the United Nations Joint Inspection Unit – Bertrand was probably unaware that regionalism had become unfashionable among the academic community. For all its merits it was unlikely to have been produced in the mid-1980s by a student of international relations in the universities in either Europe or the US, because of the climate of opinion about regionalism among the academic specialists.

Bertrand condemned the existing United Nations development arrangements with their tendency to what he called, "sectoral functionalism", and their "remote control by staff members living in the greater capitals"[22] in favour of stronger, better defined regional arrangements. What was needed was the development of a "third generation of world organisation" which transferred significant responsibility for economic development to the regional level.[23] There should be an attempt to turn the United Nations into a "centre for negotiations designed to identify and develop zones of convergence", which would be regions in Africa, Latin America and so on. As the sectoral approach, represented in the established division of labour among the Specialized Agencies, had become

altogether inappropriate for a problem which calls for an integrated approach and organised cooperation by all the parties concerned . . . the only possible structural response lies in the organisation of integrated systems of cooperation at the regional level.[24]

A greater concern with prediction, and, indeed, description, when compared with the previous approach, was reflected in Bertrand's awareness of the continued growth of regional arrangements. They had however become too numerous – there were around 280 of them – and they were irrationally organized.[25] They needed to be related to new structures which should include

an organ representing the governments of the countries of the region, another body on which outside countries contributing to the development of the region would be represented, and finally a joint council or commission to carry out the plans negotiated and adopted.

A fundamental reorganization of the United Nations was necessary in which new regional Development Agencies would take over the "resources, duties and staff of the present operational agencies, UNDP, WFP, UNFPA, UNICEF, etc",[26] whilst central institutions would be left with the research and overall supervisory functions. At the same time it was necessary to strengthen the representation of the various new regional groupings in the central institutions of the United Nations such as the Economic and Social Council. The reader will not be surprised to learn that the Bertrand prescriptions were generally greeted with a marked absence of enthusiasm in the community of international civil servants, though his diagnosis of the problems in the economic and social arrangements of the United Nations was widely welcomed. Their reception in the academic community was enthusiastic with regard to the diagnosis but also contentious as regards the practical implications of the proposals.

Bertrand's arguments, though they favoured the radical alteration of the existing arrangements of the United Nations system, were, however, in many ways reminiscent of a train of argument which was very evident when the United Nations was established. This held that regional arrangements regarding defence and economic and social questions should be encouraged, if, in Burton's words, they were associative between those with common interests, and were not dissociative in that they created new divisions in international society. An associative security arrangement would concern the maintenance of security as between members whilst a dissociative one would be directed against outsiders. One advantage of this development would be to relieve the central system of a burden of administration and responsibility, in security and other matters, which would otherwise become excessive. Associative arrangements would lessen that burden, whilst dissociative arrangements, such as the two great alliance systems which emerged in the forties and fifties, would have the opposite effect. Burton pointed out, however, that it was unfortunate that the government representatives at San Francisco and Dumbarton Oaks had not clearly asserted the associative version of regionalism.[27]

A fifth category of writing upon regionalism completes the list. Roger Masters' article on a multi-bloc model of the international system may be taken as illustrative of this style.[28] It accepted the possibility that regions might emerge more clearly without examining in much detail the evidence for this, and without specifying any indicators of regionalism; nor was it explicitly prescriptive though it is arguable that such a concern was implicit. Rather it focused upon the implications for the international system if regions *were* to emerge more clearly, and considered such questions as how far general security and stability would be affected by such developments. Masters drew upon Kaplan's work on "system and process" in international politics and also upon the theory of oligopoly, and used rigorous a priori reasoning in its specification of assumptions and in the logical development of its arguments. It is not necessary to discuss these in detail here. The conclusions were, however, encouraging from the point of view of those who might support regionalism for other reasons. Masters concluded that a multi-bloc world, one which in effect contained stronger regions, would possess significant stability-inducing elements. In other words there was no reason to fear such developments, and some grounds for supporting them, as they could make international society more stable and peaceable. Once again, however, the reader will not be surprised to learn that Masters' outstanding article was not from the academe of the eighties: it dates from 1961.

A number of questions emerge from the preceding discussion. That writing on regionalism entered into a period of decline in the late 1970s has been established and some of the reasons for this have been discussed. But academic writing in the field of international relations, as elsewhere in the social sciences, is capable of setting a mode of thinking which becomes partly detached from the real world. It sets a fashion on occasions which is in itself an impediment in the way of an academic response to developments in the evidence. It is certainly the case that Russett's book attracted such a barrage of criticism in the academic journals as would be likely to deter for a while all but the most intrepid or foolhardy of scholars. This was mainly because of the cumbersome methodology but also because of the negative findings: that there were no multi-dimensional regions to be found.

Nevertheless after a decade it is perhaps time to challenge the fashion and to ask whether the real world has changed. What is the evidence on the practice of regionalism at the beginning of the 1990s? Does it still support the judgements of those who wrote in the early 1970s? If it is found that the world has indeed become more sharply demarcated in regional terms how is this to be explained? On the face of it the evidence would seem to be overwhelmingly in support of the proposition that it had. All over the world there is a tendency for states to be more involved in regional arrangements and the argument that they were safe as free members of the international system has become progressively less convincing to their own governments. Hence in Europe all the states on the periphery of the Community were moving towards membership in the early 1990s. Even ten years earlier it would have seemed impossible that the Swedes and the Swiss would have so compromised their neutrality. But similar tendencies were observable elsewhere in the developed and the developing worlds, North America, Africa, and Asia alike. An explanation is therefore called for.

*

The empirical evidence at the global level is considered in the next chapter, but at this point a general explanation is proposed: there are underlying reasons why regionalism has become more prevalent, though its increasing visibility is probably attributable to changing academic interests as revealed in the literature discussed above.

There are three different dimensions of regional space, and distinct arguments about the tendency to regionalism are suggested by each dimension. These will now be tackled in turn. They are: area (the region exists as a plane, or surface, more usually in international relations referred to as territory); contiguity (the area may be fragmented or unitary, its parts immediately proximate to each other or remote); and size (each has a given extent, and there may be arguments about whether the region should be larger or smaller, or local, intermediate or global). It should be noted that these dimensions though related, are analytically distinct: size may vary, the tasks may be organized according to a functional need, rather than within an area; and an area may be regarded for some purposes as a unit, though its parts are distinct and widely dispersed.

It should be stressed that economic, and administrative/technical criteria are the focus here: the following discussion rests upon an idealized view of a process of the rational planning, management and execution of projects and programmes, through national and international institutions. The first phase is one in which the tasks are identified, the scale of resources evaluated, research into technical aspects carried out, and a mandate agreed for the appropriate organization. A crucial part of this phase should be that of reconciling the scale of resources allocated with the needs identified, a process which typically involves negotiation, and the "confrontation of policies" of the providers and the recipients: if successful, an agreed programme is the outcome. A second stage is the "operational" one: technical assistance may be called for, the details of projects made specific, and the actual implementation of the programme begun. The third involves supervising and relating achievement at any moment to the goal which is to be obtained so that necessary adjustments in management or resources can be made: the impact of the operation is studied, reports of progress are delivered to those with overall responsibility, and the immediate tasks are altered in the light of experience to serve the overall purpose. It is this phase of the process which has seemed by observers such as Bertrand to be a major source of the ineffectiveness of the United Nations economic and social arrangements. The sectoral arrangements have been pursued by too narrowly based organizations without much regard on a day-to-day basis for any *general* purpose.

The process of rationally planning and executing a progamme – hereafter referred to as the rational process – can be described without any necessary reference to regional space in any of its dimensions. The next step in the argument is, therefore, to establish such links. In the first place the necessity for the dimension of area is to be discussed.

A single sector can be subjected to the rational process only if it is regarded as an end in itself, and is not related to the need to achieve an integrated programme in an area about which a prior decision has been made. This is a crucial point in functionalism: the area is to be determined by the dimensions of the particular task. The possibility is therefore raised that the integrated character of the various needs of individual human beings will be at odds with the requirement that each individual task should be tackled in its own space. For some individuals these different spaces may completely overlap, but at the interstices this may not be the case. Hence two problems are likely to arise in a single sector approach. First the third phase of the rational process is difficult to carry out satisfactorily with reference solely to intra-sector criteria: evaluation and monitoring usually require trans-sector comparisons and contextual evaluations. For example, a sectoral project which focused, say, upon providing or maintaining proper housing has inevitably to be evaluated by reference to a wide range of other sectors of activity such as transport, communications, available employment for inhabitants, and other facilities. Similarly an industrial policy can only be effective if considered in the context of policies such as transport, training, and housing. Very few functions are not dependent upon a wide range of others for their successful implementation, and it follows that the individual function cannot be monitored in a satisfactory way in isolation. The explanation of this is probably a more superficial manifestation of the integrated character of individual human needs, that no function is an end in itself.

Second, however, the fact that new tasks continually appear makes it essential to obtain the effective coordination of the work of existing organizations in order to succeed with the new purpose. It is not possible to start with, as it were, a clean administrative slate. Rather it is in the nature of things that what has to be done is to alter and build upon existing arrangements. Once again, therefore, the tendency is for a number of functions to be dealt with together rather than separately, those that reflect the functions of the earlier organizations and those which have more recently become evident. In the United Nations system, for instance, there are a large number of examples of new tasks appearing which had simply not been anticipated when the Specialized Agencies were established. Existing administrations dealing with identified problems were forced to deal with each other in order to tackle new problems which overlapped their various spheres of competence. Hence the Funds and Programmes were set up which were intended to cover, however imperfectly, some of the functional gaps between the Specialized Agencies. This explains in large part the creation of UNDP, UNFPA, and UNICEF.[29] UNFPA, for instance, needed to work with UNESCO, WHO and the World Bank in developing a number of population control programmes after the mid-1970s when the goal of population control was widely accepted.[30] In other words, once again there were considerable pressures towards establishing integrated programmes, rather than dealing with individual sectors, which derived from the fact that it was necessary to have coordination.

What is striking though is that both effective coordination and the satisfaction of the range of integrated needs of individual human beings are more likely to be attained if a prior decision has been taken about the appropriate determinate space; that is that some notion of a single area in which these things are to be done together is needed, as distinct from trying to find that space which would be best for the individual function. The felt-need sectors cannot provide trans-sectoral evaluative criteria precisely because they do not necessarily overlap. The lack of a natural coextensiveness amongst sectors, seen as a virtue of functionalism, which is discussed further below, in fact becomes a major difficulty in the way of effectively implementing integrated programmes. The question always has to be put of precisely where this or that programme is to be, or has been, achieved. A programme has to be about a specific territory. Similarly any notion of coordination demands a clear spatial reference: it is impossible to evaluate the extent to which there has been or has not been effective coordination without referring to a particular space.

If the above argument is accepted significant progress in the defence of regionalism against sectoralism has already been made. But the determined sectoralist might argue further that the territory within which functions are organized does not have to be contiguous: the argument about the necessity of space can be accepted without conceding that regionalism as defined in this chapter is necessary.

Significant costs do, however, arise if the territory is not contiguous and there are three ways in which these are produced. First, effective administration and decision-making is dependent upon what has been called by Krasner, and others, regimes.[31] These include sets of principles, norms, rules and values, which are frequently unstated, but which guide and facilitate decision-making. They constitute "injunctions on behaviour of greater or lesser degrees of specificity", a tool box of established practices, which are generally accepted among those involved in a regime; their existence helps to maintain cooperation between members by, for instance, allowing decisions about new problems in the areas in which they have already emerged to be made more quickly than would otherwise have been the case, and by encouraging actors to accept short term costs in order to increase their chances of long term benefit. They exist in addition to, and apart from, the formal stated laws and regulations of a society. There is, of course, a lot more to regimes than this, but it is only necessary here to suggest that they are a useful, and probably essential adjunct of effective decision-making, not only among, but also within states.

Large communities of people having similar principles, norms, rules and values are more likely to emerge in a contiguous territory, than in areas that are remote from each other. The regime may be rooted in compatible cultural values: it is not necessarily an aspect of socio-psychological community, but is stronger if this is the case, and if a territory is contiguous, and the people within it are, therefore, proximate, time and opportunity for the growth of such values are more likely to be available. It is itself a reflection of the unfashionable character of regionalism that this point has not been made in the literature on regimes. Conversely, dispersal is likely, over time, sooner or later, to lead to a weakening of common culture, and beyond that to the erosion of regimes. One reason for this is that despite modern technology communication over longer distances remains more difficult and slower than over shorter distances. In illustration of this point it is only necessary to think of the Commonwealth, where despite a surprising durability, regimes have nevertheless been weakened, compared with the European Community, where they have been strengthened. A British observer might be tempted to assert that the cultures of say, New Zealand, Australia, and Britain had remained similar. But the point is that they have steadily become less so, and those of Britain and her European neighbours have moved closer together. One reason for this is that the level of transactions with Europe in comparison with the old Commonwealth has greatly increased.

It is striking that it is not simply a matter of deciding to do something, and creating a regime, but rather that a regime appears over a period of time as a result of the pursuit of common activities; as a consequence, however, the common activities are sustained. In the European Community the increasing level of integration supported the gradual consolidation of regimes; practical cooperation in turn encouraged the development of an underpinning of common values. Whilst it would be foolish to assert that regimes always arrive in regions, it is, nevertheless, the case that once a significant range of common practice and a supporting array of regimes have appeared, it is more likely that these will survive and expand in a contiguous territory than in a dispersed one. The attempts by the larger local states to establish themselves as regional powers may, of course, also be part of a process of consolidating regimes at the regional level. In the parlance of regime theory they may be seen as regional hegemons.

A second advantage of contiguity is that it avoids a wide range of transaction costs which arise if the territory is dispersed. Communication systems are in this case likely to be more expensive, despite the reduction in costs which have resulted from more advanced technology; indeed the

significance of this development as a factor which would reduce significantly the advantages of proximity was overestimated by many in the
1960s. But non-contiguity is also likely to increase the costs deriving from
greater uncertainty about political and economic circumstances; and the
movement of goods, and people, is also likely to incur financial penalties
and to run into a greater range of physical barriers. Third, contiguity is
desirable because it facilitates the internalization of the market: it is easier
to introduce a single market and the necessary supporting arrangements in
adjacent territories and to encourage business enterprises to conduct their
activities in those territories in ways which are similar to those within the
participating domestic economies. For instance the problems in creating and
managing arrangements for a liberal capital market or a monetary union
among non-adjacent territories are much greater than where such territories
are contiguous. If a common market is to survive and develop such
arrangements are, however, necessary.

For a number of reasons, therefore, the attempt to meet the major
welfare needs of individuals should not be exclusively through narrowly
defined sectoral activities, but more through integrated programmes located
on a particular and contiguous space. At this stage, however, a crucial
question has not yet been addressed: whether from the technical point of
view a judgement can be made about the appropriate dimensions of that
territory. A first reaction might be to say that the larger the territory the
better, and that the best integrated programme, the one in which the
maximum effectiveness would be reached, would be at the global level
when every function, no doubt with the aid of giant computers, could be
related to every other function. But obviously the technical and
administrative problems involved in carrying out global integrated
programmes would be overwhelming, and cross-sector monitoring at that
level would be daunting. A second reaction should be perhaps to distinguish
between the research and planning, and resource gathering phase on the one
hand, and the operational and monitoring phase on the other. It cannot be
denied that there are indeed global issues and a real need for research into
the problems of "space-ship" earth such as those of the Club of Rome.[32]
These are in the first category. But when it comes to the operational side,
as Bertrand has pointed out, there are stronger reasons for moving from the
global to some other lower level.[33] Very little has been written, however
about the question of how the optimum scale of that lower level might be
judged. This is not to say that if it could be done it would overwhelm the
more obvious considerations such as identitive, political or security factors;
but it would enter into the argument as a normative element and exert a
continuing pressure.

What technical considerations might be reasonably taken into account
when making a judgement about whether the size of a particular region is
appropriate? This question is put at this stage in the argument not in order
to demonstrate that this or that size is best in Africa, Europe or elsewhere,
but rather to list arguments which seem to be relevant. There are three
kinds of criterion: administrative, economic and functional, which will be
discussed briefly. A judgement about the most appropriate size of the

territory follows from the observation that larger territories generally require larger administrations for given sectors or integrated programmes, which are more remote from their operation, whilst smaller territories require smaller administrations, which tend to be more immediately involved. This remark may appear to be somewhat banal but it nevertheless sums up a sentiment that often drives movements for regional devolution within countries, and may equally sustain an interest in larger regions: on the one hand people may be more closely involved and the administration more responsive to their needs, and on the other the administration may have greater capacity and reflect larger interests. Yet large administrations are more likely to be inflexible and slow to adjust in response to changes in local circumstances. They are more likely to be subject to bureaucratic politics, that is, more given to organizational survival and expansion rather than to the setting up and efficient conduct of operations. They may, however, have the benefit of more sophisticated research programmes, and be more capable of developing a well-informed expert overview of particular problems at a higher level. Local administrations, on the other hand may be too small to generate, or respond to advanced research, and they may operate on a scale which is too small for the effective management of an integrated programme.

Small size may also be associated with inefficiency where there is a duplication of administrative provision in the same sector in adjacent areas and an inability to coordinate at that level among sectors. The ideal level of adminstration, and the ideal scale of territory, is, therefore, self-evident: big enough to play a useful role in development programmes and research, even though the activities of several administrations which perform satisfactorily in these respects may need to be coordinated by another administration at a higher level; adequate for the management of integrated programmes, but small enough to be responsive to changes in local circumstances; big enough for the efficient use of available resources, but small enough not to waste them in excessive bureaucratization.

Economic criteria also give general indications of optimum size. One complication in this context is, however, that economic criteria may be concerned with an infrastructure, which can be defined in a wider sense as including not only tangibles, such as transport facilities and power stations, but also the range of regulations and laws about economic conduct; or they may be concerned with performance, which is more a matter of the energy, skills and attitudes of the people who inhabit that infrastructure. A regional space which is the right size to create an adequate infrastructure is no guarantee of an adequate performance.

Two kinds of economic criterion affect judgements about the minimum size of the regional space. There are, first, productivity criteria: the range of goods, both consumer and capital, should be reasonably comprehensive in terms of the standards of a modernized economy: the variety of locational and geographical circumstances in the space should be sufficient to permit a wide range of specialization. These are some of the conditions which are assumed in the theory of economic integration developed by Meade, Viner et al.[34] and they are also stated on page 31. What they imply in basic terms is that the region should be big enough, rich enough and varied enough to provide for an adequate standard of living for its inhabitants without undue dependence on outsiders: this is not, however, to reject interdependence but rather to point to the need to place some limit upon the vulnerability to other states which it creates.[35] This is a crude political fact based on economic criteria which could shape a judgement about whether a particular region had an appropriate size.

A second kind of economic criterion of size may be called a performance criterion. There are certain activities which for technical reasons, and/or for reasons of social convention, are not performed adequately if a facility is below a certain size. Again the need for a certain level of performance indicates a need for a certain scale of territory. Sometimes this may be a fairly straightforward matter, as with transport systems: it is obviously unsatisfactory if a railway network is confined within a minute territory, and desirable to integrate it with other modes of transport in a larger one. Sometimes, however, the scale of territory is indicated more by the requirement, based on values and conventions, that a particular standard of performance is mandatory, as is the case with regard to, say, health provision: the problem of finding the resources to pay for this may be eased if the size of a territory is increased. Again the notion stands out that there can be a scale of territory which is optimal for this purpose. Indeed experience suggests that a wide range of provision cannot be sustained in the long term in a small region. Advanced research, in medicine and other matters, simply cannot be afforded within "small" state finance; it needs sustenance from larger economic units which can only exist if they can operate within a larger space.

Of course it is possible for a unit in a smaller territory to obtain special assistance from outsiders, or to be larger than could be financed solely from that small territory because it in practice provided for and was supported by a larger functionally specific region. But in both of these cases the support will be perceived by insiders as being less reliable than if the support base were internalized. In justification of this view is the less secure legal underpinning of external support, and its relative insulation from domestic political instruction. This was a persuasive argument in favour of the EEC in the sense that it was argued that research in general could be supported more fully and at a more advanced level in the larger market. It might be argued that there are multinational companies which can afford such provision and that these are often global in scope. On the other hand they have established themselves in reasonable numbers in the Community precisely because of the size of that market, compared with others around it. They would have been far less enthusiastic about this if the dominant markets were still national ones. Again the unreliable character of support from beyond the region was indicated in the late 1980s by companies' increasing anxiety to be within the frontiers of the Community as the deadline for completing the market by 1992 drew nearer.

The third criterion by which the size of the region might be judged is indeed the functionalist one, but it should be stressed that this is only one of the three kinds of criterion. There are problems which have a specific geographical extent, though not as many as Mitrany assumed, and there is a case for tackling them in that area. For example, soil erosion in the Tennessee Valley had a clear geographical extent, as does the requirement of disease control amongst plants or animals – or people – and there are various industrial activities such as coal and steel production which can be more effectively organized on the basis of the distribution of their raw materials, or sources of power, as with aluminium smelting, or of skilled labour. This was one of the reasons for Mitrany's support of the European Coal and Steel Community.[36] But, it should be repeated that the functional imperative is only one of the indicators of appropriate space. This argument and its implications for functionalism are considered further later.

These then, are the main general arguments against sectoralism and in favour of the development of stronger regional arrangements. The costs of sectoralism are one of the explanations of the growth of regional organization, as it indicates the source of a tendency in decision-making about technical matters in modern times which cannot be disputed. There has been a continuing, if spasmodic, concern with finding the appropriate area within which to attempt the solution of particular problems, which has frequently led to participation in regional organization; the first three explanations related to this. But at the same time there has been the realization that it is impossible to detach one problem from a group of related other problems, so that if the first is to be solved in a particular area so must all the others: they are functionally linked. A natural inclination on the part of decision-makers to deal with single issues is, therefore, constantly frustrated. It turns out that problems are all too often bigger than they seem, and a start cannot be made without risking the generation of pressures towards the expansion of the functional territory. This stresses the importance of the element of process as an explanation of the growth of local sectoralism; one regional organization tends to lead to another. But it also suggests a further pressure towards regionalism in the sense defined earlier: a tendency towards the contiguity of functional boundaries beyond the state.

The anti-sectoralist argument was, therefore, not only part of an explanation of the development of regional organization: it also implied a prediction about the future development of regionalism which is explored further in the next chapter.

Notes

1. For discussions of the nature of regionalism see Ronald J. Yalem, *Regionalism and World Order*, Public Affairs Press, Washington, 1965, and Bruce M. Russett, *International Regions and the International System: a Study in Political Ecology*, Rand McNally and Co., Chicago, 1967.
2. Ernst B. Haas, *Beyond the Nation State: Functionalism and International Organization*, Stanford University Press, Stanford, 1964, especially Chapter 14.
3. Kenneth Boulding, *Ecodynamics: a new Theory of Societal Evolution*, Sage, Beverly Hills, 1978.

4. David Mitrany, *A Working Peace System*, Quadrangle Books, Chicago, 1966. For an extensive bibliography on functionalism see Margot Light and A.J.R. Groom (Editors), *International Relations: a handbook of current theory*, Frances Pinter, London, 1985, Chapter 12.

5. A.J.R. Groom, "Functionalism in World Society", John W. Burton, "Functionalism and the Resolution of Conflict", in A.J.R. Groom and Paul Taylor (Editors), *Functionalism: Theory and Practice in International Relations*, University of London Press, London, 1975.

6. See Robert W. Cox, "Social Forces, States and World Orders", in Robert O. Keohane, *Neorealism and its Critics*, Columbia University Press, New York, 1986, Pp. 204–254 especially Pp. 208–209.
   Cox distinguishes between problem-solving theory which focuses upon the solution of specific problems whilst assuming that other things are constant, which is, therefore, conservative; and critical theory which "unlike problem-solving theory, does not take institutions and social and power relations for granted but calls them into question by concerning itself with their origins and how and whether they might be in the process of changing" (P. 208). In other words critical theory is concerned with the wholes rather than the parts. The argument in this chapter is in these terms critical theory rather than problem-solving.

7. Ian Clark, *Reform and Resistance in the International Order*, Cambridge University Press, Cambridge, 1980, especially Chapter 2, "Kant and the Tradition of Optimism".

8. See A.J.R. Groom, loc. cit. in note 5 above.

9. Yalem, loc. cit., passim.

10. Russett, loc. cit.

11. Ibid., P. 11.

12. Ibid., P. 168.

13. Leon Lindberg and Stuart Scheingold, *Regional Integration*, Harvard University Press, Cambridge, Mass., 1971.

14. Ernst B. Haas, *The Obsolescence of Regional Integration Theory*, The University of California, Berkeley, 1976.

15. Joseph S. Nye, "Regional Institutions", in Cyril E. Black and Richard A. Falk, *The Structure of the International Environment*, which is Vol. IV of their *The Future of the International Legal Order*, Princeton University Press, 1972; reproduced in Richard A. Falk and Saul H. Mendlovitz (Editors), *Regional Politics and World Order*, W. H. Freeman and Company, San Francisco, 1973.

16. Ibid., P. 92.

17. Ibid., P. 90.

18. Oran R. Young, "Political Discontinuities in the International System", *World Politics*, Vol. 20, No. 3, 1968, Pp. 369–392.

19. Andre Gunder Frank, "The Development of Underdevelopment", *Monthly Review*, September 1966, Pp. 17–30.

20. Rajni Kothari, *Footsteps Into The Future: Diagnosis of the Present World and a Design for an Alternative*, The Free Press, New York, 1974, P. 135.

21. Joint Inspection Unit, *Some Reflections on Reform of the United Nations*, prepared by Maurice Bertrand, JIU/REP/85/9, Geneva, 1985. Henceforth referred to as the Bertrand Report; reproduced in Paul Taylor and A.J.R. Groom (Editors), *International Institutions at Work*, Pinter Publishers, London, 1988.

22. Ibid., P. 54.

23. Ibid.

24. Ibid.
25. Ibid., P. 55.
26. Ibid., P. 64.
27. See J.W. Burton, "Regionalism, Functionalism, and the United Nations", *Australian Outlook*, Vol. 15, 1961, Pp. 73–87.
28. Roger Masters, "A Multi-bloc Model of the International System", *American Political Science Review*, Vol. 55, No. 4, Dec. 1961, Pp. 780–798.
29. For an account of the establishment of the UNDP see R.G.A. Jackson, *A Study of the Capacity of the United Nations Development System*, UN Doc. DP/5 1969, Geneva, 1969. See also the Bertrand Report, loc. cit. in Paul Taylor and A.J.R. Groom (Editors), *International Institutions at Work*, Pinter Publishers, London, 1988.
30. Jason L. Finkle and Barbara B. Crane, "Ideology and Politics at Mexico City: the United States at the 1984 International Conference on Population", *Population and Development Review*, Vol. 11 (March 1985) No. 1. See also Chapter 8 below.
31. Stephen D. Krasner (Editor), *International Regimes*, Cornell University Press, Ithaca, 1983; see also his *Structural Conflict: The Third World Against Global Liberalism*, University of California Press, Berkeley, 1985.
32. See Donella Meadows et al., *The Limits to Growth*, New American Library, New York, 1972; and Mihajlo Mesarovic and Eduard Pestel, *Mankind at the Turning Point*, Dutton, New York, 1974.
33. See note 28 above.
34. For a discussion of their work and a bibliography see Peter Robson, *The Economics of International Integration*, George Allen and Unwin, London, 1980.
35. The terms *vulnerability* and *sensitivity* are used here in the special sense developed by Robert O. Keohane and Joseph S. Nye in their *Power and Interdependence*, Little, Brown, Boston, 1977.
36. David Mitrany, "The Functional Approach in Historical Perspective", *International Affairs*, Vol. 47, No. 3, 1971.

2 The practice of regionalism

In this chapter the empirical evidence about the emergence of regional organization is considered, and the more specific reasons for its appearance discussed. On the one hand regionalism as a general phenomenon had received relatively little attention after the mid-1970s. On the other hand, however, evidence from the 1980s and later suggests that governments were becoming relatively more involved with regional than with global organizations (see Table 2.1). This was true not only of Europe but also of Africa, Asia, and North and South America. The growth of regional organization is not, however, the same thing as regional integration; the quality of the arrangements and their implications for the scope and level of integration will be considered later.

A number of aspects of the evidence on the growth of regional organization which was available to the present writer should be pointed out. First, the main source, which is the highly prestigious *Yearbook of International Organizations*, has only been presenting its quantitative data in a form which permitted the identification of regional growth since 1980; such a range of data was not available to earlier students! Second, the figures are about the number of organizations of which a country, or groups or individuals within a country, were members at the dates indicated. These are not numbers of organizations, but numbers of memberships. There is, however, separate information, discussed later, to suggest that the number of intergovernmental organizations in regions such as Africa, has increased faster than the total number of organizations (see Table 2.2). Third, the evidence does have the disadvantage that it takes the grouping of countries, which it places together in the region, as a given, and looks at the growth of organizations within that space. It is not possible from this information to plot regions from memberships in the various regional organizations. The evidence may, therefore, fail to reveal the emergence of sub-regions within the major regions selected, which are Europe, Africa, Asia, and America.

The main feature of the evidence set out in Table 2.1 is a comparison of the total number of memberships in international organization of countries in a region with the number of regional memberships. Both intergovernmental and nongovernmental organizations are included. Two important overall conclusions emerge from the evidence in the Tables: first, that the total amount of international organization has increased at an astonishing rate since the early 1980s; and, second, that the weight of regional compared with total organization has also increased remarkably.

The figures for a series of years indicate a declining ratio of regional memberships to total memberships so that for Europe the total number of

Table 2.1 Number of organizations of which a country is a member, added together for each named region

Europe (E. and W.)

	A Total	B Total ngos	C Regional total	D Regional ngos	Ratio C to A	% C in A
1981	31765		10965		2.89	34.5
1982	37229	35323	15290	14539	2.43	
1983	38205	36201				
1984	39466	37392	17104	16256	2.3	
1987	41885	39883	18519	17819	2.26	44
1990	49243	47321	24703	24107	2.04	50.1

Increase in regional memberships as a percentage of total memberships 1981–90: 45.2

Africa

	A Total	B Total ngos	C Regional total	D Regional ngos	Ratio C to A	% C in A
1981	10662		1949		5.47	18.2
1982	12943	11056	3070	2351	4.21	
1983	13632	11602		2602		
1984	14362	12292	3731	2898	3.84	
1987	15904	13605	4476	3504	3.55	28.1
1990	19101	16722	6597	5559	3.43	34.5

Increase in regional memberships as a percentage of total memberships 1981–90: 89.5

Asia

	A Total	B Total ngos	C Regional total	D Regional ngos	Ratio C to A	% C in A
1981	11484		1839		6.24	16
1982	13687	12453	2849	2516	4.8	
1983	14190	12892	2888	2574	4.91	
1984	14914	13553	3199	2831	4.6	
1987	16592	15166	3905	3529	4.24	23
1990	19552	18085	5775	5375	3.64	29.5

Increase in regional memberships as a percentage of total memberships 1981–90: 84.3

Table 2.1   cont.

America (N. and S.)

	A Total	B Total ngos	C Regional total	D Regional ngos	Ratio C to A	% C in A
1983	17114	15732	4843	4278	4.0	28.2
1985	18632	17136	5800	5201	3.21	31.12
1987	19738	18218	6087	5530	3.24	30.8
1990	23044	21555	8468	7963	2.7	36.7

Increase in regional memberships as a percentage of total memberships 1983–90: 30.1

Total: all memberships, regional and non-regional, intergovernmental and nongovernmental.
igos: intergovernmental organizations.
ngos: nongovernmental organizations.

Source: *Yearbook of International Organization*, Edited by Union of International Associations, Munchen, New York, London, and Paris, Published by K.G. Saur, in a single volume until 1982. 19th Edition, 1981; thereafter volume two, of three volumes, 1st Edition, 1983, 9th Edition 1991–92.

Table 2.2   Increase in total number of intergovernmental and nongovernmental organizations, and regional intergovernmental and nongovernmental organizations, 1981–91

	1981	1984	1985	1986	
All	4602	4980	5054	5018	
Regional	3246	3666	3736	3667	

	1987	1988	1989	1990	1991
All	4546	4827	4921	4939	4917
Regional	3245	3489	3597	3623	3603

Percentage Increase since 1981: All +6.84%; Regional +10.99%

Source: *Yearbook of International Organization*, loc. cit., 1987, and 1991–92, Vol. 2, Statistical Appendix

memberships was 2.89 times greater than the number of regional member-ships in 1981, but only 2.04 times that number in 1990. Although the strength of regional organization measured in this way may be judged to have increased modestly in Europe over the period it had nevertheless increased to some degree and the percentage change in the ratio of regional to total memberships was 45.2%. Nevertheless this relatively modest increase was to be expected in view of the relatively high level of regional organization reached before the period of study in an area which was dominated by the European Community. It was also striking that the changing ratio was explicable mainly in terms of increases in the number of memberships in nongovernmental organization. In other words societal interdependence seemed to have been increasing though participation by governments in intergovernmental organizations did not increase. Indeed the total number of memberships in regional intergovernmental organizations reported in the *Yearbook* decreased between 1984 and 1987 from 848 to 700.

The trend towards regional involvement in the period 1981–90 was, however, more striking in Africa where, despite a significant increase in overall involvement in international organization, the ratio of regional to total memberships increased from 5.47 to 3.43, a remarkable percentage increase of 89.5%. Both the number of nongovernmental regional memberships and the number of intergovernmental regional memberships had increased, the latter from 719 in 1982 (figures for 1981 were not included in the *Yearbook*) to 1,038 in 1990. Regional organization in Africa seemed to be considerably strengthened through the eighties in terms of these indicators. In Asia too participation in regional organization increased as compared with that in global organization during the 1980s. Table 2.1 indicates an increase in the total number of governmental and nongovernmental memberships of 70%, but the number of memberships in both kinds of organization at the regional level had increased by a striking 214%. The weight of regional memberships in total memberships was 84.3% greater in 1990 than it had been in 1981.

A glance at the evidence in Table 2.1 about America indicates the same general trend: the states in that region seemed to be more involved in regional organization compared with total international organization in 1990 than a decade earlier, despite a very striking increase in total involvement. Here, as elsewhere, membership in regional organization was increasing faster than organization in general. This interpretation is reinforced by data about the numbers of organizations in Table 2.2: the total number of organizations increased by 6.84% in the ten years 1981–91, but the number of regional organizations increased by almost 11%, i.e. almost twice the rate of the overall increase.

The pattern of increase in Africa already revealed may be rather surprising. Further evidence is in the highly respected yearbook called *Africa South of the Sahara*.[1] In its list of international organizations in that region in 1987 were 71 which the present writer identified as being intergovernmental, as not having a headquarters outside the region, and as containing at least three members. All organizations which formed a part of the United Nations system were counted as constituting a single organization. The comparable figure for 1988 was 76, but that for 1975 was 46. In other words the number of intergovernmental organizations defined in these terms had increased in Africa south of the Sahara by 39.4% in the period 1975–88.

It is hard to resist the conclusion that the 1980s was a period of remarkable growth in regional organization, though perhaps not quite as rapid as that reported by Nye for the shorter period 1957 to 1963, referred to in Chapter 1. The obvious point should be made, however, that the evidence for the latter period was likely to have been affected by the pace of creation of new states and by the general development in international economic arrangements after the period of economic recovery in the industrialized world in the 1950s. This makes the evidence for the eighties seem even more remarkable.

The evidence presented so far includes nothing about the quality of the organizations, in terms of the powers of their controlling committees or the salience of their areas of competence. Nor did that used by Nye in his 1972 article.[2] The best evidence now available about such powers derives from the experience of the European Community, which is discussed in the following chapters.

Some qualitative evidence about another area can be added at this point, taken from the yearbook *Africa South of the Sahara*.[3] In the 1980s 12 or 13 organizations attracted attention in that they were judged by the experts to be worth individual accounts. These were the United Nations and its 15 subsidiary agencies then working in Africa, the African Developmemt Bank, the Arab Bank for Economic Development, the Commonwealth, the Communauté Economique de l'Afrique de l'Ouest (CEAO), the Conseil de l'Entente, the Economic Community of Western Africa (ECAWOS), the Lomé arrangements, the Franc zone, the Islamic Development Bank, the Organization of African Unity, the Organization of the Islamic Conference, and the Southern African Development Community Conference (SADCC). In addition to the central core of organizations there were in 1975 five further listed organizations working in what could be regarded as areas of high salience under the heading *Trade and Industry*, whereas there were 15 such organizations in 1988. In 1975 there were nine entries under the headings *Government Politics and Economics*, whereas in 1988 there were 14 items under these headings. This evidence at least suggests that the tasks dealt with in the increasing number of regional organizations were not trivial: they were dealing, whether effectively or ineffectively, with issues of great importance from the point of view of the member states. This point does not need to be laboured with regard to European regional organiza-tions, and it is also valid for Asia and America.

The salience of the issues dealt with by the regional organizations may also be suggested in the motives of decision-makers for creating and joining them. Such motives vary in the degree to which they are explicitly recognized by the leaders and also in the circumstances which lead to their being suggested. It is, therefore, useful before discussing them to construct a typology in terms of which they might be arranged which recognizes these possibilities.

Incentives to join regional organizations are derived from a variety of sources:

First, from the immediate political circumstances of the state. These might be called contingent incentives.

Second, the leaders might be pushed towards regional organizations as a way of solving the pressing specific economic or social problems of the state or of pursuing longer term social or economic goals. They may, of course, sometimes be steered in that direction by a civil service or other advisers who have not made their intentions explicit: in this sense the leader is not fully aware of the motives for his/her action, which is more a consequence of continuing pressure, of social and economic propensities, than of explicit demands.

Third, decision-makers might wish to join because they are responding to the kind of consideration which realists would place under the general heading of the pursuit of the national interest: they wish to expand or consolidate the power of the state which they govern and see in regional arrangements a way of achieving this.

Finally are pressures which derive from the perception that there are fundamental deficiencies in the way in which attempts are made to solve problems within the state or in the general character of its relations with others. In other words there are structural problems which the decision-maker may attempt to rectify by joining regional organizations.

For these various types of reason decision-makers may seek membership in regional organizations, and they will now be further considered and illustrated in turn.

Among the immediate political circumstances of the states outside the Western capitalist world which have contributed towards their leaders' involvement in regional organizations since the mid-1970s the central feature must be the failure of the earlier efforts to bring about the alteration of the global system so that their economic interests were better served. The attempt to create a New International Economic Order in 1974 had faded by the early 1980s mainly because the developed states recovered from the shock of the first oil crisis and became increasingly reluctant to grant the concessions demanded by the Group of 77, such as the setting up of a Common Fund which would have been large enough to stabilize commodity prices at an acceptable level, and the creation of a link between inflation and the price of commodities.[4] The work of the Conference on International Economic Cooperation held in Paris in 1976 was largely futile from the point of view of the Group of 77. The rich states refused to accept any significant alteration of the existing arrangements in the international economic system. Hence for the developing states there was a need for an alternative strategy: that was an increasing resort to regional organization in the absence of anything better.

A number of other problems were associated with the failure of the New International Economic Order. Global international institutions, including those which had been set up as a consequence of Third World pressure, proved relatively ineffective. Chief among these was UNCTAD. As the debt crisis worsened in the early eighties a number of other organizations began to appear as positively hostile. In particular, of course, the International Monetary Fund, in pursuit of monetary stability, imposed harsh conditions upon the debtor states which were seen as essential by the lenders if further credit was to be extended.[5] These developments contributed to the growing feeling that global organization was at best only a part of the solution to the various economic problems of the less well-off states. The European Community also encouraged a greater resort to regional arrangements with specific measures to encourage trade between the developing states in the Lomé Three agreements; Lomé One in particular had been criticized for discouraging such intra-Group of 77 links.[6] A further pressure in the same direction came from the Brandt Report which can be seen as reporting an emerging consensus amongst the international development community: that regional arrangements among developing states were to be encouraged as their growth depended mainly upon increases in South–South trade.[7] Although efforts at the global level had to continue, by the mid-1980s there was a feeling among the Group of 77 that, far from radicalizing the global system, they would have to make concessions at that level. By the late 1980s these had come to include the acceptance of the right of the main contributing states to increase their control of economic and social policies in the United Nations.[8] A retreat at that level was accompanied by greater efforts at the regional one.

The second category of pressures upon governments in the Third World to participate in organization at the regional level was a range of economic and social developments within their states. Chief amongst these was the emergence of a somewhat larger number of people with higher levels of education and experience of the outside world who expected higher standards of living, and modernization, and who were prepared to exercise pressure upon their governments to achieve these goals. Accordingly more people became involved in nongovernmental organizations because they were ways of expressing the new aspirations and of pursuing them. The large number of nongovernmental groups at the conference on women's rights at Nairobi in 1976 was one illustration of this.[9] It was to be expected that a good number of these would involve people from a number of contiguous states: regional nongovernmental organizations were therefore in part a consequence of the rising tide of expectations.

Once such organizations began to appear there was set in train, however, a self-sustaining process which had as its main dynamic an inclination to emulate arrangements which seemed to have been successful in other parts of the world. The tendency towards emulation should not be underestimated as a reason for new economic and social developments once a particular stage of awareness has been reached amongst a people. The European Community was probably the most powerful role model of the freeing of trade, if only because it had seemed to provide for economic growth in Western Europe. Similarly pressures upon governments to create regional development banks were likely to increase regardless of the arguments about their specific technical merits: there were equivalents elsewhere such as the European Investment Bank which were more likely to be imitated as the World Bank was seen more frequently as an instrument of exploitation by the richer states.

Emulation was a very important political fact. But it was, of course, encouraged by its association with a very persuasive literature about the advantages of regional economic activities, in particular of common markets. The theories of economists, such as James Meade, Jacob Viner et al. do not require extended discussion in this chapter.[10] Suffice it to say that they argued the benefits of establishing freer trade within a larger area rather than a smaller one, as this would allow more efficient producers to prosper at the expense of the less efficient ones. Larger producers would be able to lower unit costs and would be able to spend more on research. One implication of this was that there would be trade creation between members of the market and trade diversion between members and outsiders. These various factors would boost economic performance in the larger regional economy, and encourage import substitution, which was a popular ambition seen as a way of saving valuable export earnings.

Kuznets added a further point which was very much in favour of the creation of regional markets.[11] He argued that, despite trade diversion, as development proceeded the value of external trade in Gross National Product (GNP) always increased. This could be interpreted as meaning that GNP could only increase if external trade increased. But the same theorist also recognized that although his argument held for all states regardless of their size the proportionate value of external trade for larger states was smaller at any particular level of development. Hence regional common markets had two interrelated advantages: they not only helped with the efficiency of businesses within the area – they helped the economy to grow – but they also meant that a lesser amount of external trade had to be created in order to attain a specific level of GNP. Writing in the early eighties, Sarkesian comfirmed the impact of these various practical and intellectual incentives when he noted that in sub-regions "plenty of specific accomplishments are evident", but "the institutionalization of such cooperative efforts may increase their effectiveness".[12] Such institutionalization proceeded apace, as has been shown, through the 1980s.

A third category of incentive towards the creation of regional organization was that which was particularly stressed by Nye. The traditional realist ambitions of statesmen were reckoned to have been to do with the acquisition of possessions especially in the form of territory. In modern times, however, it was more likely that statesmen would pursue what had been called milieu goals, such as those which were intended to change the environment in which a state operated so that it would be found more congenial. For instance governments might see participation in regional organizations as providing a context in which leadership at that level could be sought. It is also probable – perhaps more so in Africa or Asia than in Europe – that governments would seek to establish such organizations on their own territory in order to facilitate the exercising of influence, or to gain revenue. It was striking that the headquarters of regional organizations tended to be set up in the capitals of a small number of states, Kenya, Nigeria, Senegal, Egypt, and less frequently in Ethiopia, Algeria and Côte d'Ivoire, though the *Yearbook* figures between 1983 and 1988 showed a marked increase in the total numbers in the lead states. Another factor was that regional organizations could be seen as an element in a local regime, as discussed by Krasner et al., which once in place would make it easier to conduct negotiations about matters of mutual interest with neighbours, and as has been mentioned, would facilitate direct communications between a government and the attentive public in the other member countries.

These general inclinations were, however, also subject to guiding principles. For instance, the evidence about regional organizations discussed above suggests that the traditional associations arising from the experience of colonialism still affected the choice of partners. The Francophone countries tended to do things together – the prominence of the Côte d'Ivoire illustrates this – as did the Commonwealth countries, and as Sarkesian mentioned, at the *continental* level "it is very difficult to do anything concrete . . .".[13] Nevertheless there was some evidence to suggest that organization which cut across the sub-regions was growing stronger.

Another guiding principle was likely to be the urge to minimize intervention by the superpowers in the affairs of the region. In the 1970s and 1980s United States, and developing states', policy on this went through a long cycle which was not without its ironic aspects. In the early seventies, precisely when developing countries, spurred on by the success of OPEC and the radicalism of dependency theory, were concentrating upon trying to alter fundamentally the global system through an international strategy, Kissinger and Nixon tried to encourage a higher degree of regional self-reliance in defence and other matters. Conversely, states in Africa and Asia pursued regionalization more vigorously in the early to mid-1980s, when Reagan argued that the Soviet "evil empire" should be resisted in its pursuit of a global strategy, through the adoption of a global counter-strategy involving more direct intervention in states which seemed soft. The prospect of superpower intervention sharpened the appetite for doing it locally. One illustration of this was the Indian action in support of the government of the Maldive Islands after it had been attacked in November 1988 by mercenaries. Mr Gandhi pointed out explicitly that the success of Indian forces on this occasion confirmed the efficacy of regional arrangements. Their involvement in Sri Lanka reflected a similar interest. Superpower involvement would have been undesirable and unnecessary. This is not to say, however, that the idea of alliance with outsiders had now been rejected in Africa and Asia, but rather that there had arisen an inclination to seek security more actively at the regional level.

It is in conformity with the point that states more frequently pursued milieu goals that security was less often seen as being just a question of military capacity and strategy. There was a heightened realization of the need to seek economic defence against possible exploitation by outsiders, and against turbulence in the international economic system,[14] though abject economic circumstances often made the effective pursuit of such goals problematic. More specifically defensive mechanisms were thought necessary to lessen dependence on external suppliers of essential materials, including food; to reduce dependence on a narrow range of exports, which created high sensitivity, even vulnerability, to adverse movements in particular product or commodity markets; to avoid excessive dependence on a particular market, which generated power for the recipient state over the supplier – the Marks and Spencer syndrome;[15] and to increase the level of trade dependence upon insiders, thus reducing economic and political risks. One plausible response to this list of economic defence requirements would be to strengthen regional economic arrangements. It is not argued here, however, that such goals always had the highest priority in the thinking of statesmen, but that nevertheless they were a source of continuous pressure to move in the direction of greater economic security.

The three categories of incentive towards participation by governments in regional organization which have now been discussed were in support of local sectoralism. Regionalism in the sense of seeking a single space in order to facilitate the performance of a range of *interrelated* functions may be encouraged by three further kinds of pressure. First is the much discussed one of the appearance of a regional sentiment which persuaded statesmen of the need for a move towards greater regional unity. Second is the appearance of a belief among statesmen that a union would be desirable because it was seen as a grand enterprise as was the case with the Founding Fathers in the US. A third kind of pressure may, however, now be added: as was demonstrated in the preceding chapter regionalization may also result from the continuous demonstration not only that specific benefits resulted from its intensification but that conversely costs consistently arose from its alternative, the sectoral approach. Of course, in practice a regionalization process will probably be fuelled by a mixture of these elements, but it was useful to identify the third more clearly as it has been underestimated. For instance, in Nye's article, mentioned above, regional sentiment was posed as the only counterweight to sectoralism.

The failure of sectoralism may be reflected in leaders' views on their failure to reach particular developmental goals, or in marked inefficiencies in the way in which limited resources are used. It may also be noted in the intuitive judgements of observers such as Bertrand or in the previous practice of development programmes as with the Marshall Aid programme in Western Europe from 1948 to 1952, in which the US Congress specifically rejected a sectoral approach in favour of an integrated regional programme, or in the attempts to introduce regional devolution in France in the late 1960s. The effects of the failure may, therefore, be observed and on this basis alternative development strategies may be chosen which were represented, for instance, in the setting up of the UNDP or in the appointment of Round Tables of advisers by the World Bank.[16]

But the political elites of developing states must also be aware that pressures towards regionalization are also being created by the long term evolution of international society. That regional instititutions are growing is evident. The question arises, therefore, of whether there are not also pressures in favour of that process which derive from the international system. What is the nature of these pressures and to what kind of international system will they lead?

Before discussing this it is worth returning briefly to the question of the unfashionability of regionalism, even in the form of local sectoralism, in the academic literature in the 1970s and 1980s. It was striking that in much of the later writing on international organizations, such as that on regime theory or on North–South relations, there was little or no reference to regionalism. Part of the explanation for this must be the fashion of the times, or, to put the matter more pretentiously, the emerging patterns of the sociology of knowledge. The development of regime theory was motivated in part by the need to discover factors which would make for international stability as US hegemony declined.[17] For Americans, however, it was easier to see internationalism as the alternative to US hegemony, and more difficult to contemplate a future in which rival centres of power, and more self-contained economic blocs, emerged. For American regime theorists in the 1980s internationalism, not regionalism, was the ideologically accept-able alternative to American hegemony.

In some cases a different view was presented, which also just missed the case for regionalism. This view was to be noted in the writing of Robert Gilpin who in his admirable text described the processes of international capitalism as naturally involving the decline of particular economies and their succession by rival centres.[18] The United States was to be *succeeded* by the European Community and Japan. The assumption here, and it is hard to see why it was necessary, was that the process of development in some part of the global system was necessarily related inversely to the process of decline in some other part of that system. There are strong arguments, as Gilpin explained, in favour of the globalization of capitalism – and events in Eastern Europe in the early 1990s, as well as the decline of socialism in the Third World, bear this out – but its consequences could as easily be the emergence of islands of more or less equal development on a regional basis as a process of creating new hegemons.

Neither the neorealists nor the regime theorists, therefore, have been led to notice a resurgence of regionalism, the first because even when they dealt in the forces of global capitalism they tended to see these as undermining old hegemons and creating new ones, whilst the latter were disposed to see existing hegemons as being merged into a new internationalism sustained – by implication – by global regimes. The arguments in favour of the appearance of a tendency towards separate islands of regionalism therefore need to be examined and this is what follows.

Nye has argued that local sectoralism would be extended but implied that this would not alter the international system in any significant way.[19] The prediction ventured here is different. It is that functional regions will emerge increasingly clearly in particular territories over the next few decades and that their members will more frequently act together in dealings with other states. It is not suggested that there will be any necessary merging of sovereignties or that this process will be fuelled by the appearance of regional nationalisms. Pan-Africanism, for instance, is unlikely to become a significant force, and it is difficult to detect anything analagous in Asia. Neither will the creation of these regions be the result of any enthusiasm for federalism. Rather the emergence of more distinct regions will be the result of attempts to solve practical problems within and to achieve security against military attack and economic domination in relations with outsiders.

The example of the European Communities was one reason for supposing that this would be the way of the future, and the events in Europe are worth considering in some detail because of the general lessons which they contain. This is the task of the next chapter. In this chapter, however, the major conclusions may be outlined. In the 1980s, and especially since 1984, it became increasingly evident that there had come a point when it was increasingly difficult for member states, such as Britain, which wished to place firm limits upon the pace of increasing integration, to resist the process.[20] Viewed from the perspective of the British government the argument went on the following lines: in order that the British economy should continue to grow it was essential to be in the Common Market: the completion of the Common Market would increase the scale of benefits for the British economy; therefore there was a need to accept arrangements which would make it possible for British companies to act in the market in general as if it were the domestic market, such as those which were included in the Single European Act of 1986 and the Maastricht Agreement of 1991; these in turn made it necessary to introduce legislation on such practical matters as the specifications of goods and the simplification of the documentation required for trade between the member countries. But it also set up pressures for going beyond these immediate measures to the harmonization of the levels of taxation on goods and services, and, indeed, to the establishment of a common monetary system leading to the setting up of a European Central Bank. This is discussed in relation to its implications for sovereignty in Chapter 5.

There were, in other words, a series of practical further measures which were seen as necessarily arising from having reached a particular scale in the scope of integration. What seemed to have happened was a version of what the neofunctionalists had called "spill over" with the significant difference that in this new form the expansive logic applied directly only to the scope rather than to both the scope and the level of integration. It placed states in the position of having to face major pressures to go forward in order to keep what they had, and indeed of having to go further forward than they really wanted to go in order to obtain a perceived benefit, in this case a Europe without Frontiers:[21] this was a formidable pressure to expand the scope of integration. It derived from having reached a kind of critical mass of previous cooperative measures. A qualitative change had taken place in the pressures towards their further extension.

There was, however, a further force that was conducive to the strengthening of the regional arrangements with which the British had to deal. That was the realization, probably deliberately enhanced by the French, that a coalition of states from the inner core could move ahead of them in achieving a more extensive integration unless they were careful to stay with the process. They could not opt out lest they be relegated to what in the terminology of the Communities would be described as the second tier of a two-tier system. The only course of action which was acceptable on both economic and political grounds was, therefore, to remain party to negotiations about further integration, even though this could be at the risk of having to make unwelcome concessions. The dynamic of integration within the region therefore included not only a perceived need to take steps to obtain specific benefits, but also a political

element: a reluctance to be placed on the sidelines in the emerging
system.

This argument may be put in terms which make it applicable to regions
in general as follows: that as the scope of integration is increased the
chances of that scope being further extended are enhanced by the fear of
any one partner that, unless they accept this, a more progressive coalition
of their partners could emerge. This integrative dynamic therefore contains
elements both of economic self-interest and of political fear. Its underlying
condition is probably the appearance in the state of the widespread conviction that the benefits arising from integration are real and important, and
that the costs of even partial exclusion would be considerable, resulting not
only in economic disadvantage but also in political enfeeblement. This, it
should be stressed, does not imply the kind of progressive fusion of
sovereignties that was foreseen by the neofunctionalists, but, as will be
argued in Chapter 4, rather the emergence of what could be called a
symbiotic relationship between the state and the region: the well-being of
each is seen as being necessary for the sustenance of the other.[22] If the
trend towards increased participation in regional organizations discussed
above continues, the judgement that they generate significant benefits must
become a valid one in a number of regions outside Europe, and the
emergence of modified "spill over" in these other areas is, therefore, to be
expected.

These are incentives towards the strengthening of regional arrangements
which were contained within the area. But there were also pressures in that
same direction which derived from relationships between that area and
international society. Some of these were contingent. They depended on
assumptions about likely developments in that society: that there would be
continuing turbulence in the international economic system in the sense that
liberal trade arrangements at the global level would remain under threat
and pressures towards protectionism and special trade deals – the new
mercantilism – would remain; and that the superpowers would tend, as
seemed probable, despite their involvement in the Gulf War, to be less
activist in their preparedness to intervene militarily outside their own areas,
and, indeed, would become indifferent towards, or supportive of, the playing of a greater role by other states in the latter's own locality.[23] Given
these assumptions the prediction ventured would be that there would be a
tendency among the various emerging regions to equalize upwards – not
that they would all become equal but that there would be pressures deriving
from international society which pushed in that direction. The pattern of
relations with the outside world would enhance the regions' internal
consolidation and tend to increase the size of the smaller towards that of
the larger units in the system. In practice, of course, this meant once again
a tendency to emulate the dimensions of the European Communities and
the US.

The history of the European Communities suggests that as the scope of
integration increased so did the tendency to increase membership. The three
stages of expansion, in 1973, in 1981 and 1986, all suggested that governments sought to join because they thought that members were completing

the phase of negative integration – removing barriers on exchanges between them – and going beyond that to positive integration, namely the setting in place of new common arrangements. In all cases the evidence about political commitment to unification in the states seeking membership was ambiguous. There was little enthusiasm for joining a political union, though there was an anxiety not to be marginalized either economically or politically. On the other hand had the scope of integration remained at a low level there was little evidence to suggest that the British and the others would have been much bothered about joining or that the Scandinavian countries, Switzerland, and others, would have been so anxious to join the same economic space, whilst stopping short for reasons of their own from full membership. So it seemed probable that increasing scope amongst the core of original members set up pressures towards expansion.

The question arises, however, of when that expansion might be expected to stop. The general answer to this question must be that this happens when in the judgement of members the costs of further expansion are seen as being likely to exceed the benefits of not doing so. On the one hand the costs in terms of the draining of the resources of the regional organizations are likely to increase with expansion, because the core states are likely to be richer than later applicants, and because the latter are likely to seek the help of the former with their economic development.

Founding members – core states – have in practice been richer than later candidates for admission but according to Karl Deutsch this is also probable for theoretical reasons.[24] On the other hand the case for further enlargement, from the point of view of existing members, in order to enhance economic security – to provide for economic defensive needs, which were discussed earlier – is likely to become weaker as size increases. These are some of the reasons for resisting further expansion beyond an optimum point; in Europe by the early 1990s a tension had appeared between pressures towards the admission of new members because of what had been achieved within – and what was missing without – and a resistance to this by members on the grounds that it might damage that achievement. It was striking that in an earlier period of modest regional achievement, when enlargement would have been less damaging to the achievement, there was less interest in joining and greater stress on the benefits of staying outside; but that with a greater achievement, when enlargement would be more damaging, the wish to join by contiguous states was universal. It was also striking that the advantages of further enlargement tended to be stressed by those member states which were least impressed by the internal achievement, such as the British.

The goal of economic security is an incentive to enlarge regional organizations until that size has been reached at which members together judge that they are capable of withstanding turbulence in a relatively less managed international economy – their vulnerability has been lessened. The net increment in the effectiveness of economic defence is likely to become smaller as size is increased until a point is reached at which costs incurred outweigh any further benefits. At this point prospective members are likely to get a cool response, especially if, like Turkey in the case of the European

Communities, their accession threatens to impose serious burdens upon the resources of the region.

Equalization is therefore driven by the perception by governments that it is in their interest to reduce vulnerability and, beyond that, to equalize the degree of mutual sensitivity.[25] It is not denied that other considerations may get in the way of this process in the short and medium term. But nevertheless it must be regarded as a constant in the international economic system. It should also be stressed again that it has not been assumed that states involved in this process are being required to sacrifice their sovereignty. Indeed precisely the opposite is the case. The symbiotic relationship between the region and the member states may encourage governments to see the strengthening of the region as a way of enhancing their own sovereignty. The only important caveat in this context is that as scope expands it is inevitable that perceptions of what is necessary in that sovereignty should also change.

It is also necessary to look at the way in which regionalization is related to international coalitions, alliances and spheres of influence. The experience of the European Community suggests that the emergence of the region changes the dynamics of any alliance of which it is a sub-unit and the idea of a sphere of influence in which regional states were previously subordinate is weakened. This is because economic interests and military strategic interests are on a continuum: as governments acquire a wider range of common economic interests it is likely that incentives towards creating a common defence would also increase. Hence after the late 1970s the idea that the members of the European Community should strengthen their common defensive arrangements was more frequently proposed and discussed than had earlier been the case,[26] and in the Maastricht Agreement the possibility of building a common defence in the future was spelled out. One idea which had become current in the mid-eighties, and which was incorporated in 1991 in the Agreement at Maastricht, was that the West European Union should be reactivated – thus ensuring a link with NATO – but there were other proposals for giving the Community itself a more independent defence capacity, so that it would become a military power rather than being merely a civil one.[27] This again was a logical outcome of the expansion of the scope of integration; it was likely that any region would be more liable to seek a stronger common defence as its range of common economic interests expanded.

In the Third World regionalization would necessarily only appear at the expense of the grand coalition of the Group of 77 which had solidified around a consensus about anti-colonialism and support for the New International Economic Order. After the late 1970s, however, there was increasing evidence to suggest that this consensus was under pressure. Peterson concluded that

it is possible that in the 1990s politics in the [general] Assembly will return to conditions prevalent between 1955 and 1964 when ad hoc coalitions controlled proceedings and decisions on different issues . . . the tendency to link as many issues as possible by insisting on the need for "new international orders" of similar characteristics across them would also decrease.

She added that

the next few years is likely to see the third world coalition limp along, trying to bury disagreements by keeping them out of the Assembly or taking very vague general positions . . . once discussion gets beyond generalities to specifics, intra-third world divisions surface

as in "comprehensive North–South negotiations, the law of the sea, or UN restructuring".[28] The implication of Peterson's remarks was that as the larger LDC coalition was under threat it would become more likely that smaller coalitions would emerge in time among contiguous territories in response to the various pressures towards regionalization. The attempts to preserve the fiction of Third World harmony, which had earlier got in the way of such developments, would be given up.

In the major alliance of the developed world, NATO, the dominant power, the US, began in the 1980s to push much more vigorously the idea that the junior partners, the Europeans, should, given their greater economic prosperity, contribute more to their own defence within the alliance. There should be a more equitable burden-sharing.[29] At one and the same time, therefore, there appeared at this particular stage in the development of regional integration in Western Europe incentives from within and from without to emerge as a regional military power. Of course the United States Government and some commentators had seen such a prospect as not damaging the NATO alliance but rather as a way of getting the Europeans to play a more active role within it. It is, however, difficult to see how encouraging Europeans to pay more to the defence budget would do any such thing: they would be more likely to be encouraged to consolidate their own distinctive arrangements and pursue more actively their own distinctive interests. NATO may survive but with a greater tendency towards bifurcation and the idea of an American sphere of influence extending over the Atlantic would look distinctly less credible. The collapse of the Soviet Union and the disappearance of superpower rivalry have made such developments more probable.

In other parts of the world these pressures towards the adding of a military dimension to regional economic integration were more remote and may take different forms. But the conclusion that the organization of military defence is likely to follow close behind that of economic defence, wherever there is regionalization, is hard to resist. The developments within regions in the late 1980s and early 1990s therefore seem to justify the conclusion that the kind of multi-bloc world discussed by Masters in the 1960s could yet emerge.[30]

*

The argument has moved from showing that the level of involvement in regional organizations in various regions of the world had increased in the 1980s and early 1990s, and explaining this development, to an argument which suggested that international society, for reasons which related to what happened within the regions and also to what happened between them and the outside world, would become dominated by a small mumber of regional blocs. As the argument was developed so the time span in which their validity might be demonstrated was increased. Nevertheless it seemed to the present writer that pressures towards regionalization were inherent in international society and that grounds for doubt arose only with regard to the time span in which they might be expected to succeed. In other words they would lead to the transformation of international society, and not its evolution as was suggested by Nye.

A number of conclusions about the development of international organization and society may be deduced from the preceding discussion. There is, first, a point to be made about the reform of global international institutions which derives from the evidence of emerging local sectoralism. That is that discussion of the reform of the major controlling intergovernmental committees of states now needs to pay much more attention to the development of regional representation. In the Security Council this already seemed to be emerging in that in the 1980s there began a tendency to elect more frequently the various major regional leaders to the non-permanent positions. Conversely it was much less likely that states which were too minor to be able to bring any real diplomatic assets to the role would be treated in this way. This was the emerging practice. It might be argued, however, that such a practice, which could only strengthen the global institutions, should be formalized. Certainly any scheme for the reform of international institutions now needed to take account of this and Bertrand was surely correct to do so.[31] Once again the European Community indicated the way of the future: the issue of whether Britain and France should represent common EC positions in the Security Council, where they were permanent members, became more pressing in the early 1990s, and in the Maastricht Agreement of 1991 a move in this direction seemed to have been conceded.[32]

A number of points about the implications of the preceding discussion for the approach to international organization called functionalism should be made, since in Chapter 1 it was argued that it was an example of sectoralism, the main alternative to regionalism. The question needs to be put of whether it would be possible to produce a modified version of functionalism, so that as a version of sectoralism it would nevertheless be compatible with the notion that regional space was necessary. Could it in some sense be softened, as with the other two major alternatives, nationalism and globalism, so that it could be reconciled with regionalization?

Such a reconciliation begins with the observation that there always was in functionalism a certain discontinuity between its premises and the way in which the arguments were developed by Mitrany. This dicontinuity has been sharpened by the use of the word "cobweb" to describe the kind of world which the functionalists allegedly wished to create and, indeed, predicted.[33] The problem with the analogy of the cobweb, however, was that it suggested that the pattern of international transactions would develop in such a way as to show no relative discontinuities: states would be progressively subsumed in this web. There is, however, something misleading about the analogy which might be revealed in a brief examination of what a spider's web actually looks like. It is not, in fact, a continuous seam but rather has a whole series of discontinuities. There are clusters of denser webbing which are linked together with weaker and sparser threads, and, of course, at the centre of each cluster sits in his or her own territory the individual spider. The cobweb is, therefore, a highly differentiated system with sub-units, highly territorial, easily identified. It is only necessary to recall the evidence about the increasing number of regional organizations in the world to draw the conclusion that the spider's web is about as misleading an analogy of what the world is in fact like, or what it is turning into, as is that of billiard balls.

As with the cobweb a closer examination of functionalism reveals a degree of differentiation which is often ignored. The point is often missed that Mitrany did not intend the state to disappear: instead, like Gulliver in the land of the Lilliputians, it was to be tied with a myriad of functional ties to other states in the system. But it was also unclear what the functions of the state were to be. In the early days of the functionalist process it could be a political umbrella for the new international institutions, and it could also be a kind of residual category of functions in which "form" had not yet followed "function". At various points in the functionalist writings it was also implied that the state could have a role as custodian of cultural values: Mitrany was anxious that it should not be understood that he was advocating the abandonment of cultural diversity, and seemed to think that different culturally defined groups could prosper in the new functionalist world.[34] So functionalism also admitted at various points a compromise with sectoralism: at the beginning of the process, as a residual category and with regard to cultural values.

But a further kind of compromise was implied in the early arguments derived from the experience of the Tennessee Valley Authority, which was, according to Mitrany, the archetype of the functionalist approach.[35] This was that the area of the valley was chosen, not because it was the result of a happy coincidence of a number of applications of the rule that "form should follow function", but rather of the judgement that it was necessary to choose a single area in which to base an integrated programme of social, economic and ecological activities. In this case the functionalist imperative was decisive only in the sense that there was an overriding need to tackle the problem of soil erosion in that particular valley, but, beyond that, sectoralism in Mitrany's arguments, and in the practice of the Authority was largely ignored. The deriving of the analogy of the undifferentiated cobweb from this experience was, therefore, unfortunate. Rather it supported the argument that the choice of that territory which was most appropriate to the integrated programme must take priority over form follows function if the primary task was to be achieved: the cobweb had to be differentiated. The example of the Tennessee Valley Authority illustrated the pressures in favour of regionalism rather than the virtues of sectoralism.

Where does this leave the doctrine that "form follows function"? As was suggested earlier this is one – but only one – of the considerations which affects and should affect the choice of a particular size of regional space. As is implied by the example of the TVA the size which is ideal for the attainment of one functional goal may need to be adjusted to suit the integrated programme: ideally, therefore, it is a question of balancing the costs of not following the doctrine in the particular instance against the benefits which this produces for the integrated programme.

These modifications to functionalism reinforce a view about the pattern of development of international society in the long term which was episodic rather than evolutionary. Three stages are indicated. The first was the loose bipolar world of the period from the 1950s until the late 1960s. Second was a period of increasing regionalization emerging out of an enhanced local sectoralism such as was postulated above for the late 1980s and 1990s. In this period the ratio of interactions and organizations in international society would decline in comparison with that at the regional level. The world would become increasingly differentiated, as regional interactions became more intense. A third stage would be reached when a small number of multi-bloc systems had emerged.

At this third stage the links between the blocs were likely to increase in comparison with those at the regional level: the cobweb would become less differentiated. The functionalist argument could also be interpreted as being applicable at the global level only when this stage was reached. As Inis Claude pointed out in his excellent critique of functionalism the approach seemed to be irrelevant in a world in which a large number of states were underdeveloped:[36] there was not much upon which to base transnational functional activities. It was a paradox that a period of modernization, of development and, therefore, of the consolidation of the state had to precede the functionalist epoch: states had to be strengthened in order to be transcended.

The points could now be added, first, that the creation of multi-bloc regionally based systems had the advantage of helping with development and with the creation of the hooks upon which the myriad ties of the Lilliputian analogy could be anchored; second, that it also had the very considerable advantage, as the experience of the European Communities suggested, of allowing individual states to be strengthened at the same time as the region as a whole had an increasing propensity to act as a single unit in relations with the outside world – the sovereignty of the individual states did not appear to be threatened despite the fact that they increasingly seemed to be a single actor in the eyes of the outside world; and, third, that the regionalization process, through equalization upwards, would also counter the problem that global sectoral arrangements were frequently seen as benefiting the bigger and richer states more than the smaller, poorer ones.

There were, therefore, a number of reasons for supposing that in the third phase the cobweb was more likely to become less differentiated at the global level. This would also be a reflection of the modified functionalism outlined above – an appropriate compromise between sectoralism and regionalism. Yet there was also in this, of course, an intimation of a fourth phase which could appear in the distant future, one in which out of the relative inefficiencies of inter-group sectoralism arose new pressures towards the creation of an increasing range of global integrated programmes.

There is, of course, a further vitally important question which will be dealt with all too briefly in this chapter: would a world dominated by a relatively small number of regions be a stable and orderly one? The present writer agrees with the conclusions reached by Masters that it probably would be more stable and orderly than the current system, and it is not proposed to repeat Masters' arguments here. The theoretical arguments of the Introduction to this Section further support this view. The dynamics of the new regionalism suggest that the new groups would not be expansionist or highly active in their external policy. Again the experience of the European Communities is relevant; that was that a considerable proportion of governments' total available diplomatic energy was expended in managing the regional system of which they were members; there would be little inclination to actively seek new possessions in the external environment.

Mancur Olson developed a number of further arguments on similar lines which reinforced Masters' conclusions.[37] He reasoned that a larger number of smaller groups, such as lobbies, professional associations, and trade unions, were more likely to seek to acquire a greater share of a particular pie for themselves, whilst a smaller number of larger units, which he labelled "encompassing organisations" were more likely to make common cause in increasing the size of the pie. These arguments seem to have a number of important implications for cooperation between states even though there are obvious differences between international society and domestic society.

On the one hand, as regionalization must mean that there were fewer units in the international system, they would be more easily persuaded both of the "pay-offs" from cooperation, and of the need to participate in international arrangements in order to obtain them. This naturally assumes that global sectoralism is perceived as being capable of producing significant benefits. As with "encompassing organizations" the governing systems of the larger units would be more likely to judge that cooperation would increase the size of the pie, and that their positive involvement was necessary for this to happen. In other words the process of regionalization makes a positive contribution to the maintenance of international regimes.

On the other hand, there would by definition be a reduction in the number of smaller units, which may be seen as the equivalent of Olson's special interests and collusions, and, following his reasoning, there would, therefore, also be a reduction in the weight of the pressures directed primarily towards the redistribution of wealth, as, for example, through the radical reordering of international society, rather than towards its creation, and of the numbers of "free-riders" in the system. Olson's thesis, therefore, also suggests that an international society dominated by a smaller number of regional blocs is likely to be an orderly place. But these are very much arguments about the longer term.

There is now evidence to show that in the 1980s regional organization, for a number of reasons, had continued to grow at an impressive rate in

Africa and Asia. This in itself was a significant development. But there were also grounds for supposing that this would go beyond local sectoralism and would evolve on the pattern of the European Communities into a number of regional blocs in which there was an increasing tendency to expand the scope of integration whilst at the same time maintaining a symbiotic relationship between the state and the collectivity. A crucial part of the argument at this point was that the sectoral approach produced, for technical reasons, a number of costs which could be overcome by a greater measure of coordination in integrated programmes. These costs were the source of a continuing underlying pressure towards expanding the scope of integration, and hitherto they have been rather neglected in the academic literature about regional integration. All of this had important implications for functionalism, and the future of international society.

The relative unpopularity of regionalism in the literature in the 1970s had been overtaken by events. The time had come to reexamine the empirical and normative aspects of the subject which had been blocked by a sense of what was fashionable among the community of scholars.

Notes

1. *Africa South of the Sahara*, Europa Publications, London, 1988.
2. See Joseph S. Nye, "Regional Institutions", loc. cit., note 15, Chapter 1.
3. Ibid.
4. Joan Edelman Spero, *The Politics of International Economic Relations*, Third Edition, George Allen and Unwin, London, 1985, especially Chapter 7; Gautam Sen, "UNCTAD and International Economic Reform", in Paul Taylor and A.J.R.Groom (Editors), *Global Issues in the United Nations Framework*, Macmillan, London and Basingstoke, 1989.
5. Robert Gilpin, *The Political Economy of International Relations*, Princeton University Press, Princeton, 1987, especially Chapter 8.
6. Carol Cosgrove Twitchet, *A Framework for Development: The EEC and the ACP*, George Allen and Unwin, London, 1981.
7. The Brandt Commission, *Common Crisis North–South: Cooperation for World Recovery*, Pan Books, London and Sydney, 1983.
8. Paul Taylor, "Reforming the System: Getting the Money to Talk", in Paul Taylor and A.J.R. Groom (Editors), *International Institutions at Work*, Frances Pinter, London, 1988, Pp. 220–235.
9. R.J. Harrison, "Women's Rights: 1975–85", in Taylor and Groom, *Global Issues . . .*, loc. cit.
10. Their ideas are ably discussed in Peter Robson, *The Economics of International Integration*, George Allen and Unwin, London, 1980.
11. Simon Kuznets, *Modern Economic Growth: Rate, Structure and Spread*, Yale University Press, New Haven, 1966.
12. Sam C. Sarkesian, "African Community Building", in Gavin Boyd (Editor), *Regionalism and Global Security*, Lexington Books, D.C. Heath and Company, Lexington, 1984.
13. Sarkesian, loc. cit., P. 64.
14. Michael Handel, *Weak States in International Relations*, Cass, London, 1981.
15. Marks and Spencer, a major British high-street retailer, had a reputation for

acquiring power over suppliers by taking most of their product, though this was generally in order to be able to insist upon high standards.

16. Douglas Williams, *The Specialized Agencies and the United Nations: The System in Crisis*, C. Hurst and Company, London, 1987.

17. Regionalism is ignored in Robert Keohane's classic text, *After Hegemony*, Princeton University Press, Princeton, 1984.

18. Robert Gilpin, *The Political Economy of International Relations*, Princeton University Press, Princeton, 1987.

19. Joseph S. Nye, "Regional Institutions", in Cyril E. Black and Richard A. Falk, *The Structure of the International Environment*, which is Vol. IV of their The Future of the International Legal Order, Princeton University Press, 1972; reproduced in Richard A. Falk and Saul H. Mendlovitz (Editors), *Regional Politics and World Order*, W. H. Freeman and Company, San Francisco, 1973.

20. Paul Taylor, "The New Dynamics of EC Integration in the 1980s", in Juliet Lodge (Editor), *The European Community and the Challenge of the Future*, Pinter Publishers, London, 1989; and Chapter 3, below.

21. *Europe without Frontiers* was the popular description of the proposal to complete the liberalization of the Common Market in the European Community by 1992.

22. This argument is developed in Chapter 4 below.

23. For a number of reasons it looked as if the Gulf involvement was an exceptional action, and that the US would scale down its defence effort in the early 1990s and, whilst not withdrawing from attempts to build a new world order, would expect in a wider sense a greater degree of burden-sharing from partners.

24. Karl W. Deutsch et al., *Political Community and the North Atlantic Area*, Princeton University Press, Princeton, 1957.

25. The terms *vulnerability* and *sensitivity* are used here in the special sense developed by Robert O. Keohane and Joseph S. Nye in their *Power and Interdependence*, Little, Brown, Boston, 1977.

26. Hedley Bull, "Civilian Power Europe: a Contradiction in Terms?", in Loukas Tsoukalis, *The European Community: Past, Present and Future*, Basil Blackwell, Oxford, 1983, Pp. 149–164; Bernard Burrows and Geoffrey Edwards, *The Defence of Western Europe*, Butterworth, London, 1982.

27. See Christopher Brewin and Richard McAllister, "Annual Review of the Activities of the European Community in 1991", *Journal of Common Market Studies*, Vol. XXX, No. 3, September 1991.

28. M. J. Peterson, *The General Assembly in World Politics*, George Allen and Unwin, Boston, 1986, P. 204 and P. 257.

29. David Calleo, *Beyond American Hegemony: the Future of the Western Alliance*, Wheatsheaf, Brighton, 1987; and Andrew J. Pierre (Editor), *A Widening Atlantic? Domestic Change and Foreign Policy*, Council on Foreign Relations, New York, 1986.

30. Roger Masters, "A Multi-bloc Model of the International System", *American Political Science Review*, Vol. 55, No. 4, Dec. 1961, Pp. 780–798.

31. Joint Inspection Unit, *Some Reflections on Reform of the United Nations*, prepared by Maurice Bertrand, JIU/REP/85/9, Geneva, 1985; referred to as the Bertrand Report and reproduced in Paul Taylor and A.J.R. Groom (Editors), *International Institutions at Work*, Pinter Publishers, London, 1988.

32. In Articles J.2(3) and J.5(4).

33. A.J.R. Groom, "Functionalism and World Society" in A.J.R. Groom and Paul Taylor (Editors), *Functionalism: Theory and Practice in International Relations*, University of London Press, London, 1975.

34. David Mitrany, *The Functional Theory of Politics*, Martin Robertson, London, 1975.
35. David Mitrany, *A Working Peace System*, Quadrangle Books, Chicago, 1966, Pp. 157–158.
36. Inis L. Claude Jr., *Swords into Plowshares*, New York, Random House, 1971.
37. Mancur Olson, *The Rise and Decline of Nations*, Yale University Press, New Haven and London, 1982.

Section 2
The Lessons of the European Community*

Introduction

In the two chapters in this section attention is focused much more closely on the example of the European Community. In Chapter 3 the factors pressing for greater integration are considered, as they appeared in the late 1980s and early 1990s. In Chapter 4 the indications of the limits of regional integration are examined in the European context, and some implications for the international system discussed.

The underlying assumption is that these arguments have a general relevance in that they address fundamental problems which are likely to arise in regional integration throughout the world: what specific dynamics of regional integration are likely to arise, and can integration be reconciled with the survival of sovereignty in the existing states? In this sense the European Community is the laboratory within which the model is tested before application elsewhere. Students of regionalization processes in other areas need to pick up the signs and symptoms from the European experience. In Africa, Asia, and elsewhere, particulary because the states are new and caught up in a process of state-building, it is vitally important to show that integration and sovereignty are compatible.

The European Community is the most advanced experiment in peaceful regional international integration the world has ever seen. Section 1 demonstrated that regionalization processes are at work generally; but Europe is ahead of the rest, and what is believed to be happening in that context establishes precedents which may smooth the path, or stiffen the resistance of others. In any discussion of regionalism it is, therefore, essential to look very closely at the European experience. The precise way in which the lessons of Europe are applied elsewhere will depend upon the different national and continental settings, but their relevance is beyond doubt.

---

* Chapter 3 is a version of Chapter 1 of Juliet Lodge (Editor), *The European Community and the Challenge of the Future*, Pinter, London, 1989; Chapter 4 has at its core "The State in the European Community: assumptions, theories and propositions", *Review of International Studies*, January, 1991.

The theory which is stressed in this section, and which is discussed in particular in Chapter 4, is the theory of consociationalism. This sees integration as being concerned with the intermediation of the interests of segments of society which have a high degree of autonomy. Decision-making in the consociation is dominated by a cartel of elites, within which decisions can only be made on the basis of consensus. Readers may be surprised to be told in the Europe of the early 1990s, when majority voting had been formally introduced into a wider range of Community decision-making, that this was still the case. But the reader needs to be very cautious about assuming that majority decision-making at the Community level, which is seen as an area of international relations, is the same as majority voting in the so-called Anglo-American version of democracy within the state.

These arguments are much developed in Chapter 4. It is shown that the two related concepts of consociationalism and symbiosis have great significance for understanding the process of regional integration. They are derived from the modified realism discussed in the Introduction to Section 1.

But although they are developed and in this section discussed in the regional context, the reader should note that they also have relevance to the understanding of international organization in general. This is a crucial step in the development of the argument of this book, and it is discussed further in the introduction to Chapter 5. This is not just a theory of regional integration, but is also a contribution to a general theory of international organization.

3 Integration in the European Community in the 1980s and early 1990s: the new dynamics

In the late 1980s, it looked as if the pace of integration between the member states of the European Communities had once more begun to accelerate. This followed a period of turbulence in the early 1980s.[1] In this chapter, the reasons for this development are examined. The main changes in the relationship between the state and regional organization in Western Europe, which they imply, are discussed. And the question of where the new balance is to be found between integration and autonomy is considered.

The main events in this phase are well known. They include the settlement in 1984 of the British complaint about what were judged to be excessive budgetary contributions, a problem which had previously been a source of considerable animosity between Mrs Thatcher's government and, in particular, that of President Mitterrand;[2] the initiation of a campaign for the strengthening of the powers of the European institutions, especially those of the European Parliament, which culminated in the adoption by the latter of a Draft Treaty on European Union on 14 February 1984;[3] the agreement of the Single European Act at Luxembourg in December 1985, and the instigation of a new programme for the achievement of a Europe without Frontiers by 1992;[4] and the agreement about a package of budgetary measures on 11/12 February 1988, which increased the scale of resources available to the Communities, imposed restraints upon spending on the Common Agricultural Policy, doubled the size of the Funds, and introduced new procedures for exercising financial discipline.[5]

There came a point in the mid-1980s at which President Mitterrand realized that expressions of support for a higher level of integration, such as had been proposed by the European Union Treaty, were a very good strategy for putting pressure upon the British to accept a compromise in the settlement of their budgetary grievance. Helmut Kohl's government in West Germany, partly in response to the French, and partly on its own initiative, acted in ways which gave credence to this strategy. Its effectiveness rested upon the vulnerability of the British government, particularly a Conservative one, to the apparent threat to move a core of original members to a higher level of integration, if necessary to the exclusion of the British. A Conservative government had ignored comparable threats to its cost in the late 1950s, when the EEC had been formed without Britain.[6] British diplomacy, therefore, now had to balance two objectives: that of satisfying specific interests, and that of staying in the game. A measure of compromise in the former had become necessary to achieve the latter.

The various developments in the European Community since 1984 are discussed primarily from the British perspective. The justification for this stress in discussing the general character of the integration process in the Community is that it was the British who determined the pace of integration in this period, as it had been the French in the period 1958 until the mid–late 1960s and the West Germans from then until the late 1970s. Progress depended primarily upon solving British problems and upon finding ways of exerting pressure upon Britain. Two closely interrelated arguments are developed: that the key to further integration was getting the British to move, and that the perception of the need to do this, particularly in the calculations of the French, was itself a crucial factor in placing high on the agenda of the Community items which involved extending the scope of integration and strengthening the central institutions.

A glimpse may be obtained of a curious symbiosis emerging between national interest and the Community: regional processes and systems are seen to be reaching the point at which increasingly frequently the former could ironically only be satisfied by making real concessions to the latter. Mrs Thatcher's speech at Bruges of 20 September 1988, in which she scorned the idea of European unification was no evidence to the contrary:[7] indeed it indicated that the weight of the pressures towards greater unity was being felt. The implications of the speech are evaluated in the conclusions below.

These arguments are developed in three interrelated contexts in what follows. In the next section, the diplomacy about the British budgetary rebate in 1984 is considered. Then the causes and character of the Single European Act in 1985/6 are discussed. In a final section, the budgetary problems in 1987/8 and the budgetary settlement of February 1988 are considered. It is shown that patterns of diplomacy may be identified in 1984 which dominated the whole period under discussion.

*

The Thatcher government and the rest had been quarrelling since the time of the Dublin Summit in 1979 about the interrelated issues of the allegedly excessive net British contribution to the Community Budget, the question of the permanent adjustment of the budgetary mechanism and the reform of the Common Agricultural Policy (CAP). Relations moved towards crisis point just before the outbreak of the Falklands War in 1982, but then on 24 May a short term solution was hastily cobbled together.[8] In 1983, however, the scale of diplomatic pressure was again increased by the British, but despite valiant, though perhaps not very well managed, efforts by the Greeks during their six months of the Presidency in the second half of that year, the Athens Summit in December 1983 ended in deadlock. When the French took over the Presidency for the first six months of 1984 there was, therefore, a general sense that now was the time for a massive diplomatic effort to get the British problem out of the way once and for all, which the French government skilfully orchestrated. In this context the failure of the March 1984 meeting of Heads of State and Government in Brussels – The European Council – was particularly disastrous.

For a few hours after the breakdown of that meeting the two chief protagonists, Mrs Thatcher and President Mitterrand, with his Foreign Minister, Claude Cheysson, behaved as if they had looked into the abyss, and were shocked into an awareness of the desperate need to hold themselves back. There was initially talk on the part of the French of excluding the British from various meetings of EEC states set up to discuss new initiatives, while the British Cabinet actively discussed ways of unilaterally, and probably illegally, holding back payments to the Community.[9] But quite quickly the two leaders changed their tone: the need for quiet reflection and further patient diplomacy was asserted. It is striking though that when agreement was eventually reached at the Fontainebleau Meeting in June 1984 the deal was only marginally different from that which had been rejected in March, and that all sorts of loose ends were left which would not have been tolerated earlier.

Though the British government, one suspects deliberately, made it difficult for a period of weeks after the settlement to judge the Fontainebleau deal – they were very slow to produce any detailed accounts – it was soon apparent that diplomacy between March and June had achieved very little. What had changed was the attitude of the leaders in Britain, particularly, of course, senior foreign policy officers and Mrs Thatcher, to what they had. The latter had even turned up at Fontainebleau with a billet-doux for her partners called "Europe: The Future" in which she claimed that "periodic expressions of pessimism about the future of the Community have never turned out to be justified. . . . Progress that has been made is unlikely to be reversed"[10] (Europe: The Future, 1984). This letter was described as having been "given to the European Community Heads of Government by the Prime Minister as a contribution to discussion at the European Council held at Fontainebleau 25/26 June 1984". Mrs Thatcher had clearly decided that a softer line was necessary.

The flavour of the failure at Brussels in March and the measure of the achievement at Fontainebleau in June 1984 can only be appreciated in the light of a closer look at the details of what happened on those two occasions.[11] At Brussels a deal was tantalizingly close: there had been broad agreement to introduce quotas on milk production – though the Irish had held out for special treatment – and to impose a greater degree of financial control over spending on agriculture; there had been agreement to increase the ceiling on Community resources from VAT from 1% to 1.4% though this was conditional, on German instance, upon enlargement to include Spain and Portugal; the French and the others had accepted the principle of the so-called "formula" which they had strongly resisted in earlier years, that allowed for a permanent adjustment in the budgetary arrangement to ensure a fair return to Britain; and the British conceded that in calculating the scale of the return only payments out of VAT would be taken into account. The latter concession reduced the agreed scale of the British deficit

– called the GAP, from almost 2 billion ECUs to 1.6 billion ECUs (1 ECU = approximately .6 of £1 Sterling). The one question about which there was disagreement was the amount of the British contribution to the Community budget which was to be returned to the British. This was a vital issue since the proportion would apply, according to the "formula", for the next few years, and since the members insisted that agreement on this issue was the condition of acceptance of the whole package.

The negotiations about the amount to be restored to Britain conducted mainly late on Monday the 19th, through late Tuesday the 20th of March 1984, were extraordinary for the obduracy revealed by the leaders in the pursuit of relatively trivial sums, and for the light they threw on the style of negotiation followed by Mrs Thatcher. The latter was to be a matter of some importance throughout the period under consideration. The French had conceded that they thought around a billion ECUs should be restored; Mrs Thatcher's first bid was for 1.35 billion ECUs out of the GAP of 1.6 billion ECUs. In bilateral discussions with the British on Tuesday afternoon President Mitterrand said that they would accept 1.1 billion. Mrs Thatcher declined to compromise, however, and soon found herself in a minority of one in pressing her claim, which the others resisted with increasing irritability. It was her against the Nine. Eventually German Chancellor Kohl said in effect that he had had enough and that the British would get back not a penny more than 1 billion ECUs that year without the formula. He rose and indicated that he was about to leave. At this point Mrs Thatcher said she would take 1.25 billion ECUs but by then it was too late.

The meeting broke up without agreement and with a great deal of annoyance on all sides.[12] The difference between the highest offer by the French and Mrs Thatcher's late bid was 150 million ECUs, around £86 million at the current sterling rate. For this sum, which is paltry by the standards of national budgetary expenditure in even the smallest developed states, the British and the rest had taken the Community to the brink of disaster. Indeed, this was probably the lowest point in relations between the British and the others, especially the French, of the 1970s and 1980s. It follows, of course, that this meeting also marked the beginning of an improvement.

In some ways Fontainebleau represented a stepping back from the brink. It was agreed that the British should get a single payment of £600 million in 1985 and that afterwards the sum returned would be 66% of the gap between Britain's VAT contribution and the share of expenditure in Britain by the Community. The arrangement was to apply only while the own resources ceiling remained at 1.4% of VAT: if the resources level changed, as it did in February 1988, the scale of the rebate was open to renegotiation. For 1983 this formula produced a return to the UK of 1.07 billion ECUs, about £631 million. In other words the British government gained no significant improvement over what would have been within fairly easy reach in March had they conducted themselves differently. But the atmosphere was different and Mrs Thatcher's letter to the other Heads of Government suggested a more positive spirit on her part. A number of elements were added to the Brussels package which would strengthen the identity of the EEC in the minds of the European people, and an Ad Hoc Committee on Institutional Affairs, intended to consider ways of strengthening the Community's institutions, was set up. The latter proposal was apparently rather slipped in by the French and the British accepted it, as it were, before they could catch their breath.[13]

By late 1984 and early 1985, therefore, there was some evidence to suggest that the Community had moved into calmer waters, despite, rather than because of, British diplomacy in that period. Quite a number of squall clouds were still visible, however, not the least of which was that the Community was still under severe financial pressure. Special contributions from member states outside the legal budgetary framework were required in late 1984 and the European Parliament refused to release the rebate already agreed for 1984 until the extra sums had been provided.[14] The Council also proposed a budget for 1985 which covered only ten months of the year, and which made no allowance for the British rebate: this the European Parliament rejected.[15] Negotiations with Spain and Portugal ran into difficulties which raised doubts about whether they could be admitted in January 1986, and the West Germans continued to insist that unless this happened there could be no increase of the VAT ceiling to 1.4%.

In early 1985 the European Community was in a financial mess; it was desperately short of money, dependent on uncertain handouts from governments, and no one knew where the much fought-over rebate for the British would come from. The striking thing, again reflecting the change in tone in 1984, was that there was now a measure of confidence, in the absence of any hard evidence, that it would all come out more or less all right in the end. The conclusion was hard to resist that the one concrete achievement of those who conducted British diplomacy towards the European Community in 1984 was to frighten themselves into a more conciliatory attitude. Certainly any substantive gains from this investment of diplomatic energy were very hard to detect.

What explains this change of tone, which was particularly marked between the Brussels and Fontainebleau meetings, was in part that the French government was no longer benefiting from the operation of the Common Agricultural Policy to the same degree as it had previously, and the accession of Spain and Portugal could probably have the effect of turning France, amongst others, into a net contributor to the Communities' budget. The French were, therefore, more prepared to compromise with the British than they had been earlier. Nevertheless, the settlement at Fontainebleau was possible because the British, and not the French, had changed their positions compared with Brussels – though the Thatcher government tried to conceal this – and it is this change which needs to be explained. The key point was that it was at the time of the March meeting that the strategy of implying support for higher levels of integration, from which the United Kingdom could be excluded, occurred to the French President as a way of dealing with the British problem. This strategy could rest on the seeming reality of the special relationship with West Germany. This strategy was a central element in Franco-British relations from then into 1988, and was certainly a crucial factor in shaping the Single European Act, and the February 1988 budgetary agreement.

The strategy probably emerged accidently in the few hours immediately following the breakdown of the European Council meeting at Brussels, 20/21 March 1984. Mitterrand could hardly help perceiving a link between his initial reaction of calling for a conference of those in the EC who would "stand up and be counted"[16] – which amounted to keeping the British out of discussions about ways of taking the Communities forward – and the rapid retreat from intransigence by Mrs Thatcher and her colleagues. Later, of course, the themes could be developed. On 24 May 1984 – after Brussels and before Fontainebleau – the French President spoke to the European Parliament and expressed support for the European Union Treaty: indeed, he explicitly called for a new treaty and suggested a conference of governments to negotiate it.[17] It is crucial to understand that the idea of a new treaty, which had been included in the European Parliament's original proposals, was itself likely to be seen as a threat by the British. It meant that those governments which agreed with its terms would not be subject to the veto of dissenting members, as is the case with the amendment procedures of the Treaty of Rome as laid down in Article 236. It opened up the prospect of a more supranational inner core, which the United Kingdom could only join at the expense of its sovereignty.

But the French President was prepared to sharpen further the horns of the dilemma for the British, and to do so in a manner which completely escaped the notice of the British press at the time. No doubt Mrs Thatcher's "letter of conciliation" was welcomed, but the arrangements at Fontainebleau were carefully orchestrated to rub the message home. What happened was that the act of beginning the negotiations, of getting down to business, was delayed for several hours whilst President Mitterrand informally confessed what *The Times* (27 June) described in scoffing tones as his "dreams of Europe". These included acceptable things, like a Europe with no customs barriers, but also slightly "wild" things like a European flag, a European anthem, TV station, and so on. Even *The Times* could not resist the implication that here was a somewhat unpredictable, though quaint foreigner, who was getting between us and the serious work. The point was missed that Mitterrand was using the arts of high diplomacy: he was letting Mrs Thatcher see the future. No doubt the message was not lost on her. No doubt, also, the chances of reaching a settlement on terms which were very close to those which had been negotiated but rejected in March were also enhanced. The British press welcomed the settlement, and paused only to pour a little cold water on the agreement to set up what became the Adoninno Committee on a People's Europe. Very litle attention was given to the decision with which the British government reluctantly went along to set up an ad hoc committee on institutional reform.[18]

The West German position was generally supportive of the French. Helmut Kohl invariably made efforts to patch up disagreements with the French whenever they occurred, as happened before the Milan summit in June 1985. Indeed, on the latter occasion the British reaction was one that by then had become typical; there was the implication that the West German government had somehow sacrificed its true interests, which would have led it to side with the British, in order to butter up the French.[19]

German initiatives on European union were seen as being somehow un-
worthy because it was attributable to the West German wish to stay close
to their chum, rather than to any genuine conviction. The Franco-German
Treaty of Friendship of January 1963 had, however, been given a new lease
of life with an extension of the consultative procedures on political cooperation between the two states. Measures were also taken to ease trade relations between France and West Germany ahead of the practice of the
others, and there were reports of Franco-German efforts to create a "core"
of more integrated states.[20] Kohl was also prepared to make sympathetic
noises about the European Union Treaty, and in the election to the European Parliament in 1984 the Treaty was probably higher on the agenda in
West Germany than in any other state. The CDU/CSU governments' views
towards France, and a more united Europe, were not without their
contradictions and ambiguities: but from the British point of view it was
significant that Kohl was prepared to express his attachment to both ahead
of immediate calculations of interest. When the latter got in the way, as
they sometimes did, efforts were made to recover the bearing.

In one particular respect, however, Helmut Kohl's conduct was arguably
decisive. When he rose from the table in anger at 6.30 on the afternoon of
20 March 1984 in Brussels, he revealed a carelessness about British reactions which carried an unmistakable and ominous warning for the latter.
They could, as it were, "take it or leave it". The implication was that at
the end of the day they could indeed leave it, and that this was a course
of action which though unpleasant could be contemplated, and which might
have to be faced. No doubt President Mitterrand also caught the psychological chill of that moment, and shortly afterwards began to fathom its
implications. Kohl's action was indeed decisive in revealing the flaw in the
British diplomatic armament – that they were prepared to make sacrifices
in order to avoid being excluded from the inner sanctum – and more than
any other single act it changed the direction of movement of the tide of
European integration in the mid-1980s. Perhaps this was the underlying
reason for Mrs Thatcher's publicly acknowledged dislike of the West
German Chancellor, a sentiment which was obviously reciprocated.

*

The character of the Single European Act, which was negotiated at Luxembourg in December 1985, may be explained in terms of judgements and
interests which derived directly from those revealed at Fontainebleau in June
1984. The British found themselves under pressure to make concessions in
the direction of European Union, and of European policies about which
they had serious misgivings, in order to keep themselves in the game, and
in order to obtain specific objectives of their own. These goals were of
equal and vital importance.

The British wanted no truck with any of the several variations of future
development in the Communities which were then being discussed – except
one.[21] They disliked the idea of a two-tier Europe very much indeed. One
reason for this position was that it would reduce their ability to exercise

influence in the EPC framework which they very strongly supported. They also, however, disliked strongly the idea of Europe à la carte or the idea of graduated integration as general principles of future European organization: the existing example of this, the EMS arrangement, and the proposal to reactivate West European Union, were to be regarded as exceptions to the rule. That everyone should go forward at the same gentle pace, one ideally suited to British capacities and inclinations, was the future most earnestly to be desired.

One problem for the British was that by early 1985 the various items on the agenda of integration, the completion of the Common Market, the strengthening of the machinery for political cooperation, and the rather ambitious proposals for institutional reform, had been refined and increasingly firmly linked together in a single package. The British had tried to prevent this. In the discussions of the Ad Hoc Committee for Institutional Affairs, which became known as the Dooge Committee, after its Irish chairman, the pattern was set. It established a "convergence of priorities" in the particular sense that the need for a "homogeneous internal economic area", the "promotion of common values of civilisation", and the "search for an external identity" was spelled out, and made conditional upon the achievement of "efficient and democratic institutions", meaning "a strengthened Commission", the extension of the powers of the European Parliament and the reform of the Court of Justice.[22] A method for obtaining these goals was recommended in the Report: it was held that a

conference of the representatives of the governments of the member states should be convened in the near future to negotiate a draft European Union Treaty based on the "acquis communautaire", the present document, and the Stuttgart Solemn Declaration on European Union, and guided by the spirit and method of the draft treaty voted by the European Parliament.

President Mitterrand indicated his approval for this general line by appointing a known Euro-enthusiast, Maurice Faure, as the French member of the committee.[23] In other words, it proposed an explicit and detailed programme for action leading to a new treaty.

The best that the British representative, Malcolm Rifkind, could do in the face of this enthusiasm was to enter a number of reservations which were noted in footnotes. Together with his Greek and Danish colleagues he held that the proposals should be the "subject of consultations between the governments before the June European Council", and opposed the idea of the conference of government representatives. The latter probably looked to the British suspiciously like the constituent assembly of a federal union.[24] Elsewhere in the Report, Rifkind alone entered reservations on proposals to strengthen the European Parliament – at most it should "make more use of its right to put forward proposals for community action", and there should be "improvement and extension of the conciliation procedure";[25] he opposed the proposal that the incoming President of the Commission should nominate his own team of Commissioners for approval of the governments.[26] Governments should continue as at present to nominate and approve unanimously what Mrs Thatcher now frequently referred to as "our Commissioner(s)" in flat defiance of the stipulations of the Rome Treaty. And together with the Greek and Danish representatives he insisted that the January 1966 Luxembourg Accord, which required that there should be consensus voting in the Council of Ministers if a state held that a matter concerned its vital national interest, should continue to operate.[27] No reservations on the policy objectives were entered.

This pattern of doubts on the proposals for institutional reform, and support for the policies, remained the British position through until the meeting of the European Council at Milan in June 1985. It had, however, by then been somewhat refined in that the need for a state to justify in detail its wish to invoke the Luxembourg Accord was asserted by the Thatcher government, and the appeal was addressed to the others that majority voting should be used more frequently in the Council of Ministers' decision-making.[28] The apparent contradiction between these two aspects of British policy on institutional reform will be considered below. But, as William Wallace has pointed out, the British reluctance to accept that institutional arrangements mattered was a problem: British exhortations to better behaviour in the use of the veto had little appeal.[29]

By the time of the June Summit, a further element had, however, been introduced into the package with British agreement, which nevertheless had the effect of further increasing the difficulties for the British of steering a way between either accepting the package as a whole or risking the appearance of stronger pressures towards a two-tier Europe. This was the attachment to the package of an explicit time constraint, namely, the achievement of a Europe without Frontiers by a specified date, 1992. This meant that agreement about the institutional changes, as well as the detail of the programme, had to be reached in the near future: there would be less scope for the British to escape from the horns of their dilemma by procrastination.

In the draft treaty establishing the European Union, the stress had been upon constitutional and institutional aspects, with only an outline statement of the programme. No specific deadline was mentioned. In the Ad Hoc Committee's Report the programme was described in greater detail, but again no date was attached. The first mention of the 1992 deadline found by the present writer was in the President of the Commission's statement to the European Parliament, 14 January 1985, in which, speaking of the next meeting of the European Council, he said: "now that some Heads of State and Government have decided to set an example . . . it may not be over-optimistic to announce a decision to eliminate all frontiers within Europe by 1992 and to implement it."[30] This ambition was approved by the European Council at its meeting at Brussels on 29/30 March 1985. The government's response then was to ask the Commission "to draw up a detailed programme with a specific timetable" for its meeting in June. The result was the preparation of the much discussed White Paper on Completing the Internal Market which was presented to the heads of government at Milan.[31]

On 1 July 1985 it was reported in Britain that the Milan Summit of

28/29 June had been "extremely bad-tempered" and that Mrs Thatcher's "anger and frustration" even "undisguised fury" had shown through.[32] Unfortunately, however, from the British point of view, when viewed in the longer perspective, the dice can be seen to have been loaded against a favourable outcome. The French strategy, the refinement of the proposals for Europe without frontiers in the White Paper, and the pressure of deadlines, meant that it was odds on that the British would now have to accept the establishing of an intergovernmental conference which would have on its agenda the amendment of the Communities' decision-making procedures. Only the Greeks and the Danes joined with the British in voting against the Mitterrand proposal for a conference. Again, Helmut Kohl attracted Mrs Thatcher's particular wrath by supporting the French. Mitterrand said that the outcome had "sorted out those in favour of a strong united Europe from those who were hanging back". *The Times* said disingenuously that his comments had "rekindled speculation about a two-tier Europe".[33] Precisely so! From the point of view of the British the awful irony, however, was that making the concessions demanded of them on institutional reform had by now become a way of keeping such speculation alive. The more they conceded, the more the supranational tendency would be fed and the greater the demands which could be made upon them.

In the subsequent discussion of the outcome of the Milan Summit in the British House of Commons, Jonathan Aitken MP mischievously asked Mrs Thatcher if the time had come to consider President Mitterrand's proposal for a two-tier Europe (*The Times* 3 July 1985). The answer was short and simple: she disagreed. The obvious concession, therefore, had to be made. At a meeting of the General Affairs Council of Foreign Ministers, 22/23 July 1985, Britain went along with the others in agreeing to the convening of an intergovernmental conference by the Luxembourg Presidency, in office in the second half of 1985, which was explicitly asked to consider the "revision of the Rome Treaty" and the drafting of a treaty on political cooperation and European security.[34] The British had at least gained the important concession that there would not be a new treaty. It was reported, however, that early on in the discussions of the intergovernmental committee, some governments, especially the Italians, the Belgians and the Dutch, sought to put pressure upon the British by speaking explicitly of the possibility that some of the Ten could go ahead of the others.[35] It was, therefore, perhaps not surprising that in early October the British Foreign Secretary, Sir Geoffrey Howe, gave the "first indications that Britain would accept treaty amendments on a pragmatic basis".[36]

The underlying dynamics of the negotiations leading up to the conclusion of the Single European Act are now clearly visible. On the one hand were a group of states, which included in particular the French, the Italians, the Dutch, Belgians, Luxemburgers and the West Germans, which inclined to support a more ambitious set of changes for the European institutions, though probably Butler was correct when he pointed out that no member actually wanted to give the European Parliament the sole right both to initiate and approve legislation.[37] The French government by this time did not need to lead this faction at all stages, and, indeed, it was the Italians who in practice in 1985–86 usually carried the Euro-banner. The West Germans sometimes dragged their feet but generally and eventually inclined to this group much to the irritation of the British. A further instance of this resulted from the meeting in London, 27 November 1985, between Kohl and Thatcher at which they agreed that economic and monetary union should not be included as a goal in the Single European Act. Later, however, Kohl changed his mind when the French and Italians liberalized their exchange control provisions and these goals were eventually included in the Agreement's Preamble.[38] Again, presumably, Mrs Thatcher was furious!

The British headed a group of doubters which included the Greeks and the Danes. It was vital to realize, however, that the outcome of the negotiations between this group and the others cannot be completely explained by reference to the specific interests and exchanges on particular policies. The longer term dynamics which have been outlined meant that the British group was necessarily and invariably on the defensive in the negotiations, particularly with regard to the institutional questions. They were placed in the position of having to make specific concessions in order to avoid incurring non-specific and longer term costs and of having to fight a rearguard battle to prevent fundamental alterations in the structure of the Communities of which they did not approve. Thanks to the Mitterrand strategy, success in this depended paradoxically upon making concessions on precisely those questions, whilst at the same time struggling to make them as small as possible. The character of the Single European Act was largely explicable in terms of the outcome of this struggle and this feature was captured in Mrs Thatcher's extraordinarily arrogant remark to the House of Commons on the 5th December 1985, on her return from Luxembourg: "Part of our task the whole time has been to diminish their expectations and draw them down from the clouds to practical matters" (The Times, 6 December 1985). The reader should consider the likely reactions of Kohl, Mitterrand et al. on reading about this comment by the British Prime Minister.

There is a sense in which the Single European Act of December 1985 was a considerable achievement for the British negotiators. A central feature of that achievement was that a way was found to make what appeared to be major concessions to those who wanted stronger European institutions, whilst at the same time introducing such qualifications as to significantly mitigate their implications. Much depended upon the discussions at Luxembourg between the heads of government: they took 21 hours over settling the main questions, 11 more than had been planned; this was one measure of the difficulty in finding agreement. As a result, however, the British negotiators could comfort themselves, for the time being at least, with the judgement that what they had wanted all along had been achieved: a system which depended for its success upon the convergent interests, and political goodwill of governments rather than upon some constitutional relocation of the metaphysical bases of power. This judgement does not need to rest upon the assumption that the British took the lead in positively seeking and obtaining outcomes in all cases where they benefited. In some cases, indeed,

British advantage was a product, gratefully accepted, of negotiations in which others lead.

Much depended upon the nature of the new powers of the European Parliament and upon the implications of the extension of majority voting in the Council of Ministers, and the policy areas to which these changes were to apply. The proposal to introduce co-decision-making for the European Parliament in its relations with the Council – in effect to give each of the partners a veto – was successfully resisted. Instead, a cooperative procedure was introduced which allowed a second reading to the European Parliament, as a result of which it could now either reject a Council proposal, or amend it. If it did the former, the Council could only overcome its rejection by a unanimous vote; if the latter, the Commission was required either to incorporate Parliament's amendment into a new proposal for the Council, or, if it disagreed, send Parliament's amendment to the Council together with its own proposal. In this case, the Council could only accept the Parliament's amendment on the basis of unanimity.[39]

Richard Corbett concluded that the amendment procedure was "in essence a second consultation of the European Parliament in more difficult conditions (needing an absolute majority to propose amendments and unable to use delaying tactics) than current practice in its single reading".[40] On the other hand, the ability to reject legislation from the Council could strengthen the European Parliament's hand in that the requirement of unanimity in the Council to overcome the rejection would strengthen the ability of governments which sympathized with the Parliament's view, to introduce the proposed changes. In this case, therefore, Parliament's role seemed to have been increased. But a further alteration in the Single European Act was that if the Council had not acted within three months, which may be extended by one month by "common accord between the Council and the European Parliament" (Article 7 Single European Act, paragraphs F & G), the proposal could be "deemed not to have been adopted". This in effect severely curtailed the power of the European Parliament which had been confirmed by the Isoglucose case, which depended upon its ability to delay.[41] In other words, in the ten areas to which this new procedure was to apply, the member governments could as a last resort avoid taking action which they did not like by vetoing attempts in the Council to overcome Parliament's wishes. The most important area to which the cooperative procedure applied was the legislation covered in the new Article 100a, under which the Council was to take decisions by majority vote, on its first reading, to implement the establishment and functioning of the internal market – Europe without Frontiers. If the members had the will to work for the latter, it was to be assumed that as a matter of good sense, and to avoid unnecessary delays, they would not use what amounted to a veto by inaction. But the arrangement, nevertheless, meant that states in extremis could stop the European Parliament from getting what it wanted.

In view of the British government's appeals to the others to rely more upon majority voting in the Council of Ministers, it might seem odd that the British Prime Minister should have made it clear on her return from Luxembourg that "the Luxembourg compromise [allowing a national veto] was unaffected." She also said, however, that there had been "no transfer of powers from Parliament to the Assembly". She even avoided the use of the term "European Parliament", which had been formally accepted in the Single European Act. And only a little earlier she had asserted that she did not believe "even in the concept of a United States of Europe" (*The Times*, 6 December 1985).

The apparent inconsistency in the British position may be discussed with reference to Article 69 of the Treaty of Rome on the liberalization of capital movements. This was not included in the Single Act as being subject in the future to the cooperative procedure, though according to the Treaty such movements were to be taken by a majority vote after the first two transitional stages. Article 69 carried an implication that was of great importance for the British in that according to Article 61(2) (Rome Treaty) "the liberalisation of banking and insurance services connected with movements of capital shall be effected in step with progressive liberalisation of movements of capital." In other words, banking and insurance services were to be liberalized also, as the Rome Treaty had intended, by majority vote, without the involvement of the European Parliament. What seemed to be revealed was a British strategy for attempting to disarm those states, such as Greece, Spain and West Germany, which might have wished to place difficulties in the way of liberalizing banking and insurance, by appealing for their acceptance of majority voting, whilst at the same time retaining the right to invoke the Luxembourg Accord if necessary to protect their own interests. Paradoxically, therefore, majority voting was now seen by the British as a means of national leverage. It was to stop the others from preventing the British from getting what they wanted, rather than a mechanism for facilitating the easier definition of a European interest as was believed by some Euro-enthusiasts.

It was also in the British interest that 1992 was not to be a legally binding deadline, but more of a date for measuring the achievement. This is not to deny that there was an ambition to move significantly forward by then – Lord Cockfield had been placed in charge of the programme and was after all our Commissioner! But the state of British industry, though its improving condition had created an increased confidence by late 1985, was not such as to justify the removal of a safety net. Indeed, allowing the European Parliament to use the cooperative procedure with regard to Article 100a decisions could be seen as one strand in the latter: it was a way of working which would inevitably slow the process down. Article 100b provided other strands. In effect, the remaining detractions from the internal market were to be listed by the Commission in 1992, and decisions about their equivalents in the various member states, and about their removal if there were no equivalents, were then to be taken on the basis of majority decision in the Council (first reading) and the cooperative procedure. Recalcitrant states then had ample opportunity for endlessly protracting the negotiations to complete the process of achieving a Europe without Frontiers if they then deemed this necessary.

Other aspects of the Single European Act illustrate the theme of Britain's wish to minimize concessions to the European centre, whilst avoiding accentuating centripetal tendencies in other members, and obtaining desired specific ends. Many of these relate to a broad disagreement between those who were inclined to include in the Act explicitly what was thought necessary to complete the internal market, and those who wished to move forward in a more pragmatic fashion by only accepting the general principle now, and making further adjustments later in the light of experience. Amongst the latter group, naturally, the British occupied pole position, whilst the former included the Commission, Italy, France and the Benelux countries, with the support usually of the West Germans. The point has already been made that the British eventually accepted reluctantly the reiteration of the goal of the "progressive realization of economic and monetary union" (Preamble, Single European Act). But the list of exclusions from the range of specific goals linked with the completion of the internal market and the obtaining of monetary union, also reflected British interests. In Article 6, "policy on credit and savings, medicines and drugs" was carefully excluded from the cooperative procedure. Similarly, in Article 18, according to paragraph 2 of the agreed new Article 100a of the Rome Treaty on the approximation by the Community of Laws, regulations and administrative actions in member states to achieve "the establishment and functioning of the Common Market" – a process which was also to involve the cooperative procedure – "fiscal provisions, and those relating to the free movement of persons" and the "rights and interests of employed persons", were to be excluded. The latter was, of course, a sensitive political question in Mrs Thatcher's Britain as the free movement of persons would have involved removing boundary controls which Home Secretary Douglas Hurd in May 1988 insisted were necessary in order to control terrorism. On this the British government was the most resistant of the Twelve. In any case, such concessions to the idea of a united Europe were likely to be highly contentious in the Conservative party of the 1980s. They might also have eased the movement of political undesirables.

Article 17 may also be seen as being essentially a British compromise in that it held that Article 99 of the Rome Treaty should now be modified, apparently to the least possible extent, in order only to allow the European Parliament to be consulted about provisions for the harmonization of legislation concerning turn-over taxes, excise duties, and other forms of indirect taxation. It is, indeed, hard to understand why such a miniscule adjustment should have been at all necessary, except in terms of pressure upon the British to make some kind of concession, and their reaction in feeling that some attempt had to be made at drawing a line over which they would not step. The question of the introduction of standard rates of VAT – encompassed in the Article 99 reference to turn-over taxes – had become politically sensitive in Britain in the mid–late 1980s. In particular, politicians on both sides of the political divide were determined to resist attempts to introduce VAT on a number of items including children's clothes, food, and books, partly because there was some public feeling against it, though no doubt this could have been mitigated by politicians had they been so minded, and partly because some of the latter felt that to go forward would undermine one of the fundamental, and ancient rights of the British

Parliament, that of taxation. So the cooperative procedure was excluded from the new Article 99 – the European Parliament was only to be consulted – and as before the Council would act "unanimously on a proposal from the Commission", and Mrs Thatcher assured the British public that VAT could not be introduced on items in the event of their objection.

From the British point of view, indeed, the new arrangements on cooperation in economic and monetary policy had advantages. A new section on these matters was introduced into the Rome Treaty, which meant that the Commission now had responsibilities in the operation of the European Monetary System. This could be regarded as a further consolidation of the arrangements of the Community, as EMS mechanisms had previously formally not been a part of these. On the other hand, paragraph 2 of the New Article 102a EEC explicitly required that "in so far as further development in the field of economic and monetary policy necessitates institutional changes the provisions of Article 236 shall be applicable." Proposals for new institutional arrangements for the EMS would, therefore, from then on be subject to the amendment procedures of the Rome Treaty, and could therefore be vetoed by dissenting states, even those, such as the British, which had not yet joined the EMS. The British had now acquired the means of preventing the others from creating a two-tier Europe with regards to money, a significant development in view of Mrs Thatcher's opposition to the British membership in the EMS, and her hostility to a Franco-German initiative in 1988 in favour of moving towards a kind of European central bank.[42] (The latter proposal was indeed criticized by the Bundesbank in West Germany.) They had more than clawed back the concessions they had made in accepting that the goal of economic and monetary union should be included in the Act.

On some matters it is not difficult to become somewhat cynical about the attitude of British diplomats during the negotiations. On the environment, for instance, they agreed that the "polluter should pay" and that the Community was now to have a role in protecting the "quality of the environment", "the protection of human health" and "the prudent and rational utilisation of natural resources" (Article 25 SEA; New Treaty of Rome Article 130r). But, having made that gesture, the reservation was entered (New Article 130s) that any Community action should be decided on the basis of unanimity in the Council of Ministers. Such behaviour may be judged as being no more than commercial caution; it became a matter of bad taste, even moral error, when set beside Britain's major failure regarding control of omissions which produced acid rain and other pollutants, widely accepted as gravely damaging forests in Germany and in Scandinavia, and the generally obstructive attitude of the Government towards legislation on environmental and analogous questions. Indeed, the Duke of Edinburgh was moved to take the injudicious step, for a member of the Royal Family, of admitting his difficulty in justifying British policy on environmental pollution to his European colleagues in the World Wildlife and Nature Protection Fund. In late September 1988, the British Prime Minister indicated, however, that new global efforts to solve environmental problems should be made. Her speech was greeted with astonishment, which was hardly surprising in view of the earlier record of the British government. By the time of writing, there had been no practical outcome of this initiative.

Britain had also agreed to a Community effort to strengthen the "scientific and technological basis of European industry", but insisted that the Multi-annual Framework Programme in which it was to be embodied, should be subject to unanimity in the Council. In this they were supported, in particular, by the West Germans. Only a few months later the British revealed their underlying attitude to this great European enterprise: they refused to countenance anything other than a minimum budget, and, at the same time limited their participation in the European space programme. The general British posture seemed to be to encourage technological innovation and the use of venture capital but not at the European level and not out of the public purse. Indeed, they seemed prepared to enter into commitments at the European level which they had no intention of honouring in order to ensure that they could be more easily frustrated. One illustration of this was the British behaviour with regard to the financing of the Horizon 2000 project of the European Space Agency, which was described by Lord Shackleton a respected Labour member of the House of Lords as constituting "apalling bad manners and arrogance" (*The Independent*, 5 October 1988, p. 2). The British had procrastinated about the level of finance for the Agency, and were currently refusing to endorse a 5% increase in the budget to support Horizon 2000, which represented a core science programme. The British were alone in opposing the increase but held a veto as the decision according to the Single European Act was subject to unanimity in the Council of Ministers.

There is, therefore, no doubt that in the circumstances of 1984 and 1985 the Single European Act can be judged as a considerable British achievement. In its details it reflected British interests in a remarkably nuanced and comprehensive way. On the other hand, the British, and, of course, the varying coalitions of states with which they were involved, had been placed in a situation in which they had indeed been required to make concessions. They had not wanted the Dooge Committee, the Intergovernmental Committee, formal amendment of the Rome Treaty, changes in the role of the European Parliament or Commission, or, indeed, any truck with the kind of *brouhaha* approach which led up to the Luxembourg meeting. They wanted the completion of the internal market but even in this there was an element of ambiguity: they were pushed onto the bandwagon because of the others' apparent willingness to go on ahead. The few areas where there was unambiguous enthusiasm were the liberalization of the capital market, and of the related arrangements for banking and insurance, and the EPC. In these areas, however, the method preferred by the British, in their usual way, was one of low key negotiations between governments leading to specific commitments with no immediate implications for institutional change.

Despite its modest immediate effects, the Single European Act stands, however, as a symbol of the constraints which had now been placed upon those governments which preferred a minimalist approach to Europe. The question arises of whether the concessions would, despite the conscious intentions of these states, further strengthen those constraints, and it is with this question that the next section of this chapter is concerned. In other words, it is now necessary to evaluate the extent to which the constraints upon British action, deriving from the regional system, were evolving in the longer term.

*

In 1987 to 1988 four interrelated issues rose to the top of the diplomatic agenda in the European Community. They were the questions of the controlling of farm spending which, by general consent, had got out of hand, that of the strengthening of budgetary discipline, that of changing the procedures for revenue-raising so that new sums could be found to cover the Communities' expanding expenses, and that of increasing the amount of regional aid to the new Mediterranean member states. These matters were discussed in particular at three meetings of the European Council, at Brussels in June 1987, which ended in great acrimony; at Copenhagen, 4–5 December 1987, at which no settlement was reached, but which, much to everybody's surprise, was characterized by "remarkable good temper" (*The Times*, 7 December 1987); and at a special meeting, planned at Copenhagen, at Brussels 10–12 February 1988, which produced a settlement. As in previous years the battle lines were drawn between the British, in occasional alliance with one or more other members – but in increasing danger of being isolated – on the one side, and a larger group, led by France and West Germany on the other.

The immediate appearance of the outcome in February 1988 was that the British had conceded. "Against all expectations, and in defiance of the Prime Minister's most deeply entrenched instincts, the Summit had ended in success" (*The Observer*, 14 February 1988). Indeed, if attention is confined to the specific details of the outcome it is hard to avoid this conclusion. On each of the major items on the agenda there was either "no change" or a major British concession, compared, say, with the Copenhagen Summit. It also seemed fair to conclude that the outcome represented a triumph of what has been called in this chapter the "Mitterrand strategy": the judgement might even seem reasonable that Mrs Thatcher had "at last been brought to realise her European destiny". Hugo Young introduced a qualification of this interpretation, however, when he wrote

the Brussels agreement . . . may come to be seen as the most momentous retreat of Mrs Thatcher's career . . . Where all earlier encounters have been represented as a matter of total victory or defeat . . . a different perspective is necessary to explain the kind of fudge Mrs Thatcher was defending in the Commons yesterday. . . . There really is no alternative but for Europe's senior statesperson at last to show that she belongs to the continent in which we live.

In other words, though Mrs Thatcher had compromised she had in Young's view, yet to realize where she stood in the world (*The Guardian*, 16 February 1988).

The compromise needs to be considered in the light of the constraints discussed earlier in this chapter and the hierarchy of issues which they suggest. Most analysts explained it as an outcome of diplomacy about an explicit, visible agenda, and there is naturally scope for doing this as will shortly be demonstrated. A second kind of explanation is concerned, however, with diplomacy about a disguised, yet implicit agenda. At the meetings in 1987 and 1988 negotiations had implications for the pattern of the future development of the structure of the Communities, and the British gained concessions in this area which at the time were not fully appreciated by the others but which nevertheless encouraged the British to make concessions on the visible agenda. There was a hidden trade-off between items on the two agendas which obviously had not been possible at Luxembourg in December 1985 because all items then, structural/constitutional and specific, had been placed on the visible agenda. A third level of diplomacy concerned items on what might be called an emerging agenda: this included the longer term implications of the agreements about specifics, which were being realized and accepted at a relatively gradual but uneven pace by governments. They included adjustments in the scope of integration, which were required to allow the internal market to be completed, such as the adoption of stronger monetary arrangements, and strengthening the mechanisms for managing the business cycle in common. These three levels of diplomacy and the links between them will now be considered.

The item which occupied pride of place on the visible agenda was the level of spending on the common agricultural policy. Mrs Thatcher said during Friday the 12th February, when it looked as if the Brussels Summit would again, for the third time on these questions, end in deadlock: "we came here to get agricultural spending under control" (*The Times*, 13 February 1988). The British, initially with the support of the Dutch, wanted in particular a ceiling of 155 million tonnes on the production of cereals in the Community coupled with rather severe penalties for farmers who exceeded that target. The British also insisted that the rate of increase in spending on agriculture should be limited to 60% of the Community's national output growth, whilst the West Germans argued for 70–80% and the French 100%. The latter also wanted a higher ceiling on cereal products initially at 165 million tonnes, and weaker stabilizers in the event of over-production. At an Anglo-German summit in London in January 1988, Mrs Thatcher announced that even 160 million tonnes a year was "totally unacceptable" (*The Observer*, 14 February 1988).

Yet in the early hours of Saturday the 13th February "this was precisely the figure she presented to the doubting journalists as evidence of peace in our time". Details of the agreement also revealed that the British had accepted "an annual growth rate of EAGGF guarantee expenditure of 80% of GNP".[43] A relatively soft system of stabilizers was also accepted: in each marketing year an additional co-responsibility levy of 3% above the intervention price would be paid by the first buyer, which would be refunded if production was at or below the agreed ceiling. If production was above the ceiling, this levy would not be refunded, and the intervention price for the following year would be reduced by 3%. This amounted to a modest disincentive on over-production (see Note 5, p. 7). In addition, a set-aside programme was agreed according to which producers would be induced to take "at least 20% of arable land used for cultivating products covered by the Common Market organisations" out of production. A formula was derived for compensating farmers for income lost which provided for the minimum payment of 100 ECUs per hectare and the maximum of 600 ECUs per hectare.[44]

Greater discipline in spending on the agricultural intervention system was, however, agreed. For instance, states were obliged to provide more detailed information about spending "within each marketing organisation so as to ensure that the rate at which appropriations in each chapter are used is known with precision one month after expenditure has taken place" (see Note 5, Section 2, p. 6). The Commission would then compensate states for their actual expenditure on agricultural support within two months. This represented an extension of the payment period compared with the earlier practice by one half a month. In this way the Commission could be more confident that states could not in future profit by claiming amounts above what they had actually paid. Other measures for increased control over agricultural spending were also introduced. The conclusion is hard to avoid, however, that the overall balance of the agreement on agriculture was closer to that supported by France and West Germany, and rather distant from the position earlier adopted by the British.

With regard to the Structural Funds, the pattern of support and opposition to increases in allocated resources varied somewhat from that on agricultural spending. But for most of the period of the negotiations Britain appeared to be the most adamant in resisting increases above 50% by 1992. France gave some support to this position for a while though West Germany wanted a greater increase (*Financial Times*, 10 February 1988). It was reported, however, that when negotiations seemed deadlocked on the afternoon of Friday the 12th February, Mrs Thatcher struck a deal with Felipe Gonzales, the Spanish Prime Minister, whereby the British would make concessions on the financing of the funds, which were particularly to the advantage of the Southern countries, in return for their support on the agricultural side (*The Times*, 13 February 1988). This deal obviously fell apart when it became clear that Britain could not get its way on agriculture. In the event, it was the British who eventually conceded most ground. It was agreed that "commitment appropriations for structural funds will be doubled in 1993 by comparison with 1987" (see Note 5, p. 2).

In view of these various retreats when compared with earlier positions, it was surprising that Britain also accepted largely without alteration the Commission's original proposals on how to increase the scale of own resources. Mrs Thatcher's government had earlier insisted that any increase should be tied to a significant tightening of controls on farm intervention, "the problem which has faced us for eight years" (*The Times*, 13 February 1988). Relative failure in this area did not, as might have been expected, lead to increased opposition to the budgetary changes, and, in the agreement a fourth resource, which would ensure that own resources for commitments would increase to 1.3% of GNP by 1992 was accepted.[45] The three other "resources" remained unchanged. The implications of a range of further steps to achieve discipline with regard to both regulated and non-regulated expenditure, in other words, the budget as a whole, are considered shortly, though it was striking that these received relatively little attention either in the initial reporting of the agreement in Britain or in Mrs Thatcher's preliminary announcements. The "hot" items were agricultural spending and the structural funds.

Why were the British brought to make such a significant range of concessions with regard to items on the visible agenda? It would seem that the change of mind came rather late in the day. On December the 11th, *The Times* carried a singularly bellicose leader which warned of the dangers of giving way on the various matters which were to be negotiated, and on the afternoon of that day, British officials seemed to be prepared for failure. "We seem to have taken a step backwards since the Copenhagen summit in December" (*The Times*, 13 February 1988). "This thing is headed for the rocks. It is just a question of which rock it crashes against" (*The Observer*, 14 February 1988). By late on Friday, however, the British had back-pedalled enough to allow a settlement. It seems likely in view of these comments that responsibility for the change of position rested firmly with Mrs Thatcher and a relatively small group of her closest advisers. A key period may have been mid-afternoon on the 12th February, when according to officials, Mrs Thatcher did something which for her was quite extraordinary: during the conference she retreated by herself to a room for an hour's solitary contemplation. Afterwards her position was conciliatory.

One reason for the change of mind could be that during the previous week, and during the Brussels conference itself, the British had become progressively more isolated. This had not mattered on previous occasions: indeed the British had seemed to take pleasure in their singularity. At Copenhagen, however, British officials for the first time went out of their way to express their delight that Mrs Thatcher had "succeeded in avoiding the impression given at the last Summit that she was isolated in an 11–1 minority" (*The Times*, 7 December 1988). It was "for Britain especially a relief not to have to take the blame" (*Financial Times*, 7 December 1988). But confidence that rather more balanced, diplomatic groupings, varying with regard to specific issues, could emerge gradually, disappeared in early 1988. The West Germans once more veered towards the French, as, for instance, at a meeting of agricultural ministers in January, and on Friday the 12th "there were signs that the Dutch were moving to join the majority leaving Mrs Thatcher isolated 11–1 as in previous summits." The Dutch had previously supported the line of the British with regard to the ceiling on agricultural production (*The Times*, 13 February 1988). The apparent failure of the attempted deal with the Spanish confirmed this isolation, and the reaction of the French and German diplomats to Mrs Thatcher's personal style must have sharpened British appreciation of the dangers of being alone. "Seldom has German and French distaste for Mrs Thatcher and her methods been so clearly expressed as it was here" (*The Observer*, 14 February 1988). At one point the French Prime Minister Chirac allegedly uttered "an enormous obscenity" in comment upon the behaviour of the Lady (*The Observer*, 14 February 1988). The significance of psychological factors should not be underestimated.

Another part of the explanation of British behaviour was the more obvious one that there was a risk, if the British maintained their position, of losing all or part of the British rebate. The Commission had argued in 1987 that the scale of the rebate should be related solely to imbalances arising from the operation of the Common Agricultural Policy. The governments had refrained from bringing up the question of the British rebate at Copenhagen, though according to the terms of the June 1984 agreement, this was formally a possibility as the level of own resources was now to be adjusted. This possibility was held as a kind of sword of Damocles over the heads of the British diplomats as the February 1988 summit approached. For instance, on 10th February, it was reported that the French government was expected to press for a phasing out of the compensation to the British (*Financial Times*, 10 February 1988). Mrs Thatcher pointed out "triumphantly" at her press conference on 13th February that the rebate had saved £3 billion for the British taxpayer over the preceding three years.

It seemed fair to conclude, therefore, that

what determined her to settle at the last minute was a negotiator's judgement, which could only be made on the spot. It was that any further delay, postponing the decision to the Hanover summit in June, would have imperilled what Britain cares about even more than farm surpluses, namely the Fontainebleau agreement on the British rebate. (Young, *The Guardian*, 16 February 1988)

Accordingly, it was agreed, with some minor adjustments that "the European Council conclusions of the 25th and 26th June 1984 on the correction of budgetary imbalances remain applicable for as long as the new decision on own resources remains in force" (European Council, 1988, p. 15). A postponement until the Hanover summit might also have interrupted progress towards the completion of the internal market by 1992, and no doubt this was also a consideration which pushed the British towards a settlement. It was a package of agreements about specific interests, which reflected a British determination to avoid raising the question, in any form, of whether Britain was in the game.

And yet these various gains and losses about specifics somehow still fall short of a fully convincing explanation of the British retreat. Another element needs to be added. This is that Mrs Thatcher gained concessions in the particular area of budgetary discipline as a result of the diplomacy of 1987–88, and the decision taken at the February 1988 Summit with regard to this discipline carried major implications for the future development of the structure of Europe which were not fully appreciated by the negotiating partners. As Nichol has pointed out, concern with budgetary discipline became prominent on the agenda relatively late in 1984, in other words at a time of renewed movement towards strengthening the Communities.[46] This coincidence suggests the realization on the part of the

British that the matter of budgetary discipline had structural implications. It also coincided with the realization by the West German government that budgetary discipline could be used to reduce agricultural spending, without launching a full-scale attack on the West German farming lobby, which would have been electorally damaging for the CDU-CSU coalition.

It should be added, however, that the question of budgetary discipline had entered into the pattern of relations between major contributing states and the international institutions of which they were members in at least one other major context at the same time. The United States had after the Kassebaum Amendment of 1985 also stressed the need for budgetary discipline in the central system of the United Nations, and also with regard to the Specialized Agencies.[47] In this case, as with the British and the European Communities, the apparent objective was to use resources more efficiently, to relate decisions about finance more directly to decisions about policy, and to place responsibility for decisions about new tunes more firmly into the hands of those who paid the piper. Yet, certainly with regard to the United Nations, and arguably with regard to the Communities, the issue was also used to attempt to get a grip on the pattern of the future development of the organization. In other words there was a disguised agenda. That there was linkage between approaches to such analogous issues within governments is highly likely.

A significant implication of budgetary discipline, and the reason for its popularity with those who were opposed to the strengthening of Europe, was that it allowed prior judgements about finance to constrain the choice of policy, rather than the other way round. If policy had the lead in this relationship there would be steady pressure towards the expansion of the budget in the light of new proposals which had integrative implications. If finance led, however, pro-integration policies could be more easily constrained. Efficiency in the use of resources, if taken as a conscious primary goal, was to be regarded as the enemy of integration.

The cornerstone of budgetary discipline was the laying down of an overall own resources ceiling and annual ceilings for payment appropriations, that is, those sums actually to be paid in each year, up until 1992. These sums were to increase from 1.20% of GNP in 1988 by annual increases up to 1.30% of GNP in 1992. Ceilings for commitment appropriations, that is the sum of promises made for future payments, were also to be agreed, maintaining a "strict relationship" with appropriations for payments; there were to be increases, which were required to be regular, up until 1992 (see Note 43, p. 3). Decisions about the sums to be allocated were to be made before each financial year according to a "medium-term financial perspective"; implications for the particular year were to be "submitted for approval to the Council and Parliament not later than the 15th February" (see Note 45, p. 9). It was stressed that "the Communities' annual budget for the financial years 1988–92 shall be kept within the ceilings" (see Note 5, Section 2, p. 3).

A wide range of new procedures were adopted to help achieve these goals. The much more careful distinction between payments for appropriations and payments for commitments was one of these, as it was obviously helpful from the point of view of budgetary discipline to know about obligations to pay which had been entered into, as well as actual payments that were required to be made during the given period. But this distinction should be understood in the context of a further change, namely an insistence upon what were called "transparency" and "annuality". The specific implication of the application of these principles was that "carry overs of differentiated appropriations shall no longer be automatic" (see Note 5, Section 2, p. 10).

The effect of these changes was that they produced a more complete – and transparent – annual statement of finances and they, therefore, mitigated the problem of not being able to see at any point what sums in the budget were a carry over from the previous year, for what sums the community was liable at any particular point in time, "and which must be paid", and those sums which could perhaps be paid. This problem had allowed the Council to agree to policies which involved expenditure which could not be covered without agreeing to new money, precisely because there was uncertainty about how much was in the kitty. Conversely, there was no system by which the Council could be required to pay for expenditure to which it was committed. Lack of clarity about the "certainty" of existing commitments made this worse. Hence, there were continuing threats of incipient bankrupty in the 1980s, which were solved by creative accountancy, such as the "negative overdraft". This actually meant not paying for policies which had actually been agreed. The European Parliament concluded that "the permanent and growing imbalance in the Community budget is essentially a product of decisions by the Council" and agreed that "therefore budgetary discipline was absolutely necessary" (see Note 48). The part of the agreement of February 1988 which concerned budgetary management also limited the size of future "negative reserves".

On the other hand, this uncertainty about the budget also made it more likely that the Council would indeed adopt policies which had the implication that the Communities' budget would need to be expanded. The picture at Brussels in February 1988 was complicated by the need to reform the agricultural policy, and increase the structural funds, as well as cover existing debts. The budget would therefore have to be increased, and, at the same time, room found for the larger structural funds by reducing spending on agriculture. But the new arrangements also meant that after 1992 a brake could be applied to future expansion, though a means of controlled acceleration was needed until then. As Parliament itself concluded "the budget would no longer be drawn up in terms of expenditure but would be established purely on the basis of revenue."[48] From now on no policy with budgetary implications could be agreed unless a decision about revenue was taken at the same time. This was a significant strengthening of the hand of the anti-integrationists, such as the British. The Community had been delivered into the hands of the accountants.

The genuine complaints about agriculture opened up the opportunity to do something about budgetary discipline in general which, as Parliament recognized, also threatened to limit its own small capacity to increase the budget in the area of non-regulated finance. Indeed, Mrs Thatcher's team must have been somewhat encouraged by their success in keeping the Commission's support, and by the seeming preparedness of the Commission to attach blame to the European Parliament in this area with allegations of Parliament's "over allocation in many budgetary headings, resulting from over-estimates of spending capacity" (Commission, 1987, p. 10). Parliament refuted this allegation by pointing out that the Commission's own estimates in the area of non-regulated finance had usually been higher than its own (European Parliament, 1987, pp. 14–15). Nevertheless, it was clear that non-compulsory expenditure would be subject to the new ceilings, though it was argued by Commission and Parliament representatives that in this area tighter budgetary management was largely a matter of presentation. The amount of waste was negligible compared with the average national administration. There was, however, a "need to persuade the paymaster that it was under control" (Interview, MEP, December, 1987). The British, as well as the West Germans, deliberately and grossly exaggerated the problems in controlling Community expenditure, for instance, with regard to the research budget.

But the consequence was that the Parliament was left on the defensive with regard to the February 1988 agreement. There was the fear that "should effective control of agricultural expenditure and agreement between Council and Parliament on the financial forecasts for implementing the Single European Act fail to materialise, non-compulsory expenditure would be in danger of becoming a budgetary reserve for the EAGGF guarantee section" (European Parliament, 1987, p. 14, para. 24). Parliament's legal right to increase expenditure in the non-compulsory area would be squeezed between the new ceilings, and the possible marginal failures of budgetary discipline regarding agriculture. Parliament could be forgiven the cynical view that "it is by no means certain that Council's political commitment to implementation of the Single European Act . . . would prevail over the temptation to oppose any increase in the maximum rate particularly in cases where additional resources would have to be found for the EAGGF guarantee section" (European Parliament, 1987, p. 14, para. 25).

The Single European Act could in principle involve more expenditure under the non-compulsory heading, and the maximum rate referred to the pace of increase in that context. Parliament complained that this amounted to an illegal amendment to the Treaty of Rome. Despite some concessions by the governments regarding consultations about the necessary sums, and indeed an explicit commitment to find sums necessary to carry out the terms of the Single European Act, Parliament's budgetary role seemed to have been weakened by the new arrangements. There was, indeed, some evidence that the Commission had moved into a more critical stance as regards the European Parliament's budgetary powers in the course of these discussions, a development which must have given further encouragement to those who wished to find in budgetary discipline a measure of compensation for the concessions made on specifics.

The budgetary discipline agreements were, therefore, implicitly about the future structure of the Communities, and amounted to a significant strengthening of the hand of those who preferred an intergovernmental rather than a more supranational approach. Not only were governments now to be brought more rapidly in the Council to a realization of the budgetary implications of their choice of policies, a good recipe for a minimalist approach, but the hand of those who wished to place a cap upon Community spending by 1992 was strengthened. Nothing much about the growth of the budget could be done until then. The integrative strategy implied, for instance, by the McDougal Report back in 1977, which involved a steady expansion of the European budget with a slow accretion correspondingly of powers to the European Parliament, was again not taken up.[49] Of course, the effectiveness of this approach remained to be seen, but a British government under Mrs Thatcher could not but have been encouraged by the new arrangements. They seemed to mirror some of the rearrangements achieved by the United States in its diplomacy with the United Nations system and the Specialized Agencies. These gains on the disguised agenda surely facilitated the surprising concessions on the visible one.

A distinction has to be made, however, between the diplomacy of the time, and what could be called the emerging agenda. Items on the latter were touched obliquely, and were not a part of the currency consciously used at the negotiations. It has been shown in this chapter that Mrs Thatcher could have concluded that she had on balance gained adequate concessions at the February 1988 special meeting of the European Council when both the visible and disguised agenda were taken into account, though the fact that she could not explain the nature of her victory implied that there was also a sense in which she had failed. The need to claw back surreptitiously some of the assets of the supranational tendency was itself an admission of the continuing strength of the latter. A more overt approach risked placing the British in the position of having to go even further in the direction they disliked. Indeed, any direct discussion of the structure of Europe now necessarily raised the spectre of two-tier Europe, a danger which had been evident since 1984.

*

As has already been explained the general situation in this chapter is examined primarily from a British perspective. But it should not be forgotten that finding a way forward in the European Community was crucially dependent upon the building of successful coalitions. This had become a more complex process as the number of members increased and as some of these gathered into formal groups – a Southern group, a Northern group, etc. Indeed with the extension of majority voting in the SEA the possibility of various arcane permutations of votes in the Council was noted, such as blocking minorities. It has not been necessary to discuss in detail the way in which such coalitions were formed with regard to the various issues discussed in this chapter, though attention was naturally given to the behaviour of the big four, Britain, France, West Germany and Italy.

Successful coalitions need, however, to attract the support of the smaller states. Their behaviour also showed underlying tendencies, or a sense of role, which had to be reckoned with in specific contexts. In brief the Dutch and the Belgians had to steer a very careful course between a natural sympathy for Britain, which was a product of history, and a general support for advanced forms of supranationalism. On occasions, therefore, these two governments tried to mediate. More usually they attempted to use their special relationship to present the case for stronger central institutions to the British in a sympathetic way. The Danes and the Greeks formed a second group which generally supported British preferences for weak Community institutions; the Danes in particular resisted any concessions to supranationalism, and sometimes were more fundamentalist in this than the British. A third group of weaker states included Spain and Portugal, which as yet seemed to take a pragmatic line on the underlying constitutional issues, preferring for the time being to place primary stress on obtaining specific economic returns from the Community.

The way in which the coalitions of larger and smaller states was formed depended, however, primarily upon the pattern of diplomacy between the big four, and among these it was the British who were the litmus test of the chances of future integration. Stress is, therefore, now again placed upon developments in Britain.

Hugo Young wrote that "Mrs Thatcher's concessions on the European Community budget were concessions to the idea of Europe. They were made in order to sustain the very notion of the Community" (*The Guardian*, 16 February 1988). There was, however, considerable doubt about whether she and her senior advisers intended this to happen. But the longer term tendencies in the development of the regional system, both before the Brussels 1988 meeting, and when they are projected into the future, were such that such concessions might be seen to have become progressively more difficult to avoid. Despite British intentions, the British concessions on the visible agenda can be seen as Young implies as sustaining "the very notion of the Community". In the longer term, the political relationship of Britain with Europe may be seen to have been progressively consolidated. The political cooperation procedures were slowly acquiring new substance, and the British Foreign Office was increasingly committed to these. There had occurred a sea-change in British thinking about where it stood in the world: that it was a European state was increasingly hard to dispute, and a gradual alignment of its interests with those of the continental states was evident. The decision to complete the internal market by 1992 also carried with it major implications for both the level and scope of regional arrangements in Europe. If the British wanted the first, the pressures to accept the latter would inevitably grow.

Within Britain this underlying trend was recognized. Within her Cabinet there was evidence of Mrs Thatcher's increasing isolation with regard to the level of her doubts about Europe. The Foreign Secretary and the Chancellor of the Exchequer have both openly expressed their disagreement with her about the need to join the European Monetary System. The Home Secretary, though prepared to drag his feet on some matters, such as easing restrictions on the movement of people, as at a meeting of the Trevi Group in June 1988, was also inclined to support closer links with Europe. In the Labour Party, too, change was evident. The new party document explicitly referred to the need to stay in Europe, though one reaction was the election of an anti-marketeer as leader of the Labour Party group in the European Parliament. For the first time it was likely that the question of membership in the EEC would no longer be a major issue in future elections to the British Parliament. The regime of the Communities' system was on the way to being consolidated within Britain.

These developments were linked with a noticeable alteration in the tone of the public debate about Europe. The need to plan for the new internal market was necessarily accompanied by a public relations strategy directed at business by the government. The visibility of Europe increased. But there was also evidence of a growing realization that there was an insistent tendency towards stronger European arrangements such as a European monetary authority, or even a kind of European central bank as proposed by Kohl and Mitterrand (Samuel Brittan, Interview, BBC News at One, Friday 3rd June). There may have been startled reactions and hostility to the prospect of, say, closer military cooperation between France and West Germany, but British reactions were now more generally not, as they used to be, that this was rather a silly irrelevance, but rather anxiety that this was yet another game in which they would now need to join (*The Guardian*, 28 December 1987). Increasingly, the others went on ahead, but Britain had to tag along behind.

Mrs Thatcher made a speech about the future of Europe at the College of Europe in Bruges on 20 September 1988, which attracted considerable attention. It was sharply criticized as being "unrelentingly negative" by those who favoured a more supranational Europe, in the Commission, and states such as Italy and Holland, and enthusiastically welcomed by opponents of a stronger Europe (*The Times*, 21 September 1988). It was certainly a speech of major importance. It was, however, also an excellent illustration of the major theme of this chapter: that in the 1980s a new balance between the autonomy of the states and the integration of the European Community had been struck. It was particularly revealing to find this balance in the remarks of someone who was the most forthright and indeed nationalistic of European leaders.

The speech contained clear indications of the perception that the extension of the scope of integration was necessary in order to promote the well-being of the various separate nation states: the latter had a symbiotic relationship with the former. Therefore "willing and active co-operation between independent sovereign states is the best way to build a successful European Community", and

Europe will be stronger precisely because it has France as France, Spain as Spain, Britain as Britain, each with its own customs, traditions and identity. It would be folly to fit them into some sort of Identikit European personality.

The states were to be served by the achievement at the European level of a wide range of policies which "encourage enterprise" – "if Europe is to flourish and create the jobs of the future, enterprise is the key." The *acquis communitaire* and the various initiatives in the European Community of the mid-1980s were, therefore, necessary and important, but not in Mrs Thatcher's view because of their contribution to strengthening regional arrangements, but because of their reinforcement of the distinctive life of the separate states.

Accordingly the European Community was definitely not to be a framework within which new regional administrative and governmental arrangements were to be nurtured. Indeed Mrs Thatcher's image of Europe seemed to be of a kind of macro enterprise zone, free of regulations which could increase the cost of labour and impede the movement of capital, and equally of the kind of centralized supervision which could be the product of "arcane institutional debates". In this fashion Mrs Thatcher justified her opposition to a European Central Bank (this was not "the key issue" – this was rather to "implement the Community's commitment to free movement of capital"). Similarly those who wished to see stronger institutions in Brussels were derided:

it is ironic that just when those countries such as the Soviet Union, which have tried to run everything from the centre, are learning that success depends on dispersing power and decisions away from the centre, some in the Community seem to want to move in the opposite direction. . . . We have not successfully rolled back the frontiers of the state in Britain only to see them reimposed at a European level with a European superstate exercising a new dominance from Brussels.

Yet even Mrs Thatcher's view implied that regional arrangements had to be strengthened and the balance between integration and autonomy restruck. If the goal of a Europe without frontiers was to be achieved a major extension of the scope of integration would necessarily follow. Business organizations in the various member states were to be permitted and encouraged to operate in the Common Market as a whole as if it were their own domestic market: hence the major effort to remove the range of restrictions and barriers which had previously discouraged this. To cope with the new competition and use the new opportunities companies would need to "Europeanize" themselves. In short what was being contemplated even by the most ardent intergovernmentalists was something that went far beyond the traditional practice of international cooperation between states: it amounted to the creation of a single economic space. A further range of interdependencies would inevitably follow. Mutual trade would be increased to levels closer to that within the US and a new range of transnational organizations and connections would emerge. The balance could be said to have changed even if only the scope of integration were taken into account.

The more interesting question, however, is about the implications of these developments for the level of integration, in other words for the powers of the central institutions. Mrs Thatcher denied that there were any such implications. The President of the Commission, Jacques Delors was of a different opinion. He said that over the next few years the European Community would be responsible for some 80% of all legislation in the

Twelve, during which time an embryo European government might emerge (*The Guardian*, 21 September 1988). Though it was difficult to decide precisely what powers should be transferred to the centre, the truth of the matter probably lies closer to the latter view than the former. As this chapter has demonstrated there was certainly an increase in the powers of the central institutions in the 1980s, in the form of the cooperative procedure, majority voting in the Council, and also an extension of the executive powers of the Commission. It was also the case that pressure in favour of further increases in these powers had continued, and even increased, and it is difficult to see how the new European economic space could be managed unless further transfers in that direction were made. The alternative, an attempt at cooperative management by governments of the range of complex and urgent matters which would arise would be inefficient and liable to failure.

Mrs Thatcher's speech reflects the increasing pressures in favour of increasing the level of integration and fits very well into the pattern of British diplomacy described in the preceding pages. It suggests a sense of having been overtaken by the new dynamics of European integration, whilst at the same time seeking to slow down processes which could not be halted, and salvage whatever could be salvaged for national sovereignty. The Mitterrand strategy gave at least a significant push to these processes, but they also acquired momentum because of dynamics recognized in the mid-1960s by the neofunctionalist theorists. For instance any explanation of the continuing high position of the issue of the development of the European Monetary System on the European agenda would need to include elements of neofunctionalism; spill over from a Europe without frontiers was one cause of increasing interest in many quarters in a European Central Bank, and regardless of Mrs Thatcher's intentions, such interest would continue. It will become increasingly likely that such a bank will be created and that Britain will be a member.

The student of the European Community in the 1980s therefore needs to return to the writings of a group of scholars – the neofunctionalists – whose writings have for many years been unfashionable. They provide the essential context of theory in which to place the practice of diplomacy and even the speeches of Prime Ministers so that they might be better understood. But this chapter has noted a variation on the old themes: in the 1980s an underlying dynamic was evident that was less likely to appear when the number of members of the EC was fewer. It is that diplomatic relations can emerge between core and peripheral states in such a way that all are subject to greater incentives to integrate. This argument will be explored further on a future occasion.

Notes

1. William Wallace, Helen Wallace and Carole Webb (Editors), *Policy-making in the European Communities*, Wiley, 2nd Ed., London, 1983.
2. Geoffrey Denton, "Restructuring the EC Budget: Implications of the

Fontainebleau Agreement", *Journal of Common Market Studies*, Vol. XXIII, No. 2, December 1984: pp. 117–40. Stephen George, *The British Government and the European Community since 1984*, University Association for Contemporary European Studies, Occasional Papers 4, Kings College, London, 1987, especially Pp. 2–18.

3. Otto Schmuck, "The European Parliament's Draft Treaty establishing the European Union (1979–84)", in Roy Pryce (Editor), *The Dynamics of European Union*, London and New York: Croom Helm, 1987, pp. 188–216. Commission of the European Communities, "Draft Treaty establishing the European Union", Bulletin of the European Communities, Vol. 17, No. 2, 1984: pp. 7–28.

4. Juliet Lodge, "The Single European Act: Towards a new Euro-Dynamism?", *Journal of Common Market Studies*, Vol. XXIV, No. 3, March 1986: pp. 203–223. European Parliament, *A New Phase in European Union*, General Secretariat, Luxembourg, 1985.

5. European Council, *Texts of Agreement reached at European Council*, 11/12 February 1988, including documents SN517/88 and SN461/88, P. 7.

6. Miriam Camps, *Britain and the European Community*, Princeton University Press, Princeton, 1964.

7. *The Times*, September 21, 1988.

8. Robert Stephens, "Britain's other War", *The Observer*, 23 May, 1982.

9. *Financial Times*, March 22, 1984, had article headed "Cabinet debates block on EEC payments".

10. *Europe – the future*, para. 26, unpublished, dated 25/26 June 1984.

11. John Wyles, "So near and yet so far", *Financial Times*, March 22, 1984: p. 24.

12. Peter Jenkins, "Behind the lines at the battle of Brussels", *The Guardian*, March 22, 1984: p. 17.

13. Paul Cheeseright, *Financial Times*, June 28 1984: "The ad hoc committee . . . was pushed through by France in the last hour's discussion at the summit during what appears to have been a cursory consideration of new policies."

14. *The Guardian*, October 5, 1984.

15. *The Times*, October 23, 1984.

16. Wyles, 1984, loc. cit.

17. Commission of the European Communities, *The Inter-governmental Conference: Background and Issues*, London, 1985, (a) p. 1.

18. *The Times*, June 27, 1984.

19. *The Times*, June 29, 1985.

20. *The Sunday Times*, March 3, 1985. *The Sunday Times*, 3 March 1985 had a front page article headed "Super-EEC plan leaves Britain in the cold".

21. Helen Wallace, *Europe: the Challenge of Diversity*, London: Routledge and Kegan Paul for the Royal Institute of International Affairs, 1985, pp. 29–49; Bernd Langeheine and Ulrich Weinstock, "Graduated Integration: a Modest Path Towards Progress", *Journal of Common Market Studies*, Vol. XXIII, No. 3, March 1985.

22. Ad Hoc Committee for Institutional Affairs, *Report to the European Council*, Brussels 29–30 March 1985, SN/1187/85.

23. Ibid., P. 33.

24. Ibid.

25. Ibid., P. 30.

26. Ibid., P. 28.

27. Ibid., P. 26.

28. *The Times*, June 27 1985.

29. William Wallace, writing in *The Times*, July 2 1985.
30. Commission of the European Communities, *Bulletin of the European Communities*, Supplement 1/85, "The thrust of Commission Policy", Strasbourg, 14 and 15 January 1985, P. 6.
31. Commission of the European Communities, *Completing the Internal Market: White paper from the Commission to the European Council*, Luxembourg, Office of Official Publications, June, 1985.
32. *The Times*, July 1 1985.
33. Ibid.
34. Commission of the European Communities, *The Inter-governmental Conference: Background and Issues*, London, 1985, p. 2.
35. Richard Corbett, "The Intergovernmental Conference and the Single European Act", in Roy Pryce, (Editor) *The Dynamics of European Union*, Croom Helm, 1987, p. 242.
36. Ibid.
37. Sir Micheal Butler, *Europe: More than a Continent*, London: William Heinemann, 1986, p. 156.
38. Corbett, loc. cit., P. 247.
39. Commission of the European Communities, *Bulletin of the European Communities*, Supplement 2/86, Single European Act, Luxembourg, Office for Official Publications, 1986, Title II, Section 1, especially articles 6 and 7.
40. Corbett, loc. cit. P. 262.
41. T.C. Hartley, *The Foundations of European Community Law*, Oxford: Clarendon Press, 1981, pp. 519–20.
42. John Palmer, "Hard Pounding for the EMS", *The Guardian*, May 18 1988.
43. Presidency, *Making a success of the Single European Act: a Note*, SN 461/1/88, Brussels, 1988, p. 3.
44. Ibid., Pp. 38–39.
45. Commission of the European Communities, *Communication on Budgetary Discipline*, Com(87) 430, Final, Brussels, August 1987, p. 3.
46. William Nichol, "From Rejection to Repudiation: EC Budgetary Affairs in 1985", *Journal of Common Market Studies*, Vol. XXV, No. 1, September 1986.
47. Paul Taylor, "Reforming the System: Getting the Money to Talk", in Paul Taylor and A.J.R. Groom (Editors), *International Institutions at Work*, London: Pinter Publishers, 1988, pp. 220–236.
48. European Parliament, *Session Documents*, Series A, Document A 2-200/87/Part B, November 7, 1987, p. 5.
49. Commission of the European Communities, Report, *The Role of the Public Finance in European Integration* (MacDougal Report), Brussels, April 1977.

4 The limits of European integration: the concepts of consociation and symbiosis

Students of the European Community in the early 1990s could not but be struck by an apparent paradox: that, on the one hand, pressures towards an increasing centralization of arrangements under the heading of political and monetary union seemed to have increased, and were frequently linked in public discussion with the concept of federalism;[1] whilst, on the other hand, a number of members, most obviously Spain, Portugal and Greece, even the new Germany, were obviously using the Community to develop their sense of their own identity as separate states, and, although the British had been most prominent in opposing federalism, no member government had shown any inclination in specific terms to abandon its sovereignty. This paradox is hard to understand and is perhaps too easily dismissed with the retort that the Community is *sui generis*, or that the supporters of further integration had simply not understood its constitutional implications, as the Bruges group argued.[2]

Running through the argument in this chapter are, therefore, two themes which might appear to be mutually exclusive: the survival and even entrenchment of the state on the one hand and the extension of the range of international organization in the European Community on the other. Does not any development in the latter inevitably lead to the weakening of the former by, for instance, challenging its sovereignty? The conclusion is that this is not necessarily the case: indeed there are now reasons for supposing that at the regional level, where the challenge might at first sight appear to be at its strongest, the state and international organization are capable of being mutually reinforcing.[3] Thus the regionalization process, which was shown to be a general phenomenon in the earlier chapters, need not get in the way of state-building. Indeed, in the European Community, states such as Spain and Portugal have sought membership in order to rediscover themselves as states, not to lose their identity.

Judgements about the implications for sovereignty of life in an interdependent world are too often naive and sharply polarized: the slightest practical adjustment to the need for greater cooperation between states may be resisted as representing too great a compromise with the ideal of statehood, or stronger international organizations are hailed as a step towards a federalist millennium. In this chapter an attempt is made to challenge this perception.

In the following discussion a theory is developed about the implications of regional integration in the European Community for its member states, and a number of underlying assumptions and concepts are made explicit. The argument is developed that integration in the 1980s and early 1990s had a symbiotic character: that the state and the regional system were mutually supportive – each lived off the other. Particular kinds of government behaviour arose which demanded appropriate institutional arrangements.

The theory of consociationalism, developed in the field of comparative government is, in the judgement of the present writer, very relevant for explaining the symbiotic process in regional government. It gives insights which qualify aspects of those suggested by the more traditional theories of integration, such as neofunctionalism, functionalism and federalism. Students of international organization and comparative government have frequently shared concepts. Most prominent have been the grand theories of constitutional arrangement such as federalism and confederalism, but the list of shared analytical concepts, pluralism, balance, hierarchy, and the like, is enormous. Consociationalism should now be added to this list.

It is a relatively recent addition to the literature of comparative government, having been developed by Arend Lijphart in his book on *The Politics of Accommodation: Pluralism and Democracy in the Netherlands*[4] which was published in 1968, and was identified as a major contribution to the literature.[5] Its primary original purpose was to attempt to understand the workings of democracies which seemed to be unusually divided, such as Holland and Switzerland; these were generally polities which had compromised with mainstream democratic forms in the sense of "one man one vote" with majorities prevailing at all levels of government, in the sense that they accepted a "blocking minority". In subsequent years the theory was used in developing proposed solutions to the problems of societies in which there was inter-ethnic violence such as in Northern Ireland or Israel.[6] It seems appropriate, therefore, to ask at this point what this theory contains for the theory of international organization. International organization is also about managing relations between groups which may be sharply divided and amongst which democratic forms are much modified.

*

What are the necessary features of consociation? This question should be distinguished from that of the nature of the conditions in which it might arise or survive. It has been described by Lijphart as having four features.[7] First there must be a number of groups which are in some sense insulated from each other, in that their interests and associations are more inwardly directed than overlapping with those of members of other groups in the same state: there are relatively few cross-cutting cleavages, and authority within that state is segmented in relation to such groups. Second, the state is dominated by what Dahrendorf called a *cartel of elites*:[8] the political elites of the various segments are each involved in some way on a continuous basis in the process of decision-making and decisions are the product of agreements and coalitions among the members of that cartel. None is placed into the ranks of the opposition in decision-making, as, for instance, in the event of defeat in an election, which would be the case with a majority system. The cartel need not necessarily require that all actors be positively involved in the same way on all occasions: variations on the theme would be an arrangement, as in Switzerland, where it is agreed that each member of the central council acts as leader or President for a specified term, or in the Lebanon before the civil war where there was an agreed division of responsibilities between Muslim and Christian leaders.[9]

The third feature is a logical extension of the cartel principle: it is that all the political elites must have the right of veto over decisions of which they disapproved. In other words the majoritarian principle in the system as a whole, which is characteristic of other forms of democracy, is suspended in favour of the requirement of consensus, though it may apply within the segments, or, on some issues which are contentious, among the members of the cartel. Finally there must be a law of proportionality, which means that the various segments of the population must have proportionate representation among the major institutions, the bureaucracy, legal systems, and so on, of the state. These features then ensure that the rights and interests of the subordinate sections of society, as interpreted by or filtered through the members of the cartel of elites, are safeguarded. Indeed political arrangements are so contrived that each minority is protected from the dictatorship of the whole.

The central problem of consociation is the maintenance of stability in a situation of actual or potential mutual tension. Indeed the problem implies an irony which is more characteristic of international relations than of stable democracies: the need to generate enthusiasm for stability precisely because of the continuing threat of fragmentation. As Lijphart put it

The leaders of the rival subcultures may engage in competitive behaviour and thus further aggravate mutual tensions and political instability, but they may also make deliberate efforts to counteract the immobilizing and unstabilizing effects of cultural fragmentation.[10]

The imminence of mutual tensions is revealed in the determination of the segments' leaders to defend the separate interests of the groups in the common forum. In the more conventional democracies – called Anglo-American systems by Gabriel Almond – in contrast, "because the political culture tends to be homogeneous and pragmatic, the political process takes on some of the atmosphere of a game. A game is a good game when the outcome is in doubt and when the stakes are not too high. When the stakes are too high the tone changes from excitement to anxiety. . . . But in consociational democracies politics is treated not as a game but as serious business."[11] The leaders are faced continuously with the dilemma of acting to preserve the general system whilst at the same time seeking to protect and further the interests of the groups which they represent.

With regard to their own groups, therefore, elites must be able to rely on a high degree of homogeneity, and be capable of backing this up on occasion with techniques for the maintenance of internal discipline. This explains Lustick's contention that within segments control may sometimes be so powerful as to appear to challenge the judgement that they are internally democratic. The stability of the whole may require the discipline of the segments, even in ways which move towards the limit of what is acceptable – controls upon the press, limitations upon freedom of association, fixing public appointments, and the like.

Ian Lustick succinctly described the main aspects of the behaviour of elites in consociational arrangements which may be conveniently highlighted where appropiate by comparison with his parallel account of hegemonic control.[12] There were seven such characteristics and the present writer is heavily indebted to Lustick for the following discussion.[13]

First, the criterion that effectively governs the authoritative allocation of resources in the consociational system is the common denominator of the interests of the two segments as perceived and articulated by their respective elites.

Second, linkages beweeen the two sub-units or segments in the system take the form of political or material exchanges, negotiations, bargains, trades and compromises. In the control system, however, the segment which has dominance extracts what it needs from the subordinate segment and delivers what it sees fit.

Third, in the consociational system hard bargaining between sub-unit elites is a necessary fact of political life, and this is a concrete sign that it is operating successfully. In the control system, however, precisely the opposite is the case: hard bargaining signals the failure of the control mechanisms.

Fourth, the role of the official regime, the civil service, law agencies, public education system, armed forces, etc., in the consociational regime is to act as an umpire, or interpreter, of the bargains which have been reached; but in the control system the official regime is the legal and administrative instrument of the superordinate segments. It is there to act as the instrument of control.

Fifth, the normative justification for the regime adopted by authorities in the consociational regime is likely to be couched in terms of vague and general references to the common welfare of both sub-units, whereas in a control regime it is more likely that there will be an elaborate ideology to justify the subordination of one group to another.

Sixth, the central strategic problem that faces elites in the consociational system is symmetrical for each sub-unit: each must strike bargains which preserve the integrity of the whole system, but which can also be enforced within the respective sub-units which they represent. In a control system, however, the superordinate sub-unit elites strive to devise techniques for manipulating the sub-group, whilst the subordinate group's leadership attempts to minimize concessions to the superordinate group. "In spite of this asymmetry, however, the strategic concern of elites of both sub-units in the control system is much more externally focused than that of sub-unit elites in the consociational system."[14]

Finally the visual metaphor for the interaction between the sub-units in the consociational system is that of a set of scales, delicately but securely balanced, while that of the control system is that of a puppeteer manipulating the stringed puppet. "Though reflective of the basic differences between the two sorts of relationships, both images contain a suggestion of the separateness of sub-units, of the specificity of the linkages that join them, and of their overall stability."[15]

Lijphart summarizes as follows the conditions which are needed in order to sustain such behaviour on the part of the elites: they must, first, have the ability to accommodate the divergent interests and demands of the subcultures. This requires, second, that they have the ability to transcend cleavages and to join in a common effort with the elites of rival subcultures. Third, they must therefore be committed to the maintenance of the system and to the improvement of its cohesion and stability. And, fourth, "all of the above requirements are based on the assumption that the elites understand the perils of political fragmentation."[16] Such is the political conjuring act which the elites of stable consociation systems are expected to perform.

What are the implications of these arguments for our understanding of regional international integration as among the members of the European Community? The theory suggests that the effects of functional cooperation may be both positive, in the sense that links are fostered, attitudes modified, and community strengthened, but also negative in that integration itself produces pressures which tend to reinforce segmental autonomy. At the same time a framework may be created within which dissenting minorities can be allowed eventually a measure of autonomy.

Indeed when translated to the international level the theory of consociationalism in its various aspects suggests something rather startling: that comprehensive international arrangements may in some ways challenge rather than reinforce the process of developing a transnational sociopsychological community. They may release pressures that encourage the encapsuling of nations, and the firmer definition of ethnic and cultural minorities, as well as countervailing pressures towards greater community, regional decision-making, and in the terms of Seymour Martin Lipset, "cross-cutting cleavages".[17] Consociationalism fundamentally alters the teleology of integration theory by indicating an end situation which has built into it pressures for the maintenance of segmental autonomy within a cooperative system, i.e. a symbiotic arrangement.

In contrast integration theories such as functionalism and neofunctionalism suggest a progressive, linear view of integration.[18] There is an accumulation of tendencies which point in the same direction. The same is true of federalism, though it has in common with consociationalism a capacity to accommodate sharp cleavages in society as long as these are clearly geographically demarcated. In view of the apparent similarities between consociationalism and federalism they are compared more fully below.

*

Consociationalism is useful in that it presents a conceivable outcome of the integration process which differs from those indicated by other theories and allows the identification of aspects in the current situation which could be seen as tending towards that outcome. The use made of the theory in this essay is a modest one: it is used to highlight and place in a particular perspective what has been happening in the European Community over the last few years. As has already been stated the implication is that integration in the sense of the strengthening of the regional functional systems may help to sharpen rather than soften the cleavages in the existing society of nations.

One reason for this is seen to be that members of the cartel of elites are likely to be faced with a dilemma: they will have an interest in increasing the size of the pie, and the share obtained by their own segment, whilst at the same time protecting the distinctiveness of their segments in comparison with others, since they serve as each member's individual constituency and power base. The process of increasing the size of the total pie, which is the essential condition of larger shares, tends, however, to encourage the development of intersegmental social and cultural links, alongside the economic ones, which may have a cost in terms of the chances of maintaining the segment's viability in the longer term. Integration may, therefore – apart from committing them to enlarging the pie – also generate in the elites an increasing anxiety about the implications of the stengthening of the horizontal links between the segments since that would also tend to weaken their constituencies. The status and authority of the members of the cartel are dependent upon their capacity to identify segmental interests and to present themselves as leaders and agents of a distinct clearly defined community. Unlike other theories of integration consociationalism, therefore, highlights the politics of the relationship between leaders and led, and the way in which the interests of the former may depart from those of the latter during the process.

The theory suggests two ways in which the special interest of the elites may be stressed by them in the integration process. The first is where members of the cartel of elites make agreements together for their own purposes, even when these conflict with those of the segments which they nominally serve. This would be, indeed, the apotheosis of the danger that was advertised by the left wing of the political spectrum in Britain and elsewhere: that European integration was essentially a bourgeois conspiracy of elites and big business – in alliance with governments – against the interests of the mass of the people.[19]

The second is when a particular elite seeks to use the context of the common arrangements to promote changes which suit the interests of their key supporters in their particular segments, so that their power within it is consolidated. In the early 1990s Prime Minister Thatcher's opposition to the Commission's proposal to introduce a social charter into the EC to protect the interests of workers seemed to some commentators to suggest an intention to make the Community a happy hunting ground for capital.[20] There must be no hindrance in the way of capital's exploiting differences in the cost of labour and the level of welfare provision in the various parts of the EC, even though this also meant keeping social security provisions for British workers at a lower level.

Two sub-themes could be detected in the British position, both of which could be related to its anxiety about preserving its status in its own segment. First, a European Social Charter would enhance the cohesion of labour at the Community level, and therefore had to be resisted; second, reducing the level of social provision would enhance its authority in relation to a key group – business, industrialists – within its own segment, and therefore was to be encouraged. In that it points to the special interests of elites as opposed to publics, consociationalism highlights these points. To put the matter in more general terms the theory of consociationalism adds something to our understanding of regional integration when it points to the way in which the process could be reconciled with the existing interests of elites. It could be seen by them as providing a means by which their power base could be consolidated; not only would their capacity for rewarding as far as was necessary the key sub-groups within the distinct segments be enhanced, but their capacity to influence the definition of such interests would also be increased. This lends support to the view that integration has a double effect: it creates special opportunities for elites to resist the development of "cross-cutting cleavages".

The theory is also suggestive, however, about existing elites' attitudes towards minorities in the integrating system and the attitudes of the leaders of those minorities. The appearance of the regional arrangements provides the leaders of dissenting minorities with a forum within which to push for increased specific returns and separate representation. The traditional theories of integration, functionalism and neofunctionalism, have no way of coping with this observable political fact.[21] Scots, Welsh, Basque, Irish and even Catalan nationalists have all seen the Community as an opportunity for furthering their cause. The minority seeks to consolidate direct contacts with regional level organization whereas the existing elite cartel members seek to limit such contacts. One test of this hypothesis could be found in the attitudes of governments towards permitting or preventing direct links between local groups and the Community when seeking support from the latter's structural funds.[22] The British government has tended to oppose such contacts, and this certainly has modest implications for the perceptions of folk in the non-English areas in Britain of themselves as forming distinct communities. Even more striking in the context of consociation was the strength of the opposition to the free movement of people in the Dutch Parliament in the late 1980s, despite the traditional support of the Dutch government for European union, and their commitment to going ahead of the others in that direction with the French, West Germans and other Benelux countries. Segmental autonomy had to be preserved!

Similarly the British government sought to raise the patriotic temperature regarding the EC, whilst denying that this was really a challenge to the latter – a circumstance which also fits with consociationalism.[23] In this context O'Leary suggested the generation of cross-frontier programmes to be financed by the Community as a way of softening the sectoral tensions in Northern Ireland.[24] The logic of consociationalism in its application to the integration process is, however, that national governments would resist this approach until a late stage. This point is discussed further below.

It provides, however, a small further part of the explanation of the observed pattern of behaviour of the minorities in the European Community. The universal habit was for them to see the Community as the context in which they could obtain a greater level of independence and at the same time increase the level of specific returns to their groups. This suggests that contrary to first impression the tendency might be for successful integration to sharpen divisions between minorities and the dominant segments, rather than lessen them. In that it stresses the propensity of leaders of the dominant segments to increase their countervailing resistance to minority dissent, consociation theory seems to raise the possibility that integration might serve to exacerbate intercommunal tensions. In the early 1990s the assertion of the principle of *subsidiarity*, which was formally included in a Community treaty for the first time in the Maastricht Agreement,[25] contained a fundamental flaw from the point of view of those who simply wanted to use it to resist a further flow of competences to the Community from the national level. The principle, in that it held that nothing should be done at the higher level if it could be done at the lower, also seemed to justify a flow of competences down to the local communities within the state. In Britain it was not only an argument against further flows to the Community, but also an argument in support of the claim by the Scots, the Welsh, and the Irish, for autonomy.

There is, however, a more optimistic scenario which may be valid in the longer term, which is also suggested by the theory. This is, however – it must be admitted – a rather pale dawn. Leaders may quite suddenly decide that the game of keeping a minority within the dominant segment was not worth the candle. This outcome would arise if the level of tensions within segments rose to an intolerable level, But it would also be encouraged by the integration process in that the latter amplifies the separate expectations of minorities and provides a focus for them, whilst at the same time sharpening the identity of the cartel of elites as a forum to which non-members might aspire. The theory of consociation does not suggest on the other hand that attempts to strengthen cross-frontier functional arrangements between members of the same minority are likely to be acceptable to national governments until the level of tensions within the segments has risen to a very high level. We are therefore faced at best with a two-stage process: a first stage of increasing resistance to change, but then a sudden giving way to the demands of minorities for autonomy. In the context of this argument the interesting point is that the integration process is itself a variable in such outcomes in two senses: first in that it sharpens the identity of the cartel of elites, and, second, that it encourages the clearer definition of minorities and the articulation of their separate interests in the larger framework.

The process of decision-making at the centre of the system is also illuminated by the theory of consociationalism. The theory suggests that in this context members of the elite cartel will become more inclined to insist that they retain an ultimate veto on decisions of which they disapprove and more resistant to decision-taking on the basis of majorities. Decision-making would become more difficult because of the success of the process. At first sight the Single European Act, and the Maastricht Agreement, seemed to be evidence against the proposition that this was true of the European Community, but the informed reader will at least entertain a rather cynical view about its terms regarding majority voting.[26] This argument is discussed in greater detail later in this chapter. On the whole the states reserved the right, either explicitly in the Act or in terms of stated intentions, to veto anything which affected their vital interests. Further it appears to have been generally accepted that the Act did not supersede the Luxembourg Accord of 1966 which allowed the veto. There was evidence to suggest that majority voting was more frequently used after the Act and that the Council's work had consequently been speeded up, but the underlying circumstances remained the same: states could veto what they did not like. This point is discussed further below.

The members of the Council of Ministers and of the European Council did indeed behave like the members of an elite cartel in a consociational multi-party government, with enormously complex consensus-building and a marked tendency to express profound doubts about the others' intentions. Whereas within stable "Anglo-American" democracies the norm of political conduct is not to impune the honour and integrity of the other politicians until late in the game, in the European Community this was almost the first thing that happened when there was a dispute. In 1990 an example of this concerned the scandal of "mad cow disease" in Britain. Protests by the French, the Germans, the Italians, and the Luxembourgers were immediately treated in Britain as illustrations of the tendency of foreigners to cheat.[27]

The Council's working style was indeed more like an amplified version of that of the Swiss confederation or the government of the Netherlands than of the Anglo-American democracies. The great initiatives of the 1980s invariably began elsewhere: in the Commission, the European Parliament, or a particular government, or small group of like-minded governments, such as France and West Germany. And the building of consensus tended to be dominated as much by a fear of being left out, as by an enthusiasm for new benefits. As the consociational model suggests, the condition for retaining the common decision-making system is that the fear of fragmentation is greater than the fear of weakening segmental authority. Indeed the consociationalism model of the working of the European Community has precisely the opposite implications for the working assumptions and background conditions of decision-making from those which are suggested by traditional functionalism or even neofunctionalism: these indicate the prospect of greater accord as integration proceeds, the former promotes a more complicated arrangement which might be better described as one of confined dissent. The implications of this for the central bureaucracy – the Commission – are also worth considering. Consociational theory sees the state apparatus as being an umpire rather than a promoter of any specific ideology. Within an existing consociational state the bureaucracy is an umpire in that it must avoid attaching itself to the ideology of a particular segment. This was also true of the Commission of the European

Communities, and this of course is not a particularly original point. But there is a more interesting development of this idea which is suggested by consociationalism. It is that integration has the effect of compelling the central institution to adopt more frequently, and at an earlier stage of the decison-making process, the role of umpire. The task of presenting initiatives which reflect the general community interest is by no means eliminated, but what tends to happen is that the grand designs are more frequently compromised out of recognition and are at continuing risk of being entirely lost to sight as decision-making proceeds. Members of the pro-European lobby held that this was the consequence of the close involvement of government representatives in decision-making at a very early stage in the formulation of policy by the Commission, as in the Committee of Permanent Representatives.[28] It is hard to see how this could be avoided in the light of the way the decision-making process had evolved over the years. The theory suggests, however, that pressures to enlarge the role of the Commission as umpire are increased rather than diminished as integration proceeds. As the stakes rise so the members of the elite cartel become more careful to protect their interests and insist that the condition of movement is consensus.

A further insight from consociationalism concerns the staffing of the Commission. Whereas integration theory predicts an increasing preparedness to accept appointments to the central bureaucracy on the basis of ability, regardless of geographical or social distribution, the theory of consociationalism suggests an increasing determination to insist upon proportionality in the central institutions, and indeed an increasing tendency for particular elites to identify their nationals in those institutions as their representatives. In the late 1980s and early 1990s the British government took to making a careful count of the number of its nationals in the Commission and of complaining if it judged that it was underrepresented.

This is a useful theoretical perspective upon the tendency for the collegiate principle in the Commission to become weaker – dissenting members became much more frequently identified than they had been – and for state governments to act as if Commissioners from their states were their representatives. For instance, Leon Brittan was reported in the United Kingdom as having taken particular positions in Commission meetings and was judged in terms of how far such positions reflected what could only be described as British elite interests, namely those of the government and the business community, despite the rule that Commission meetings should be in camera and decisions taken on the basis of the collegiate principle, i.e. all are bound in public by a majority vote of the college. (It is not suggested here, however, that Brittan has been explicitly told what to do by the British!)

In June 1990 it was evident, however, that Brittan had been placed in a difficult position with regard to the Commission's handling of the British government's "sweeteners" to British Aerospace when they took over Austin-Rover precisely because of a high level of publicity for the Commissioner in Britain and the perception that he was the British representative.[29] He had to steer a very careful line between a strict application of

Community competition rules, which had been transgressed, and appearing to do what he could for the current British political and business establishment. Another indication of an increasing nationalization of the Commission was Mrs Thatcher's habit of referring to British Commissioners as "our commissioners". It was widely accepted that the collegiate principle and the Treaty of Rome's requirement that Commissioners should not be instructed by governments had always to some degree been transgressed, but as integration proceeded there was in the press and the statements of politicians a more general acceptance of this as the routine.

What are the main differences between federalism and consociationalism? Lijphart has pointed to the way in which they may work in rather similar ways within stable democracies, the crucial difference being that Federalism requires that the various segments be readily identifiable on a geographical basis whereas consociationalism allows for degrees of overlap in the physical location of the segments.[30] When viewed as integration processes, however, the two emerge as having rather different implications. Federalism is by definition a single-step process relying upon a meeting of political leaders – a constituent assembly – and the agreeing of a constitution which reconciles regional differences. In classical federalism the product of this process, the constitution, is seen as a political solution to the problems of diversity.[31] Consociationalism does not, however, require such a conscious act of political creativity and there is no need to reconcile diversities: it can be a process proceeding beyond the control of specific political actors. Indeed the dynamics of integration which were identified by the neofunctionalists may proceed alongside the processes of consociationalism. What the latter adds is a view about a set of pressures which shape the political process which derive from its social and cultural setting.

The Federalist integration process requires the establishing of two levels of government – separate but coordinate – being the government of the whole, the federal level, and the government of the parts, the state or local level. Such levels may also arise in a consociation. In the latter, however, the idea of a central government in which there is a habit of identifying and acting upon a common interest is relatively weak. Federalism tends to the upgrading of the common interest in the general system whereas consociationalism tends to the reinforcement of the search for the lowest common denominator at that level. More precisely: the general interest, in so far as it emerges, is as likely to be a limited consensus among elites as a common interest of segments: as has been pointed out earlier, consociationalism underlines the potential for divergence between the interests of elites and publics in a political process such as integration. Similarly the assumption behind federalism in its mainstream form is that the system will over time gradually strengthen the perception of the common interest at the general and elite level, whereas the logic of the consociational approach suggests that elites will strive to promote constrained inter-group rivalry, and will judge that they are victims rather than beneficiaries of developing crosscutting cleavages. It follows that in the consociational model the segments expect their leaders to be activist and politicized in their pursuit of interests in the cartel of elites. As was pointed out above in a consociational system politics tend to be a serious business as the stakes are seen as being high: there is no tendencey towards depoliticization. In the federalist process of integration, however, there is an expectation of depoliticization and of the transmuting of politics into a game.

What keeps the consociational system alive is that the costs of fragmentation, in terms of internal tensions and the risks of intervention from outside, are seen to exceed those arising from the cumbersome internal arrangements, and the range of specific benefits arising from the latter are seen as being sufficient. Indeed an awareness of the external implications of internal failure is more pressing than with other constitutions: in the case of several of the existing consociational systems in Western Europe, such as Holland and Switzerland, there had been experience of intervention, or undue pressure from outside, at times of internal weakness. An awareness of this danger is part of the political ideology of these countries. It is striking though that as international integration in the European Community evolved a parallel argument, even a sentiment, appeared. This is reflected in the strengthening perception that for all the tedious burdens of EC decision-making, and the undignified horse-trading, the breakdown of the Community would be horrendous in its international implications. The fear of vulnerability in international society is a powerful incentive towards maintaining the viability of the cartel of elites as a management coalition. Consociationalism sharpens this point.

In sum, consociationalism highlights the ways in which existing political elites might pursue international integration for their own selfish reasons at the cost of community solidarity – it is in a sense a dynamic view of intergovernmentalism – whereas federalism and other integration theories expects them to act in the interests of the greater number in the longer term. There are very few instances in which politicians have in fact acted in the interest of the larger number in the longer term, and this might add credence to consociationalism.

The theory undoubtedly helps to highlight many aspects of the integration process in Western Europe, though the tone which it lends is often bleak in the eyes of those who would prefer to see an emerging European federation on the model, perhaps, of Almond's Anglo-American style of government, with decision-makers and publics equally involved in an increasing range of cross-cutting cleavages between the segments of the European society, and an emerging socio-psychological community, in which majority decision-taking in a real sense – as opposed to the quasi-majoritarianism indicated by the Luxembourg Accord – was increasingly the norm. These things may yet emerge but consociationalism helps to identify some of the roadblocks that are in the way.

On the other hand the theory may be regarded as more optimistic by those who see the good life as involving the freeing of dissenting minorities and the admission of their representatives to the conferences of statesmen. There is a sense indeed in which consociationalism challenges the doctrine of national self-determination: it permits in some circumstances the detachment of national groups from larger segments with which they have been housed, without requiring that the fabric of the technical/functional arrangements of the state are similarly relocated. National detachment – the segmental autonomy which is a building block of consociationalism – is possible in part because such systems have already become non-terminous with nations: self-determination has fewer implications for what the nation does or can do. This is a modern version of the doctrine of national self-determination, and in acccepting this Western Europe seems to be ahead of Eastern Europe, where in the early 1990s there was a worrying tendency to insist upon the accumulation of technical competences in the territory of the state. The abandoning of the dogma of the necessary coextensiveness of technical and national frontiers is one of the conditions of the success of regionalization processes throughout the world.

If in Birch's terms nationalism is by definition a search for polical autonomy any list of the purposes to which such autonomy would be put is bound in Western Europe to get shorter and shorter as integration proceeds.[32] This can only be to the advantage of minorities seeking a greater say about their own destiny. The irony of their position, however, is that integration both increases in some ways their chances of achieving autonomy, but also reduces the range of purposes to which it could be put.

*

Consociational theory has important implications for the development of international organization at the regional level because it points to the way in which the regional system could develop as a framework for cooperative activity without the implication that the governments' concern to protect their sovereignty, the equivalent of segmental autonomy within states, would be lessened. This is the theme of symbiosis between the participating segments and the collectivity, which is implicit in consociationalism, and which will be explored further in this section. A concern with sovereignty was very evident in the European Community in the early 1990s, but one of the problems was that the debate about furthering integration was too frequently in the out-of-date terms of the rival claims of federalists and intergovernmentalists. As Leon Brittan said, this debate was like a wrestling match between two elderly sumo wrestlers.[33] The pattern of the claims and counter-claims about the prospects of further integration tended, therefore, to have two principal features: first was the appearance of the pattern of interests typical of consociationalism, a paradoxical assertion of separateness at the same time as a determined adhesion to the collectivity; and second was a tendency on the part of those who disliked federalist outcomes to exaggerate the risk that these might arise.

It is not difficult to find equivalents at the regional level of the calculations of the segments within the consociational states. The sense of needing to promote the common system in order to increase security, both in the face of possible economic threats, but also of a military or strategic kind, was clear in Western Europe. Similarly the realization that essential utilitarian/economic returns were to be gained from the common system was evident. The neofunctionalist dynamics had certainly reemerged in the context of the drive towards the establishment of the single market by

1992, as was indicated in Chapter 3 above. It was also shown, however, that the political element is probably more important than the economic one: once scope reaches a certain level, states are pushed to accept some constraints in their struggle to promote their own interests by the fear of being marginalized in the common system. The possibility that a coalition could emerge within the cartel of elites which would pursue stronger arrangements amongst themselves to the exclusion of the reluctant partners is a powerful incentive to stay in the game. Hence although Mrs Thatcher may have behaved badly in the cartel of elites she was determined to remain a member. This circumstance encouraged the French in their use of a particular diplomatic weapon against the British, which again reveals the character of the Community as a consocation. President Mitterrand was quite prepared to remind the British of the possibilities of setting up a two-tier Europe with the British demoted to the lower tier, if they proved too unreasonable in the context, for instance, of the proposal for Economic and Monetary Union.[34] At the same time it was apparent that senior members of the British government, such as Hurd, Howe, Major, and Lawson, were fearful about being marginalized.[35] Both Lawson and Howe resigned at least in part over this issue.

There was also evidence of the way in which the strengthening of the common system could reinforce the distinctiveness of the participating units. In the machinery in the Communities for defining and managing a common foreign policy, it was clear that what was likely to emerge for the foreseeable future was not a common European foreign policy, or, indeed, a coordinated foreign policy in the technical sense, but rather a policy made by harmonizing the various separate interests of the member states. A balance was to be struck between using membership in the Community to promote the separate interests of each individual state, as with Britain and the Commonwealth, or France and the Francophone states, or even Britain in its special relationship with the US, and the maintenance of the appearance of the potential for common action. It was paradoxical that the latter had to be convincing in order to preserve the capacity for individual action, and a continuing investment in the common enterprise was, therefore, necessary. At the same time it was apparent that each state was anxious to preserve the system whereby it took over the Presidency every six years: it created an opportunity for making an impact on the common arrangements, but, at the same time, appearing as a distinctive power within the system and in relations with outsiders.

A second feature of the debate was, however, an exaggeration of the risks of federalist outcomes.[36] Such fears seemed to arise from a misunderstanding of the nature of the legal and constitutional arrangements of the European Community. It is, of course, the case that as integration proceeds an increasing range of common rules apply over wider areas of economic and social life in member states, and that around 60% of legislation made at the national level involved European Community issues. These were developments that greatly affected the procedures of administration and legislation, and the need to agree such rules in common with the partners certainly placed limitations upon the individual country's ability to go it alone. But the assertion that this need in itself constituted a limitation upon sovereignty was misleading when it suggested that this was happening because of the special legal character of regionalization, rather than because of what was happening in general.[37]

The practice of sovereignty has always involved a compromise with the level of interdependence which prevailed at a particular time, or in a particular area. The fact is that all modern states are now required to arrange their economic systems in cooperation with other states: as Leon Brittan said in the speech referred to above, the need for the British authorities to "chase after" West German interest rates was hardly an illustration of free choice on the part of the British. But in a wide range of areas, ranging from decisions about the safety of medicines to the accept-ability of standards of civil liberties, states are subject to pressures from outside the state and quite frequently these are strong enough to constrain the choice of national governments. The European Community may be seen as a special case of such constraints, but it is important to recognize that, in so far as it is a special case, this is because of the national policies which the separate governments have each freely chosen. It would be entirely unreasonable of, say, the British government to choose to join the Community in order to achieve certain objectives, like increasing mutual trade, but then to resist the introduction of the procedures necessary to obtain those ends on the grounds that they implied joint action. The greater degree of interdependence has heightened the need for cooperation, but this is nothing to do with the special character of the Communities' legal arrangements. Indeed it is arguable that policy-making in the Community has not in itself detracted from national sovereignty: what is changed is the wish of national legislatures and governments to do certain things rather than their legal or constitutional right or capacity to do them.

These points may be sharpened by looking more closely at the legal and constitutional arrangements of the European Communities, which might at first sight appear to challenge sovereignty. In the late 1980s and early 1990s two major revisions of the Treaty of Rome took place, the Single European Act, which eventually came into force in 1987 after ratification by the member states, and the Maastricht Agreement, also an amendment of the Treaty of Rome, which was agreed in the Dutch town by the Heads of State and Government in December 1991. The question of how far these agreements changed the underlying constitutional and legal aspects of sovereignty, will now be discussed in some detail, since these agreements represent the frontier challenge to the sovereignty of member states. This is the point which the European Community has reached and where the general arguments of this chapter are finally tested.

It should be stressed, however, that the arguments which follow contain the details of the institutional and constitutional changes of the two agreements, and that they reinforce the general views already presented. If the reader prefers not to deal with such intricacies he/she may move on rapidly to the chapter's conclusions.

The overall constitutional relationship

The Maastricht Agreement did not fundamentally alter the relationship in constitutional terms from that established by the Single European Act. The main point is that although there had been changes in the conditions of sovereignty, and the way in which it could be exercised, the case against the view that sovereignty had been ceded either by the Treaty of Rome itself, or by its successive amendments, remained very powerful. This case received little or no attention in Britain in the public debate before the meeting of the European Council at Maastricht, and the false argument that integration and sovereignty were necessarily opposed concepts prevailed by default. But sovereignty had not been lost although it may not have been exercised effectively.

In support of this view the main arguments are as follows:

1. The Community was based upon a Treaty from which any member state could withdraw under international law – the Treaty of Rome was not a constitution. For instance, if the British Parliament had made it clear, *without any ambiguity*, that it intended to nullify a particular decision made by the European institutions, the British courts would have followed the dictates of Parliament. The essence of the situation was that Parliament had unilaterally agreed to bind itself to a treaty, and there was no legal or constitutional impediment in the way of Parliament's changing its mind. In practice, therefore, the doctrine of the primacy of Community law over national law rested upon the *willingness* of Parliament to accept the current situation and its implications.

   The situation in the other member states was more complicated but not fundamentally different. Indeed the situation there, as in Britain, underlined the point that the Community arrangements rested on separate national constitutional orders not on a supranational European one. If a continental government wished to withdraw from the Treaty of Rome it would act under the terms of general international law, just as in Britain, but if its Assembly issued a specific instruction to its national courts to negate a Community Act, it would have been acting unconstitutionally in terms of its own constitution. In order to be effective, therefore, the procedure for amending the constitution would have to be followed, as opposed to the procedure for producing ordinary legislation. If this were done continental courts could also apply a national law ahead of the Community law.[38]

2. The doctrine of the sovereignty of Parliament in Britain is the basis of the argument that Parliament could have nullified an individual Community Act by an Act of ordinary legislation, if it so wished, without contravening the British constitution.

   Because each Parliament is sovereign there is no difference in Britain between Acts of constitutional amendment and ordinary acts of legislation. British courts would, therefore, regard a specific instruction by Parliament to nullify a Community Act as being, at one and the same time, an amendment of the constitution and an Act of legislation: apart from issuing a specific instruction to the courts in Britain Parliament would also in the same Act be changing the terms of the constitutional arrangements, which it established in the European Communities Act of 1972, under which it was required to give priority to the law of the Communities. British courts would do what they were told to do by Parliament because Parliament had combined a specific instruction with a constitutional means. The European Court of Justice (ECJ) would, of course, complain about this, but it would be ineffectual because the Communities were not based upon a higher constitutional order, but rather on the separate individual constitutional orders of the member states.

3. There were, however, a number of reasons why National Assemblies in the Community were unlikely to try to nullify a Regulation or Directive set forth by institutions of the Community.

One of these is that such decisions would already have been approved by one or more national Ministers in the Council of Ministers who had, except in very unusual circumstances, the support of a majority of elected representatives in their own countries. In normal circumstances, it was unlikely that a majority could have been found at home to negate a decision made in Brussels, particularly where that meant following the procedures for constitutional amendment, which normally require a two-thirds majority. But this was a political impediment rather than a legal one.

Another impediment is the fact that members of national Assemblies, such as the UK Parliament, were rather poorly informed about the nature of the Communities and the details of their business. However, the governments could, in principle, have made it easier for elected representatives to exercise sovereignty by altering procedures to enable proposed legislation to be more fully debated at home and amended according to their wishes. An extreme example of this possibility would be if Ministers were to have been given a mandate which tied them to a specified policy in Brussels. At least one other member – Denmark – had such arrangements. In such a situation, the claim that sovereignty had been lost would be hard to sustain, because Assemblies would be effectively giving instructions to their representatives in Brussels as Community legislation was being formulated. Conversely the failure of Assemblies to exercise their sovereign powers did not mean that this could not be done. Failure to exercise a sovereign power did not mean that it had been lost.

4. This may be thought to ignore the possibility that governments might be outvoted in the Council of Ministers according to the majority voting arrangements in the Treaty of Rome, in the Single European Act, and as discussed below, after its ratification, in the Maastricht Agreement.

There are three arguments against the view that majority voting had fundamentally eroded governments' powers to veto action of which they disapproved.

The first is quite simply that the national systems, in their various ways, could nullify acts which proved objectionable, as has been pointed out above. Such a course might damage relationships with the Community, but that political or economic costs might arise is irrelevant to the constitutional and legal possibilities.

Second, the governments retained, even in areas where the formal arrangement was majority voting – because they speak for a sovereign state – a *reserve power* in the Council to veto any *proposed* legislation of which they disapproved. Although it was highly unlikely that this would be a part of the routine arrangements of the Community after the Single European Act, it nevertheless remained as a power to be used *in extremis* by member governments which objected to a particular course of action.

The conclusion of the Single European Act and the Maastricht Agreement somewhat complicated, of course, the operation of the Luxembourg Accords, though they did not lead to their abandonment, as Mrs Thatcher was anxious to point out after her return from negotiating the SEA in December 1985. The two amendments to the Treaty of Rome introduced majority voting into a relatively narrow, if important, range of legislation: in the SEA the main reference was A100a legislation which concerned the area of the single market. In the Maastricht Agreement further areas of legislation were added, in particular concerning cultural questions, education questions, and some aspects of environmental and research and development policy.

But even in these areas it would be a mistake to suppose that majority voting had the same implications which it would have in decision-making within a stable democracy. At the end of the day there was little likelihood that a sovereign state would be regularly outvoted on issues which it regarded as vital to its national interests.

Even in areas where majority voting was a formal possibility every effort was made to reach consensus. Indeed its main effect was to put greater pressure on states to compromise so that a general agreement could be found. No government likes to be outvoted, and would do everything in its power to avoid this. In any case these questions arose in the context of the implementation of decisions the principles of which had already been approved on the basis of unanimity in the Council of Ministers, or in the "grand" agreements such as the Single European Act or the Maastricht Agreement. When formal voting was used it was likely to concern technical issues, where major issues of principle were not at stake, and in this sense majority voting, when it took place, was usually not about first order questions.

One difficulty in this area, however, was that it was difficult to get accurate information about the distribution of support on particular issues, and about how states voted if formal voting took place. This was partly because of the general principle that the meetings of the Council of Ministers were in camera, but also because governments did not like it being generally known how the bargains had been struck. It might be uncomfortable for ministers sometimes if it were known in precisely what circumstances concessions had been made and in exchange for what. This is particularly the case when majority voting is a lubricant of the consensus-forming process.

But it was known in early 1992 that there had been two occasions on which states had invoked the Luxembourg Accords when they could have been outvoted. One such occasion concerned the Spanish government on an issue which concerned the modification of an aspect of VAT. On both occasions, however, the request was turned down on the insistence of the Presidency, and majority voting was used: the states who wished to argue the issue until consensus had been reached were outvoted.

What is to be made of this? Once again the events recorded do not seem to be strong evidence that the Luxembourg Accords were no longer applicable, because they concerned only two occasions, which, in the area to which majority voting applied since 1987, was remarkably infrequent. A further point is that the reaction of a number of states to the requests having been turned down was of shock; and the two governments sought to conceal the episodes from their home constituency. In other words there was the sense that this was an aberration and that there would be trouble if it got out.

The most important point, however is that it happened on two occasions only and not to one of the bigger states. It seems quite unlikely that if one of these states had appealed for resort to the Luxembourg Accord procedure more than a few times, and had not got its way, that there would not have been major trouble. To avoid the terms of the Accords would be highly damaging to the Community, and in practice the formal arrangement would be evaded. To do otherwise would not be in the interest of the states which formed the majority. For these various reasons the argument that the Luxembourg Accords were still applicable, which is a view frequently repeated by government ministers in Britain, seemed to be well founded. The need to promote the 1992 process meant, however, that governments were now less likely to resort to such thinking because, as sovereign states, they had accepted an overriding goal.

Third, governments had another kind of reserve power. Even though it may be accepted that a particular institution should have the power to act in specific areas without being subject to instructions from government, governments retained the right to negotiate a different set of powers for institutions in other areas. They were not subject to any general principle, e.g. a federal principle, according to which the powers of future institutions were to be allocated. Indeed, as shown above the opposite principle, that of subsidiarity, was asserted at Maastricht: powers were to be kept at the lowest level possible. That governments retained the right to pursue their own strategy in these matters meant that they could seek to balance the loss of powers in one realm against the gain or retention of powers in another: supranational powers to the Eurofed could be balanced against unanimity in the area of economic coordination. It might be argued that, even though they might continue to seek such countervailing powers, they would be increasingly condemned to accept supranationalism: there was a federalizing process. As will be shown below there was little in the Maastricht Agreement to substantiate this view, and this writer sees little evidence to support it. The availability of this strategy was another indication that states had retained their sovereignty.

The conclusion must be that neither accession to the European Communities, nor the terms of the Single European Act or the Maastricht Agreement, had altered the underlying legal and constitutional circumstances of national sovereignty. Indeed, the fear that this had happened was strikingly less in member states other than Britain.

The adjustments introduced in the Maastricht Agreement

The broad pattern of the development of the institutions proposed in the Maastricht Agreement was one of increasing the involvement of institutions other than the core institutions in the decision-making process. There was no blanket extension of new powers to institutions such as the European Parliament, but rather a careful extension of a right to participation in carefully designated areas. This adjustment was seen as the continuation of the efforts made hitherto to create a European Union, a term which was included in the preamble, and which appeared at a number of other places. The phrase "ever closer Union" was retained in the revised Common Provisions, which seemed to indicate further integration to come. Another broad direction of development was towards the inclusion of areas which were previously alongside the Communities, such as the foreign policy arrangements, more fully in the Union. The whole was to be consolidated into a single package of activities linked in systems of common management. The role of the Community in a number of new areas was also made explicit.

There were two kinds of institutional adjustment, which might be termed institutional extension, and institutional innovation.[39]

Institutional extension

This applied to the role of the European Parliament in two major respects, and one minor one. (The latter need not be discussed at length: it is that the Parliament was given a modified right to initiate legislation, but only by being allowed to call upon the Commission to "submit any appropriate proposal . . . for implementing this Treaty".) First the major changes in the Parliament's powers introduced by the Single European Act were incorporated in Article 189c in the Maastricht Agreement. This was the procedure which was called the Cooperative Procedure, which was introduced into the SEA as a modification of Article 149 of the Treaty of Rome. In the text of the Agreement it was to be followed in a number of new areas, but it should be recalled that in the SEA it applied mainly to Article 100(a) legislation which was of great importance for the achievement of the single market. It enhanced the European Parliament's say over Community business in this area but the Council of Ministers could overrule its decisions: if Parliament vetoed the Council's proposal for legislation, the Council could overcome that veto on the basis of unanimity, but if it took no decision for three months the proposal would be void. If Parliament proposed amendments to legislation, the Council could accept them, on the basis of unanimity, if they departed from the terms of the Commission's proposals to the Council.

A new form of participation by the European Parliament in the decison-making process of the Community was included in the Agreement's proposed new Article 189(b) of the Treaty. This form of decision-making was required in a number of policy areas, specifically decisions on consumer affairs, on aspects of environmental questions, on cultural, and educational matters, and on questions concerning the Communities' programmes for furthering common and joint research programmes. Article 189b gave the European Parliament a right which it previously lacked: to impose an unconditional veto on the Council's proposals for legislation in the stated areas. From some points of view this might be regarded as a significant enhancement of its powers.

The process was a complicated one and included resort to a new Conciliation Committee in the event of disagreement between the Council and the Parliament, to be made up of equal numbers from each. Whether or not the Conciliation Committee reached agreement, approval of the legislation depended on the agreement of both Council and Parliament, unless Parliament failed to respond within a six-week period. Legislation approved under 189(b) was to be signed by the Presidents of both the European Parliament and the Council of Ministers. Except when approving amendments from the European Parliament which had not been supported by the Commission, in which case unanimity applied, the Council was to take decisions in these procedures on the basis of qualified majority.

The Agreement included a Declaration on the Role of National Parliaments in the European Union, which stressed the importance of "greater involvement of national Parliaments in the activities of the European Union", and an improvement of ways of exchanging information between national Parliaments and the European Parliament; Commission proposals were to go to national Parliaments "in good time for information and *possible* examination" [author's emphasis]. Closer relations between the European Parliament and national Parliaments were also to be encouraged by providing "appropriate reciprocal facilities and regular meetings". It seems obvious that if national Assemblies responded positively to this invitation, sovereignty *vis-à-vis* the Community could be exercised more effectively.

The machinery of the member states in the area of foreign policy was also further developed, and different categories of response to the outside world were created. The European Council was to be responsible for agreeing the principles and guidelines of foreign policy, the Council, acting on the basis of unanimity, was to agree common positions, and the Council within the context of such guidelines, principles and common positions, was to decide which so-called joint actions should be subject to management on the basis of qualified majority, which in this case had to include the positive votes of eight of the twelve states, with 54 votes in favour.

A major innovation with regards to the judicial arrangements of the Communities was the introduction of a system whereby member states which did not comply with Directives could be subjected to a fine by the Court of Justice. The Commision could advise the Court as to the appropriate sum to be paid by way of the fine. This, it was thought, would be likely to encourage the more reluctant states to obey the law.

Although ideas had been discussed for streamlining the Commission by, for instance, reducing its membership to twelve, there were no specific decisions for this in the Agreement. The main concession was that the Commission was to be subject to the approval of the European Parliament after its appointment by the member governments, though what happened in the event of its being rejected was not indicated.

Institutional innovation

The Agreement included a number of new institutions. Perhaps the most interesting was the Committee of the Regions which was to be made up of representatives of the sub-regions in member states, though they were to be appointed by the governments. The Committee was given a consultative role in a number of issue areas, and could be required to produce its opinion within a period specified by the Council, but not less than one month, after which the Council was free to act.

A conciliation committee with regards to legislation was also established as indicated above. A further innovation was the creation of an Ombudsman to be appointed by the European Parliament to investigate complaints by individuals and groups about alleged misconduct by the institutions of the Community.

Implications for the constitutional principles of the Community

1. The Agreement obviously included a number of cases of the expansion of the role of the Communities. The list of common policies was much enlarged to include education and culture, consumer protection, energy, civil protection and tourism, and trans-European networks in transport. There were a number of innovations with regard to the rights of individuals including the creation of citizenship of the European Union, the right to vote in municipal elections and to stand as candidates for citizens of other EC member states – details to be produced by 31 December 1994 – and an equal right for all citizens of the Union to help by the consular and other representatives of other member states in third countries – details by 31 December 1993. The increase in the role of the Community with regard to external relations, and a limited use of qualified majority voting in that area, was also striking. But the commitment to the development of a common defence policy was extremely cautious, and it was possible to interpret it as being intended for the very distant future. It "might in time lead to a common defense" (A.D(1)). This is not to deny, however, that the allowing of a role on some aspects of defence to the WEU on the part of the members of the European Communities was a significant step in that direction.

2. In the area of external relations the French and the British seemed to have made concessions to the demand to promote European positions in their capacity as permanent members of the Security Council of the United Nations. Under A.E(4)

member states which are also members of the U.N. Security Council will concert [sic] and keep the other members fully informed . . . they will ensure the defence of the positions and interests of the Union, without prejudice to their responsibilities under the provisions of the U.N. Charter.

There was a degree of movement here in allowing the other members a right to be consulted about Security Council business: previously the British and the French had insisted on a fairly rigid separation of the two areas.

3. But apparent concessions to integration must be balanced against apparent reinforcements of the reserve powers of the governments. Much depends upon the interpretation of the significance of the various uses made of articles 189(c) and 189(b). The evidence of the Agreement suggests that this was a matter of fine judgement by the negotiators at Maastricht, with broadly speaking 189(c) being preferred if the question was one of importance to the members of the Council who wished to get their way in the positive sense of getting something done, and 189(b) being preferred if the members were less enthusiastic about an issue and were prepared to put up with a veto by the European Parliament. The latter procedure also allowed for a kind of double block by states which opposed the policy proposal under consideration. If it was outvoted in the Council where qualified majority voting applied, then it could seek to mobilize opposition in the European Parliament in order to create a majority of members against its acceptance there. This would naturally tend to encourage the more hesitant governments to whip members of their party in the European Parliament into towing the party line, and would tend to weaken the development of European parties, despite the lip service paid to this in Annex 1 of the Agreement. This is another instance of a well-established doctrine about the development of the European Communities: that apparent concessions to supranationalism were more likely when intergovernmentalism had been bolstered. The paradox should be noted, that 189(b) which appeared to give more powers to the European Parliament could be interpreted as helping the more cautious states.

4. The 189(b) procedure was introduced in some areas where 189(c) had previously applied in the form of A.149 of the Treaty of Rome. This was true for Title III legislation on the free movement of persons, services and capital, and also for Article 100a legislation under Title IV. Decisions on the Multiannual Framework programmes on research and technology cooperation under A.130i were to be taken under 189(b), though they were previously to be taken under the terms of the SEA by unanimity in the Council. Decisions on cooperation in public health matters, and in consumer protection, both brought in as specific Community policies under their own heading, were to be based on 189(b).

5. It was particularly interesting to note the discrimination between the use of 189 (b) and (c). On transport policy, guidelines were to be on the basis of 189(b) but decisions on implementation, on establishing interoperability in transport, and on agreeing technical standards were on the basis of 189(c). Under the general heading of Social Policy, Title VIII, decisions to promote cooperation on matters of education were to be taken

by the 189(b) procedure, whilst under the same heading decisions to promote vocational training to adapt to industrial change, facilitate mobility, and cooperation on training, were to be taken through 198(c). With regard to Research and Technological Development, the overall programmes, as already indicated, were through 189(b), but specific programmes were to be approved by majority vote in the Council, i.e. not even by 189(c), the equivalent of which, the procedure introduced by the SEA through A.149, had previously applied. Here was a case of regression. Decisions on the tasks, primary objectives and organization of the Structural Funds were to be taken on the basis of unanimity – no change from the SEA – but implementing legislation with regard to the Regional Fund and the Social Fund were 189(c), whilst decisions on the guidance section of the Agricultural Fund were somewhat oddly to be taken solely by qualified majority vote in the Council of Ministers.

6. The reservation of unanimity in some questions was also interesting. Article 189(c) procedures could be used to decide the actions to be taken to implement environment policy, but unanimity was to be used for provisions under this heading of a fiscal character, for measures affecting town and country planning, except measures regarding water resource management, and for measures "significantly affecting choice between different energy sources" in member states. On Title XIV questions regarding industry, cooperation between undertakings to promote innovation and adjustment to structural change were on the basis of unanimity in the Council.

There was also to be an extremely interesting innovation in giving the Communities a role in a common policy on entry visas, under A100c, but decisions on this were to be on the basis of unanimity – to establish guidelines – until 1996, when qualified majority voting in the Council was to apply – not 189 b or c – with states reserving the right to act alone with regard to law and order and internal security questions. On decisions which could facilitate exercising the rights of citizenship, unanimity was to apply. With regard to the establishment of a Community role on education decisions concerning the harmonization of laws and regulations of member states were not to be subject to 189(b), but unanimity in the Council.

Sovereignty and economic and monetary union

The implications for sovereignty of moving towards economic and monetary union need to be considered, especially as the Maastricht Agreement contained a commitment to move towards a monetary union by the late 1990s, according to specified rules, and in three stages. The crucial point to make here is that sovereignty has never been untrammelled; it has always been subject to the "givens" of international economic and political circumstances. In order to be accepted as members of international society, states have always recognized that they must acknowledge the prevailing codes of behaviour. Beyond that, however, they are constrained by the current configuration of power and, as economic interdependence increased, by a wider range of rules and prohibitions. The situation which follows from such constraints is that states are *not* constantly compelled by circumstances to limit behaviour that would otherwise go unchecked. Instead, it is a general sense of what sovereignty entails *at that particular time*.

The outer limits of freedom of action are *conventionally* defined and sovereignty is the right to act within those limits. Because sovereignty is conventionally defined, its perceived aspects change over time. For instance, states used to insist that their military contingency planning was a matter for their separate, exclusive sovereignty, but in NATO joint planning became the norm without creating the sense that sovereignty had been endangered. Indeed, precisely the opposite was the case – giving up an outmoded condition of sovereignty came to be seen as necessary in order to preserve sovereignty.

For member states, the "givens" of sovereignty included by the early 1990s a wide range of constraints on an independent ability to control their own economies – constraints which hitherto had originated in international society in a large number of different areas, in each of which the separate power of states was declining. Amongst these areas, of course, were those constraints which derived from the economic strength of Germany – a fact which would have to be faced regardless of the future development of the Community. What is striking though is that constraints had existed for a number of years and had not raised the question of the limitation of sovereignty (except in very exceptional circumstances, such as the "letter of intent" sent by the British Labour government to the International Monetary Fund in 1976). As such constraints emerged, the British simply changed their view about where the outer edges of sovereign action lay.

Two illusions persisted with regard to currency. The first was that the member states could, in fact, manage it independently when all the evidence suggested that this was not the case. (Some MPs in Britain even suffered from the delusion that Parliament controlled it!) The real situation was that all states were heavily influenced in the management of money by external factors and other states, though some, such as Germany, were more influential than others. For instance, for many years the pound sterling moved in value largely in response to international pressures. Interest rate changes usually followed changes in other countries, especially in Germany. The second illusion was that the business community always prefered to improve its competitive position by making exports as cheap as possible in comparison with those of its competitors, thus putting a premium on the currency's adjustability. In reality, what the business community actually preferred was stability even if the currency was marginally overvalued because stability gives greater predictability about sales and returns and reduces transaction costs. The pound was not only largely outside the control of British authorities, but it had also moved through a wider range of fluctuation than the business community preferred. Being outside the monetary union would not have protected sovereignty, if by that it is meant the ability to determine the value of the currency. In fact, being outside of the monetary union carried with it considerable costs deriving from the lack of currency stability.

There was, of course, a trade-off here. In the arrangements for economic and monetary union, unilateral control of policies could be exchanged for a greater part in shaping common policies and a greater say over the relevant decisions of others. In this sense, members had an unusual opportunity to expand the limits of sovereignty rather than, as is normally the case, passively accepting the givens. For instance, extending common institutional arrangements would increase rather than weaken ability to influence Germany's policy. To put the case in its weakest form: a *de jure* European Monetary System, even if dominated by Germany, was preferable to a *de facto* Deutschmark zone. If the German view of the powers and authority of the proposed European central bank, the Eurofed, won the day, then it would at least involve British and other officials in the taking of monetary decisions which applied to all members even though that body would be formally beyond direct instructions from the governments. There would in this situation be a pooling but not an abandonment of sovereignty.

But if, as seemed likely, there was a need to make further efforts to "tighten up the existing machinery for the coordination of macroeconomic policies and discipline in budgetary policy", the range of opportunities for the various states to influence common policies that were necessary for the effective working of the monetary union would also be increased. Decisions to go further and set up new machinery to promote economic convergence would necessarily either subject both Germany and Britain to a common authority, on the lines of Eurofed or the European Environmental Agency (an example of pooled sovereignty) or would involve joint management by government representatives. In all these cases, the ability of the Germans to make decisions independently and effectively which created the "givens" of the sovereignty of the others would have been reduced.

Conclusions

The above arguments suggest that the terms of the Maastricht Agreement on Political Union did not significantly alter the conclusions reached after the Single European Act. It is true that the role of the Community had been enhanced, both in the sense that the scope of integration had been broadened, and that a wider role had been allowed to institutions such as the European Parliament. There had also been institutional innovation in creating the Council of the Regions, the Ombudsman, and the new Conciliation Council. There were also some new principles, which enhanced the degree of interpenetration of the member states. But what should be stressed is that the negotiations were very carefully judged, and a somewhat arcane nuancing of the granting of powers and the reservation of powers was achieved, no doubt sometimes for political and electoral reasons, and sometimes for reasons of principle.

But in general terms no new powers were granted which could be seen as diminishing the sovereignty of states, and which provided evidence to challenge the argument presented in the latter part of this chapter. Even the decision which seemed to increase the powers of the European Parliament, A.189(b), could be seen as having been carefully judged to allow some encouragement to states which might have wished to make it easier to resist integration. And the Committee of the Regions had no powers of its own. The main principle of concessions to the Community seemed to be to extend implementing powers within the framework of agreements about principles, purposes, and major structures, which had been approved by the Council, either in a positive vote in favour by all members, or by a unanimous overcoming of the EP's opposition through 189(c). This is not to mention the various reserve powers available to states.

It is vital to recognize that the regional arrangements rested on an international treaty – in the case of the Community, the Treaty of Rome – which had validity because of its acceptance according to the different constitutional arrangements of the separate states. This document was not a constitution, and there was absolutely no reason to suppose that it was different from any other treaty in its implications for the rights of states with regard to its abandonment or avoidance.[40] For instance, unlike constitutions it could only be amended on the basis of the unanimous consent of all signatories. Despite the differences in the details of the members' constitutions it remained possible for each state to negate the effect of any of the laws of the Community within its frontiers and to withdraw altogether from the system, although the procedure would be more complicated in monist states, where the technique normally used for constitutional amendment might be required, than in dualist states, such as Britain, where a normal act of Parliament would suffice. Despite all the efforts of the Court of the Communities, if the British Parliament made it clear that it wished to negate the effects of a piece of Community legislation British courts would have followed Parliament and not the Court.[41]

As long as the Community rested upon a Treaty, and not a constitution, it is very difficult to see how the legal/constitutional situation could ever be taken beyond this point. Indeed the often repeated threat of President Mitterrand, and his Prime Ministers Michel Rocard and Edith Cresson, to use a separate treaty to move to a higher level of integration amongst ratifying states ironically confirmed this point: if a constitution bound them together this would be impossible, as it is between the states in the US Federal system.[42] The choice of this device for obtaining greater unification only confirmed the underlying separateness of the states. The argument that the Communities' institutions were, as de Gaulle had said, extensions of the administrative and juridical arms of the state cannot simply be ignored:[43] the view that Communities' legal system rested upon a higher constitutional order was inevitably a political and contentious one. The point might be made quite simply in the British case, though it applied to all other members: what Parliament had given it could equally, according to the British Constitution – which had not been superseded – take away. In the European Community the states remained sovereign, and would remain so unless a fundamentally different order was introduced.

De Gaulle made his legal/constitutional point in order to resist the Commission's claim for an extension of its competence. The point being made here is, however, that the competence of the centre could be extended indefinitely without necessarily challenging de Gaulle's argument. What is important, however, is that the form of the institutional arrangements should also be analogous with those which appeared in consociationalist states. By the early 1990s the Community's institutional arrangements had not moved in a federalist direction, and, indeed, stipulations of the Treaty of Rome which would have achieved this had been effectively resisted despite the enormous expansion of the scope of integration. As has been pointed out one enduring and crucial alteration was the Luxembourg Accords of January 1966 which ensured the continuation of the principle of unanimity in the votes in the Council of Ministers on matters thought important by any one member state. What emerges from this, however, is that there was now a need to continue to construct institutions at the centre which did not pose a federalist threat. The exaggeration of this danger could be countered by the argument that it had no basis in the underlying constitutional and legal circumstances of the Community, nor need it have arisen in future institutional arrangements. On the other hand those who were putting forward plans for future institutions needed to be alerted to the need to reflect the Community's essential consociational character.

A distinction needs to be made between decisions about policy – the creation and extension of the framework for common action – and decisions about management and coordination. The coalition necessary to take decisions about the former would always involve a requirement for unanimity or consensus, and the Single European Act and the Maastricht Agreement generally reflected this principle: the assumption in the early 1990s was that this would continue to be the case in the EC. The arrangement for common management would be within the framework of such decisions: it would be involved with the supervision and enforcement of what had already been agreed. Wherever possible that management would involve bureaucracies in which states would have equal representation. It was striking in the late eighties that the management arrangement proposed in the Delors Plan for Monetary Union involved a coordinated arrangement of national central banks. The proposal was not for a central bank under the direction of a federal independent authority.[44] This approach was reflected in the strategy of encouraging the harmonization of national standards, as with the directives on banking and insurance, and the proposals put forward for approximating national social standards in the light of the Community's Social Charter, rather than agreeing common Community standards which would be imposed from the top.

Common management could, however, involve something like the High Authority of the European Coal and Steel Community, which was very much an executive agency applying rules which had been agreed in some detail by the member states.[45] An analogy which sharpens this point concerns the differences between computers and people: a computer has something in common with the High Authority in that both are essentially rule-applying machines, whereas people are somewhat analogous with states in that both have mechanisms for deciding about future rules. What was seen was a system which was becoming stronger in that its scope was being extended, but which at the same time worked, not on the basis of what functionalists, or federalists, would call the Community interest, but much

more on the basis of the low level consensus among segment elites identified
within consociationalism. There would be a very strong sense that the
Community was there to serve the states: at the same time the community
would need to be worked for and enhanced or the interests of the sub-units
would be compromised.

The term which captures most accurately the dominant character of the
relationship between the states and the region is, therefore, *symbiosis*. Each
of the two levels, the separate states and the common system depended
upon the other. In terms of the range of integration theories the dynamics
which tended towards the strengthening of the community level are identified particularly clearly within neofunctionalism, whereas the pressures
which tend to encapsulate the segments, in the form of the states, are identified best within consociationalism. What is interesting from the point of
view of the theme of this chapter, however, is that there is no evidence to
suggest that the common arrangements could not be extended a very long
way before posing any direct challenge to the sovereignty of states.

Indeed as with consociationalism and the various segments within states
the common system in some ways helps to consolidate the sub-units. Hence
in the European Community were a number of states which joined in order
to develop their sense of forming distinctive entities, such as Spain and
Portugal, or West Germany, or arguably even Britain, and these needed to
have no fear that to strengthen the common arrangements and accept their
increasing scope was necessarily to compromise this ambition. Such states
were the more fortunate equivalents at the higher level of the dissenting
minorities within a number of existing states. Certain ways of taking decisions in the common system were, however, indicated though these
appeared to be emerging anyway in the European Community in the early
1990s. The symbiotic character of the regional system was, however, a
reflection of its consociationalism.

*

The symbiotic theme has been developed and illustrated in the chapters in
Section 1, but especially in Section 2. On the one hand are elements
conducive towards the strengthening of the regional arrangements, which
were most clearly evident in the case of the European Community, but
which, it was argued, are likely to become more pressing in other regions
of the world. On the other hand, however, are the adjustments of the states
to these pressures. Arguments developed from the experience of the European Community are also likely to apply in other regions. A crucial point
is that the demonstration of the ways in which the development of regional
arrangements might be reconciled with the survival of the state in Western
Europe has important implications for regionalism in other parts of the
world; it frees the argument of the albatross of federalism.

Such arguments are also important in that they show how the international
system of states can be fundamentally altered: as was argued in the Introduction to Section 1 a system dominated by a number of groupings of closely
interrelated states, is more radical in its implications for international society

than the emergence of new federations. As Mitrany implied, the latter merely leads to the creation of bigger states. This argument is carried forward in the Introduction to the next section.

A theme in European integration which has been consistently under-estimated, and which is recognized in consociationalism, is the way in which it has been seen in practice as a context for state consolidation and development. State building in Africa, and elsewhere, has many similarities with the processes of recovery and consolidation in Spain, Portugal, and Greece.

Notes

1. See the essays in *Contemporary European Affairs*, Vol. 1, No. 1/2, 1989, edited by David Bell and John Gaffney, under the title *1992 and After*.
2. See Alan Sked, *A Proposal for European Union*, The Bruges Group, Occasional Paper 9, London, 1990.
3. This argument is developed in Paul Taylor, "Regionalism and Functionalism Reconsidered", in A.J.R. Groom and Paul Taylor (Editors), *Frameworks for International Co-operation*, Pinter Publishers, London, 1990, Pp. 234–254.
4. Arend Lijphart, *The Politics of Accommodation; Pluralism and Democracy in the Netherlands*, University of California Press, Berkeley and Los Angeles, 1968; see also Arend Lijphart, "Consociational Democracy", *World Politics*, Vol. XXI, No. 2, 1969.
5. Hans Daalder, "The Consociational Democracy Theme", *World Politics*, Vol. XXVI, July 1974.
6. See Arend Lijphart, "Review Article: Northern Ireland Problem; Cases, Theories and Solutions", *British Journal of Political Science*, Vol. 5, 1975; and Brendan O'Leary, "The Limits to Coercive Consociationalism in Northern Ireland", *Political Studies*, Vol. XXXIII, No. 4, Pp. 562–588, 1989. These both contain extensive bibliographies.
7. Arend Lijphart, "Consociation and Federation: Conceptual and Empirical Links", *Canadian Journal of Political Science*, Vol. XXII, No. 3, 1979, Pp. 499–515.
8. R. Dahrendorf, *Society and Democracy in Germany*, Garden City, 1967, p. 276.
9. K. McRae (Editor), *Consociational Democracy: Political Accommodation in Segmented Societies*, McLelland and Stewart, Toronto, 1974.
10. Lijphart, 1969, loc. cit., p. 211–212.
11. Gabriel A. Almond, "Comparative Political Systems", *Journal of Politics*, Vol. XVIII, August 1956, Pp. 398–399.
12. Ian Lustick, "Stability in Deeply Divided Societies: Consociationalism versus Control", *World Politics*, Vol. XXXI, No. 3, 1979.
13. Lustick, 1979, loc. cit., Pp. 330–332.
14. Ibid., P. 332.
15. Ibid.
16. Lijphart, 1969, loc. cit., P. 216.
17. Seymour Martin Lipset, *Political Man: The Social Bases of Politics*, Garden City, 1960, Pp. 88–89.
18. For an excellent brief account of the theory and practice of federalism in the European Community see R.J. Harrison, *Europe in Question*, George Allen and Unwin, London, 1974.
19. See Stuart Holland, *The UnCommon Market*, The Macmillan Press, London, 1980.

20. Peter Kellner, *The Independent*, 22 March 1989.
21. For accounts of these various theories see A.J.R. Groom and Paul Taylor (Editors), *Frameworks for International Cooperation*, loc. cit.
22. For instance the British Government sought to protect its position as overseer of applications to the structural funds of the EC from local authorities and other organizations in Britain, and, indeed, appeared to be using EC disbursements not, as had been intended, to increase the size of available funds (the principle of additionality) but rather as an alternative to what would otherwise have been available from the British Treasury. It was only after the Commission had threatened to withhold funds from a development programme in South Wales in early 1992 that the British government eventually agreed reluctantly to amend its budgetary procedures to reflect the principle of additionality.
23. The rhetoric of the Thatcher administration regarding the EC frequently implied that the motives of the partners were either foolish or dishonourable. Particulary noteworthy, however – indicative of an attitude though not directly about the EC – was the Prime Minister's statement when a guest of President Mitterrand at the bicentennial celebrations of the French Revolution in Paris in July 1989, that this was not much to celebrate and that in any case the English thought of it first. A distinguished English historian, Christopher Thorne, commented in *The Guardian*, Saturday, 15th July that this had made him ashamed to be British: Thatcher's comments had been impertinent and wrong in fact.
24. O'Leary, 1989, loc. cit.
25. See Treaty on European Union, CONF-UP-UEM 2002/1/92, Brussels, 12 February 1992, Article 3b, at P. 9.
26. Paul Taylor, "The New Dynamics of EC Integration in the 1980s", in Juliet Lodge (Editor), *The European Community and the Challenge of the Future*, Pinter Publishers, London, 1989, Pp. 3–25.
27. This was a disease found in cattle in Britain in the 1980s which affected the nervous system and which it was feared could be transferred to humans. Some EC governments banned imports of beef from Britain until they were convinced that controls on the slaughter and transfer of meat had been sufficiently tightened, so that infected meat was not imported. A number of politicians and "popular" newspapers in Britain described this sensible, and legal precaution as blatant, unscrupulous opportunism to improve national beef sales at the expense of the British farmer.
28. See Fiona Hayes-Renshaw, *The Role of the Committee of Permanent Representatives in the Decision-Making Process of the European Community*, unpublished Ph.D. Thesis, University of London, 1990.
29. See *Financial Times*, 27 June 1990.
30. Lijphart, 1979, loc. cit.
31. The classic text on federalism is K.C. Wheare, *Federal Government*, Oxford University Press, London, Second Edition, 1951.
32. A.H. Birch, *Nationalism and National Integration*, Unwin Hyman, London, 1989. Birch writes on P.6: "A nation is best defined as a society which either governs itself today, or has done so in the past, or has a credible claim to do so in the not too distant future."
33. In his Granada Lecture, *Europe: Our Sort of Community*, reported in *The Independent*, 8 November 1989.
34. As on October 25th 1989. This was the lead front page story in *The Guardian*, 26 October 1989.

35. See *The Guardian*'s lead story "Cabinet rallies to Howe's EMS Flag", 2 November 1989.
36. Exemplified in Mrs Thatcher's keynote speech at the College of Europe in Bruges, 30 September 1988.
37. See note 2 above.
38. See Paul Taylor, "EC Membership: Claims and Counter-Claims", *International Affairs*, Spring 1981, Vol. 57, No. 2.
39. See the Maastricht Treaty, issued as *The Treaty on European Union*, by the Conference of Representatives of the Governments of the Member States, Political Union, and Monetary Union, CONF-UP-UEM 2002/1/92, Brussels, 12 February 1992.
40. See P.D. Dagtoglu (Editor), *Basis Problems of the European Community*, Basil Blackwell, Oxford, 1975.
41. See Geoffrey Howe, "The European Communities Act, 1971", *International Affairs*, Vol. 49, No. 1, January 1973.
42. See note 35 above.
43. J. Rosenstiel, "Some Reflections on the Notion of Supranationality", *Journal of Common Market Studies*, November 1963.
44. Committee for the Study of Economic and Monetary Union, *Report on Economic and Monetary Union in the European Community*, prepared for the European Council, 1988, Paragraph 33, Pp. 21–22.
45. Paul Taylor, "Supranationalism: the Power and Authority of International Institutions", in *Frameworks for International Co-operation*, loc. cit.

Section 3
The Development of Global Organization*

Introduction

In this section the pattern of development of international organization at the global level is considered: the focus is upon the economic and social side, which is the area with which most international organizations are concerned. The evolution of global international organization is discussed in terms of its overall structure and purpose, rather than aspects of the policies of specific institutions and their impact. Under the heading of the purpose of international organization the question is also put of whose – or which states' – interests was it intended to serve? In the next section, however, developments in the United Nations involvement with particular examples of the global agenda, namely population control, and the maintenance of international peace and security, are considered.

Arguments derived from the two linked concepts of *consociationalism* and *symbiosis* also apply in somewhat different ways to the developments at the global level which are discussed in this section. They suggest that the level and style of international organization is a function of the sub-units' (governments') perception of how their separate interests are to be reconciled with those of the collectivity (the regional or international system), rather than of the emergence of any transcendental common interest. The process of establishing rapport between two levels of interest, rather than establishing the superiority of one level of interest over the other, is seen to be the key to cooperation.

At the global level the pressures towards cooperation which derive from governments' concern about marginalization, and about obtaining the benefits produced from increasing scope, are relatively weak. Global organizations are perceived as having relatively indirect functional interconnections: there is, therefore, no incentive to stay with an integration process through which the scope of international organization is extended. Regimes are relatively detached from each other, and in so far as they are related – or in regime theory parlance, embedded – they enhance the bargaining

* Chapter 7 is a version of my article "The United Nations under Stress: Financial Pressures and their Consequences", in *Review of International Studies*, November 1991.

capacity of the participating states rather than strengthen any integrative dynamic which constrains that capacity. Elite cartels may emerge, as at present with the caucus of the five permanent members of the Security Council, but their maintenance tends to be uncertain and pressures upon individuals to stay with the game are weaker: there is no increment of attachment. Though there may be benefits from participating, the costs of non-involvement are less: marginalization is not a meaningful threat, though this might be starting to change.

In their implications for global organizations the concepts are far more radical than, say, federalism, in that they imply the survival of states within larger configurations through which the interests of the states in the larger organizations are mediated. As already pointed out federalism is less radical in its implications for international society as its vision is of larger states, constructed like the older smaller ones, behaving in the traditional way on their own account in international organizations. The alternative concepts discussed here have the great advantage that they reconcile change at the global and regional levels: they point to the emergence of new symbiotic regional arrangements, which relate to global organizations in new ways as collectives of states, without preventing any one of them from doing this separately, or denying their existence as sovereign entities.

What emerges at the global level, however, is a form of symbiosis in which the balance is the reverse of that at the regional level. Symbiosis implies a duality of national concern, with, first, the identification of the common interest – the promotion of the community – and, second, the reconciliation of that with the separate, national interests. Within the European Community, as was shown in Chapter 4, states have come to accept this symbiosis, with unity and diversity – to borrow from Montesquieu – being equally stressed. The question of whether there is any equivalent of this in the international system is an important one, but it tends to be answered rather weakly.

At the global level states are much less tolerant of attempts to strengthen the collectivity. Appeals to the contrary tend to be idealistic – to do with enhancing the common good, or in terms of recognizing self-interest in helping the less well off. There may be an international culture, as Bull has suggested, but this is qualitatively different from the kind of culture of community found in a symbiotic consociation. Even the more realistic argument in favour of participation, that it enlarges the opportunities for exercising diplomatic pressure, has not always been convincing to the world's statesmen.

The theoretical value of symbiotic consociation is revealed by the fact that any observer who was aware of that theory, and who also knew something about the pattern of issue-linkage at the global level and the nature of international culture, would be able to predict the way in which the states have imposed restraints upon international organizations at that level.

The theory indicates that global organization differs from regional in three major ways: there is only a weak integrative dynamic deriving from functional linkage between issue areas; there is little or no fear of marginalization; and the reconciliation of collective and national interests strongly favours the latter.

The three chapters in Section 3 show an entirely predictable pattern. On the one hand the growth of Specialized Agencies has been restrained since the early 1980s. This has been effected by the limitation of financial resources, in particular by the major contributor, the USA, and by resisting the creation of new agencies. Only one new agency, UNIDO, has been created since the immediate post-war period. The extension of the scope of common government was resisted as neither the sense of community nor the logic of linkage between functional areas suggested that this was necessary; accordingly concern with the autonomy of segments put a break at an early stage on the development of common organization. Conversely stronger community and stronger issue linkage would have led to stronger coordinating organization.

On the other hand the pattern of adaptation to new tasks would also be predictable in the light of symbiosis. The states tended to dislike the prospect of setting up new agencies to deal with new tasks, and had difficulty in adjusting the work of existing agencies. Accordingly the adjustment process was in the form of setting up Funds or Programmes which would have the task of coordinating the work of the existing agencies in the light of a new purpose. What was striking was that there was no sense of any common overall purpose, or any convergence in the purposes of the various separate agencies, which, of course, was much more developed in forms of advanced regionalization. Accordingly Funds and Programmes were financed on a voluntary basis and from the beginning were much more vulnerable to the wishes of the contributing states. It was much easier for funds to be withheld if policies were regarded as unsatisfactory, or, indeed, if the circumstances of the contributing states had altered.

The crucial point is that the method of adjustment to new problems at the global level – establishing Funds and Programmes – was consistent with the response since the 1970s to the problems found in the Specialized Agencies: failure to impose any radical changes upon existing institutions, but adding on new institutional gadgets in a piecemeal way; no grant of an increase in competence to international organization, in the sense of a right to manage, linked with a grant of the powers necessary to manage effectively, but rather a tinkering with the existing arrangements at the same low level of competence.

A theme which runs through the chapters in Section 3 is that the system lacked any central brain, and remained very weak in its coordination mechanisms despite the Funds and Programmes. There were numerous Reports about this, and a variety of proposals for correcting the problem were put forward, but no progress towards a solution was made, and, indeed, in the early 1990s it looked very unlikely that any progress would be made in the future. The immediate reason for this was that the United Nations system was pluralistic: its decentralized character allowed the member states to avoid the problems which would arise if the instruments of the collectivity were to be strengthened.

There would be too many awkward questions: what would be the policy of the central brain? What mechanisms would be required? How would the states protect themselves and their interests in the new system? In the absence of countervailing tendencies, such as arise within regions as scope expands, states would rather not face these questions. The need for common management was less pressing, because of the nature of the issue-linkage at the global level and the weak sense of community: it was possible, and necessary, to evade the problems concerning interests and institutions which are inherent in common management.

The inclinations identified in these arguments had three major consequences which mark the limits of cooperation. First, states at the global level never accepted the introduction of any system which involved what could be recognized in moral and legal terms as an *obligation* to international organization. For instance they refused any arrangement whereby funds could be levied by the organization upon participating members: they consistently resisted the creation of any right to finance, such as exists in the European Community. This is apparent in the response of some states to the proposal of the Law of the Sea Convention for an International Sea Authority, and for the transfer to it of sums generated by the exploitation of the sea bed by commercial agencies. It was progress of a kind that the proposal had been made and that some states had accepted it, but by the early 1990s the states which would have lost the most had not ratified the proposal. This was, of course, quite consistent with the earlier failure to accept SUNFED and the various proposals made in the Brandt Report, such as that for a link arrangement whereby special drawing rights would be allocated to the developing states. In the global system, unlike the regional, the learning curve, though it exists, is rather flat.

The financial crisis of the late 1980s and early 1990s, discussed in Chapters 6 and 7, is, however, the result of similar inclinations: the reluctance of the richer states to have to pay sums which had in a sense been levied by a hostile majority of states. From their point of view the way in which budgetary processes had evolved had created what looked like a tax, the functional equivalent of a right to finance on the part of international organizations: such a system had to be opposed.

Secondly, of course, there was at the global level no common authority which could be regarded as analogous with the Commission of the European Communities. There was no authoritative centre for the development of proposals for common policy, despite the appeals made by observers such as Bertrand: there were many centres, the voices of which remained relatively muted and non-authoritative. A good indication of this was the view sometimes expressed that the lead in the system was taken in the absence of any alternative by the ineffectual Economic and Social Sections of the Secretariat of the central United Nations! As will be shown below the development of the system had been marked by frequent alterations to these central arrangements, none of which had any positive effect.

Thirdly there were no mechanisms for system-level supervision of the global organizations in that there was no centre within which binding decisions could be taken about the efficiency, propriety or legality of the behaviour of institutions or individuals in the various international organizations. There was no equivalent of the Court of Justice of the European Communities, or even of the Panel of Auditors. For this reason any allegation of impropriety in global international organizations, as in UNESCO or, more recently in the FAO, quickly degenerated into political squabbles marked by the absence of any agreed criteria of misconduct. It may have appeared outrageous to some but not to others. This is another crucial measure of the difference between the general system and the community of states which makes up the EEC, where there is a high level of agreement about what constitutes acceptable behaviour in the central institutions, for instance in the management of funds.

What explains the deficiencies of the global system, compared with the main regional system, in these respects is not, however, that states have compromised their sovereignty at the regional level whereas they have refused to do this at the global one. Rather it is that at the regional level utilitarian and political pressures have combined with an evolving sense of common purpose to persuade states to finds ways of protecting their sovereignty in complex management institutions, but they have found no reason to do this at the global level.

The arguments developed and illustrated in Section 3 are, therefore, that the states found a balance with international organization by resisting the further expansion of the Specialized Agencies, adjusting through setting up relatively weak Funds and Programmes financed on a voluntary basis, opposing any attempts to find more rational ways of managing the system, by, for instance, strengthening procedures for coordination and direction, and refusing to accept the levying of Funds, the emergence of any international authority for initiating policy, and the creation of system supervision. These various points are illuminated by the theory of consociationalism and the notion of symbiosis. The arguments also apply, however, to the role of international organizations with regard to the interests of individuals, and the reader may wish to turn directly to a discussion of this issue in the Introduction to Section 4 below.

At the regional and global levels the pattern of the relationships between the state and international organization is distinctive. The logic of the relationship is, however, common, though its practical implications vary. What it signifies, however, is that sovereignty in the early 1990s was still a prevailing doctrine, but that this by no means excluded advanced forms of common management within international organizations. These had in the main been necessary only at the regional level. It is clear, though, that the sense of a need for the common management of discrete units – states – together with an increasing perception that collective and national interests had a symbiotic relationship, was beginning to appear at the global as well as at the regional level. Again, these points are addressed more fully in the Introduction to Section 4.

But advanced cooperation did not mean federalism, and an involvement in a process of regional integration did not mean the abandonment of statehood. At first sight these observations may seem to be unsurprising. Their general implication is, however, of major importance: they indicate a pattern of development of international society into relatively tight groupings of states which nevertheless tend to act as units in weak global institutions.

The pattern of evolution of global organization may be divided into three phases. After the establishment of the main elements of the system, which had been achieved by the late 1940s, the main institutional inhabitants of this landscape consisted of the central system of the United Nations, together with the Specialized Agencies. By the 1960s, however, it had been realized that the system was not ideal from the point of view of dealing with new global problems as they had emerged. There was, therefore, a need to adapt the system to new tasks, a phase which was marked by the setting up of what became known as the Funds and Programmes. One of the earliest major examples of this was the United Nations Development Programme (UNDP), set up in 1969 to coordinate the activities of the older institutions with regard to the development of the Third World. A range of other such intermediate institutions emerged: their main purpose was to coordinate the work of existing institutions in the light of the need to deal with new trans-sectoral problems.

This phase of adaptation very quickly gave way to a second phase where concern was focused upon the need to make the system of international organization more efficient, in the sense of achieving its purposes on the basis of rational planning, sustained by a clear purpose, under a common management. Inefficiency, defined in terms of a range of criteria, which are detailed below, was to be reduced to a minimum. Attempts to achieve this goal are discussed below and it will be seen that despite a great deal of effort not much was achieved.

In the 1980s, however, the second phase of seeking greater efficiency gave way to a third phase of seeking greater economy. The Americans took the lead in this, though by the early 1980s most of the other major contributors, such as the British, were also determined not to increase their expenditure upon international organization, which became known as a policy of maintaining the principle of zero growth with regard to the budgets of the organizations; the view was that spending through the system had to be kept at its existing level in real terms.

A period of particularly rapid growth in terms of resources for international organizations in the 1970s came to a halt because of the imposition of a financial corset in the early 1980s. This third phase is discussed in Chapters 6 and 7, and figures about the growth of global international organizations measured in budgetary terms are contained in Chapter 7. An important observation is that efforts to control increases in spending through organizations' budgets were made in both the European Community and in the global system at about the same time.

In sum, the system has gone through three phases: a concern with achieving greater effectiveness through adaptation in a first phase, marked in particular by the creation of the Funds and Programmes; a second phase of seeking greater efficiency in the pursuit of the stated purposes of the organizations; and a third phase of seeking greater economy, and the better use of resources in the system. It should be stressed that the concerns of earlier phases were not replaced by new ones. Rather there was an accumulation of concerns from the earlier phases with a particular concern dominating in each phase.

5 The process of reform in the United Nations system: adaptation for efficiency

The task of adaptation of the system was closely linked with the so-called special conferences which were held increasingly frequently after the early 1970s. These conferences have been particularly associated with the attempt to increase the effectiveness of international programmes which have been organized through the United Nations system over the last 25 years and which have been concerned with some of the more pressing global problems of the period: population policies, problems of refugees, the problem of producing and distributing food, the issues of racial discrimination, disarmament and development, the protection of the environment, and the difficulties in the way of defining and promoting the rights of women. The most obvious question which occurs is: why did such conferences seem necessary? It might have been expected, after all, that new problems would have been dealt with adequately through established arrangements, which were already very extensive in scope and competence. Despite this, however, special conferences were arranged; the peculiar circumstances in which this happened are discussed in this chapter. A number of related questions about the way in which international institutions emerged, how they worked, and their contribution to tackling specific problems, obviously also arise in this context. They are set out in the conclusions to this chapter, and are discussed, with reference to states roles in international organizations, in later chapters.

Preliminary research also suggested that the special conferences needed to be considered as part of a process of adaptation in the United Nations system as a whole; they not only frequently led to the creation of new institutions, or the adjustment of existing ones, but also affected the pattern of relations between institutions in the system, by creating new frameworks for coordination, initiation or attempts at management. The contributors, therefore, found themselves required to address a number of fundamental questions about the relationship between the conference and the United Nations system. How did they relate to the adjustment process? How successful were they with regard to this function? And what were the implications of the adjustments for the overall efficiency of the system? In this particular chapter preliminary answers to these questions are suggested, but they are discussed further in the chapters later in this book. In view of the increasing number of complaints in the 1980s and 1990s on the part of governments, particularly the major contributors – and some academics – about the way in which the United Nations economic and social organizations functioned, the question of their adaptation is now of considerable importance. The special conferences' part in this process is relevant to a current, very lively, debate, the outcome of which could significantly affect the future scale and role of international organization. In this chapter, therefore, not only are the reasons for holding the conferences examined, but also their setting in the range of United Nations economic and social organizations, and their impact upon current problems in the rational management of the system.

What are special conferences? A preliminary definition may be taken from a current text on international organization.

The typical pattern of each conferences was to select a single topic for attention, set a time period and meeting place for the conference, arrange for preparatory work by existing or specially created agencies, hold a conference of two or more week's duration generally open to all states, and adopt a set of principles and an action plan requiring implementation through new or existing United Nations or related agencies.[1]

A Report by the Joint Inspection Unit in 1982 accepted a definition of the special conferences as

a conference that is not part of the regular recurrent conference programme of a biennium, but that is convened in response to a specific resolution of the General Assembly or the Economic and Social Council, for whose substantive preparation specific additional budgetary provisions are made, and which all States are normally invited to attend. Such a conference usually extends over a period of a minimum of two to a maximum of four to six weeks and requires an intensive level of planning and servicing.[2]

The conferences may be divided into two broad categories from the point of view of their primary purpose. A more extensive typology is developed in the next chapter. First are those which were intended to define and uphold standards of behaviour for governments or individuals and which were not intended to lead directly to programmes, projects or operations, though these could be implied, or be added later. Such conferences – amongst those in this volume – included those which focused on race relations, women's rights or disarmament. Second are those which were intended to lead directly to a range of practical activities, frequently involving setting up a new international organization, or changing established ones, and allocating financial and other resources over a long period. This category includes those concerned with population, food, and the environment. The distinction between these two types of conferences is, of course, often blurred in practice: standard setting does not take place in an operational vacuum, and operations are related to standards which have been established. The arguments in this chapter, therefore, apply equally to both kinds of conference, though the second and third sets may appear at first sight to apply more directly to the operational conferences, and more generally to those concerned with standard setting. As will become evident this is because the operational consequences of the latter, and their implications for rational management, are more remote. They are, nevertheless, real.

The conferences may be seen as a product of three kinds of development, though the impact of each varies with the business with which they were concerned. First they were a response to the emergence of new problems, or to changes in the dimensions of longer standing ones: environmental problems were largely of the first kind, whilst problems in the area of race-relations, or population control, were of the latter kind (this section). Second, it is necessary to tackle the question of why such issues could not have been considered in a routine way within existing international institutions: why was there a need for special conferences? This question leads to an examination of the weaknesses of the economic and social international organizations of the United Nations system, in particular their failure to develop procedures for identifying and tackling new problems as a matter of routine (second section). Third, the conferences must be seen as a response to the attitudes of states and bureaucrats, which emerged in various coalitions, favouring or opposing particular responses (third section). A dimension of this theme which needs to be stressed is that state attitudes also played a key role in preventing the kinds of reform within the existing United Nations system which would have permitted the "routinization" of the conferences, in the sense that they could normally be held as part of the existing arrangements of ECOSOC, and of the General Assembly. This point is discussed further later in this chapter. One point in this context should be made at the outset: the conferences were by no means always positive in the sense that they reflected states' determination to do something. Sometimes they were regarded as a way of avoiding action in the context of particular problems.

A problem, and a resulting need for action, lies as much in the eye of the beholder as in its inherent character. The first reason for calling the special conferences which concerned the nature of the problem was that groups had emerged which were in a position to command attention and which demanded that something should be done. By the 1970s a pattern of transnational interest group politics had emerged which frequently involved a coalition of groups from a number of states which had become electorally or politically significant in some other way in one or more of them, and which occasionally acted in support of a group of national governments. One example of this was the emergence of blacks in the United States as a political force, and their natural inclination to go along to some extent with governments in relatively new black states in pushing for more international action to promote racial equality. Political elites in the US were brought to accept international action on racial questions, though they subsequently qualified their position, in part because questions of race had been given greater prominence on the domestic political agenda.

Similarly international action on a number of environmental problems was encouraged by the greater prominence of groups with this concern in internal politics in a number of states. This development is also not simply

a function of the increasing problems in this area, but also of the emergence
of people with the time and inclination to be concerned with such matters:
Ronald Inglehart's concept of the "post-acquisitive society" helps to explain
this.[3] As individuals grew richer in some states there came a time when
energies previously directed to obtaining a satisfactory standard of living,
and acquiring worldly goods, were rechannelled into other less pressing
interests. A first step was an increased concern with consumer standards,
as reflected by such organizations as that headed by Ralph Nader in the US,
and the Consumer Association in the United Kingdom. Consumerism led
naturally to "environmentalism", and the appearance in a number of richer
countries, such as West Germany and Scandinavia, of politically significant
Green Parties. It was to be expected that these would appear in countries
which were rich enough to support a "post-acquisitive society". These
groups, some of which were direct participants in the political process –
they were political parties – not only pushed their own governments into
greater attentiveness towards environmental issues, but also became the
informal partners in a number of international forums of governments of
their own and other states. The decision to hold a global conference on
environmental problems in Stockholm was very much a product of these
changes in economic, social and political circumstances. In other words the
conferences were in part a symptom of changes in the underlying structure
of power.

A second reason for calling the conferences, which concerned the problem
directly, was to be found, to use Jervis's terminology, in the pattern of relationships between the operational world and the perceptual one.[4] Under
the latter heading were matching changes in the world view of the disadvantaged and of the more prosperous, which both resulted from the remarkable
extension of global communications. The former group was permitted a
comparison of what they had with what could be got, and were simul-
taneously infected with the ideology of materialism and modernization; in
consequence they were subject to what has been called a rising tide of
expectations. This applied as much to non-material standards, behaviour
and rights, as to worldly goods. The rich, on the other hand, were made
more aware of the plight of the disadvantaged and were more likely to have
their consciences stirred as they watched television or read their Sunday
newspapers.

A further perceptual change needs, however, to be added as the catalyst of
action: that was the appearance of what has been rather inelegantly labelled
the "can-do" mentality. This was the perception that complex social and
economic problems were manageable, and did not need to be met with
passive resignation. There was a procedural confidence, based upon a conviction that the underlying causes of difficulties were understood, which
sustained a belief in the efficacy of action: in some areas, the mix of attitudes
which led to the holding of the global conferences was extraordinary, and
could not have arisen before the late twentieth century. The mixture of
technical facilities, together with confidence about the rightness and effectiveness of chosen courses of action, which lay behind efforts in the area of
population control, for instance, could only have arisen in recent decades.

There emerged, therefore, perceptions that action was necessary and that available skills were adequate to achieve solutions to perceived problems. The "operational" world developed features which reinforced the propensity to act generated by these perceptions. It was not just that there were problems, but that they were often the result of a maldistribution, rather than an inadequacy of resources. If the problem had existed because of a general lack it would have been less likely that people would have been moved to an immediate response, though they may have supported research or a longer term programme. But the observation of maldistribution, which easily leads to the view that damage and deficiency in one area is in some sense a consequence of superfluity in another, is a more powerful energizer, and a number of the global conferences were in part a result of this conviction. Maldistribution, as a concept which contains two causally connected elements – gains and losses, the one causing the other – is, however, more likely to be accepted and understood, and to be a force for action, in a period of extensive and increasing interdependence. As Charles Beitz has argued, belief in interdependence reinforces a preparedness to accept transnational linkages, and concomitantly the perception that maldistribution involves moral considerations.[5] In particular these arguments reinforce the view that someone is responsible for someone else's problems, and that, therefore, something should be done. International society is seen to have acquired a moral dimension in the sense that the case for redistribution has become overwhelming.

This argument played a part in a number of the conferences in a variety of ways. With the environmental conference it took the form that some polluters were obtaining economic rewards unfairly by damaging other people's environment. Acid rain produced by the British benefited them but cost the West Germans dear. American industry benefited from lax pollution control which led to the pollution of Lake Ontario and a penalty for the Canadians. Dependency theorists have developed comparable arguments to explain the plight of the world's poorer states: the nature of their relationship with the rich ones created their poverty, and the rich were rich because the poor were poor.[6] These arguments have been a powerful incentive in the context of the New International Economic Order for moving participants to holding global conferences on development problems.[7] In the case of food problems the argument was applied in two rather different ways. First there was the view that the pattern of food consumption in the developed world, which included a relatively high level of animal products, directly contributed to shortfalls in supplies of grain, the staple diet of the Third World. Secondly, however, was the observation that shortages of food were frequently local or regional, rather than global: there was enough to go around if it could be distributed more efficiently, and though the causal element was rather more tenuous, it seemed again to be the case that one group of people were short of a good – food – because another group had too much of it.

This mixture of characteristic perceptions about standards (what is a problem?), about techniques (procedural confidence), about the operational world (the causal relationship between excess and deficiency), were a powerful incentive to global conferences in the 1970s and later; the particular mixture of ingredients could not have been concocted much earlier. It should not be forgotten, though, that the changes in the underlying structure of power also made a contribution. A third reason for their being regarded as a necessary approach to new problems, now to be discussed, was that there was an increasing degree of specialization and the pursuit of more narrow, selfish interests, on the part of individuals and organizations which were creating and applying knowledge in fields relevant to the solution of the problems.

On the one hand there was a realization of global problems and they demanded the application of a wide range of skills: they demanded a holistic approach. On the other hand was a feeling that learning and research was becoming increasingly compartmentalized and detached from the real world. Furthermore knowledge which could be used to solve problems was increasingly being used irresponsibly, and was in fact causing more and greater problems. There emerged the view, therefore, probably first revealed in connection with work on nuclear energy, that the practice of knowledge-forming was irresponsible. It was too often applied regardless of social and physical consequences in pursuit of short term gains for the few. One consequence of this was that there emerged a new concern to try to link together various branches of knowledge, which showed a tendency to go their separate ways, and to apply them to the solution of particular problems.[8] There was the need to rearrange the universe of knowledge in order to make it applicable to the real world. The conferences may be seen as one practical consequence of this need: they reflected an impatience with what were seen as dangerous tendencies in the intellectual realm and at the same time a determination to apply appropriate knowledge to practical problems.

A kind of intellectual threshold was reached in the 1960s and 1970s in the form of a critical interaction between concern and knowledge. The reaching of this threshold was perhaps revealed most clearly in the environmental conferences, but it was also evident in a number of the other conferences, such as those on population and food. They reflected a determination to take knowledge by the scruff of the neck and apply it to a problem in the round.

Another dimension of this incentive to hold special conferences was, however, the view that the existing Specialized Agencies had themselves become in various respects detached from the problems of the real world. Maurice Bertrand's perception that a sectoral approach to economic and social problems had become a liability illustrates this tendency.[9] They had become victim of what Alison has called organizational processes:[10] the problem was too often seen as a context in which they could promote their own interests. It was reported that the representatives of Specialized Agencies too often behaved like travelling salesmen competing for custom in the Third World, and even relief agencies jealously guarded the status of their own organizations in the field at a certain cost in overall efficiency.[11] The agencies would also frequently not focus precisely enough on the problems which had emerged: the division of labour between them had become inappropriate to the tasks which needed to be tackled in modern times. It is now seen to be necessary to approach problems with instruments and specializations which have by convention become the property of several of them.[12] To put the problems in the language of the functionalism of David Mitrany, the "form" of the Specialized Agencies no longer followed the required "functions".[13] There were, therefore, in the area of the application of knowledge – in this case the world of the various international organizations – problems which were very similar to those found in its creation. Both had become overspecialized and imperfectly engaged with the new problems of society.

The conference also arose, therefore, because of the need to find ways of approaching problems which could not be found in existing Specialized Agencies. Mitrany might have concluded that they did indeed reflect the ineluctable tendency for the form to follow the function in that they represented a growing pressure upon Specialized Agencies to accept change. One theme in the following chapters is the way in which the conferences sometimes defined a space between the various existing organizations.

These then are some of the factors which led to the calling of the special conferences, which were to do with the problem themselves. They reflected changes in the underlying structure of power, a new pattern of perceptions about the problems and the opportunities for solving them, and the feeling that it was necessary to tackle the increasing gap between knowledge and organization and the real world. The problem remains, however, of why the existing economic and social organization of the United Nations could not have been adjusted to take on the new problems, or why the conferences needed to be special in order to proclaim new standards. Why was it necessary to find new frameworks rather than adjusting the old ones? These questions are to be discussed in the next section.

*

That the special conferences were in part the product of certain weaknesses in the UN system is reflected in a number of prestigious reports in the mid and late 1970s. The Group of Experts appointed by the Secretary General noted in May 1975 that

it has become a recent practice of the United Nations to convene on an ad hoc basis world conferences to deal with global issues such as the environment, population, food, human settlements, international women's year, the world water problem and desertification.[14]

The Group also found that

the new practice of convening special sessions of the General Assembly to deal with major economic problems [is] potentially a very effective device – provided that such sessions are carefully planned and prepared – which should be further pursued in the future.[15]

The Group was careful to distinguish between such special sessions, which would be useful, and the ad hoc conferences, which "lead to an excessive diffusion of responsibility for global policy making for a consequent loss of coherence".[16] It concluded, therefore, that

whenever issues of global significance need urgent and separate consideration special sessions of the General Assembly on the pattern of the Sixth and Seventh Special Sessions, or special sessions of the proposed "development committee" should, after careful preparation be convened rather than ad hoc world conferences. . . .[17]

The feeling that such conferences carried the danger, amongst others, of diffusing responsibilities, was also reflected in United Nations General Assembly resolution 32/197 (1977), which was to become the main legal basis of efforts to reform the UN's economic and social organization in the late 1970s and later.[18]

The ad hoc conferences were an encouraging indication of adaptation in the UN system, but also reflected the difficulties within it, which were addressed in the various reports and resolutions, and also tended to accentuate them. The underlying problems were that the system had become polycentric, and that it contained no organization within it which could coordinate and manage its wide range of economic and social activities. The polycentric character, and the resulting failures of management, meant that it was always easier to respond in an ad hoc fashion to new problems – to create ad hoc conferences – rather than to adapt rationally within the system and to build according to the decisions of a coordinator and initiator upon existing arrangements.

In a polycentric system there are special problems in the way of internal adaptation in response to new problems: responses, such as the conferences, tend to be tentative and partially outside the system. The first reason for this is that by definition there is no central mechanism for deciding upon the nature of the response. Secondly the actors, in this case chiefly the Specialized Agencies, tend to see adaptation as requiring a reduction in their own areas of competence, or an unacceptable expansion of another's, or at best as a mutual limitation. This helps to explain the tendency of the agencies' main coordinating mechanism, the Administrative Committee for Coordination (ACC), to send reports to the Economic and Social Council (ECOSOC) which concealed inter-agency disagreements.[19] The general interest was to reject change, and to conceal the occasional pro-system response. At best the least threatening actor could be allowed a minimum coordinating role: hence Ameri's comment that: "It is in most cases true that the UN Secretariat alone can carry the ball and make inter-agency cooperation meaningful."[20] Any stronger response tended to be evaded and hence to be expressed outside the system.

A third reason for low intra-system adaptability was the lack of a single authoritative perspective on what was required, and the sheer volume of undigested material: there were many sources of information and competing evaluations in the United Nations system. Maurice Bertrand made this point particularly forcefully in 1984.[21] At meetings of the ACC the Secretary

General hesitated about taking a strong line in part because there were usually no prior consultations with senior officials and heads of the United Nations bodies beforehand. Hill commented that

There exists no means of harmonizing the thinking of executive heads and the senior staff of organs concerned with central policy issues, such as ESA, UNCTAD, UNIDO, UNDP, and directing it towards problems facing the international community and towards possible initiatives that the UN might usefully take.[22]

Research efforts in the various agencies were unintegrated. It was hardly surprising, then, that there was no authoritative viewpoint in the light of which changes could be introduced: there was no central brain.

The Economic and Social Council had, of course, been intended to manage the system, but had failed to live up to the expectations of the founders. In particular it failed, despite various institutional amendments, such as the setting up and subsequent reinforcement of its Committee on Programme and Coordination (CPC) in 1969, to coordinate the activities of the Specialized Agencies. This failure was seen by Gunner Myrdal as early as 1960 as "almost scandalous in view of the declared purposes of the Charter".[23] This judgement still seemed to apply in the mid-1980s and is one measure of the difficulty of bringing about any useful reform in the organization. A further weakness was that the General Assembly lacked the authority to instruct the agencies, though it could give them advice and address recommendations to them. It tended not to consult the agencies very closely when it considered economic and social proposals – an omission which might be considered extraordinary – and it lacked the means of effectively monitoring the performance of the agencies. For instance it lacked a way of checking the relationship between the agencies' budgets and their programmes; it was said that the General Assembly checked budgets in a vacuum.[24] Its main watchdogs over the agencies, the Advisory Committee on Administrative and Budgetary Questions (ACABQ) and the Joint Inspection Unit (JIU), though capable of providing good, hard-hitting reports, were essentially advisory. The ACC, the system's main administrative coordinator, which also, however, had a potential for developing a role in generating overall policy – and an ambition to do so – became a framework within which agencies' heads defended their interests whilst discussing ways of implementing UN programmes: its members were as much involved in justifying positions adopted within each agency as in coordinating their activities in striving for a common purpose. Ameri concluded that "towards the coordination of overall policy it cannot be claimed that the ACC has made more than a minor and intermittent contribution."[25]

Another route to effective management and policy coordination was sought when in the 1977 Resolution it was recommended that a new Director-General for Development and International Economic Cooperation should be appointed within the Secretariat to ensure "the coherence, coordination and efficient management of all activities in the economic and social fields financed by the regular budget or by extra budgetary resources".[26] The references to both regular budget and extra budgetary resources seem to imply that the new officer was to supervise the activities not only of the United Nations' own organizations – the Funds and Programmes – but also the Specialized Agencies. The post was established and was held first by Kenneth Dadzie, and later by Michael Ripert, but again it was largely unsuccessful with respect to its major goals. The problems with this office are discussed later in this chapter, but in 1992 the new Secretary-General of the United Nations, Boutros Boutros Gahli, downgraded the office in yet another reorganization of the Secretariat intended to improve its efficiency.

These various characteristics and deficiencies illustrate the lack of any overall coherent management, either in terms of administration, or in terms of policy initiatives and monitoring. They are discussed and explained in greater detail in the next section. Proposals for reform in the making of coherent overall policy and achieving effective direction focused upon ways of improving the supervisory function of the General Assembly, and upon reorganizing the work of the Economic and Social Council and upgrading the status of its members. The latter was stressed in both the 1975 Report and the 1977 Resolution: the 1975 Report identified the central problem when it argued that the

revitalization of the Economic and Social Council, through far reaching changes in its functioning and methods of work [is] one of the conditions for strengthening the central structure of the system and enabling it to play an effective role in world economic affairs . . . if the United Nations system is to contribute effectively to the solution of international economic problems there must be a central organ within the system where the inputs from the various United Nations bodies can be shaped into coherent policies for development and international economic cooperation, and where there can be a central review of the mutual consistency of actions taken sectorally, particularly of the interdependence of decisions on trade, monetary reform and the development of financing, and of decisions taken in the field of agriculture, industrialization and other areas.[27]

The past failure of ECOSOC in these respects was one reason for setting up those institutions in the United Nations which are called Funds or Programmes, and which were usually initiated at special conferences. One experienced United Nations diplomat even argued in discussion with the present writer that had ECOSOC been more effective, there would have been no call for a New International Economic Order, and UNCTAD would not have been created. Though this may be an exaggeration, the general thrust of the argument is valid.

Once they existed, however, the Funds and Programmes created new difficulties in the way of achieving agreed policies and central direction over and above those arising from the status of the agencies. They were not subject to ECOSOC supervision in contrast with the agencies, which were at least required to report to ECOSOC under the terms of Article 64. Furthermore as their name indicates they were financed out of funds to which governments directly contributed and therefore felt better able to control. Although a United Nations Pledging Conference was established as a way of raising finance, states were not subject to the same long term financial commitment that they incurred with regard to the agencies, which were financed out of a regular budget. The failure of the older system, and in particular the visible self-interest of the agencies, was likely to lead to resistance on the part of some states to the closer incorporation of Funds and Programmes in the larger system as part of a process of reform. In some cases it was particularly apparent that they were creatures of a coalition of states – UNCTAD and UNIDO, for instance, were dominated by developing countries – and subjecting them to a general manager would have weakened the coalition's influence.

Proposals to strengthen central direction also raised immediately the delicate issue of the membership of the common framework: ECOSOC had 54 members and was dominated by the richer states. Though it had been accepted that all UN members could attend and speak, only the 54 could vote. If it was to be strengthened, the developing states argued, it would also have to be representative, a view that was resisted by the developed states. It was also the case, of course, that simply increasing the range of independent agencies, each with interests of its own, was likely to make the task of creating a stronger ECOSOC more difficult: indeed some of the Funds/Programmes, in particular UNDP, and UNCTAD became major rivals of ECOSOC as candidates for the role of policy-maker and coordinator for the system. For these reasons the Funds and Programmes should be seen not only as part of a process of adaptation within the UN system: they were also a result of the failure of internal management within the UN system, and one of the causes of that failure.

The kinds of reform envisaged for ECOSOC would have strengthened the UN's internal adaptation procedures, and, therefore, reduced the range of circumstances in which there would have been a need for special conferences. The latter tended to be initiated in general terms by an ECOSOC proposal, supported by a General Assembly resolution, but then to be taken over by an ad hoc group lacking direct supervision by the United Nations. The Secretary-General may, however, have been a member of the group, and may have played a part in selecting the administrative head of the conference (as with Maurice Strong with regard to the Environmental Conference, or Antonio Carillo-Flores with regard to the Population Conference). The detailed administrative arrangements were left to the creativity of a few individuals; the relationship with the secretariat of existing agencies and funds was a matter for negotiation, though usually the conference secretariat was set up alongside, but independent of, an existing interested administration. The one exception to this was that UNCTAD serviced the Conference on the Least Developed Countries, which met in Paris in 1981. That experience if anything confirmed the point that the conferences needed to be autonomous of the agencies: it was thought that UNCTAD had occasionally detracted from the goal of finding solutions for the LDCs, by promoting its own institutional interests.[28] The location of the conference was also determined on an ad hoc basis (Bucharest for population (1974), Paris for the Conference on the Least Developed Countries (1981), Stockholm for the environment (1972)) and the procedures were worked out afresh for each conference, thus allowing considerable scope for the whims of dominant individuals. The questions of whether a particular conference would lead to a more permanent organization, and the form of the latter, was also not predetermined; it was left to the conference itself to decide.

Strengthening the ECOSOC was seen as a direct alternative to this way of proceeding. In 1977 General Resolution 32/197 the views of the 1975 Group of Experts Report were reflected closely. The General Assembly reasserted the need to give the ECOSOC greater authority, by strengthening it in two major respects.[29] First it was felt necessary to strengthen its monitoring function: better procedures were needed by which it could be informed of what was going on, and of what needed to be done. A new office was set up in the Secretariat, the office for Programme Planning and Coordination, which was to produce improved reports for ECOSOC. One version of these was called Cross Organizational Programme Analyses (COPAs) which were on a range of programmes involving several agencies and funds, and were addressed to the ECOSOC's Committee for Programme and Coordination (CPC).[30] They were to be an "analysis of the actual state of coordination".[31] The CPC insisted that it should evaluate the programmes and indicate where greater efforts should be made. This was, however, only one element in an effort to increase the range of information available to ECOSOC in a form which would allow an effective response to new problems.

The second goal was that of increasing ECOSOC's capacity for generating programme initiatives in the light of changing needs – in other words it was intended that ECOSOC would either itself carry out the work of the special conferences, or that it would be more directly involved in setting up and managing them: they would ideally be in the form of special sessions of the General Assembly. The Council was enjoined to disband most of its subsidiary committees, and instead to deal with their work in the Council itself in "shorter but more frequent subject-orientated sessions spread throughout the year".[32] The idea was that such meetings should more easily involve higher level specialists whose views would naturally carry more weight. In addition, following along the same lines of argument, it was recommended that the Council should, when necessary, hold special sessions to deal with emerging problems meriting special or urgent international attention; it would also hold "periodic meetings at the ministerial or other sufficiently high level to review major issues in the world economic and social situation".[33] The General Assembly's intention that the Council should bring conferences more directly under its wing was also indicated in its injunction that the Council should assume

direct responsibility for carrying out the preparatory work for ad hoc conferences convened by the Council itself, and as appropriate by the General Assembly, without prejudice to arrangements already agreed upon for conferences currently under preparation.[34]

The clear implication was that arrangements outside the Council's framework were to be phased out.

The view that special conferences represented a challenge to, and offered alternative frameworks to, the existing organizations of the United Nations system was also implied in the General Assembly's Resolution 35/10C of 3 November 1980, which invited

member-states and UN organs, when considering the convening of special conferences, to ensure that the objectives of the proposed conference are such that they have not been achieved and cannot be pursued within a reasonable timeframe through the established inter-governmental machinery of the United Nations and the specialized agencies.[35]

The perception is evident that adjustment in the existing situation, in the form of the conferences, could involve duplication, and, moreover, threatened existing organizations. In an excellent Joint Inspection Unit report of February 1982 the major technical, administrative and financial problems involved in holding special conferences were considered and ways of solving them were suggested.[36] Broadly it was proposed that they be more closely managed within the system as resolved in A/32/197. At the time of writing there was, however, no evidence of any positive response to these efforts. Again a great paradox is evident: that the polycentric system produces problems, frequently skilfully identified, which cannot be solved within the polycentric system. Indeed the process of identifying problems in this situation frequently makes things worse rather than better, as new organizations are usually established in consequence, and new complexities and problems in management introduced.

The various changes were intended to create an improved mechanism for monitoring economic and social developments, and the progress of programmes already established, and in the light of this to initiate appropriate policies, and necessary institutional amendments and additions according to a comprehensive strategy. The absence of such procedures was one reason for the system's minimalist response to new problems, and the tendency for them to be considered in special conferences.

The problems are a crucial part of the context of the range of special conferences, though they relate to operational and standard-setting conferences in somewhat different ways. In the best of all possible worlds – if the system were effectively managed – operational special conferences would not be necessary, as by definition there would be a smooth adjustment to new problems within the system; institutions would be altered in a rational response to pressures for adaptation, priorities would be agreed, and resources allocated. But the best conceivable practice, is, of course, short of this: special conferences would still have a role in a process of adaptation, in that they are ways of exerting pressure upon those governments and institutions which do not wish to adapt. We are, after all, dealing with sovereign states in international society, and with institutions which have the Weberian characteristics of bureaucracies. However, improved management would reduce the occasions upon which this task needed to be performed to a minimum – there would be a tendency towards the ideal – would smooth the adaptation process, and reduce its cost (financial and administrative), and would be expected to remove the need for ad hoc administration and special finance. These benefits of reform, which can only be set out here in a tentative way, should be set beside the striking costs of not doing so.

Conferences which are specifically concerned with standard-setting should not be viewed, however, as having a potential redundancy. There needs to be special results from their function: they are intended to play a part in defining a consensus about standards which necessarily are meant to be pursued in other existing organizations of states. Unlike operational conferences they do not necessarily imply structural changes in the light of new tasks, but rather they introduced higher standards in the pursuit of existing tasks. Their institutional homelessness is, therefore, inherent in their character. Their present muddled organizational setting in the United Nations system is certainly highly relevant to understanding the difficulties of getting new standards accepted and applied, but the primary contribution of reform to the preparation and conduct of these conferences would probably be technical/administrative and financial. For both kinds of conference, therefore, the failure to reform the system has major implications.

Having reported this failure it is, however, now necessary to go on to explain it. It is unfortunately necessary to explain not only why there were no adjustments before the identification of the problems in the mid-1970s, and the drawing up of recommendations by the General Assembly, but also why the latter were largely ignored and no alternative remedies found up to the time of writing. In particular the proposed changes in membership and working methods of ECOSOC were not implemented. These questions are addressed in the next section.

*

Special conferences have a good side and a bad side: they reflect a new concern with global problems and a striving for solutions, but they may also add to the problems of managing the UN's economic and social activities according to any rational and comprehensive strategy. They may produce new institutions, which add to the already heavy burden of control, and they reflect existing difficulties in the way of reform.

It has been mentioned that special sessions of the General Assembly have been regarded, for instance in 321/197, as a preferable alternative but at first sight it is hard to see why this should be so. One advantage, of course, is that there would need to be less "adhocery" in establishing and administering such sessions. It would be possible to use existing services and arrangements. But the advantage of special sessions over conferences may only be fully realized if the system's coordination/management problems were to be resolved so that their conclusions were backed by mandatory proposals to existing agencies and Funds. This point applies as much to the standard-setting as to the operational conferences. If the agencies and Funds were required to adjust in order to carry out the agreed tasks, the special sessions would have considerable merit. Even in the reformed system, however, it would be unrealistic to suggest giving such powers to ad hoc conferences as presently constituted. The need for reform and restructuring is not diminished by greater resort to special sessions of the General Assembly.

The various reports and recommendations on the reform of the United Nations system are themselves a measure of its failings. Those produced in the 1970s put forward a range of proposals for improvement. The most recent was that produced in December 1985 by the Joint Inspection Unit, a searching analysis and critique of current arrangements, written by Maurice Bertrand, reflecting in many ways the same old problems and the system's continuing failure to adapt.[37] The main themes were that the range of information on the system's success in pursuing its chosen goals was still deficient, although the extent of the description of its activities had been much expanded in the 1970s and 1980s (the literature still did not permit a well-founded estimate of attainment in comparison with defined goals); the procedures for coordinating the activities of the wide range of organizations involved in work on projects in particular countries – about 15 of them in a country receiving aid[38] – were deficient (a COPA reported in 1984 that in Barbados there had been three organizations concerned with human settlements "but none reports cooperation")[39]; the system lacked a common controlling brain, which could choose a strategy, for instance, in "joint planning", and adjust it to circumstances; and the relationship between judgements about need and the provision of resources was remote. Although the specific context of the reports is that of development, the complaints certainly applied to the UN's work in general in the economic and social field, and this point is made explicit in the various reports.

These indications of the system's failings helped to explain Bertrand's scathing comment that "the notion of an integrated approach to development, although adopted by the General Assembly of the United Nations and ritually repeated at each General Assembly, has remained for the United Nations an empty formula";[40] the various alterations in the structure and procedures of the previous 15 years had been a "useless effort at coordination", and the system showed

lack of intellectual preparation for work of programming, inadequate analysis of the role assigned to the United Nations system in the general scheme of technical assistance requirements of the various countries, absence of a unified concept of development, lack of satisfactory machinery at the centre of local levels to ensure the preliminary work of coordination of contributions of the various agencies, lack of a common methodology for defining types of projects.[41]

In other words the United Nations economic and social arrangements remained unmanaged, unfocused, and essentially irrational.

The failures of the system can be described in terms of goals and procedures: the former were uncertain and the latter inappropriate. Alternatively it may be described in terms of the specific characteristics of the present arrangements: how are its underlying failings reflected in the way that its business is now conducted? It is difficult to capture in any comprehensive way the specific failures of the system, without, of course, resorting to a long list of malfunctions which would be tedious in this context. Some characteristic deficiencies may, however, be summarized within a reasonably comprehensive typology. There is, on the one hand, a tendency to reiteration which takes two forms: first, a deliberate duplication of activities and institutions, and, second, a repetition of other activities and functions, which is more the consequence of a carelessness or lack of conscious control in management (the former is now referred to in the discussion which follows as *duplication*, and the latter as *fragmentation*). On the other hand is a tendency towards the concentration of various functions in sub-systems which also takes two forms: first is a resistance to specialization in functions, in other words, a habit of performing tasks at the same time and place which are in important respects different and disconnected; and second is a tendency to resist the concentration in the system of key functions, so that there are unresolved claims and counterclaims about where such functions should be performed (the former is called *aggregation* in what follows and the latter *reservation*).

Duplication is revealed, as was pointed out earlier, in the existence of a number of institutions within the system which claim to act as system managers and coordinators, sometimes in the central systems, sometimes in individual countries, or both. As has already been mentioned ECOSOC should perform this role at the centre, according to the Charter. But the ACC also considers that it should manage and coordinate, and has introduced in recent years new institutions to help with this, in particular the Consultative Committee on Substantive Questions (CCSQ). Bertrand comments upon

the vagueness of the terms of reference; the similarity of jurisdiction between organs as important as the Economic and Social Council, UNCTAD, the Second and Third Committees of the General Assembly . . . [which] have created in the United Nations system a state of confusion.[42]

In relation to development issues the UNDP also claims a role which it has frequently asserted is "central",[43] though the World Bank has mounted a powerful counter-claim to this position in recent years. At the country level the ACC attempts coordination through the resident coordinators, though these seem to trespass upon UNDP territory, whilst the World Bank attempts the same task through its Round Tables. Such unsatisfactory duplication and uncertainty about roles arose because of the habit of adding new institutions to existing arrangements, in order to solve a perceived problem rather than altering the arrangements. The institutions which already existed successfully resisted attempts to challenge their continuing claims to centrality. Hence "actually, the concern for coordination which over the years has given rise to a regular reinforcement and a growing complication, has remained constant since the outset only to the extent that it has always remained unsatisfied."[44]

The *reservation* of functions may be illustrated in a number of contexts. The ACC has expressed the view that a relative lack of coordination might be acceptable, and that the independence of the Specialized Agencies, its main members, should be respected. One agency was reported to have complained about ECOSOC's and the General Assembly's alleged tendency to "take decisions on matters plainly falling within the province of the specialized agencies", and "to create new specialized forums for decision making in areas of activity already covered by these organisations"[45] – a remarkable comment upon its attitude to the "World Parliament". ACC's broadly unhelpful approach towards strengthening central control is reflected in its unenthusiastic attitude towards joint planning which "should not be undertaken for its own sake".[46] ACC is seen to have the responsibility of "representing fully the positions adopted by their [the agencies] governing body".[47] There were numerous reports of squabbling between the ACC and the CPC – reported as a "sort of dialogue of the deaf"[48] – neither wishing to lose status to the other, and rather low key, half-hearted attempts to improve matters.[49] Bertrand suggested that the tone of ACC reports tended to conceal the problems of coordination deliberately in order to reduce the pressures upon it: an ACC document had recalled that

a sense of optimism can be retained in the "potentially better means to solve many of the major problems facing humanity", a view which might be judged as being "essentially intended to convince member-states that everything is fine in the area of coordination".[50]

The new Director-General for Development and International Economic Cooperation also found it difficult to exercise his coordinating function with regard to the agencies: indeed it was pointed out that the latter in practice refused to recognize his authority, a situation which was reflected in the Secretary-General's repeated appeals to them to cooperate by, for instance, sending him accounts of their work. That he was not an elected officer, but was appointed by the Secretary-General, placed him below the agency heads in the pecking order.[51] This partly explained their refusal to accept the Director-General as chairman of the ACC in the absence of the Secretary-General himself, as had been envisaged. The members were anxious to avoid any step which would suggest any lowering of their status in relation to a United Nations official. Overall the office proved ineffective and was abolished in early 1992.

The duplication and reservation of roles was, of course, a reflection of the play of bureaucratic politics, but also of the failure of the member states to counter the anti-rationalization tendencies which are inherent in bureaucracies. The governments were themselves divided, so UNCTAD survived and competed with ECOSOC, the former favoured by the developing states and the latter by the developed. Governments disagreed not merely about means but also about ends, and this permitted a variety of interpretations of such key concepts as "development" to flourish in the organization.

It could hardly be maintained today that UNCTAD and the IMF for example, have the same concept of conditions of development, or that despite their convergence at the Alma Ata Conference on primary health care WHO and UNICEF now share the same approach to health matters in the developing countries, or that FAO's approaches to food security are fully shared by the World Food Council. . . . the various organizations are a long way from having a common philosophy, vision, or approach.[52]

The interplay of bureaucratic politics and intergovernmental disagreement also explains the apparent increase in another form of duplication in the work of the institutions, namely, the repetition of discussions about the same issues at various levels in the same institution and in different institutions. For instance, ECOSOC too often simply went over the same ground already traversed in its own committees; the General Assembly repeated the debates already conducted in main committees; a US government official acidly complained "Should we accept the continuation and repetition of the experience of the last eight months, for example, during which the issues discussed at UNCTAD Six were reopened and repeated on at least three occasions?"[53] Such duplication arose because of the mistrust of governments of each other: rationalization and specialization increased the risk that a key function in the system could be "captured" by a state or group of states of the wrong persuasion. This fear explained the rejection by the developing states of the proposal made in 1977 that ECOSOC should have a number of small advisory groups on specific policy issues. The consequence was that there was a duplication, and reservation, not only of the functions of managing and coordinating the system, but also of that of defining policy, among institutions, and at various levels within institutions.

The fragmentation of the system was revealed in the tendency for available resources to be devoted to a wide range of small scale, frequently unrelated projects, a habit which arose from the feeling that all the various demands, however small, from the various states, deserved some kind of system response. Fragmentation is also closely allied with what Bertrand describes as his "fallacy number 2: that the development of the poorer zones in the world can be brought about by a sectoral and, therefore nonintegrated approach."[54] A pattern has emerged in the United Nations which is like that which was rightly firmly resisted by the United States in the late 1940s with regard to Marshall Aid, namely dealing on a bilateral basis about each individual state's particular demands without regard to a larger plan. Hence

the obligation to deal with all existing problems, in all fields, and in all sectors, because of the convergent pressure of the most diverse interests of all delegations, tends to a parcelling out, not to say fragmentation, of available resources between a very large number of small programmes and small projects endowed with extremely limited means.[55]

This multiplicity together with most states' urge to be involved and represented, has also led to what Bertrand describes as an abysmally poor quality of staff.[56]

There is also fragmentation in the financing of operational activities, both between institutions ("financing decisions are taken separately for each of the operational funds, UNDP, UNFPA, UNICEF, etc"), and between donors and beneficiaries ("no real dialogue between donor and beneficiary countries on the nature of the problems to which most attention should be paid"). "It is not even certain that within each organization there is agreement between headquarters and field personnel or between the various departments dealing with different but related problems."[57] A COPA study in 1984 on human settlements confirmed this with the astounding revelation that the "headquarters offices of many organizations simply do not know whether cooperative arrangements at the project level exist or not."[58]

Such a pattern of fragmentation is, of course, likely to be reflected and reinforced by the widely reported lack of coordination of the views of officers who come from the same country, but who are working in different institutional settings. On a number of issues the position of governments is simply not thought through so that their various representatives often adopt contradictory or, at least, not mutually reinforcing positions in the various institutions. In the field this could also arise from the sheer number of projects, and their remoteness and relative unimportance – from the perspective of the donor states. The governments are divided not only amongst themselves but also within themselves. This pattern is also repeated in the tendency already discussed for governments to give funds outside regular budgets to agencies which they favour in order to promote causes which they happen to like. The UNDP particularly was weakened by this practice, which, according to the OECD, was indulged in ironically by precisely those states – Holland and the Scandinavian countries – which were most conscientious about making financial contributions for development.[59] The activities were in effect undermining the system. The practice seemed to have declined in 1984–85 as the result of appeals from a number of sources including the OECD.

The United Nations social and economic system also showed a tendency to treat together various activities which might be judged to deserve attention in different fora, the practice here called *aggregation*. This also took a number of forms. There was a tendency, deriving from the mutual suspicion of states, to avoid what might be termed an orderly approach to negotiation in international fora as represented, for instance, in the habit of proceeding from a debate about general principles, or the philosophy of the matter, at an earlier stage, to one about the details of implementation later. This "orderly" approach had been increasingly abandoned in favour of returning to discussions of the basics, the grand issues, at every conceivable opportunity; it was also noticed that instead of reaching agreement about issues in a connected series of decisions, there had appeared the practice of endlessly qualifying what appeared to be an agreed common position, so that the latter increasingly looked like an illusion. This development is, of course, bound up with the "politicization" of issues which were previously regarded as technical or non-contentious.[60] For instance, institutions such as UNESCO began to take what were judged to be political positions, in relation to the problems in the Middle East, and in particular the status of Israel. More generally there was a tendency to confuse the various stages of developing and executing policy.

The anonymous US official quoted earlier summed up this tendency rather well in a particular context

The North–South dialogue and negotiation process has lost its coherence and structure. The original idea of separate mandates and specific areas of responsibility for individual international fora hardly describes the present state of affairs. Rather than fulfilling specific niches in a well-defined system, subordinate bodies are attempting to assume the coloration and indeed the function of the whole system. This blurring of institutional lines has led to enormous duplication of effort and the consequent waste of human and natural resources, the spread of disagreement and confrontation to other forums and the injection of purely political and theoretical economic issues into previously practical discussions.[61]

There has been a

willingness to agree to language, and indeed in some cases to appear to be negotiating on substance, for purely "political" purposes. Such a procedure may result in a temporary appearance of agreement but in fact does little to improve relations . . . eventually it becomes obvious that some "solutions" and "agreements" are meaningless and ephemeral.[62]

The point might be added that such habits of aggregation also tend to undermine the practical working arrangements within institutions, for instance by usurping the role of management in drawing it into a larger and nebulous general forum.

The range of difficulties in the system are symptoms of the barriers in the way of change which are found in the interplay between bureaucratic politics and the interests of states. Any major restructuring of the system in the light of these difficulties is strongly resisted by a coincidence of two negative and two positive inclinations: the officers, and the commentators who are close to them, have developed a pride in their familiarity with its arcane complexity and any change is seen to devalue this asset, and they assert the virtues of pluralism, whilst too many governments are too frequently indifferent and unknowing about what goes on. But these negative factors are reinforced by a fierce disagreement between governments on some matters, which leads to an active opposition to change except on their own terms, and a hostility on the part of the majority of international officials to anything which could weaken their particular organization or their role within it.

*

These patterns in the United Nations system, and the difficulties and attitudes which they reveal, explain the necessity for special conferences in the past, and form their institutional setting. They also explain the probability that the system will not be adjusted so that the operational ones, at least, become less necessary in the future, and those concerned with standard setting are more efficiently organized and more effective. The special conferences may be judged as both a helpful and encouraging response to new problems and as a product of the weakness of the existing social and economic arrangements in the United Nations.

But in the early 1990s the major contributing states, such as Britain, became somewhat disillusioned about the prospects for amending the social and economic machinery of the United Nations. The British had taken the lead in 1989 in an attempt to improve the workings of the Economic and Social Council, by reducing its meetings to one a year, to be held in New York, together with the abolishing of the more redundant of its committees. The idea was that this would reduce the extent of duplication in the discussions and make it more attractive to more senior people from national governments who would then invest it with greater authority. They might even be prepared to attend! Unfortunately the main states, even the British and the French, could not agree about the proposed reforms, and this latest effort was abandoned by the British. The expectation was then that if reform was to come at all it would result from the pressures needed to achieve success in relation to the so-called new agenda. Any direct assault upon the design of the machinery was futile.

In the early 1990s the pressures for holding more such conferences were evident, and they will presumably lead to the creation of even more Funds and Programmes. The so-called New Agenda – the need to deal with environmental problems, the problems of international terrorism, drugs and refugees, as well as the traditional problem of economic development – have further stimulated the process. For instance a major conference on environmental programmes was to be held in Brazil in June 1992 and on population in 1994. Unlike the 1970s, however, it is now to be subject to a new discipline, deriving from financial constraints, which is discussed in the next chapters.

Notes

1. A. Le Roy Bennett, *International Organizations: Principles and Issues* (2nd Edition), Prentice Hall, Englewood Cliffs, 1980, p. 310.
2. Quoted in Joint Inspection Unit, *Secretariat Organization and Procedures for Preparation of United Nations Special Conferences*, prepared by Mark Allen et al., JIU/REP/82/2, p. 1.
3. Ronald Inglehart, "An End to European Integration?", *American Political Science Review*, Vol. 61, March 1967, pp. 93–94.
4. Robert Jervis, *Perception and Misperception in International Politics*, Princeton University Press, Princeton, 1976.
5. Charles R. Beitz, *Political Theory and International Relations*, Princeton University Press, Princeton, 1979.
6. See Theotonio Dos Santos, "The Structure of Dependence", *American Economic Review*, Vol. 60, No. 2, May 1970, pp. 231–236.
7. See John P. Renninger with James Zech, *The 11th Special Session and the Future of Global Negotiations*, UNITAR, New York, 1981.
8. As in Quincy Wright *The Study of International Relations*, Appleton-Century-Crofts, New York, 1955, p. 12.
9. Joint Inspection Unit, *Some Reflections on Reform of the United Nations*, prepared by Maurice Bertrand, JIU/REP/85/9, Geneva, 1985. Henceforth referred to as *The Bertrand Report*.
10. Graham T. Allison, *The Essence of Decision: Explaining the Cuban Missile Crisis*, Little, Brown and Company, Boston, 1971.
11. Randolph Kent, "Relief Agencies at Work", in Paul Taylor and A.J.R. Groom (Editors), *International Institutions at Work*, Frances Pinter, London, 1987.

12. See Evan Luard, *International Agencies*, London, Macmillan, 1977.
13. See David Mitrany, *A Working Peace System*, republished Quadrangle Books, Chicago, 1966, especially pp. 68–73.
14. *A New United Nations Structure for Global Economic Cooperation: Report of the Group of Experts on the Structure of the United Nations System*, E/AC 62/9, United Nations, New York, 1975, para. 34, p. 11. Henceforth referred to as Group of Experts Report.
15. Ibid., para. 36, p. 11.
16. Ibid., para. 35, p. 11.
17. Ibid., para. 37, p. 11.
18. 32/197, Section II; contained in UN GA, Official Records: Thirty-second Session, Supplement No. 45. (A./32/45) Sept.–Dec. 1977, at pp. 121–127. Henceforth referred to as 32/197.
19. Houshang Ameri, *Politics and Process in the Specialized Agencies of the United Nations*, Gower, Aldershot, 1982, p. 92.
20. Ibid., p. 96.
21. *Reporting to the Economic and Social Council*, prepared by Maurice Bertrand, Joint Inspection Unit, JIU/REP/84/7, Geneva, 1984, para. 5, p. 2, and passim.
22. Martin Hill, *The United Nations System: Coordinating its Economic and Social Work*, Cambridge University Press, Cambridge, 1978, p. 95.
23. Quoted in John P. Renninger, *ECOSOC; Options for Reform*, UNITAR, New York, 1981, p. 5.
24. Martin Hill, loc. cit., p. 44.
25. H. Ameri, loc. cit., p. 93.
26. A32/197, loc. cit., p. 127, para. 64.
27. Group of Experts Report, loc. cit., fn. 12, p. 13, para. 42.
28. Thomas G. Weiss, "The UN Conference on the Least Developed Countries", *International Affairs*, Vol. 59, No. 4, Autumn, 1983, pp. 649–675.
29. A/32/197, loc. cit., Section II.
30. COPAs were instituted in 1977 by the ECOSOC in EC/2098/LXIII.
31. See M. Bertrand, 1984, loc. cit., p. 16.
32. A32/197, p. 122, para. 7.
33. Ibid., para. 9.
34. Ibid., para. 11(d).
35. Joint Inspection Unit, *Secretariat Organization* . . ., 1982. Loc. cit., p. 2, para. 10.
36. Ibid., pp. 9–29.
37. *The Bertrand Report*, loc. cit.
38. Ibid., p. 7, para. 18.
39. *Cross Organizational Programme Analysis of the Activities of the United Nations System in Human Settlements*, E/AC.51/1984/5. 4 April 1984, p. 43, para. 97.
40. *The Bertrand Report*, p. 10, para. 29.
41. Ibid., p. 10, paras. 29 and 30.
42. Ibid., p. 7, para. 20.
43. *Operational Activities for Development of the United Nations System*, A/38/258, 3 June 1983, p. 9, para. 9(a).
44. *The Bertrand Report*, p. 9, para. 25.
45. In *Annex* to *Development and International Economic Cooperation: Restructuring* . . ., Report of Secretary General, A/36/477, p. 4, para. 32.
46. *Restructuring of the Economic and Social Sector of the United Nations*, A/37/439, p. 6, para. 16.

47. Ibid., p. 9, para. 31.
48. Bertrand, 1984, loc. cit., p. 16, para. 35.
49. See A/37/439, loc. cit., p. 4, para. 10.
50. Bertrand, 1984, loc. cit., p. 15, para. 31.
51. Interview with UN official, April 1985.
52. Bertrand, 1984, loc. cit., p. 19, para. 42.
53. From an anonymous internal US administrative document, headed *North/South Dialogue and UNCTAD*, dated Feb. 16, 1984, Section 11, p. 2.
54. *The Bertrand Report*, pp. 45–46, para. 138.
55. Bertrand, 1984, loc. cit., p. 29, para. 63.
56. *The Bertrand Report*, p. 12, p. 38.
57. Bertrand, 1984, loc. cit., p. 19, para. 42.
58. *Cross Organizational Programme Analysis*, . . . E/AC.51/1984/5, loc. cit., p. 41.
59. Interview with OECD official, Paris, April 1985.
60. See Victor-Yves Ghebali, "The Politicization of UN Specialized Agencies: A Preliminary Analysis", *Journal of International Studies*, Millennium, Vol. 14, No. 3, Winter, 1985, pp. 317–334.
61. Loc. cit., in footnote 53, p. 2.
62. Ibid., p. 3.

6 Reforming the system: getting the money to talk in the central system

In this chapter two major developments concerning the reform of the United Nations system are brought together and their interrelationships explored. On the one hand is the process of attempting to reform the organization from within, an effort which has been punctuated by a number of incisive, and often brilliant, reports, such as the Jackson Report of 1969, the Report of the Secretary-General's Experts in 1975, and more up-to-date, the Bertrand Report.[1] This internal reform process also included a number of ambitious, but largely ineffective responses from the General Assembly, of which the most significant was Resolution 32/197 of 1977.[2] This was the main legal basis of the reform process in subsequent years. There have certainly been some changes as a result of the expenditure of all this energy, such as the creation of the "over-seer" post under the Secretary-General of a Director General for Development and International Economic Cooperation, but the net impact upon the system by the early 1990s was negligible.[3]

On the other hand there were attempts by the governments of the states which contributed most to the finances of the United Nations system to exert their authority, and, conversely, to resist the attempts by the minor and negligible contributors to use their voting strength to get their way. This dispute was a manifestation of an older quarrel between them – usually from the developed world – who preferred the bigger states to lead and manage the system, as in the Security Council, and those who believed that international organization should be representative, and governed according to a version of democratic principle, with each state being equal to every other in having one vote.[4] The latter view was naturally strongly upheld by the newer, and, usually, poorer states, which had been created since the 1950s, and led to attempts to expand the role of institutions such as the General Assembly, or UNCTAD, where they had a majority.

In the 1970s and 1980s the United States government, which, according to an agreed formula, contributed 25% of the funds allocated by majority decision in the General Assembly to the United Nations system, expressed increasing dissatisfaction about a situation in which it could be outvoted by coalitions of states which each contributed less than .01%. It is worth noting, though, that even this US contribution is less than that which would have resulted from the application of the formula agreed by the General Assembly in 1946, which required that the Committee on Contributions should take into account national income, per capita income, economic dislocations resulting from the war, and the ability of states to obtain foreign currencies. Decisions had been taken, however, to limit the total liability of any one member, in part because it was thought unwise to allow the organization to become too dependent upon the financial contribution of any one state.

The 15 main contributors between them contributed 84.4% of the resources, and, out of 159 members, 78 contributed less than .01%.[5] A number of other major contributors, particularly the British, and the Soviet Union, itself a major contributor, also, however, supported efforts to reduce expenditure. The major contributing states' complaints were reinforced by what they saw as gross inefficiency in the use of resources, and by related failings such as politicization, and even corruption. The first victims of their increasing dissatisfaction were the International Labour Organizations, from which the Americans withdrew in 1978 – to return in 1980 – and later, of course, UNESCO, from which both the Americans and the British withdrew in the early 1980s. The urge to seek a better use of resources was undoubtedly stimulated by the coming to power in both the United States, and Britain, of right-wing governments with monetarist inclinations, and by an increasing suspicion of international organization in general, particularly in Reagan's America.[6]

But it must also be admitted that their complaints often had a clear basis in the facts, and that the difficulties of meeting them either within the particular organization, or, within the system were formidable. Their only resort appeared increasingly to be either withdrawal, or the holding back of financial contributions.

Students of international organization, even those who were strongly supportive of its development, had increasingly been brought to admit that the budgetary process, particularly in the central United Nations system, had serious flaws. In 1972 a number of reforms were undertaken which were intended to provide a way of reconciling claims for money put forward by the various "proposing" or "policy-creating" organs, such as the General Assembly itself, and its committees, with a longer term plan for the work of the organization. A two-year budgetary cycle was introduced which began when the Secretariat, represented, in particular, by the Controller and his office, collected the various claims for money and transferred them to the Fifth Committee of the General Assembly, which in turn forwarded them to the General Assembly itself for final decision.[7] In preparing the budget the Secretary-General would seek the advice, first, of a small, and highly praised committee of experts, somewhat analogous with the Public Accounts Committee in Britain, called the Advisory Committee on Administrative and Budgetary Questions (ACABQ), which would give advice on the financial and administrative aspects of the proposals. (The role and status of this Committee is discussed in greater detail below.) The Secretary-General would also seek the advice of the intergovernmental Committee on Programme and Coordination (CPC), which had the task of evaluating the programmes on which the money was to be spent in the light of the longer term, six-year, Medium Term Plan. The CPC was peculiar in that it served and acted as a committee of both the Economic and Social

Council (ECOSOC) and the General Assembly. This procedure did not, however, work as intended: writing in 1977–78, Luard concluded that "what is wholly lacking, and what exists in most national systems, is a central decision-making body, which makes the final overall decisions about the policies and programmes to be implemented."[8] The reasons for this failure are discussed later.

One of its consequences, however, was that, rightly or wrongly, it was seen as one of the causes of a steady expansion of the United Nations budget; in the political circumstances of the early 1980s, especially in the United States, this made the organization vulnerable to attack from hostile groups such as the right-wing Heritage Foundation. In the two years 1976–77 the assessed budget was around $800 million, whilst in the biennium 1986–87 it stood at $1.663 billion, an increase of around 100%.[9] Since the early 1950s, the pattern was for the budget to double about every seven years. This sum was that spent through the central system: voluntary funding of the Funds and Programmes, and the budgets of the Specialized Agencies, were additional. The figure should, however, be put into perspective. $1.6 billion was only a little more than the amount spent on the development of one torpedo by the British government in the 1970s, and early 1980s, and equalled the gross contribution – before the Rebate – by Britain to the EEC in the mid-1980s. The proportion of the assessed budget payable by the United States was around $200m.

Despite the relative modesty of these sums, the United States Congress approved, in August 1985, an amendment to the Foreign Relations Act instigated by Senator Nancy Kassebaum, which ruled that the United States's share should be reduced to no more than 20% of the assessed budget until the system was reformed: later developments in Congress, in particular the Gramm-Rudman Balanced Budget Act of December 1985, which required the US government to balance its budget by 1991, further reduced Congressional appropriations for international organization.[10] In May 1987 the sum indicated by Congress for the following financial year was reported as being only around 50% of the assessed sum. Although the central system was the primary target the Specialized Agencies were also being squeezed to varying degrees: the World Health Organization was owed $19 million by the United States out of a liability of $62 million; the International Labour Organization was owed $7 million out of an assessed liability of $31 million. The Food and Agricultural Organization had also been placed in financial difficulties.

The precise strategy behind these varying allocations, which was being pursued by the responsible agency in the United States, an office in the State Department, was hard to fathom. The general goal could, however, be fairly summed up as reform of the system, though this laudable ambition was open to various interpretations from a United States perspective. The specific reform mentioned in the Kassebaum Amendment was the introduction of weighted voting, on the model of the controlling bodies of the International Monetary Fund and the World Bank, into the key organs of the United Nations and the other agencies. As the possibility of this being approved by the Security Council, and accepted by a two-thirds majority of members, both being required to modify the Charter, was remote, it must be assumed either that Kassebaum and her supporters had little grasp of the practicalities of the issue or that the demand was deliberately made unrealistic so that a reduction of US funding would be assured, or that there was a "hidden agenda" of other more easily attainable reforms. The demand for weighted voting was in the latter approach to be seen as part of a strategy for getting the others to make more modest concessions. The balance of the evidence suggests that this came to be seen as the correct approach by the United States Administration, whatever the views of Kassebaum and her supporters. Certainly there was no question of United States withdrawal from the United Nations, and even the views of the Heritage Foundation were described by senior bureaucrats as hard-hitting, but not "off-the-wall", and not in favour of withdrawal.[11]

There was also strong evidence to suggest that the obvious explanation, that the United States simply wanted to pay less, was also incorrect. On a number of occasions the suggestion was put forward both within the United Nations, for instance, in a speech by the Colombian delegate to the General Assembly in 1985, and outside, that it would be a good idea if the maximum assessment for all states were to be reduced to 10% of the budget, and the budgetary burden redistributed among the better-off members. The Secretary-General had also urged a reduction in the maximum assessment to 15% of the total budget. After all, the sums were fairly small. The response of the United States administration to such suggestions was, however, generally one of hostility and embarrassment, a response which was not surprising in view of Reagan's general stance in international relations of attempting to make "America great again". The hidden agenda must be interpreted as including a strategy, not for reducing payments, but rather for getting a proportionate, or greater, weight of influence in the system in exchange for the 25% assessment. The United States did not want to contribute less, but did very much want to get the money it contributed to talk more.

But these rather shorter term US views and intentions about financing the system, which were characteristic of the attitudes of the developed states in the 1980s, should not be divorced from a much longer term effort to adjust and reform the economic and social arrangements of the United Nations. The American hidden agenda also came to include the goal of contributing to this longer term reform process, in which a large number of individuals and governments had been involved, although it used the levers which had been created by the political and economic circumstances of the time: the budgetary ones. It is indeed probable that the prospects for stimulating *general* reform by using the financial weapon were not fully realized at the time of the Kassebaum Amendment. As so often happens the opportunity was created before it was recognized, and was related to purposes which were not quite the same as those which were later stressed. The nature of the general reforms which were being sought by the Americans in the late 1980s–90s will be discussed later. It is necessary, however, to outline first the various stages of the general reform process, as this was an essential part of the context of the later reform efforts.

*

Three stages in the process may be identified, each associated with the particular primary purpose then sought through reform. In each stage the range of reforms which were sought remained largely the same, but they differed with regard to the purpose which was dominant. The first phase was associated with the goal of adjusting the United Nations to the more effective pursuit of a new purpose which had not been clearly visible at the time that the central system and main agencies had been created, namely, the economic development of the less prosperous newer states. The adjustment of the organization in order to facilitate the attainment of new goals was to become a persistent theme, associated with the creation of new organizations, especially the Funds and Programmes, and with the holding of Special Conferences, both in the form of ad hoc conferences, such as the 1972 Environment Conference in Stockholm, and Special Sessions of the General Assembly, such as the 1974 Sixth Special Session on the New International Economic Order.[12] But the primary purpose of the reforms sought in the late 1960s was arguably that of facilitating the goal of development, above others, and the outstanding report then, the Jackson Report of 1969, was primarily concerned with that end. Accordingly, although other associated changes were sought, the dominating proposal was for the strengthening of the United Nations Development Programme (UNDP), and for establishing it as the manager and coordinator of the development process through the control of technical assistance programmes. Other organizations, including the Agencies, were to have their efforts with regard to development fitted into schemes decided by the UNDP. The primary purpose of the first phase was, therefore, to adjust to the emergence of a particularly important new goal, though attempts at such adjustment in the light of other new goals were to become a permanent feature of the reform process.

In the 1970s, however, reform was aimed primarily at the more effective pursuit of existing goals in the economic and social areas. In the 1975 *Report* of the Secretary-General's Group of Experts[13] and in Resolution 32/197 of 1977, the dominating image was of a polycentric system which lacked effective central direction, and rational planning. Now there was need for a central "brain", a more unified research and initiation process, more focus and better adjusted programmes, and improved monitoring of operations. Hence there were lengthy proposals about reforming the Economic and Social Council, for ensuring that conferences and meetings were better managed, and for adjusting the Secretariat's arrangements to promote a greater efficiency. As has already been mentioned, the setting up of a new post of Director-General for Development and International Economic Cooperation, was one consequence of this effort; the Secretariat was also enjoined to monitor operations more closely, and there were various rearrangements, such as the introduction of facilities for generating the Cross Operational Programme Analyses (COPAS). In effect, however, though there had been considerable success in identifying problems, the reform effort led to few real achievements, partly because of the resistance of bureaucrats, and partly because of the failure of governments, which had achieved a reasonable degree of agreement about the nature of the problems, but could not agree to specific steps to put them right. In particular the Economic and Social Council remained unreformed, and the system still lacked any central manager.

The efforts of the 1970s, therefore, led to the adding of further items to the agenda of reform rather than to useful improvement: the goal of achieving more effective management was added to that of adjustment to new tasks. The Bertrand Reports of 1984 on the supply of information in the system, and of December 1985 on institutional arrangements, essentially added new dimensions to these themes. The main contribution was the incisive criticism of an approach which was seen to have become too narrowly focused on particular sectors, at the expense of integrated programmes, and the corresponding need to deal with operations within sub-regions where they could be more effectively coordinated and managed. The 1970s proposals tried to strengthen the role of the centre: Bertrand's 1985 Report argued that this was impracticable, and that, although there should be a central economic United Nations, which dealt with research and provided a general overview of the problems, the practical work on the ground should be done through common arrangements by groups of contiguous states.[14] It is difficult, and, indeed, unnecessary to convey here the admirable range and depth of critical insight found in the Bertrand and earlier reports; but, again, the resulting practical achievement was minimal. A further sub-heading was added to the agenda for reform.

It was in this context, however, that a third phase of the reform process was instigated as the result of the United States pressure on the budgetary process. In February 1986 a group of High-Level Intergovernmental Experts was set up by the General Assembly to be appointed by the President of the General Assembly.[15] The 18 experts were selected from the world's major regions and sub-regions, and were chaired by Tom Vraalsen of Norway. Maurice Bertrand was also one of its members. In August 1986 this group, which became known as the Committee of Eighteen, produced a report in the form of a "Review of the Efficiency of the Administrative and Financial Functioning of the United Nations".[16] This added a new dimension to the agenda of reform: that of achieving greater efficiency in the use of resources. This time, unlike on previous occasions, the budgetary imperative was paramount. It did not supplant the other items on the agenda but rather led to their being approached from this new perspective.

At the time of writing it seemed that this report had given a new impetus to the reform process, and it is, therefore, now necessary to look in greater detail at the diagnoses and prescriptions which it contained with regard, first, to the budgetary process, and, then, to the institutional and administrative arrangements. The central argument, however, is that the Americans, with the possible, but unadmitted collusion of other major contributing states, saw the reform process in the 1980s as an opportunity, not only for reforming the budget and rationalizing the procedures in the economic and social areas, but also for strengthening their own control. It involved a strategy for countering the voting strength in the General Assembly of the newer smaller states. The latter had in the eyes of the major contributors too often pushed through decisions in policies and arrangements for which they did not pay.

*

The Committee concluded that the budgetary arrangements, as they had emerged since the major reforms of the early 1970s, contained two major interrelated weaknesses: first the various claims for money were not being closely scrutinized in the context of any overall plan which included goals and priorities, in this case the Medium Term Plan – intended to cover a six-year period; second the Medium Term Plan was itself not being drawn up by the governments in such detail as would have allowed them a full appreciation of what needed to be done, and encouraged their greater commitment to the stated and implicit goals. "The 6-year medium term plan should reflect the consolidated objectives and goals of member states, and should constitute the principal policy directive of the United Nations" (paragraph 58). But the "test of the medium term plan, like the programme budget, is prepared by the Secretariat in a form which is almost final, and member states have neither the means nor the time to undertake major changes in the draft medium term plan" (paragraph 66).

The Budget statement itself "in fact . . . is merely the financial compilation of a number of decisions and recommendations taken by a large number of inter-governmental bodies and interpreted in the various departments and divisions in the Secretariat" (paragraph 67). Its relationship with the plan was admirably captured in the following comments, which though expressed in discreet and measured tones, were a savage indictment of the budgetary process: "priority setting in the medium term plan takes place at the sub-programme level, while resource estimates are provided at the major programme level . . . consequently there is no clear linkage between priority setting and resource requirements, either in the medium term plan or in the programme budget" (paragraph 63). Budget decisions were, of course, eventually ratified by the General Assembly, and recommendations made by the Fifth Committee; at various stages, as already indicated, there was ample opportunity for comment. But "no central organ really monitors the overall conception of the plan on such occasions" (paragraph 67(b)). Indeed, the opposite tended to happen: claims for expenditure at the sub-programme level tended in effect to lead to modifications every two years of the medium term plan.

It was as if a tailor were to alter his measuring tape if he found the suit of clothes were too small! Claims for additional expenditure, from the Secretary-General and elsewhere, were also hard to resist, and this led to frequent supplementary budgets. The budgetary process was, therefore, vulnerable to the accusation that it allowed the poorer "spending" states to exert continuing pressure in favour of the uncontrolled expansion of the budget. This was another feature of the system which the major contributing states resented.

The Committee was prepared to accept that "over the past 15 years, the General Assembly had established principles, methods and instruments which should have made it possible to reach satisfactory results in this area" (paragraph 58). Nevertheless, the budgetary procedures had caused major problems. In the words of the Committee:

the Secretariat prepares the programme budget itself: the budget division sends the budgetary directives around June of the year preceding the year in which the General Assembly votes on the budget. Preparations last about 11 months; in May of the following year, the Committee for Programme and Coordination, on the one hand, and the Advisory Committee on Administrative and Budgetary Questions on the other, begin reviewing the programme budget: the former examines the programme content while the latter examines the administrative and financial aspects of the programme budget, after which the two committees submit their reports so that the Assembly can begin its consideration of the programme budget in September and complete it by the end of the year. The opportunities which the two above-mentioned committees have for recommending modifications in the content of the programme budget are very slight and relate almost entirely to details, because the Secretariat tends to consider the submission of budget fascicles [sic] to be practically definitive. (paragraph 67)(C)

Three problems may be found in the budgetary procedure as described above, one of which was made explicit in the Report, a second which was implicit in it, and one which was only indirectly considered there, but which has been widely discussed in other reports and studies on the coordination procedures in the United Nations. The first was the obvious point that the Secretariat dominated the early stages of the process, and took the determination of the budget to a point at which it was difficult to unravel it for close examination by the monitoring groups and committees. In addition there was naturally a certain hesitation about returning to ground already covered, especially as this could be at the risk of offending colleagues in the Secretariat. The powers of socialization processes in bureaucracies should not be underestimated!

Second, however, the dividing line between the responsibilities of the ACABQ and the CPC was not entirely clear. The former was made up of experts and its mandate was of a technical nature with regard to finance and administration. There is a line to be drawn between judgements of a political nature, concerning the kinds of goals to be pursued, and those of a technical kind, concerning appropriate mechanisms and judgements about the best use of available resources. But the frontier between the two is hard to draw precisely: knowing the extent of its mandate was made more difficult for the ACABQ by the fact that its monitoring partner, the CPC, was an intergovernmental committee and, therefore, nominally with greater authority. Conversely, the CPC, though its role was monitoring the coordination of programmes and shaping the Medium Term Plan, was somewhat uncertain of its mandate. The net result was a kind of "after-you-Cecil" problem. This was, however, reflected in the judgements of the Committee of Eighteen when it came to its recommendations: members were divided about how far the role of either should be expanded or protected.

The third problem concerned the respective status of the ACABQ and the

CPC, a question not addressed directly in the Committee of Eighteen's report. In reality the ACABQ had greater authority and a much superior reputation compared with the CPC, despite the difficulties which undoubtedly existed in the way of its increasing the effectiveness of its supervision. One indication of these was the increasing tendency for the Fifth Committee of the General Assembly to restore items which had not been recommended; another was the Secretary-General's habit of insisting upon budgetary supplements which it opposed. Its work was certainly facilitated by the fact that it was not intended to examine closely and comment upon – critically or otherwise – the declared objectives and policies of the member governments. Rather it was to check the financial aspects of the pursuit of those policies: in the central system this amounted to evaluating "the Secretary-General's financial and administrative proposals for giving effect to those decisions".[17]

The authority of the ACABQ was enhanced by a number of other considerations. Its 16 members were elected by the General Assembly in their individual capacity. Though each of the groups of states was to be represented candidates were normally chosen by consensus on the basis of their individual expertise, and it was rare for the General Assembly to be asked to choose between rivals. The one exception to this was the Western European group within which there was sometimes disagreement about whose name to put forward, in recent years mainly between the British and the French. In 1987 the French were represented but not the British; the US, the Soviet Union and the Japanese were invariably present, and accordingly its composition gave particular weight to the major contributors.[18]

Experts are, of course, not necessarily non-political. In this case, however, they were encouraged to be less so by the convention that their meetings, unlike those of the CPC, were held in camera. The chairmen of the Committee were also individually distinguished and in office for an unusually long period: there had been only four chairmen since the committee was created in 1946, and the incumbent in 1992, M. Msele from Tanzania, had been in office for 14 years. The Committee was in fact the oldest such committee created by the General Assembly. In addition its secretariat, though drawn from the main UN Secretariat, was independent from it in the sense that its head was not under the instructions of the Secretary-General. He was responsible solely to the Committee and through that to the General Assembly. It was for these various reasons that the ACABQ acquired a considerable reputation and its 40 or so reports a year had, with a few exceptions, been treated with respect. This explains the preference of a number of governments and commentators for attempting to solve the problems of the budgetary process by extending and reinforcing the role of the ACABQ rather than by reforming the CPC.

In contrast the history of the CPC was somewhat chequered, though it is essential to be aware of the details of the makeup of the Committee as they are crucial for understanding and interpreting the later US strategy. The Committee was established in 1962, but its current role was not made specific until 1969: legislation then provided that the Committee should function as the main subsidiary organ of ECOSOC and the Assembly for planning, programming and coordination.

In particular the Committee is charged with reviewing the programme of the United Nations as defined in the medium term plan, recommending an order of priorities among programmes, giving guidance to the Secretariat on translating legislation into programmes, developing evaluative procedures, making recommendations on work programmes . . . in the light of the need to avoid overlapping and duplication . . .[19]

After 1970 it consisted of 21 members, elected by the General Assembly on the nomination of ECOSOC, on the basis of equitable geographical distribution, namely 5 African, 4 Asian, 4 Latin American, 3 East European, and 5 West European and other members. The latter group naturally included the USA and the British. It was to meet for six weeks in "plan" years and four weeks in "budget" years. The practice was for its decisions to be taken on the basis of consensus, a point which should be carefully noted in view of later developments.

The CPC suffered, however, from several weaknesses and as a result failed to carry out its assigned functions satisfactorily. It suffered from insufficient and inappropriate information; hence the earlier rearrangement of the Secretariat to provide COPAS, which, however, only partially solved the problem. There remained a lack of substantial comprehensive evaluative materials. The CPC also failed to establish its status in relations with other institutions: the ACC also played a supervisory role and dealt with the CPC with such reluctance that mutual relations were described as a "dialogue of the deaf".[20] As already mentioned the limits of its competence in comparison with the ACABQ were also unclear, though this was a case of uncertainty rather than hostility. But perhaps the central problem was that its staff were never of a sufficient calibre, or from sufficiently senior positions in member governments, to allow it to develop any degree of independent muscle. It usually met at the level of Second Secretary: it also had a reputation for being overconcerned with minutiae as in early 1987 when it allegedly spent two days deciding whether it would in future meet for two weeks or three. In its joint meetings with ACC it, therefore, suffered a serious "status deficit". This explains 32/197's recommendations that the supporting committees of ECOSOC should be abolished and their functions taken over by the Council itself, where, possibly, more senior people could be persuaded to participate.[21] At least this would avoid the repetition of discussions in the CPC and the full Council, which was characteristic of the existing arrangements. In the budgetary process as it had evolved by the late 1980s the failure of governments to play an effective role in shaping the Medium Term Plan, and the lack of a rational reconciliation of resources and programmes, was, therefore, also attributable to the fact that these crucial functions had been entrusted to a weak reed.

The Committee of Eighteen also pointed to weaknesses in two other areas, though it is not necessary to go into great detail here about these. The personnel policies of the organization were severely criticized. Problems included a lack of training, a disillusionment about promotion prospects, and especially excessive numbers at more senior levels. The point was made that there had been too many appointments at the level of Under Secretary-General, and it was implied that member governments did not necessarily regard administrative talent as a condition of emplacement. The Committee also did not point out that much of this expansion had taken place during the tenure as Secretary-General of Kurt Waldheim! There were 28 posts at this level: "today's structure is both too top heavy and too complex" (paragraph 32). Many of these personnel criticisms had been made before. Indeed Shirley Hazzard produced a pungent attack on staffing policies in the early 1970s.[22] The point was also made by the Committee that "the present organisational structure is too fragmented with 9 political and 11 economic and social departments" leading to a "duplication of work" and a "diffusion of responsibility". Another area where problems were detected, though it was essentially a similar weakness to the previous one, though on a larger scale, was in the structure of the United Nations economic and social organisation: "expansion in the agenda has led to a parallel growth in the intergovernmental machinery, which had in some cases resulted in duplication of agendas and work, particularly in the economic and social fields" (paragraph 16).

The earlier discussion has shown that the personnel and structural problems were recognized in a number of earlier reports and studies. An element which was new in 1986–87, and which added a new dynamic to the reform process, was that the pressure for reform now derived primarily from the need to save money, and not from other pressures, such as the need to adjust to new tasks or to be more effective. The Americans had made this the case. Another new element was that in the process of seeking reforms to the perceived problems the Americans found an opportunity for pressing for changes which they thought would give power to the payer. This strategy will now be considered in the context of the specific reforms which were proposed and initiated.

*

The Committee put forward three sets of proposals on the reform of the budgetary process and the drawing up of the medium term plan. The first two sets were fairly detailed and in most respects were rather similar. They both sought to strengthen the role of the CPC, though the second saw this more as a matter of fully implementing its existing terms of reference, whilst the first reckoned that these might also need to be "adjusted". Both were concerned to persuade the governments to recognize the importance of the CPC's work by appointing people on the basis of their "technical competence and professional experience" (paragraphs 34 and 31). Both proposals also held that the CPC should "take part in the planning and budget procedures from the very beginning and throughout the process" (paragraphs 29 and 32). It should "consider and make recommendations to the General Assembly on priorities among the programmes" and a "calendar of procedures" in these consultations was to be drawn up by the Secretary-

General after consultation with governments and the institutions involved. The key role of the CPC with regard to the medium term plan was to be recognized.

The first two sets of proposals were also in agreement about the need for a new timetable for making the programme budget. An outline budget was to be prepared by the Secretary-General in the spring of the non-budget year, with an indication of the resources which the Secretary-General expected to be available, and advice and recommendations then tended to the General Assembly through the Fifth Committee. Decisions taken then would guide the Secretary-General in initiating a second stage of the process in the budget year. This time round the draft budget would again be subject to examination, recommendations, formulations, and then the whole referred back to the Assembly for decision. The first two sets of proposals did, however, differ in the respective roles which were to be allowed to the CPC and the ACABQ in the process of giving advice and making recommendations in the budget. The first clearly implied that the CPC would have the lead role in advising the Assembly, though it would take into account the advice of the ACABQ: this was the measure of the expected "adjustments". With regard to the budget process the second set of proposals saw the two bodies as having responsibility in particular fields – in federalist fashion, "independent" but "coordinate" – each advising the Assembly separately in those fields. The Secretary-General was to send the outline budget and the draft budget to both the CPC and the ACABQ: in the first set of proposals the budgets were to be addressed to the CPC alone. The second set reflected an anxiety about not downgrading the ACABQ, which had acquired a considerable reputation over the years, though this was at the risk of losing effective leadership by one or other institution in the budget process.

The third set of proposals seemed to reflect this fear in a somewhat exaggerated way though it also showed evidence of United States views. It asserted bluntly that the distinction between the functions of the ACABQ and the CPC were unreal, and that the new CPC should perform both. It also held that decisions about the resources which would be available for the coming biennium should be taken by the CPC in its new form *before* the Secretary-General began work on the outline budget: he would be informed about "the amount of resources that member states can and are prepared to make available to the organization" (paragraph 35). One implication of this, of course, was that the established policies and programmes of the United Nations, which the Secretary-General could be expected to support, and which would form a basis for his budgetary calculations, could in this arrangement be altered in the light of quite unrelated national financial considerations. In other words, the Medium Term Plan would in the system resulting from these proposals be no better a guide for budgetary planning than in the older inefficient one. All three sets of proposals agreed, however, that once the budget had been approved it should no longer be exceeded by special, supplementary budgets: within a biennium "additional expenditures resulting from legislative decisions . . . must be accommodated within the budget level decided upon by the General Assembly" (paragraph 34). The size of a contingency fund – called a financial envelope – was placed at 2% of the total budget, but clearly the Committee recognized that the adding of extra items to the agreed budget in an uncontrolled way, a habit about which the ACABQ had long complained, would have to be stopped. By implication the third set of proposals also accepted the new timetable outlined in the other two.

Up to the time of writing, May 1987, two sets of decisions had been taken to implement the recommendations of the Committee of Eighteen. First, the General Assembly, after a decade which was described as tense, even cliff hanging, adopted a Resolution on the 18th December 1986, which introduced a new budgetary procedure, requested that the Secretary-General should reduce the number of his staff, and that the Administrative and Financial functioning of the United Nations should be reviewed.[23] Second, in February 1987 the Economic and Social Council decided to conduct an "in-depth study of the United Nations intergovernmental structures and functions in the economic and social fields",[24] with a view to implementing, in particular, recommendation 8 of the Report of the Committee of Eighteen. This suggested that the arrangements of, inter alia, UNCTAD, UNDP, UNFPA, UNEP and UNICEF be examined with a view to their "rationalization". Recommendation 8 (3) even referred to the possibility of "merging existing bodies in order to improve their work"! But all existing organizations were enjoined to submit "within 30 days" their proposals for internal restructuring.[25] Such an approach seemed unusually energetic and ambitious by the standards of the United Nations: the final report resulting from the in-depth study was to be available for the Economic and Social Council to consider at its second regular session for 1988. It remained to be seen what the net outcome of these efforts would be, but the United Nations had probably never been closer to closing down some of its offices. There was not an unusual head of steam behind the reform process and a considerable effort would be required to resist it. It might be mentioned also, that the Secretary-General had acted upon the Committee of Eighteen's proposals on staffing: the cut of 15% within three years recommended in Recommendation 15 2a was very much in view, as was the proposed reduction of 25% in the number of posts at the level of Under Secretary and Assistant Secretary-General, requested in Recommendation 15 2b. No doubt the Secretary-General was not entirely averse to the latter. Reductions were, however, more the result of "wastage" than planning, and there were reports that staffing problems had arisen as a result.

The budgetary process agreed on 18 December 1986 could be seen as a compromise between the Committee of Eighteen's first and second sets of proposals. It rejected the proposal in the third set that the CPC should determine in advance the resources available, but accepted the CPC's primary role in considering the Secretary-General's outline budget and proffering advice on it to the General Assembly in the "off-budget" years. In the budget years, however, after the budget had been reconsidered by the Assembly, and turned into firm proposals by the Secretary-General, it would be forwarded to both the CPC and the ACABQ which were to advise the Fifth Committee "in accordance with their respective mandates". The Resolution also accepted the various proposals concerning the up-grading of the CPC and it looked as though it would now be a more formidable institution, expected to play a key role in relating the budgetary proposals to the Medium Term Plan, and in shaping the latter. It was to be involved from the beginning in the process of shaping the budget. In other words it was accepted that the CPC would be the principal "advisory" and "intergovernmental" committee on these matters.

In view of this, one particular decision in the resolution attracted particular attention, and was regarded as a breakthrough by United States officials. This was the agreement in paragraph 6 that the CPC should "continue its existing practice of reaching decisions by consensus".[26] Paragraph 7 took this further with the stipulation that "all possible efforts" should be made in the Fifth Committee "with a view to establishing the broadest possible agreement". The argument seemed to be that though consensus had been the established way of reaching agreement before the reforms, this was not significant as long as the CPC's role was modest. With the development of that role, however, there was a greater risk that voting would take place, and lines drawn between the larger number of smaller contributors, and the smaller number of larger contributors. Conversely, the requirement of consensus would greatly increase the leverage which could be exercised by the major contributing states over the others. The client states would be more frequently placed in a situation in which either they concurred with the contributing states, or they risked losing the latter's funds. The consensus approach, in other words, was viewed as a weapon in the hands of the rich which could be used to get the poor states to accept the discipline of the Medium Term Plan. The rich states would also, however, have been able to play a decisive role in shaping the Medium Term Plan in the CPC: decisions in that process would also be taken on the basis of consensus. There is evidence to suggest that the US Administration, or at least, officials within it, regarded these arrangements as largely satisfying the demands made at the time of the Kassebaum Amendment, and that they were now prepared to make approaches to Congress, with a view to restoring full funding to the US system.[27]

It is not, of course, that the CPC could be sure that its budgetary proposals would be accepted by the Fifth Committee or the General Assembly. But the richer states could be expected to exercise greater authority in the smaller CPC. The question of whether insisting upon consensus voting was compatible with the Charter – that it was legal – also remained to be examined. The appeal for consensus in the Fifth Committee would only marginally reduce the chances of adverse votes. A more important disincentive, however, would be that it would be more difficult, and, from the point of view of the poorer states, even dangerous, to unravel a carefully structured budget, relating resources to priorities, monetary commitments to programmes and intentions, which had already been agreed in the CPC. It was, therefore, more a question of tipping the balance of probabilities in favour of the richer states, of making it easier for them to lead and more difficult for the poorer states not to follow, rather than one of eliminating opposition. It would be a matter of management, not of control.

It is, however, arguable that the financial weapon, as used by the US, was likely to prove a powerful incentive for the more general reform of the United Nations system. The report of the Committee of Eighteen itself exemplified this. The proposed changes in the budgetary process may be seen as attempts at institutionalizing in the United Nations arrangements the ability of the rich to use the financial weapon to press on a continuing basis for reforms which they preferred. In other words, they were aimed at in effect incorporating the Kassebaum Amendment informally into the United Nations Charter. The discrepancy between voting power and financial power, which had long irritated the US, was to be reduced. That this prospect was in the minds of US officials was revealed by their view that improving the budgetary process in the central system was only the beginning of the reform effort. The agenda, no longer hidden, was for similar reforms to be introduced into all the Specialized Agencies: they were all to be required to accept consensus voting in their key budgetary committees as a condition of full-funding. Even the International Labour Organization, which was regarded as having reformed its budgetary arrangements after the 1978 US withdrawal, was nevertheless to be deprived of funds unless and until the consensus procedure had been introduced. This was the position taken by US officials in the summer of 1987. Consensus became the practical alternative in US eyes to weighted voting.

There are obviously a number of distinctive features about the reform process in the United Nations in the late 1980s and early 1990s. The reduction of funding, and the threat to cut further, stimulated a more energetic effort to change than had been seen before. But, as the crisis developed, opportunities for going beyond the list of potential reforms, which had emerged over the years seemed to be recognized, though these took forms that were not apparent in the Kassebaum Amendment. It remained to be seen whether consensus could be a functional alternative to weighted voting, and, indeed, whether the planned reforms would be achieved. There certainly emerged, however, a US strategy for change. The cynic might be forgiven for wondering how far a concerted strategy for change had emerged which involved not only the Americans but also the other major contributing states, such as the British, the Japanese or the West Germans. After all, the contributing governments consult each other fairly closely, and on a routine basis, about the level of their funding of the various international arrangements, in particular through the so-called Geneva Group which exists in the various UN capitals with the exception of New York. By the time of writing, no specific evidence that these other states were involved had, however, emerged.

*

The meetings of CPC in September–October 1987 did not employ the consensus principle. Members disagreed about a number of matters, including the level of the contingency fund. It was pointed out, however, that the period 1987–88 was essentially transitional, and that the new arrangements were to be introduced in the autumn of 1988. Unfortunately, as is revealed in the next chapter, it proved difficult to keep the consensus principle, particulary in the Fifth Committee, and in 1992 the US was still massively behind in payments to a number of international organizations, including the central system.

There was the view that the acceptance of the new arrangements had been part of a bargain, the other side of which was a return by the Americans to full funding. The administration in Washington favoured this, but Congress was divided on the issue and not disposed to treat it with any sense of urgency. The Senate was in favour of a higher level of funding than the House, but for both the matter was small beer compared with the budgetary crisis in the US. It looked unlikely, in view of the current strains upon the United States finances, that any serious effort could be made for the time being to find more money for the United Nations.

Nevertheless, there was still a strong sense that this was a turning point in the history of the United Nations. Continuing funding shortfalls encouraged the various efforts to adjust and reform.

Notes

1. "Jackson Report": R.G.A. Jackson, *A Study of the Capacity of the United Nations Development System*, Geneva 1969, UN Doc. DP/5 1969; Joint Inspection Unit, *Some Reflections on Reform of the United Nations*, prepared by Maurice Bertrand, JIU/REP/85/9, Geneva, 1985.
2. 32/197 Section 11; contained in UNGA Official Records, Thirty-Second Session, Supplement No. 45 (A./32/45) Sept.–Dec. 1977 at pp. 121–127.
3. For an assessment of the impact see Douglas Williams, *The Specialized Agencies and the United Nations: the System in Crisis*, Hurst, London, 1987.
4. For an account of reactions to developing states' claims regarding development see Craig N. Murphy, "What the Third World Want", *International Studies Quarterly*, 27, 1983, pp. 55–76.
5. Figures from an internal US Administration document marked IRM: 6 November 1986.
6. See the critical evaluations of the United Nations produced by the Heritage Foundation, such as *Africa is Starving and the United Nations is to Blame*, written by Roger A. Brooks, for *Backgrounder: A United Nations Assessment Project Study*, the Heritage Foundation, Washington D.C., 14 January 1986.
7. See Evan Luard, *The United Nations: How it Works and What it Does*, Macmillan, London, 1979, pp. 130–131.
8. Luard, loc. cit., p. 133.
9. Latter figure from *Report of the Group of High-Level Intergovernmental Experts to Review the Efficiency of the Administrative and Financial Functioning of the United Nations*, GA Official Records; Forty-first Session, Supplement No. 49 (A/41/49), New York 1986; (henceforth called *Report of Committee of Eighteen*); former figures from Luard, loc. cit. p. 113.
10. See the excellent account of these developments in Arthur Kilgore, "Cut down in the Crossfire", *International Relations*, Vol. VIII, No. 6, November 1986, pp. 592–610.
11. Interview with officials, US Mission to the UN, April 1987.
12. For a close examination of the role of ad hoc conferences, and GA Special Sessions, see Paul Taylor and A.J.P. Groom, *Global Issues in the United Nations Framework*, Macmillan, London, 1989.

13. *Report of Group of Experts*, E/AC 62/9, United Nations, New York, 1975.
14. See note 1.
15. In GA Res. 40/237, 18 December 1985.
16. See note 9: *Report of Committee of Eighteen*.
17. Martin Hill, *The United Nations System: Coordinating Its Economic and Social Work*, Cambridge University Press, Cambridge, 1978, p. 66.
18. Information about ACABQ was obtained in interviews with officials from its Secretariat, October and November 1987.
19. New Zealand Ministry of Foreign Affairs, *United Nations Handbook, 1986*, Wellington, New Zealand, p. 66.
20. Joint Inspection Unit, *Reporting to the Economic and Social Council*, JIU/REP/84/7, Geneva, 1984, p. 16, para. 35.
21. A/32/197, loc. cit., Section II (see footnote 2).
22. Shirley Hazzard, *Defeat of an Ideal: a Study of the Self-destruction of the United Nations*, Atlantic Monthly Press, Boston, 1973.
23. General Assembly, A/41/L.49, 18 December 1986, Section I, para. I.
24. ECOSOC, C/1987/INF/2, para. I.
25. Ibid., sub-paragraph i.
26. A/41/L.49, Section I.
27. Interviews with US officials, Geneva, April 1987.

7 The United Nations system under stress: financial pressures and their consequences

This chapter is about the United Nations system's response to the financial pressures with which it was faced in the 1980s and early 1990s. These resulted from two developments: the decision of the main contributing states to adopt a policy of zero growth in real terms in the budgets of the organizations, and the additional withholdings by the United States which resulted from the Kassebaum Amendment to the Senate Foreign Relations Act of August 1985.[1] This required a 20% underpayment by the US of its assessed financial contributions until a range of reforms in budgetary procedures, judged acceptable by the US Administration, had been introduced.[2] The impact of the resulting financial squeeze is considered with particular reference to three Specialized Agencies, the World Health Organization (WHO), the International Labour Organization (ILO), and the Food and Agriculture Organization (FAO).

The chapter goes beyond Chapter 6 in arguing that when it came to the Agencies the US policy of accumulating large arrears in payments was flawed as a strategy of reform in three senses. First, it was so generalized that it lacked any sensitivity to the needs of the system: the WHO, accepted even by the Americans as a worthy organization, was punished as much as the poor performers. Second, it lacked a capacity for positive feedback in that it was incapable of rewarding or recognizing improvements when they arose: the ILO had gone a long way towards reform, but received no encouragement. And third, the specific goals of the strategy were muddled with larger issues of principle and philosophy. The US complained that some organizations, such as the FAO were performing functions, i.e. economic development, which were not their proper role, but failed to commit themselves to a clear view about where, or indeed, whether, such functions should be performed in the system of multinational organizations. Critics were entitled to believe that the issue of practical reform was an irrelevance.

In order to understand the reasons for the crisis in the system, and the nature of the pressures upon the organizations, it is necessary to look, first, at the scale of the arrears, and then at the way in which the Administration lost control of the strategy. These issues are considered in the first section. In a second part the consequences of these developments for the organizations are discussed; and, in a third, issues concerning the

Table 7.1 Total assessed contributions of the United States to international
organizations, and total assessed and voluntary contributions, since
1971, in current dollars and adjusted for inflation

	assessed contributions (thousands)		assessed plus voluntary contributions (thousands)	
	current dollars	adjusted	current dollars	adjusted
(1)				
1971	119559		436407	
1.		119559		436407
1973	146734		406816	
1.097		133175		370844
1974	154834		414348	
1.217		127225		340466
1975	172255		475052	
1.328		129710		357719
1977	243671		629125	
1.496		162881		420538
1980	322204		893312	
2.034		158402		439189
1981	376784		1019656	
2.245		167832		454189
1982	439068		1051014	
2.383		180053		441046
1983	385289		959144	
2.460		156621		389895
1984	363854		1153478	
2.564		141908		449834
1985	329183		1003200	
2.656		123939		377710
1986	360761		956027	
2.707		133269		353168

(1) Date and value of inflation indicator. Latter calculated from consumer price
index in *Economic Report of the President*, February 1988, US Government
Printing Office, 1988, P313.

Source: 29th–36th Annual Report, *United States Contributions to International
Organization*, Report to Congress, United States Department of State, Bureau of
International Organization Affairs, October 1981 through 1987

reform of the method of financing the United Nations system are
considered.

*

Figures about the pattern of development of United States contributions to
international organizations are presented in Tables 7.1, 7.2 and 7.3. In
Table 7.1 it is shown that when adjustment for inflation is made both
assessed contributions and voluntary contributions by the Federal Government reached a peak in the late 1970s and early 1980s, but that through

Table 7.2 United States contributions to the assessed budgets of the United Nations and the main specialized agencies adjusted for inflation in relation to the US Consumer Price Index, by calendar year

	share payed by US (1)	FAO	IAEA	ICAO	(in thousands of dollars) ILO	ITU	UNESCO	WHO	UN
		25%	25.26%	25%	25%	7%	25%	25%	25%
1971	1	10083	3977	2167	7816	703	12018	23741	56312
1974	1.217	11118	6391	2309	9271	1241	15236	26071	52154
1977	1.496	12398	7029	2493	11604	1290	20052	26026	66441
1980	2.034	14073	10503	2281	11618	1356	16440	24756	73522
1981	2.245	15104	10697	2495	11294	1462	23170	25635	74571
1982	2.383	23117	8228	2289	12684	1170	23653	28313	82765
1983	2.460	18576	7177	2489	12554	1031	20158	23828	68519
1984	2.564	19490	7058	2641	12434	1161		23847	72928
1985	2.656	13840	7185	2612	11487	956		22032	63548
1986	2.707	14717	8526	2782	11892	1219		22799	69130
1987	2.806							23199	
1988	2.905				13978			24504	74427

(1) Date and value of inflation indicator. Latter calculated from consumer price index in *Economic Report of the President*, Feb. 1988, US Government Printing Office, 1988, P313. 1988 indicator projected from earlier data.

Source: 29th–36th Annual Report, *United States Contributions to International Organization*, Report to Congress, United States Department of State, Bureau of International Organization Affairs, October 1981 through 1986. 1987 and 1988 figures (except for ITU and UNESCO) from interviews with officials September 1989

Table 7.3 United States assessed *and* voluntary contributions to international organizations as a percentage of (1) total programme expenditures and authorizations by international organizations, and, of (2a) outlays through the US Federal Budget, and of (3a) Gross National Product, set beside (4) changes in US per capita money income in constant 1971 dollars (all races). Columns (2) and (3) are percentage of assessed contributions *only* in Federal budget outlays and GNP respectively.

	(1)	(2)	(2a)	(3)	(3a)	(4)(a)
1971	33.4	.057	.207	.010	.039	3417
1972	34	.058	.207			
1973	29	.059	.166			3774
1974	24	.057	.154			3652
1976		.056	.210	.011	.043	
1977	24	.059	.153			3866
1979	23	.056	.167			
1982	22	.058	.141	.012	.033	3768
1983	20	.0476	.119			3881
1984	24	.0426	.135			4028
1985	20	.0347	.106	.008	.025	4146
1986	20	.0363	.097	.008	.022	4311

(a) Inflation indicator as in Table 7.2.

Sources: For figures on GNP, *Economic Report of the President*, transmitted to Congress, February 1988, US Government Printing Office, Washington, 1988, p.272. Money incomes from *National Data Book: Statistical Abstract of the United States*, 1988, US Department of Commerce, 108th. Edition, Washington, DC, 1987, P.430. Contributions to international organizations, and expenditures and authorizations of international organizations, from 29th–36th Annual Reports, *United States Contributions to International Organizations*, cited in Table 7.2 above

the eighties the level of assessed contributions declined; figures in Table 7.2 for the assessed contributions of selected institutions, ILO, WHO and the UN, suggest a minor upturn in 1987–88 but, as is discussed below, these amounts were not paid in full. Table 7.1 also shows that until 1986 there was no making up of the decline in assessed contributions by greater contributions on the voluntary side. By 1986 the total level of contributions in real terms had only returned to what it had been in 1973–74. Indeed Table 7.3 indicates that contributions to international organizations made up a declining proportion of Federal outlays as the decade progressed; this pattern is also found when the contributions are compared with Gross National Product. Table 7.3 also indicates that as this decline was taking place the value of the real money incomes of individual Americans was increasing.

Table 7.2 examines the consequences in budgetary terms of this decline for the major agencies. Major losers in the 1980s seemed to be the WHO, the Food and Agriculture Organizations (FAO) and the UN, but the WHO and the UN had increased their level of contributions in the 1970s to a lesser extent than the FAO, which then declined more rapidly. The WHO had in fact increased its level of spending through the 1970s rather modestly, as had the ILO. The level of assessed contributions to the ILO fell through the 1980s up until 1986 but rather less steeply than that of the other losers.

These figures reveal that the impression given to the American public that there was an accelerating rate of contributions to international organizations, which was to be reined in by the Kassebaum Amendment, was false. Figures presented in current dollars helped to justify a political case for reducing contributions, but on this evidence Kassebaum was as much a symptom of a decline in the level of financing as a cause: the downward trend started well before 1985, and the effects of Kassebaum was to make a financial situation which was already serious very much worse.

Nevertheless during the 1980s the US Administration had complained with increasing vehemence that they were required to pay excessive sums, being a fixed percentage of a budget which they had been unable to control. Too frequently, it was asserted, the Secretariats of the international organizations consulted the major donors too late in the biennial budgetary cycle at a point when the budget had become difficult to unravel. And too often states which paid very little outvoted the major donors in the plenary meetings in approving such budgets.

This complaint was dealt with in the central system of the United Nations in the General Assembly Resolution of 18 December 1986, when the US government and the other major donors accepted a compromise whereby they would be consulted earlier, in the first year of the budgetary cycle, about both programmes and finance, and decisions about the budget would be taken on the basis of consensus in the Committee on Programme and Coordination (CPC), on which the major contributors were always represented, before being forwarded to the plenary, which in the United Nations was the Fifth Committee of the General Assembly. The original objective as stated in the Kassebaum Amendment was the introduction of weighted voting, on the lines of the International Monetary Fund and the World Bank, into the other organizations.

The expectation was, however, that a budget which had been approved by a consensus of donors and beneficiaries in the smaller committee, was unlikely to be unravelled in the plenary: what had been achieved was a functional equivalent of weighted voting. In 1989 consensus was indeed found on all issues facing the Fifth Committee, thus appearing to vindicate the changes. In 1990 the consensus barely held because of increasing discontent among the Group of 77 (G77), about the US inability to return to full funding. In the meantime, however, the US government sought to extend its strategy for reform to other parts of the UN system: as will be shown below it was next the turn of the Agencies to be put under pressure to give committees which were analogous with the CPC comparable status and powers.

This policy reflected in large part a mood of anti-internationalism in the United States, as was evident in the arguments of groups such as the

Heritage Foundation which had become influential under Reagan, fuelled by grievances such as the belief that the United Nations was anti-Zionist, and that too often technical questions were politicized.[3] Now, however, the dispute was overtaken by a disagreement between the Administration and Congress about the United States budgetary deficit.[4] That deficit had indeed risen at an extraordinarily rapid rate in the 1980s. According to figures released in 1988 between 1980 and 1988 it had increased by almost 200% from 914.3 billion dollars to 2581.6 billion dollars. The response of Congress was the requirement laid down by the Gramm-Rudman Resolution that the American Budget be brought into balance, which had the effect of squeezing contributions to international institutions. The conduct of US policy on relations with the economic and social organizations of the United Nations system now became an incidental victim of a quarrel between the two arms of government about the Federal budget.

The more sympathetic stance of the Administration was indicative, according to Puchala and Coate, of personnel changes in the State Department which brought in more flexible people.[5] The situation was graphically described in a letter written in October 1987 to the Director-General of the World Health Organization by Acting-Secretary at the Department of State, John C. Whitehead, who said that:

the present difficulties surrounding our domestic budgetary process continue to perpetuate uncertainties regarding the level and timing of funds that will be appropriated in Fiscal Year 1988 to pay for our assessed contributions to international organizations. The Administration has made a strong effort with personal letters from all concerned members of the Cabinet to secure full Congressional funding for such outstanding agencies as the WHO.[6]

A number of other governments, including the British, were reported to be lobbying on the Hill, though no country initiated serious discussions about ways of making up the shortfall caused by the American actions. Indeed European Community countries adopted a policy of excluding any making up of shortfalls in the budgets of the institutions. Some governments – Australia was reported to be taking a high profile on this – reacted with anger: they might end up having to pay the arrears arising in the Agencies' budgets.[7]

But as the Administration became more liberal Congressional doubts seemed to be hardening: there had been a shift to the right, which had "brought into key positions more Congressmen and Senators who are disposed to be sceptical of US participation in multilateral organizations".[8] In Fiscal Year 1988 the Administration had requested 571 million dollars as contributions for international organizations of which only 84%, or 480 million dollars had been appropriated.[9] The present writer calculated that this allowed a total of around $302 million for the UN and the Agencies. (The sum allocated included contributions to NATO, OECD and GATT inter alia.) And at the end of 1987 there had been an explicit agreement between the Administration and the Congress at which it had been agreed that "in order to achieve the Gramm-Rudman-Hollings ceilings, overall fiscal year 1989 requests would be no more than 2% over the Fiscal Year 1988 proposals."[10] Accordingly the Fiscal Year 1989 request was for only $490 million. The sum available for the UN and the Agencies was $308 million, which might be compared with the sum provided by the US at current dollars in 1982, the year of the highest contributions, of $439 million.

By early 1988, therefore, the Administration had to reconcile itself to a longer term shortfall in available resources. A set of guidelines for doing this were contained in a statement by Richard S. Williamson, Assistant Secretary for International Organization Affairs at the Department of State, to the House Foreign Affairs Committee, on 23 February 1988.[11] These guidelines have been the general framework of US payments policy ever since. As from Fiscal Year 1988, according to Williamson, the Administration had employed a formula for the allocation of available funds to international organizations, which introduced a system whereby the US would seek to save money by underpaying its share of an agreed budget in the organizations, rather than working to contain a budget in which its share was constant.

A list of four categories of institutions was drawn up. In the top category were those which were regarded as being of overriding strategic importance and which were to receive full funding at all times (NATO and ITU). Second were institutions which had been defined as being "good boys", as they had introduced various alterations in their budgetary procedures which the Administration had required. These would also normally be given full funding, namely 100% of the assessed contributions (OECD, GATT, IAEA, WHO, ICAO and WMO). A third priority cluster was deemed to be less deserving for a mixture of reasons, usually but not invariably being to do with inadequate internal reforms, and were to get 85% of the full assessment (OAS, PAHO, ILO, UNIDO). Finally, a fourth cluster "included organizations which have been the least responsive to US calls for budgetary reform or to other US concerns" (the UN, and the FAO). These were to receive 75% of the assessed contribution. No explanation was given of the decision to place the United Nations in the category of the undeserving, though there was some evidence to support the categorization of FAO. The treatment of the United Nations seemed particularly odd in view of the General Assembly Resolution of December 1986, on the basis of which the Administration had earlier requested a return to full funding.

Congress failed to agree to this in its discussions about appropriations in the autumn of 1988 and 1989. It was not until late 1990 that it was accepted that for the organizations which had responded positively to the demands for reform there would be a progressive reduction of arrears over a five-year period. The problems remained at the time of writing – April 1991 – that although the principle of full payment had been conceded, Congress had failed to release sufficient funds to pay all the sums owed, and that some organizations, chief amongst which was the FAO, were still seen as needing reform and accordingly were still subject to a deliberate shortfall.

*

Table 7.4   US assessments and arrears owed to ILO, WHO and the UN 1986–89

	ILO assessment	ILO arrears due	WHO assessment	WHO arrears due	UN assessment	UN arrears due
1986	32000	–	62800	–	187137	
1987	37000	29500	62800	38000	191500	
1988	40607.5	24956	71187.8	27674	216287	495000(b)
(a)1989	48648.3	24956 + 1989 assessment	71187.8	27674 + 1989 assessment	216287	279000 + 1989 assessment
1991		47,366,893 (Swiss francs)		27,236,635		approx. 530,000

(thousands of current dollars)

(a) Sum of accumulated US arrears at September 1989. Some payment expected when new US financial year starts in October 1989.
(b) Represents an accumulated deficit of $524 million less $29 million paid in February 1989.

Source: Interviews with officials in budget sections of WHO, ILO and UN in September 1989, and April 1991. The FAO was owed $140 million

In this section the flaws in the US strategy outlined in the opening paragraphs will be discussed with reference to the experience of three Specialized Agencies. These organizations were chosen because they represent the three main standards of possible behaviour in the eyes of the US: a good performer, WHO, a reformed miscreant, ILO, and an unreformed character, FAO.

Despite innovative ideas by individual officers US efforts to increase accountability in the institutions amounted to an indiscriminate and poorly targeted assault. Alterations to budgetary processes were pursued without regard for their actual condition, what changes had been introduced in recent years, and the programme problems facing the particular organization. WHO, a good performer, was punished as much as FAO, a poor one. The policy seemed to be driven as much by the need to mollify prejudices in the US as to achieve practical improvements.

As Table 7.4 indicates, in September 1989 the United Nations was owed an astonishing $495 million dollars in accumulated arrears. WHO and ILO were both owed significant sums in accumulated arrears in September 1989, though WHO was relatively somewhat better off than ILO. The latter was owed around 50% of the current assessment from previous years, whilst the former was owed around 38%. Neither agency, nor the UN, had received any part of sums due in the current calendar year, though as the US financial year begins in October some payment could be expected then. By early 1991 attempts were being made to pay the sums owed, but WHO was still owed, the central system, the ILO, and FAO.

The response of the three institutions to the crisis will be analysed under three headings. First, the effects upon budget-making procedures. This was the area of the arrangements of the Agencies which was of greatest concern to the US Administration, as it was its policy to seek adjustments here which emulated those achieved in the central system. Second, the consequences of the crisis for the financial situation of the institution and the efforts made to cover shortfalls. And third, the consequences for activities and staffing levels.

These themes provide a reasonably comprehensive account of the effects of the crisis upon the selected institutions.

1. Effects upon the budget-making procedures

Since the early 1970s all the agencies applied the same general principles with regard to the budgetary process: the budget is produced on a biennial basis and should be related to a six-year *medium term plan* about programme priorities, divided into three two-year periods. What was at issue was the way in which the general principles were applied in the various organizations.

The crisis in the late 1980s seemed to have the effect of accelerating developments in WHO which were already underway, and, indeed, which could be traced back at least as far as the mid-1970s.[12] On 21 January 1987, in Williamson's words, "just two months after the UN General Assembly decision" (in December 1986), "the Executive Board of WHO adopted its own resolution on 'cooperation in programme budgeting'. This resolution asked each of the WHO governing body units to work toward consensus in reaching conclusions on budget proposals."[13] The Executive Board had, however, done little more than clarify existing arrangements, though of course it was in the circumstances prevailing in the US politically important to do this.[14] Broadly speaking it confirmed that the procedures introduced into the UN's central system in December 1986 now also existed in the WHO.

The equivalent in the WHO of the CPC in the central system was the Programme Committee of nine government representatives. This was instructed to review "the Director-General's proposed guidance to regional offices and headquarters regarding the development of the next biennial programme budget proposals" and recommend a budget to the Health Assembly, to be produced as "the result of a cooperative process aimed at reaching consensus".[15] Williamson had obviously wished to suggest to Congress that this was a startling change, a product of decisive American diplomacy, but the reality was less dramatic: in effect it had been necessary only for the Executive Board of 31 representatives to confirm the role of the Programme Committee and the practice, which had long been accepted in the Programme Committee as in the Executive Board, of voting on the basis of consensus. Indeed, as Jacobson had explained, one of the intentions behind the complex procedures for electing the members of the Executive Board, and the other main committees in WHO, was to ensure that consensus, among what was called by one official the "public health mafia", was the norm.[16] That no contentious changes had been required was the real reason for the Executive Board's prompt response.

There is no doubt, however, that the crisis led to a further stage in the rather longer term trend towards the tightening of earlier procedures. Priorities had been confirmed and extended. Now guidelines about budgetary ceilings were more firmly indicated than earlier, and claims for finance from the various parts of the system were more carefully related to the overall budget. Hence the role of the Geneva Group, with regards to WHO as well as the other agencies, seemed to have been sharpened: in the early seventies it had indicated a "general order of magnitude" for budgets,[17] but by the late eighties it had come to establish ceilings beyond which budgets could not be increased. This naturally led to the Programme Committee's issuing firmer guidelines to those responsible for producing claims upon the budget.

The weight had shifted somewhat from defining the right policies and attaining benefits on the ground to a concern with financial discipline in the context of more centralized overall management. One excellent indication of this was the development reported to the present writer in late 1988: whereas the Executive Board used to spend most of its time on technical questions, now it was mainly concerned with finance![18]

With regard to the ILO the changes in the procedures affecting the budget also had a certain cosmetic quality. It looked as though conformity with the procedural principles agreed in the central system in December 1986 had been placed ahead of the actual record of good behaviour. This explains the resigned acceptance in the organization of the need to undertake reform whilst implying that this was more a matter of form than substance: officials felt that this was a charade that had to be played.

Two major committees of the organization were to have a role. One was the Governing Body of 56 members elected on the basis of the ILO's unique tripartite system of representation – governments, management and workers – but with the major industrialized countries always represented. In June 1986 a constitutional amendment had increased membership of the Governing Body to 112 divided among four regional groups, but at the time of writing this had not been ratified by a sufficient number of states.[19] The Governing Body was essentially the main administering committee of the plenary International Labour Conference: the former met in February–March and November whilst the latter met in November. The second was the so-called Programme, Financial and Administrative Committee (PFAC), which was a standing committee of the Governing Body, on which the major contributors also sat. This was the committee which was destined to play the part in the ILO taken by the CPC in the central system in the modified budgetary procedure.

The formal reforms were initiated immediately after the report of the Group of 18 had been published in August 1986, but the first acknowledged specific stimulus was a discussion at the meeting of the PFAC in February–March 1987 to which the Director-General said he would respond.[20] It appears that at that meeting there were complaints about procedures, pressed by the Americans, and the Director-General did indeed confess shortly after to two budgetary sins. There had been in the "tight production schedule" no time for the PFCA "to examine fully and take a position on, the programme adjustment proposals when they came before the Governing Body."[21] The six-year Medium Term Plan had also hitherto given "broad illustrative estimates" or "indicative statements" which "were not reviewed by the Committee and the Governing Body with a view to translating them into specific resource guidance for each of the three programmes and budgets covered by the six-year plan."[22] In short the budget had not been scrutinized very closely by member governments before it had reached a near final form and been placed before the Conference in November. In addition, because of the way in which the Medium Term Plan was drawn up it was difficult to relate policies reasonably clearly to resources.

The Director-General proposed solutions to these problems to the meeting of the Governing Body in May 1987. The first problem was to be addressed by consulting with the PFAC much earlier in the budgetary process. The second was to be tackled by specifying in much more detail on a rolling basis the next two years of the Medium Term Plan: "to forge a direct and close link between the Medium-Term Plan and the biennial programmes and budgets . . . ."[23] It was confirmed that decisions in the PFAC would continue to be taken on the basis of consensus. The proposed changes were accepted by the Governing Body in May 1987 and by the Conference in November 1987.[24] The points hardly need elaborating that, on the model of events in the United Nations in December 1986, these alterations were seen as satisfying the main American Administration demands.[25]

But there was to be no return to full funding. What followed was described by one official, observing the budgetary process in February–March 1988, as "making a mockery of the budgetary process".[26]

The remarkable feature was that those in the US State Department who took part in the reformed budgetary procedure knew that, whatever the level of funding which was agreed, the US would only pay at most 85% of their share, according to the Williamson guidelines. A logical strategy would, of course, have been to request more than it expected to receive: in other words, the withholding of 15% could be allowed for in the initial bid. But budgetary proprieties and the zero growth principle prevented this. Conversely the bitter pill could not be swallowed and a lower realistic budget submitted. This would have appeared to condone the non-payment of due contributions and could set up a process of continual contraction at the rate of 15% of the US 25% assessment each year.

Thus the process in 1988 was doomed to aim with the help and cooperation of American officers at a level of funding which these same officials knew would not be paid. This procedure was repeated in 1989. The description of this situation as a mockery seems in some ways too gentle.

Despite good behaviour the Administration, which had requested the form of the improvements in the first place, refused to give the ILO a higher ranking in the Williamson categories when this was requested by the organization in April 1988.[27] This was odd in that in the Williamson statement the ILO had been given a clean bill of health.

In sharp contrast the FAO proved slow to change in response to the pressures from the main donors. In the spring of 1991 the complaints were still that the Secretariat under Mr Sauma continued to prepare the budget, and in general to conduct its financial affairs without sufficient consultation with its main donor states, and the result was that consensus in the main committees with responsibility in this area was rare.[28] It was only in 1991 that Mr Sauma had accepted the idea of zero growth, and this was the first occasion for many years on which there had been consensus in the Finance Committee of nine members meeting in April and May: the budget was next to be considered by the 59-member Council in June and then finally approved by simple majority in the Conference of all members in November. In the latter forums the pattern was for discussion to be acrimonious and the outcome in recent years has been for the US not to pay its assessment. Despite expressing strong reservations, and voting against the budget, the British always paid their assessment: even the Nordic countries have, however, expressed doubts about the procedures, though usually by abstaining rather than voting against.

The budgetary process still did not involve the contributing states until the beginning of the second year of the biennium, and the documentation about the budget was regarded as unhelpful. The organization had introduced the practice of releasing an outline budget in January of the second year of the biennium which was judged to be inadequate: there were complaints about the lack of transparency in the system. Financial Reports were to be issued every three months, but were hard to obtain. The Finance Committee was said to be slow to distribute such information. This committee in some ways had become more politicized in recent years: it had been made up of financial specialists nominated on the basis of their expertise (like ACABQ), but were now government representatives.

Indeed the process of reform in the FAO seemed in early 1991 to have hardly begun, despite the considerable pressures exerted by the US by withholding funds. Problems included disagreements about the underlying purpose of the organization: was it a development organization or was it mainly concerned with regulation and "governance"? The US and the other hard line states preferred the latter view whilst the developing countries supported the former, and the Director-General saw himself as their spokesman.

The US position was, however, complicated in Rome by the fact that the contributing states were themselves divided. This was a city where the Geneva Group did not necessarily stick together. The French in particular got on well with Mr Sauma, whilst the Southern tier of the EC countries tended to support him too. Even the Germans had broken ranks recently. There were, however, signs of a gathering momentum in a process of consultation outside the organization between moderate developing countries and the main contributors – 25 states in all – about the reform of the system. It was striking though that at this late stage it was still necessary to expend diplomatic energy on preparing a Medium Term plan, an exercise seen by the Nordic countries as the right way forward, within which programme priorities could be agreed: this issue was high on the agenda of reform in early 1991.

2. The crisis and resources

The squeezing of the WHO's resources by the underpayment of assessments in the late 1980s should be seen in the context of the acceptance by the Organization for several years of the principle of zero growth and, indeed, as reported above, of a slight reduction in real terms each year in the scale of its budget from 1982 to 1987. Over a number of years considerable effort had been devoted to improving the administration and efficiency of the organization.[29] 1987 shortfalls had nevertheless required that WHO programme implementation worldwide be reduced by $35 million.

In early 1988 the prospects for the coming biennium looked bleak: the budget had been increased in nominal terms, solely to cover cost increases – a concession which the hardline contributors strongly opposed in FAO in early 1991 – and, in planning for the next 1988–89 biennium it was assumed that despite the Administration's preferences there would be further unavoidable shortfalls, and that beyond that period it was likely that the US would continue to press for severe budgetary restraint. There would accordingly be a "contingency" reduction in programmes to the value of $50 million in 1988–89.[30]

The shortfall in resources was dealt with by the organization in two major ways.

First, there were reductions in spending as noted in the previous paragraph. The WHO had three levels of operation, the global, the regional and the state. The organization had sought in the past to put particular stress on the task of maximizing the provision of resources at the state level, as that was where the programmes were carried out and where the more immediate effects could be achieved. Now, however, that situation could no longer be maintained. Country programmes would have to share in the general package of reductions, and this meant that for the first time the work of WHO on the ground would be reduced.[31]

Second, it was decided to support current spending from two reserves, the Working Capital Fund and the casual income fund. The source of the latter was the sale of services, technical publications and the like. To cover shortfalls in 1986–87, $11 million was borrowed from the Working Capital Fund and $10 million from the casual income reserve, to be repaid later.[32]

As is suggested in Table 7.4 the implications of the late 1980s crisis for the International Labour Organization were, however, in some ways more serious, although their costs in human terms were less tangible and immediate. It will be recalled that the ILO was in the third category on the Williamson list and, therefore, was to get at most 85% of the United States assessment: this was indicative of the relatively unsympathetic attitude on the part of the American Administration and did not bode well for the future.

This was despite the strong feeling in the organization that the ILO was a "financially responsible organization": the budget had not grown in real terms between the mid-1970s and the mid-1980s. Indeed a senior official stated that the budget in 1986 was 10% less than it had been in 1976, and that there had been no return to the *status quo ante* when the Americans returned in 1980 after their withdrawal in 1977. There had also been a 10% reduction in the number of staff in that period, and a further 18% was now to be shed.[33]

In his discussion in early 1987 of the next Medium Term Plan, that for 1990 to 1995, the Director-General accepted that the programme budget for the biennium 1990–91, at $331 million, would be based on the principle of zero growth compared with 1988–89, and cost increases such as those resulting from inflation would be absorbed.[34] But a senior official in the budget section suggested that even this was an over-optimistic expectation. And there was a resigned conviction that "he may propose further programme reductions to the Governing Body at its 239th Session, February–March 1988."[35] The large scale of US arrears in late 1989, still applying in summer 1990, and early 1991, is indicated in Table 7.4.

In the FAO the US position in April 1991 was that it would not pay more than the minimum contribution needed to avoid losing its vote until the changes it preferred had been introduced. Indeed a decision not to pay the assessed contribution in the next financial year had already been taken by the Administration. In April 1991 $140 million was owed in arrears in addition to the assessment for the current year of $73 million: a minimum of $65 million would have to be paid by the end of the year to avoid losing voting rights. The British had resorted to the ploy of paying their contribution in three tranches rather than two in 1990, i.e. payment was slowed down, though made in full, in order to put pressure on the organization.

The Secretariat had been reluctant to propose a budget based on zero growth in real terms, despite having "felt the pinch" in 1986: in 1986–87 the programme budget had been cut by $25 million, and in 1988–89 $20 million had been cut. Even though Mr Sauma had accepted the principle of zero growth in 1991, there were several issues about which disagreement remained. By using a formula based upon the rate at which vacancies in the organization were refilled, known as the lapse rate, he succeeded in getting in effect 34% growth. In the last biennium a .25% had been obtained.[36]

The Director-General was, however, still insisting that cost increases should not be subject to the zero growth principle. He was also seeking increases of at least $4 million in the budget for the Technical Cooperation Programme – 11.8% of the Budget, which was less than the 17% increase demanded by the developing countries in the 1990 Conference. An increase here was seen as part of a bargain: it was the G77's reward for accepting zero growth.

3. Activities and staffing levels

It is not surprising that the implications of all this for the work of WHO were serious. There is little evidence to suggest, however, that the cuts led to staff reductions in the organization, though there were inevitably reductions in the numbers employed in member states in WHO pro-grammes, e.g. an 18% cut in the staff of health manpower development. There is also little evidence to indicate that the US Administration attempted to influence decisions about where cuts should be made. This was attributable in part to WHO's decentralized structure, in part to its concern with specialist health programmes, and in part to the esteem in which the organization was held by responsible officials in the Administration.

For the first time, however, it was now necessary to reduce WHO programmes. A list with 22 headings under which cuts had to be made was issued in 1988. These make for disturbing reading: they included "activities in developing countries for the control of such diseases as malaria, tuberculosis, leprosy and rabies" "drastically reduced to budget cuts" "The attainment of the water decade target of clean water and safe sanitation for all people throughout the world by 1990" "adversely affected by the cuts with all the negative implications for infant mortality" "The target of providing immunization to all the children of the world by 1990" "revised due to the budget cuts" "targets for the reduction of mortality and morbidity from diarrhoeal diseases . . . seriously affected" "The safety and quality of vaccines to prevent diphtheria, whooping cough and rabies . . . endangered".[37] In early 1991 an early restoration of these cuts looked unlikely.

For the ILO there would also have to be cuts and economies: e.g. major meetings, on labour market flexibility and employment, the social protection of home workers and the possibility of reforming social security, had been postponed from 1988–89; and there would need to be more cuts. A further 15% of staff were to be shed. In June 1986, after a long period of consideration, an amendment to the constitution of the organization had been approved which established a procedure for preventing the introduction of motions of condemnation to the International Labour Conference on matters outside the organization's field of responsibility. A new committee was to decide on the admissibility of such motions. This would seem to have been a satisfactory response to the demand made by a number of the major contributors, but especially strongly by the Americans, that irrelevant, politicizing resolutions, such as those condemning Israel, should be disallowed. These various illustrations of good behaviour did not, however, have any positive results as regards funding.

In 1989 the Director General was prepared to say that he had every hope that there would be a return to full funding, but in 1991 it looked as though there would be financial shortfalls at least until 1995. In consequence the ILO seemed set for a period of severe restriction in its operations and, as already mentioned, further reductions in its staffing levels. The irony was, of course, that the organization had put right its internal problems – even meeting the complaints about politicization – beginning even before Kassebaum, and that in any case its behaviour through the eighties had been financially responsible.

The Director-General of FAO was determined to maintain the level of programmes at all costs. There would be no further planned reductions in the programmes of the organization, but an ad hoc fashion response to resource shortfalls by, for instance, postponing payments. In 1989 he received the backing of the Conference for this policy. It was indeed accepted even by the main contributing states that the organization had stayed within 8–10% of its normal level of programme funding in the early 1990s.

The main contributing states nevertheless had damaging complaints about the FAO programmes. There were more than 2000 of them, they were hard to monitor, probably too small and over-sectoralized, and were not subject to any set of priorities. As with finance this was an area of loud complaints by donors about a lack of transparency and accountability in the organization. Even the numbers of FAO personnel in the field could not be discovered! A difficulty was that the G77 countries were opposed to the establishing of priorities as it was obvious that some would be losers in the resulting ranking of claims for resources.[38]

A good performer, WHO was needlessly damaged in its capacity to provide services which were regarded as necessary even by the US: the ILO failed to obtain any clear benefit from compliance with US demands; and the FAO remained defiant, and slow to change, capitalizing upon the ideological brawl about the role of international organization in the development process between the major hard line donors and the rest. Such were the flaws in US strategy on the reform of the agencies. In the next section their implications for the reform of the United Nations system will be considered.

*

In many ways the future of the United Nations looked brighter in the early 1990s than it had for many years.[39] The very favourable signals on the security side – Security Council cooperation in the settlement of the Iraq–Iran war, the Namibia problem and experience of the Gulf War – were, however, beside the point when it came to the future role of the Agencies and the Funds.

Their experience suggested the need to find ways of making it more difficult for a single major contributor to act as the US had done. That meant adjusting the budgetary arrangements so that more states paid roughly equal contributions: as an insurance against rogue behaviour there should be no outstanding single contributor.

Of course attention has to be given to the question of how to get states that have not paid to do so. Here the answer is simple: either assessments have to be paid in full or they need to be altered by common consent using the relevant legal procedures. States have to recognize and accept their legal obligations, though they might be given some encouragement in this. One suggestion was that states should be given a rebate if they paid early and incur a penalty if they paid late. It had been noted that in the ITU, where there was a penalty for the tardy, there were fewer late payers.

The current enthusiasm for increases in voluntary contributions by member states was, however, to be regretted.[40] The US experience revealed that voluntary contributions did not increase as assessed contributions declined (see Table 7.3). In the short term they may add to the pot. In the long term, however, they greatly increase the problems of coordination. For instance, the effectiveness of UNDP was damaged by the tendency for even the internationalist states such as those in Scandinavia, and Holland, to give money directly to the Agencies for programmes in which they were specially interested.[41]

The problem was that such money could encourage particular agencies to go it alone in attempts to expand their particular realm outside the UNDP framework. Voluntary contributions also created unpredictability in finance and too great a dependence on the satisfaction of particular donors. In effect voluntary contributions increased the risk of placing institutions in the thrall of those who gave them the money. There was, of course, also the great problem of the uncertainty of finance. It is, therefore, greatly preferable to limit the size of voluntary funding in relation to the total budget of an institution.

The most immediate expression of the general political problems facing the agencies, however, is the nature of the relationship between policy and finance. The issue is whether finance dominates, in the sense that the decision is taken first about the money which is available, and the choice about desirable policy fitted into that frame of reference, as was proposed by the US in the FAO in 1987; or whether policy is chosen first and the funds found later. If the former course is followed policy choice will be constrained, and budgets will not expand.

On the other side, of course, there are always excellent reasons for increasing budgetary claims at an accelerating rate. It follows that the management of the budgetary process should include a forum in which proposals for the budget are confronted with the policy programme: decisions about each should be made in the context of decisions about the other. The financial constraints of the late 1980s and early 1990s at least pushed the reform of the policy instruments, and clarified their relationship with finance. On the other hand, the extreme hardline donor position of placing a prior limit on spending, to which the US sometimes inclined, must be resisted, as such a procedure would encourage contributors to guarantee national priorities at the expense of international ones.[42]

Alteration of the scale of assessments for contributions to international organizations is necessary. In testimony to the House Appropriations Subcommittee on 29 March 1988 George Shultz, then Secretary of State, expressed his concern over the "growing shortfalls in our payments". But he then said that

there are some who view the solution to this problem as negotiating a reduction in our assessments, while others argue just as forcefully that for the US to seek an assessment reduction would be tantamount to accepting a diminished US role in world affairs and that such negotiations would most probably be contentious and provide our adversaries with another opportunity to attack the United States.[43]

There is, however, a good cause for reducing the scale of US contributions, and precisely for the reasons Shultz adduced for keeping them at the present level. It seems morally unacceptable that such large contributions to the institutions of the international community should be seen as an instrument of national power. But this is only one element in the argument, supported by an increasing number of observers and participants, including the Secretary-General, in favour of reducing the maximum contribution to 15% or even 10%. It should be recalled that the scale of finance in question is small compared with the domestic budget of even a small developed state.

A change would detract from the US sense that the world owed them something as they carried the major burden, and would also reflect the modification since 1945 of the international hierarchy – that the United States has declined in comparison with other entities such as the European Community (EC) and Japan. It would also be right for the others to pay more in the light of their increasing prosperity. The complaints of some governments about US behaviour – such as the European Community – contrasted with their reluctance to do anything about the shortfalls themselves, are hypocritical.

The model of the EC suggests further ideas about reform. For instance the contributions could be denominated in SDRs, the equivalent at the global level of ECUs in Europe, which is the common denominator there.[44] In this way one of the major hazards of the financing of international organizations in the 1980s, exchange rate fluctuations, could be reduced. Changes in the value of the dollar caused major problems in altering the value of contributions. Such an adjustment would not be minor but would be appropriate at a time of floating currencies. Awareness of possibilities is at least a first step to reform.

The reform of the system for financing international organizations is necessary both because of what the Americans did, but also what they failed to do. The illegal withholding of payments was not matched with any coherent vision of what effect they intended for the system. In one sense, however, there was a concealed agenda. There was an intention on the part of the hard line governments to challenge the ideological basis upon which the establishment and growth of international organizations were founded: the idea that the needs of the international community should be recognized and every effort made to find the money to satisfy them. Such an intention is demonstrated in the idea of zero growth and it was evident well before Kassebaum.

But despite the fact that the Charter was negotiated in the name of the world's peoples such a fundamental alteration in approach never appeared in any election manifesto, and was never subject to public debate. Its consequence was that the weight in budgetary terms of intergovernmental international organization reached its zenith in the early eighties, after a period of more or less continuous growth since the war, and has not increased since. This alteration in the universe of international organization was never brought into the open.

Notes

1. See Douglas Williams, *The Specialized Agencies and the United Nations: The System in Crisis*, D. Hurst and Company, London, 1987; and Paul Taylor, "Reforming the System: Getting the Money to Talk", in Paul Taylor and A.J.R. Groom (Editors), *International Institutions at Work*, Frances Pinter, London, 1988.
2. See "Kassebaum and Gramm-Rudman", Chapter VIII of Williams, loc. cit., contributed by Arthur Kilgore.
3. See the various reports on the United Nations produced by the Heritage Foundation under the title *A United Nations Assessment Project Study*. Something of the flavour of the enterprise may be gleaned from the opening sentence of No. 487 issued under the heading *The United Nations Library: Putting Soviet Disinformation into Circulation:* "The Dag Hammarskjold Library at the United Nations Headquarters has become a Soviet outpost"!
4. See Donald J. Puchala and Roger A. Coate, *The State of the United Nations, 1988,* The Academic Council on the United Nations System, Hanover, N.H., 1988.
5. Ibid., p. 24.
6. Quoted in full in World Health Organization, EB 81/42, Annex, 13 November 1987, at p. 3.
7. Interview, Geneva, April 1987.
8. Puchala and Coate, loc. cit., p. 22.
9. Document marked: Statement of Richard S. Williamson, Assistant Secretary for International Organizations Affairs, Department of State, before the House Foreign Affairs Committee, Subcommittee on Human Rights and International Organizations and Subcommittee on International Operations, February 23, 1988; figures found at p. 20.
10. Ibid. p. 24.
11. Ibid., Appendix, p. 2.
12. Executive Board, 79th Session, *Summary Records: First Meeting,* in PB/88–89, loc. cit., annex.
13. Williamson Statement (see footnote 16): p. 10.
14. World Health Organization, Executive Board, *EB79/ 1987/ REC/1,* 18th Meeting, 22 January 1987.
15. Ibid., Paras 2(1) and 2(2).
16. Harold K. Jacobson, "WHO: Medicine, Regionalism, and Managed Politics", in Robert W. Cox and Harold K. Jacobson (Editors), *The Anatomy of Influence: Decision Making in International Organization,* Yale University Press, New Haven and London, p. 189; and interview in Geneva, April 1988.
17. Jacobson, loc. cit., p. 189.
18. Interview, December 1988.
19. Reported in International Labour Conference, *Provisional Record,* Seventy-second Session, Geneva, 1986, Part 11, 3/17.
20. International Labour Office, Governing Body, *GB.236/PFA/5/10,* 236th Session, Geneva, May 1987, Para. 1.
21. Ibid., Para. 3.
22. Ibid., Para. 5.
23. Ibid., Para. 6.
24. International Labour Office, Governing Body, *GB.236/9/22,* 236th Session, *First Report of the Programme, Financial and Administrative Committee,* Para. 112.
25. See Williamson Statement, loc. cit., Pp. 11–12.

26. Interview with a senior ILO Budget official in April 1988.
27. Interview in April 1988 with officials at ILO, Geneva.
28. Information about the FAO here and later is the product of interviews with officials in the FAO Secretariat and national representations in April 1991.
29. PB/88–89, loc. cit., Para. 52.
30. Ibid.
31. World Health Organization, Regional Committee for the Eastern Mediterranean, *EM/RC34/3.1*, September 1987, especially paras 4 and 12.
32. *EB81/ 42 Add.1*, January 1988, Para. 2.
33. Interview, April 1988.
34. International Labour Organization, *Medium-Term Plan 1990–95*, International Labour Office, Geneva, 1988, p. 118.
35. Ibid., Para. 6.24.
36. Interview with FAO official, April 3 1991.
37. WHO Memorandum, available April 1988, no document identification.
38. Interview with a G77 FAO representative, Rome, April 5 1991.
39. See Mikhail Gorbachev, *Realities and Guarantees for a Secure World*, Novosti Press Agency Publishing House, Moscow, 1987, especially section V. p. 14.
40. See Peter Fromuth, *The UN at 40: the problems and Opportunities*, UNA-USA, New York, June 1986, Pp. 53–55.
41. See the very firm statement about the dangers of fragmentation arising from voluntary funding in Organization for Economic Cooperation and Development, *1984 Review, Development Cooperation*, OECD, Paris, November, 1984, p. 99.
42. See GA A/41/49, Supplement No. 49, *Report of the Group of High-Level Intergovernmental Experts to Review the Efficiency of the Administrative and Financial Functioning of the United Nations* (henceforth called the *Report of the Committee of 18*), New York, 1986.
43. Testimony of George P. Shultz, Secretary of State, before the House Appropriations Subcommittee on Commerce, Justice, State (Congressman Neal Smith), March 29th, 1988.
44. See Juliet Lodge (Editor), *The European Community and the Challenge of the Future*, Pinter Publishers, London, 1989.

Section 4
Global Organization and the New Agenda

Introduction

The arguments deriving from consociationalism and symbiosis discussed in Chapter 4 and the Introduction to Section Three, also have striking implications for the role of international organizations with regard to pressing global problems which affect individuals directly. Examples of this would be the AIDS problem, or the environmental crisis, or the crisis caused by the apparently dangerously rapid growth of global population, but the provison of physical security for individuals also comes into this category. At first sight it might be supposed by the Western observer that such problems should self-evidently be managed by a supranational approach as they seem to be of such overwhelming importance. But the state has found particular ways of protecting its interests, and indeed, of using the urgency of the problems to strengthen its own internal arrangements. The discussion of the population issue in Chapter 8 below illustrates this response very clearly. Similar conclusions emerge, however, from the discussion of the UN's role in the 1990–91 Gulf crisis discusssd in Chapter 9.

As is shown, it is common for a transnational coalition to emerge with regard to such issues, which demands a supranational approach to the problem, and produces a global plan of action. Such an approach was also followed in the preparations for the Environmental Conference held in Rio de Janeiro, Brazil, in June 1992. But the response hitherto has been far from supranational, and indeed is better described as *statist*; it emerges from the clash between the pressures to apply a supranational solution, involving detailed and binding targets for achievement within specified periods, and the determination of states to protect their sovereignty. The outcome tends to be for the global plan to be eroded. General goals are substituted for specific and binding targets, and national plans are drawn up to move towards the general goals. What started out as a drive towards setting up an authoritative international institution to manage a common plan ends up as a programme for coordinating a series of national plans for which national authorities are responsible and within which they decide their own targets.

The global effort becomes one of providing a general impetus, helping to provide resources, and monitoring progress. Despite the appearance of a global problem the result is the strengthening of the role of the state: in this case the balance between the state and the claims of international organization again emerges in a distinctive way, and understanding it is helped by the consociational model of international organization. The claim that a particular interest is transcendent, that in this case the community's claim has priority, is challenged according to the iron law of consociation; that the validity of interests at either level is inevitably qualified in the light of countervailing claims at the other. There are no purely global interests, if by this is meant a global agenda which has absolute priority.

It is fascinating that, in the late twentieth century, the pattern of the relationship between the state and the development of international organizations of the nineteenth century was in some ways reversed. In the nineteenth century governments of advanced states created international organizations because without them they could not do things within their frontiers which they wished to do, particularly, of course, with regard to the working of increasingly sophisticated economic and technical arrangements. Later, as Morse pointed out, pressures towards increasing policy interdependence were strengthened for rather similar reasons. In an interdependent world the internal affairs of states simply could not be managed without increasing intergovernmental coordination, but it was the involvement of governments internally which drove the external cooperation.

More recently, however, problems have appeared which in a sense are outside the state in that they have obvious global dimensions, and have little to do with the management or facilitating of internal arrangements. For new states, however, such problems have provided an opportunity for increasing internal involvement and thus furthering the consolidation of the national regime. In the first case increasing involvement internationally was the result of something which required to be done internally, in the latter case the thing to be done internationally was the opportunity for increasing internal involvement.

Comparisons between thinking about the states over a longer period of time are in some ways even more fascinating. In the seventeenth century Hobbes and others argued that the primary purpose of the state was to provide for the security of individuals; the latter's interests justified the former. In the late twentieth century, however – when the apocalypse seems much nearer – the relationship sometimes appears to be the other way round; the pressing interests of individuals, for instance, with regard to environmental damage, are to be compromised in the light of the needs of the state. Indeed the cynical observer may be permitted the bleak conclusion that this is an area where the state itself has become in some sense a parasite; it insists upon its entrenchment as a political and institutional form at the expense of the survival of its citizens, something which was far from the ken of Thomas Hobbes. The doomsday scenario is conjured up of a world of states which exist metaphysically without citizens.

8 Working for global population control

This chapter discusses the way in which the issue of population control entered the agenda of international organization, so that it became an acceptable item for cooperative action. The way in which states, particularly developing states, responded to this development is of particular concern, because it is evidence of their likely response to other items on the new agenda, such as the protection of the environment. The discussion deals with these issues in the context of the World Population Conference which met in Bucharest, Romania, 20–30 August 1974, and the International Population Conferences, intended to evaluate progress since its predecessor, held in Mexico City 6–14 August 1984, and due again in 1994.[1]

Three major questions arise. First, why were the special conferences held in preference to discussion of the questions with which they dealt in, say, ECOSOC, or the General Assembly, or in one of the existing Agencies? Second, what was the impact of the conferences, intentional or otherwise, upon the population policies of government? It is necessary to consider the policy differences which were revealed during the conferences, and to measure the achievements reflected in their conclusions, which in this case took the form of a World Population Plan of Action agreed in Bucharest, and re-affirmed in 1984. And, third, the question is to be considered of what the conferences achieved in the longer term: what was their contribution, if any, to the practice of population policy, and the means for its implementation.

A definition of special conferences was attempted in Chapter 5 of this volume. They are arranged outside the regular framework of the United Nations and its agencies, although they frequently involve inputs in the form of proposals and secretarial provision from those bodies, and, indeed, are formally initiated by either the Economic and Social Council or the General Assembly. In 1980 a Report, prepared by the Secretary-General stressed that they were conferences that did not form a part of the regular recurrent conference programme of a biennium and that they attracted specific additional budgetary provisions for their substantive preparation and that all states were invited to attend.[2] They frequently occur when a new problem has been identified, demanding action, which is not the clear responsibility of any of the existing Specialized Agencies, and in consequence they often initiate a new institutional arrangement in the form of a fund or programme, or, as in this case, adjustment of existing institutions. They are, however, intended to be unique occasions, not seen as beginning a routine series of such meetings, although they frequently, as in the case of the World Population Conference, lead to a second "follow-up" conference. In the 1960s and 1970s the number of such conferences began to increase, and indeed, the General Assembly laid down a number of rules about them in 1967.[3] The various case studies in this volume illustrate the wide range of subjects with which they have been concerned.

It is not intended in this chapter to evaluate in detail the technical aspects and problems of population policy, or of its impact: the stress is upon the conferences and their role, the changing significance of population policy in the agendas of governments – essentially a political rather than a technical question – and the related changes in the economic and social organization of the United Nations system. Nevertheless, it is necessary to indicate briefly the meaning of population policy in the eyes of those who are population specialists who are involved in its administration. The usual caveat has to be centred: as Halvor Gille, Deputy Executive Director of UNFPA (the United Nations Fund for Population Activities) wrote in 1978 "a clear-cut and generally agreed upon definition of the term 'population activities' is not available."[4] Nevertheless, they are "classified by the United Nations organization concerned into the following major subject areas: (1) basic population data; (2) population dynamics; (3) population policy formulation, implementation and evaluation; (4) family planning; (5) bio-medical research; (6) communications and education".[5] By 1984 the specific substantive areas concerned, as indicated by the division of labour among the major committees set up to prepare for the Mexico conference were: fertility and the family, interpreted to include such questions as family planning, factors affecting family size, and the status of women; population distribution, migration and development, involving questions about the location and movement of peoples; population, resources, environment and development, in particular the big question of the relationship between population growth, and the adequacy of resources (Malthus and Marx, and so on), and habitat (urbanization versus rural development); and mortality and health policy, including such questions as infant mortality and the implications of increasing life expectancy.[6] Clearly the area of concern to population specialists had become a very wide one.

It is also necessary to describe briefly the events which led to the conferences. Developments in three contexts seem to be relevant: the increasing acceptability of population policy by governments and people and the progress of thinking about such matters within the "population community" of experts and involved administrators; the developing organization of "population activities" at the international level; and the specific events leading up to the holding of the population conference in 1974. The dynamics behind the first conference carried over to the second: the first was the unusual development which needs to be explained. The conference titles are indicative: the second was called less ambitiously the International Conference on Population, whilst the first claimed in a grandiose fashion to be a World Conference.

Between the early 1950s, and the early 1990s, the need for population policies came to be generally accepted by governments, and the scale of scientific research into, and knowledge about, population problems had considerably expanded. This is not to imply, of course, that there were not still serious difficulties in the way in which such policies were executed, and deficiencies in knowledge about them – such as the relationship between population size and development. But there had developed a broad consensus about the need for such policies. This was indeed an astonishing development: in 1952 the threat had been made by around a third of the membership of the World Health Organization to walk out if that organization were to involve itself in population activities.[7]

In 1973, although anxiety was expressed about the "acceleration of world population growth" seen as the "direct result of the acceleration of population growth in less developed countries",[8] some progress was reported. In 1970 35 developing countries had "policies and organized family planning programmes" whereas pre-1955 only three countries had such policies (India, China and Pakistan)[9]; another 34 tolerated family planning programmes sponsored by private organizations, such as the International Planned Parenthood Federation (IPPF).[10] Three-quarters of developing countries had no research institutions on which the governments could rely for the development and implementation of their policies.[11] By the late 1960s and early 1970s, the period of preparation for the 1974 conference, there was, therefore, a sense of a task begun, needing a great increase in resources and effort, and anxiety about what might happen if population growth could not be curtailed. Progress in accepting and implementing population policies between 1974 and the mid-1980s is evaluated in greater detail later.

The modest expansion of population activities within the countries was matched by a growing concern within international organizations about such questions, and an increase in the number of specialists conducting research in the area. There had, indeed, been two earlier international conferences on population questions, in Rome (1954) and Belgrade (1965), and for a while the 1974 conference was referred to, somewhat ambiguously, as the Third World [sic] Population Conference. But the two earlier conferences had been for experts acting in their individual capacities, rather than as government representatives: a group of population experts appointed in 1969 by the Secretary-General to advise him about the desirability of holding a further meeting (described hereafter as the 1969 Group) stated that at the time of the 1954 conference "demographic matters and relevant research techniques were little known",[12] and that the 1965 conference had been geared mainly to the development of knowledge.[13] One reflection of the development of population studies was an article in Le Monde in January 1974 in which Leon Tabah, Head of the Population Division (UN) wrote that

primitive demography is in the act of coming of age as demographers start to look beyond simply counting heads to the impact of numbers on social and economic betterment and on the carrying capacity of our life support systems.[14]

There had, furthermore, been inadequate representation of developing countries at the earlier conferences, despite the complaint that they had been too large.[15] It is also a reflection of the rather low level of involvement on the part of the United Nations and its member governments in population questions before the mid-1960s, that both earlier conferences were co-sponsored by a nongovernmental international association of population specialists, the International Union for the Scientific Study of Population (IUSSP), which had been established in the 1920s. The 1969 Group explicitly decided that the 1974 conference should not be a third specialist conference, and it followed that the IUSSP could not, therefore, be involved in its organization.[16]

The 1960s saw a considerable expansion in the involvement of international organizations in population activities. In 1965 the World Health Organization "obtained its first limited mandate from member governments"[17] and a year later a formula was agreed within the World Health Organization by its Assembly which allowed it a more active role: fertility control was defined as a health problem, and technical assistance in family planning was accordingly authorized.[18] The decade saw a series of such authorizations and injunctions to action. In 1962 the General Assembly passed a resolution that called on the United Nations system to expand its research in population and development, and to increase technical assistance to countries carrying out demographic studies; in 1970 the Assembly included in its resolution on the Second United Nations Development Decade a Declaration on the need to reduce the average annual rate of population increase to 2.5% in the following decade.[19]

In addition to the 1965 Belgrade Conference there were also a number of institutional innovations and other international conferences. There had, indeed, been a successful Asian conference on population involving government representatives in 1963, which was "the first to call on the UN to expand technical assistance to countries carrying out 'family welfare planning programmes'".[20] In the early 1970s there were regional conferences in Latin America (1970), Africa (1971), Europe (1971), and a second Asian conference (1973).[21] These had been planned before the decision had been taken to hold the 1974 conference but became part of its planning process. In 1967 the institution which was later to become the United Nations' principal organ in the field of population activities, the United Nations Fund For Population Activities (UNFPA) was created under the Secretary-General, and in 1969 it was placed under the general surveillance of the Governing Council of the United Nations Development Programme (UNDP) by the General Assembly.

It will be shown later that the emergence of this organization, under its distinguished Executive-Director, Raphael Salas, was one of the main elements of the institutional adjustment of the United Nations to the expansion of population activities. It is striking, however, that in a major article on the origins and conduct of the 1974 Bucharest Conference, published in 1975, UNFPA was hardly mentioned: it was not included in the list of "important resolutions and milestones" in the development of the UN's role in population questions.[22] The article did, however, appear in the first volume of a journal, *Population and Development Review*, that was to become a major organ of the population community: this is perhaps a further indication of the latter's enlargement and growing status, moving in parallel with the organizational developments.

One of the peculiarities of the sequence of events leading up to the decision to hold the world Population Conference in Bucharest in August 1974 was that strictly speaking no such decision appears to have been taken, if by that is meant that there was a deliberate act of initiation. Of course, there was a formal granting of a mandate, in the form of a decision by the Economic and Social Council (ECOSOC) Resolution 1484 (XLVIII) in 1970: the Conference was to be held in 1974, was to be at the governmental level, and was to "consider basic demographic problems, their relationship with economic and social development, and population policies and action programmes needed to promote human welfare and development".[23] But this decision was but the culmination of a series of discussions: it reflected an agreement which had emerged gradually through 1968 and 1969, and at no point could it be said that "*there* it was agreed to go ahead".

In the United Nations system the proposal to hold a conference may be first identified at the Fourteenth Session of the Population Commission in 1968: this is an organ of the Economic and Social Council, and is made up of the representatives of states.[24] In the discussion of the Commission, the main pressure towards holding a conference on population seems to have come in particular from the United States, and "to a lesser extent from a small group of Western European and Asian nations".[25] (The coalition of support for the 1984 conference was quite different: it was dominated by UNFPA and a group of developing countries.) However, the Population Commission's Fourteenth Session merely requested that the Secretary-General should "re-evaluate the purposes and functions" of such a conference and "submit proposals for the consideration of the Population Commission at its 15th session", "taking account of the UN's work programme and of the programme of the IUSSP".[26] The Secretary-General then established the 1969 Group of Experts to advise him and it was this group which in effect confirmed that there would be a conference. But it achieved this goal by simply assuming that it would take place, rather than proposing explicitly that it should happen, and by concentrating instead upon its character and timing. The Fifteenth Session of the Population Commission, to which the Secretary-General addressed the Group's recommendations, acted as if a conference had been proposed, and in turn in November 1969 recommended to a full Council that a Third World Population Conference should be held.[27] The deliberations of the 1969 Group are, therefore, of key importance in the events leading to the 1974 conference.

The Group was made up of senior population academics and administrators. They were Jean Bourgeois-Pichat, Head of the National Institute of Demographic Studies in Paris, General William Draper, Chairman of the United States Population Crisis Committee (and described as one of the founding fathers of the population movement),[28] Simon Ominde, Professor of Geography, University College, Nairobi, Peter

Podyachikh, Director of the USSR Department of Censuses, and Asok Mitra, who was then Secretary, Tourism and Civil Aviation Department, New Delhi, but also one of India's most distinguished demographers. Their discussions determined the character, scale and timing of the conference. "The Third World Population conference should have a purpose which would go beyond those of earlier conferences."[29] A meeting of government representatives rather than of experts was favoured and it was proposed that the year of the conference should be designated "World Population Year" to "focus world opinion".[30] Notice that the year was designated because of the conference, not vice versa! (The General Assembly confirmed this proposal in 1970.) There was to be adequate provision for press and mass information media.[31] It was clear, then, that the Group intended that the conference would be so arranged as to have a maximum of political impact, combining politicians and publicity.

This potent mixture was given additional fizz in October 1973 when it was decided to hold a Population Tribune of nongovernmental organizations alongside the conference[32] and later it was decided to precede the conference with an international youth population conference "which cost governments and the UNFPA $300,000".[33] The question was considered of whether a series of regional conferences could not be held as an alternative, but

it was emphasized that the world population problem is unique and that it involves all nations of the world regardless of their respective levels of economic and social advancement. As such, the problem should be discussed at the world level, irrespective of regional and institutional grouping . . . World and regional population meetings were not mutually exclusive.[34]

Two features of the conference were, therefore, now decided; it was to be "political" and it was to be "global".

The 1969 Group also commented upon the timing of the conference. It noted that the General Assembly had ruled that there should be no more than one major special conference a year and that 1971 had already been taken with an international conference on atomic energy, and 1972 by an international conference on the human environment.[35] The argument was also used that the results of the UN's 1970 round of population censuses should be available to the conference and this requirement indicated a date in 1973 or 1974. The various conferences should also be slotted into the programme of preparations and time was necessary to complete the necessary arrangements. In the light of this advice the decision was taken by ECOSOC in Resolution 1484 (XLVIII) to convene the meeting from 19–30 August 1974.

In the event, of course, 1974 became crowded with world conferences, especially the Sixth Special Session of the General Assembly held earlier in the year. This was to be of considerable significance for the World Population Conference. The Group was not able to come to a firm conclusion about the location of the conference, though it inclined towards the United Nations headquarters in New York as existing facilities there could readily cope with a conference of this size and political significance. Indeed, the offer by the Romanian government to house the conference in Bucharest was not made until the autumn of 1973: the agreement between the United Nations and Romania was signed on 18 October 1973.[36] The Group's recommendations about the timing and character of the conference were, however, decisive.

The political character of the conference was considerably enhanced by a resolution of the ECOSOC in June 1972 consciously to adopt an activist role, a development which was very much in keeping with the inclinations of the Population Community. It was decided to place on the agenda of the World Population Conference "Draft World Population Plan of Action",[37] and the Secretary-General, with the support of an Advisory Committee, was to be responsible for formulating the Plan. The first draft of this was presented to the Seventeenth Session of the Population Commission in November 1973, and it was to become the main focus of discussion during the conference itself.

It was in keeping with the "special character of the conference" that a Secretary-General was appointed from outside the United Nations system as head of the Conference Secretariat. He was Antonio Carillo-Flores, a Mexican Professor of Law, author and administrator, who was appointed by the Secretary-General, Kurt Waldheim, in September 1972.[38] A Conference Secretariat was then appointed under his charge, and the additional cost of this was estimated at $392,000.[39] The contribution of the Preparatory Committee, which was to advise the UN Secretary-General about formulating an agenda and making the necessary arrangements for the conference, will be discussed later. It met in 1971 and was appointed in accordance with ECOSOC Resolution 1484 (XLVIII). The Population Commission exercised general supervisory responsibility for the preparations for the conference: the Secretary-General reported to it.

The evidence suggests, therefore, that the World Population Conference of 1974 was a product of an interaction between three variables. First was the development of thinking about population problems, and the strengthening of the population community. By the late 1960s, knowledge appears to have reached the point at which there was increasing pressure among specialists to accelerate the process of "operationalizing" population policy. More could be done, and there was a certain impatience about translating thought, and intentions into action. Second, there had been crucial changes in thinking among governments and other relevant elites about the acceptability of population policy. The fierce moral objections which had been decisive in the early 1950s could no longer prevail by the late 1960s, and this opened the door to those who were inclined to act. It is striking, though, that the conference was held, and arguably could only have been held, after significant movement in thinking both about the practicality of population policies – it could be done – and about its acceptability – it should be done. The conference, therefore, did not open the door, but acted rather as an accelerator for the moving vehicle.

The third variable was that population policy had no uncontested institutional home in the late 1960s into the mid-1970s. Indeed, once it became acceptable, and more active, the cause was the object of dispute between the institutions. Such quarrelsome behaviour is, of course, a frequent occurrence in relations between the various agencies in the United Nations system. The WHO greatly resented the expanded, though still modest, role of the UNFPA in the area, and struggled to establish itself as the lead organization with regard to population. One illustration of this was a wrangle between WHO on the one side, and UNFPA and the World Bank on the other about a plan for population activities in Indonesia which originated in 1969.[40] In the years leading up to the 1974 Conference, therefore, population policy was a contested area. It was also held just prior to the passing of Resolution 32/197 by the General Assembly in 1977, which held that special conferences should be regarded as exceptional, and that they should be brought into the routine arrangements of the Economic and Social Council.[41] The Population Conference was, therefore, special in that it was outside the routine arrangements of the United Nations system, partly because it had no institutional home, and, indeed, related to territory disputed between the Agencies, and partly because such arrangements had not yet been discouraged.

The 1974 World Population Conference was, therefore, a product of a critical interaction between three kinds of development: in policy, in attitudes towards action, and the institutional arrangements. In the first two the stage had been reached at which the urge to practical achievement in the specific area of Population Policy had been greatly enhanced. The conference was the consequence of the realization that having moved this far, a determined push in particular with regard to the politicization of the issue, could produce major results. But, as the institutional setting of this effort was contested, the conference had to be "special". In any case, its special character also helped politicize the issue, though the implications of this for action need to be further considered. This will be attempted in the next section.

As already indicated the main focus of discussion at Bucharest was the draft World Population Plan of Action. The striking feature of this was that the draft proved to be highly contentious, much to the surprise of those involved in its preparation, and the conference was a forum of fierce exchange between its proponents and its critics. Indeed on 27 August the conference newspaper reported that "there were fears last night that the slow progress of formal negotiation would defeat the effort to reach agreement on the 93 paragraphs of text".[42] Over 300 amendments had been put forward by dissenting states, compared with 35 in Mexico in 1984. It was with general relief that the amended plan was eventually approved on 30 August 1974.

Three sets of questions are suggested by this development. First what was proposed in the Plan, and why were those who formulated it unaware before the conference of the criticism it would attract? These issues are of considerable interest to students of international organization, because it is often assumed that the development of collegiality among specialists favours agreement: in this instance, however, the college appears to have become "enclosed".[43] Second, what was the response of the dissenting states in their actions in the conference, and in their arguments? The latter were much influenced by the perspective of the New International Economic Order (NIEO), which had been propounded only a few months earlier at the General Assembly's Sixth Special Session, but, as will be shown, this was not the only source of their reaction. Third, what was the resulting impact upon the plan which was eventually agreed? In the following – third – section of this chapter the practical achievement will be assessed in broad terms, and this includes the Mexico Conference of 1984, and the impact of the two conferences upon institutions, and procedures, will be evaluated.

The Plan was a substantial document of four major sections and 109 paragraphs reproduced in 18 standard journal pages.[44] It contained background materials and a range of problems considered to be of relevance to population issues and was not narrowly concerned with fertility control: for example, the integration of Population Policy into Development Policy; current rates of growth; inequities in development; mortality rates and their reduction; the problems of fertility control; individual reproduction and social needs and aspirations; growth and control of urbanization; the revitalization of rural areas; and issues in international migration. The links between population control and other issues such as development and resources, migration and urbanization, were recognized, although there was a tendency to see these as being conditional upon success with population control, rather than as distinctive goals of equal importance. A number of population specialists have, however, been led to argue that the Draft Plan focused upon "population variables", recommended direct action in fertility, and was specialist rather than political, whereas the plan's critics "contaminated" the purity of the interest of the population specialists by introducing spurious political considerations.

The significance of Bucharest is thus to be found in the new politicization of population – not within the terms of the classical debates between Marx and Malthus, but in the contemporary context of the struggle over the distribution of resources and power between the industrial nations and the developing nations of the Third World.[45]

This judgement misses the points that the Draft Plan, for all its apolitical pretensions, was indeed highly political in a number of respects, and that the developing world's political reaction was by no means solely based on the claims for a New International Economic Order.

There is indeed some merit in the view of Alfred Sauvy expressed on the eve of the conference, that ". . . at Bucharest, a World Population Plan of Action will be proposed that will take aim, whatever may be said to disguise it, at the Sovereignty of Nations."[46] He went too far, perhaps, in suggesting that the whole thing was a plot invented by the Americans and the Swedes,[47] but the plan showed evidence of a managerial attitude: for all its assertions about the importance of sovereignty it sought to fit national responses into a global pattern, and to lay down constraints upon national actors in population questions, for instance, with regard to numbers and timing (Section C was the activist element: it contained 50 recommendations for action). In other words the plan could be reasonably interpreted as carrying the threat, in the eyes of new states, that a supranational approach to their population development could evolve unless it was effectively opposed: their reaction could be described as a "statist" response to the supranational ambitions of the international population community. But it was also not neutral politically in the sense that at several points it implied implicitly or explicitly a preference for Western values and institutions. This impression was reinforced by the fact that the United States and the Western states had indeed been the leading champions of the cause and by their apparent lack of sensitivity to the susceptibilities of the new states both in the Draft Plan and at points during its preparation. The planners invited a political reaction from the client states precisely because it revealed a holistic awareness. That is, population was related to a wide range of economic and social issues. It did not concentrate upon fertility. This, as Tarbah asserted, reflected a growing maturity in the subject. But in stressing the economic, social and political context it conceded the point that population control was also essentially political and legitimized a hostile response on other, equally valid, political grounds.

It is not suggested, of course, that there was any attempt to force the developing states to adopt more effective population policies. Such an approach would have been entirely impracticable. There was, however, a "programmatic emphasis"; the procedure resembled that upon which the Americans had insisted to administer Marshall Aid in Western Europe from 1948 to 1952 – a coordinated overall plan, rather than individual "state" arrangements, with states specifying "quantitative-targets" and formulating and implementing "policies for achieving them" as part of the process for determining the overall plan (paragraph 16, section c). The West European states accepted, of course, these American conditions in the immediate post-Second World War period: one reason for this may be that they lacked the sensitivity of so many of the new states about their independence. To assist in the drawing up of the state programmes, states had been previously asked to submit country statements, and required, in a somewhat headmasterly fashion, to provide a 500-word summary,[48] and to decide upon targets. The targets which were agreed would be used in the review and appraisal of this plan. (There was to be a major review every five years.) States were expected to commit themselves to specified achievements by the indicated dates: for instance, "All persons who so desire . . . but not later than 1985" should be provided with the "necessary information and education about family planning and the means to practice".[49] "Countries which have a very high birth rate may consider taking action . . . to reduce these rates by about 5 to 10 per 1000 before 1985."[50] Where population was thought to be insufficient the desired increase should be through "a reduction of mortality" and "encouraging immigration",[51] that is, not by fertility increase (in the agreed plan increasing population by slackening fertility control was permitted). It was advisable that a suitable international body lend its offices "to protect the rights of international migrants".[52] This selection of recommendations from the Draft Plan can only give a general indication of its style. Nevertheless, the judgement that it was managerial seems to be justified, as can a developing country's fear that such specific plans for action could at some future date be backed by richer Western states with economic or indeed political pressures; the proximity of the Sixth Special Session increased the likelihood that such fears would arise.

The developing states' reaction, therefore, was to insist upon not committing themselves to specific targets, reserving their separate right to determine population policies in their own territory. The plan that was agreed, the World Population Plan of Action (WPPA), was judged by population specialists as "not really a plan of action"; "the implications of the Plan for implementation, particularly by the international community, require subsequent interpretation against institutional and organizational objectives".

The international community has tended to work on the direct approach, the Plan tends to recommend the indirect; the international community has emphasized family planning as a demographic instrument, the Plan accepts it for reasons of health and human rights, but de-emphasizes it in general; the international community has focused on fertility, the Plan focuses on social change, equity, on migration, and on mortality (this last, incidentally, containing the only quantitative and dated target in the Plan, except, perhaps, for census-taking); and so on.[53]

A detailed account of the changes in the agreed Plan from the draft is not necessary here. Their flavour may be gauged, however, by one example: "Setting quantitative targets and implementing policies for achieving them" (draft, para. 16) was replaced with "states are invited to consider adopting population policies within the framework of socio-economic development" (final, para. 17). Clearly the developing countries were determined to dampen the population community's urge to action.

Their resistance cannot but have been reinforced by evidence of paternalism and an apparent, but probably unconscious, promotion of Western values and arrangements. (No awareness of this has been shown in any of the specialist "population" sources consulted by the present writer for this chapter.) The Preparatory Committee was a little insensitive when it concluded in 1971 that the

World Population Conference would provide a forum in which the developing countries could exchange experience in regard to population problems . . . but that it was desirable to have European experience . . . in order to obtain a complete review . . . and to promote knowledge, policies and action programmes.[54]

That is, the Europeans would point the way and hold the torch! Comparison of the Draft Plan and the final version also reveals political preferences and the developing countries response (Draft Plan first).[55] Clause 37 (d(c)) contained an injunction to "reduce . . . polygamous practices": this was omitted. Clause 25 (c) favoured "small family size norms". Clause 27(c) does not recommend *any* world family size norm. Clause 29(c) held that affecting fertility . . . "may imply major social, institutional and structural reforms"; in the corresponding Clause 31 (c) is a sharp rejoinder, which ignores the Draft, but states that "international co-operation is called for to give priority to assisting *national* efforts". An amusing and instructive, alteration was imposed on Clause 75 which required that there would be "co-operation with . . . labour unions, co-operatives, and other similar institutions and programmes . . . in the role which they as individuals can assume in resolving population problems"; the rejoinder was Clause 89 which far from involving cooperation between institutions within the state (as perhaps in a pluralist society?), held that work should be "through the assistance of *governmental* agencies"! The developing countries seemed to be resisting what they interpreted (rightly) as efforts to use population policy as an instrument for their social and political reform as judged from a Western standpoint.

The conclusion is hard to avoid that the Bucharest Conference was the scene of a collision between, on the one hand, an activist and managerial approach towards population policy, which suggested a preference for a coordinated programme at the international level, which tended towards supranationalism, and which reflected Western values; and, on the other hand, a "statist" view, seeking to keep the hands of national governments relatively untrammelled in pursuing population policies, and, indeed, seeing the population area as one in which national autonomy could be further developed, and preferring the approach of the harmonization of individual national actions. In the first approach, the key words are coordination, tending to supranationalism; in the second, harmonization tending to autonomous national action. The attempts by the developing world to promote the goals of the new international economic order at Bucharest were, therefore, only in part a continuation of the offensive mounted at the Sixth Special Session, intended to wrest economic concessions from the richer, mainly Western states. They were also part of a defensive strategy: to argue that the important question was to achieve economic development, rather than directly controlling population, and that this would in itself control population ("a scholarly interpretation of the factors underlying the demographic transition (in the West)" . . . "transformed into an ideological statement"),[56] was also an obvious and convenient way of saying that they would do it their way. On the other hand, to concede that population policy was an independent variable could have been to further strengthen the hand of the managerial incrementalists, such as the Americans, and weaken that of the statists.

The arguments of the majority of developing states at Bucharest were, however, couched in the terms of the new international economic order. There were within this group two rather different kinds of stress.[57] One group of states, which included those from Sub-Saharan Africa, Algeria, Argentina, China, Albania, Romania, Cuba and Peru, asserted that population problems were essentially symptoms of other difficulties, and that direct control of fertility was unnecessary. Indeed, it was if anything a diversion from the key issue of achieving economic development which would itself produce a natural decline. The "Malthusian" arguments were now being used as part of a "rich man's plot" to evade economic change and in some instances to deprive developing states of people who could help with the more important goal. A second group, which included India, Egypt, Mexico, Yugoslavia and some Latin American and African states, accepted that population problems could hinder economic development, but insisted that fertility control was only one component of a programme for developing a new international economic order. The former could only be effective if the latter were conceded, and could not be given priority. The key committee of the conference was the Working Group on the World Population Plan of Action and the more radical group among the redistributionist states scored a major tactical victory when M. Oubouzar from Algeria was elected its Chairman in the face of Western opposition. It was reported that the population activists were consistently outmanoeuvred: the Secretariat, represented by the officials from the Population Division under Leon Tarbah, was deliberately bypassed by Oubouzar, and the United States as leading activist was "curiously ineffective and isolated".[58] Indeed, the states which had led the new International Economic Order Movement, and which had dominated the Sixth Special Session, also emerged as controllers of the population conference.

Clearly those who had formulated the draft World Population Plan of Action had failed to anticipate the political problems which it would encounter. The scale of the preparations, and the number of people consulted and involved, make the omission of the political dimension especially peculiar. Part of the explanation must be that the agency which took over major responsibility for the draft, the population division of the Secretariat, was itself isolated from other parts of the Secretariat which could have provided stronger political inputs. The specialist isolation was also observable, however, in the work of the Population Division, and even in the regional conferences, which preceded Bucharest. There participants tended not to be senior government representatives; they were lower level officials, and, therefore, were more narrowly concerned with technical questions. In other words the problems were caused in part by that same narrow sectoralism which had been identified as a more widespread problem in the United Nations system by Maurice Bertrand in the 1985 Report of the Joint Inspection Unit.[59] It was not challenged in the stage of preparation, even by those governments and other international actors, which were actively involved. Even the Inter-Agency Committee, set up by the US State Department, to prepare the US position, which met over a period of more than a year, failed to anticipate the anti-sectoralist reactions. One possible reason for this, suggested by Finkle and Crane, is that the specialization of labour within the administration of modernized states, including that concerned with foreign policy, increases the difficulties in the way of formulating "overall" or "holistic" approaches, and similarly in anticipating such reactions in others. The US stress upon the need for the separate treatment of issues during the conference, and its resistance to the "overall" resolutions introduced by the redistributionist states were also a consequence of the way its own administration was organized.[60]

On the one hand was a tendency towards the insulation of population specialists from political circumstances; on the other was the detachment of the political context from the specialist discussions. Leon Tarbah believed that the redistributionists had deliberately held fire until the conference was underway.[61] The conference Secretary-General, Carillo-Flores, failed to have any discussions with the two leading "wreckers" at Bucharest, Algeria and Argentina, and the Chinese had not attended any of the regional conferences.[62] At the conference the Chinese declared that the World Population Plan of Action was a plan by the superpowers for "economic plunder and political blackmail".[63] Certainly at the various regional conferences there were few signs of trouble, and the argument that some delegates were instructed not to muddy the waters, or were chosen in the expectation that they would not do so, is plausible. There were redistributionist governments, it may be supposed, which were anxious not to disabuse the population community of their fond belief that the population issue, and the conference, would be handled the same way that the environmental issue and conference had been handled two years earlier. The prepared plan had been given a very smooth passage through the conference. They wished to maximize the political advantages to themselves of a conference which the sectoralists were working to make as effective a political instrument as possible.

Several ironic aspects to the interplay between politics and specialist interests at Bucharest are, therefore, revealed. Had the specialists known about the others' intentions they would have taken care to control more carefully those institutional arrangements which could have allowed a greater degree of politicization. Had the redistributionists been faced beforehand with the prospect of such constraints being placed upon their politicization of issues, they would probably have made a much more limited investment in it of time and resources. Had there been "perfect information" it is difficult to know what kind of conference Bucharest would have been: but it would certainly have been less political. Another irony is that the failures of the preparatory process – its insulation from a number of relevant, wider political concerns – were themselves indicative of a need for the political content of population policy to be acknowledged. The conference was in the event a useful forum in which the implicit political preferences of the activists could be revealed, and confronted with the alternative political values of the redistributionist states. Such a confrontation was necessary, as it produced an ideological stand-off behind which practical population policies, stripped to their ideological minimum, could be formulated. Bucharest was an occasion on which a particular kind of activism was frustrated, and the redistributionist states used their particular form of holism as a shield behind which to begin pursuing practical unilateral sectoralism. The conference in this way stimulated the pursuit subsequently of increasingly active population policies by the separate states. Yet another irony, therefore, was that the frustration of the activists on this occasion may have been the key to increased activity.

This view was strongly supported by the fact that the vast majority of states at Bucharest wanted a form of the World Population Plan of Action: it was not regarded as dispensable in the search for modest gains in the pursuit of the new international economic order. As Finkle and Crane point out "conciliation was the 'residual position' of almost all participants".[64] The effect of the redistributionists efforts was to weaken the Draft's operational stress, to remove policy priorities and strategies, and to be noncommittal about the relationship of population policy to other issues, such as development and human rights (policy linkage!). Once this effect had been achieved, however, there was in the last few days of the conference a rush to achieve agreements, in which Sweden, Mexico and Egypt played a leading part. The very blandness of the plan permitted the "residual positions" to be brought forward. The West accepted it as the best that could be obtained; the East European states, led by Romania, eventually supported it as a sign of the success of a conference held on their territory; and the redistributionists supported it as a mechanism which promised Western financial support for population policies which could now be adjusted to their various separate interests.

In this, the third section of this chapter, the achievements of the 1974 World Population Conference are assessed, and the additional contributions of the 1984 Conference in Mexico City are evaluated. It is impossible to prove that either conference directly caused an extension of national efforts, though the range of these were certainly greatly extended after 1974. It seems safe to infer, however, that the conferences at least provided a stimulus to the more active pursuit of such policies. They helped to change attitudes, and encouraged institutional change. Developments at the Mexico Conference are themselves, indeed, an indication of the extent to which attitudes had changed since 1974.

One of the major background papers to the international conference in 1984, the Review and Appraisal of the World Population Plan of Action, prepared by the Secretary-General, described the trends as "highly encouraging", although it stressed the need for continued effort as "the momentum of population growth remains an extremely powerful force".[65] Despite a small decline in financial support from international agencies in the 1980s,[66] which was confirmed in an OECD Report, "most notable has been the tendency of developing countries to commit increasing shares of their own resources", "an average $US2 for every $1 from international sources" and "$US4.6 for every $US1 from UNFPA for UNFPA projects".[67] This tends to confirm that states had at least been stimulated to pursue more energetically their national efforts by the 1974 conference. Encouragement was also found in the slowing down of the rate of population increase, and, although it was expected that population levels would continue to rise, projections suggested that there would be a "levelling off" near the middle of the twenty-first century: an estimate for global population then, which assumed a general life expectancy of 78.7 years, and fertility levels at about replacement level, was 10.5 billion. A high "variant", however, was 14 billion, and a low variant was 7.7 billion.[68] According to the *Review and Appraisal*, however, the actual rate of increase until 1984 corresponded to the low variant of increase estimated in 1974, at 1.7% per annum.[69] By 1992 it had been concluded that there "had been an increase in the use of contraception in developing countries from 40% in 1980 to 49% in 1990", and that population growth had declined to 1.7% per annum from 2.1% in 1980. According to a World Bank base case projection, population growth would decline to around 1% per annum by 2030.[70] If this rate of increase persisted the population of the globe would reach 12.5 billion by the middle of the twenty-second century. This rate of increase was of course still dangerously high: but it was much lower than in the early eighties, and some of this change must be attributed to the efforts of the international community.

This was not to dispute that the population situation in some areas, especially Africa, was disastrous, and that the predicted total number was uncomfortably high. But on the whole the optimistic general picture was reflected in a fairly even spread of favourable developments; indeed, Africa was the only region where the rate of increase has risen between the early 1970s and the early 1980s, (from 2.7% in 1970–75, to 3% in 1980–85), and this was "very largely due to a slow but continuing decline of mortality rates". The most significant decline was in Asia (from 2.4% to 1.7%), but even in Catholic Latin America, the trend was downwards (from 2.5% to 2.3%). There had been an increase in the rate in 58 countries, a decline in 49, and no change in 16, but the declining countries had 73% of the global population.[71] The views of governments, it was reported, had also shifted markedly: there had been a decline in the proportion of countries where the growth rate was explicitly seen as too low. Ten per cent thought this way, compared with 20% ten years earlier.[72] By 1984 around three-quarters of all developing countries had set up "units dealing with population aspects" related to the development process, and more than half of these had been established in the 1980s.[73] The value of dealing explicitly with population policy seems generally to have been acknowledged, a truly remarkable shift of opinion since the 1952 debate in the WHO. Changes since 1974 in the People's Republic of China, as the world's most populous state, were particularly striking: in 1982 population control was referred to explicitly in the new constitution. By the mid-1980s, therefore, both the general pattern and the country and regional variants showed favourable trends: the evidence seemed to justify the view that the promotion of population policies had been worthwhile, and that further efforts were both necessary and could produce results. Although their precise impact was difficult to assess, the judgement that the two population conferences made some contribution to these trends seems justified.

The Mexico Conference was itself in various respects an indication of what might be called the *routinization* of population policy. One measure of this was the reaction of the conference to the astonishing performance there by the United States delegation, which was yet another illustration of the way in which responsible United States foreign policy may be sacrificed on the altar of electoral expediency. It will be recalled that the United States authorities had a long tradition of supporting more active and responsible population policies, had provided significant support for intergovernmental and nongovernmental international agencies involved in this area, and had been a leading advocate at the Bucharest conference. Unfortunately, however, the Mexico Conference was timed to take place a few months before the American Presidential election, and in essence the role of the established United States population community, centred on the State Department under the eminent David Benedick, was hijacked by a right-wing coalition intent upon using Mexico to confirm the President as leader of the moral majority.[74] The delegation was placed under James Buckley, who had worked for the "right-to-life" movement in the United States, and planning of the delegation's strategy and mandate was moved to the White House. David Benedick was excluded from the delegation and shortly afterwards he resigned.

The most remarkable aspect of the American position at the 1984 Conference was that it was a mirror image of that of the more radical of the redistributionists at Bucharest. The influence of the Heritage Foundation, as reflected, for instance, in its tract headed "Africa is Starving and the United Nations Shares the Blame",[75] was easy to detect. Population problems were seen as essentially a result of underdevelopment, and too much government intervention was to blame for that. "There is no global population crisis that requires drastic forms of intervention by government."[76] These views were strengthened with an admixture of "right-to-lifeism". It was asserted that the United States would not extend population assistance to or through any international organization that supported abortion, although the United States eventually agreed at Mexico to a resolution which recommended only that abortion should "in no case be promoted as a method of family planning".[77] Earlier the United States had withdrawn financial support from, *inter alia*, the highly respectable International Planned Parenthood Federation – through its Agency for International Development – and the UNFPA was required to say that it did not approve of abortion. It was not, however, that any serious objection could be made to attempts to encourage a responsible attitude towards abortion, but rather that there was the unpleasant sense that the issue was being exploited by the Americans for their own internal political purposes. They had gone to Mexico to make political capital rather than to encourage responsible population policies. It was also pointed out that the United States delegation made no reference to the rights and interests of women in America or elsewhere – another illustration of this kind of conservative persuasion. Many independent American population specialists at the conference disagreed strongly in public with the official delegation's general stance on abortion, and other matters, but naturally the latter achieved their intended publicity.

The response to the United States position at the conference was itself indicative of the routinization of population policy. Unlike 1974, the general response to the United States ideological out-pouring was to concentrate upon what had emerged as the major technical and operational issues. There was a low key consensus, which included the older redistributionists and the West Europeans, that the Bucharest World Population Plan of Action was to be accepted and built upon; indeed that had been the position of the respectable United States population community and of the State Department. If anything, the extreme US position at the Conference reinforced the propensity of the others to agree. Only about 24 governments this time proposed amendments, and the draft set of recommendations for strengthening the WPPA was overwhelmingly approved.[78] It was the official US delegation which made the biggest waves during the conference; in addition to their stand on abortion, they also insisted upon putting their

opposition to Recommendation 36, which opposed settlement in unoc-
cupied territories – without mentioning Israel – to a vote.[79] Only Israel
supported the US in this. They also deleted Recommendation 5 which
"supported disarmament". Even the West Europeans were disappointed that
the United States had not adopted the usual practice of entering a formal
reservation about these issues rather than insisting upon a formal vote.
Although it was obviously sensible to encourage international organizations
in general to avoid introducing extraneous political issues into technical
discussions, in Mexico the Americans seemed to be trying to create a drama
out of the issue for domestic purposes, rather than in order to achieve practical improvement.

The general view was that the Americans had to be humoured and gently
encouraged to support the consensus position at the end. This effort was
largely successful. Amendments to the World Population Plan of Action were
insignificant and its character as determined at Bucharest was unaltered. It
was felt that the population issue had, however, been given "heightened
visibility"; the consensus was extended, and the World Population Plan of
Action was seen to have become a "document of enduring value",[80] and the
population community was given a stronger mandate. Having achieved the
desired publicity the United States delegation joined with the others in
approving by acclaim (the Holy See dissociating itself) the agreed recommendation for the further implementation of the World Population Plan of
Action, and a Declaration on Population and Development, drafted by a
group of 29, on 14 August 1984. The Americans had to face the fact that
for the overwhelming majority of states population policy had become a
relatively non-contentious issue by 1984. It had been routinized.

The Mexico Conference affected a number of developments in addition
to routinization. The coalition which had pushed for it was markedly
different from that which had promoted Bucharest: it included officials of
the United Nations, particularly the UNFPA, and the Population Division,
together with the Third World countries. The "political circus" aspects of
Bucharest were curtailed: there were no parallel conferences of nongovernmental organizations or of young people, the attempt was made unsuc-
cessfully to limit delegations to four participants, and the conference was
scheduled for six days only. The Western states were in general on this
occasion rather muted in their support for the conference, and insisted that
its finances should be firmly managed, and that it should take the Bucharest
WPPA as its starting point. Indeed, this time it was the Third World states
which were the enthusiasts, a change reflected in their insistence upon
greatly expanding the role of the UNFPA. It was on their insistence that
Recommendation 83 was approved which held that:

In view of the leading role of the UNFPA in Population Matters, the Conference
urges that the Fund should be strengthened further, so as to ensure the more effective delivery of population assistance, taking into account the growing needs in this
field. The Secretary-General of the United Nations is invited to examine this recommendation, and to submit a report to the General Assembly on its implementation
as soon as possible but not later than 1986.[81]

The conclusion seems justified that the "punters" – those who were to be inveigled into activity – had become the "pushers" – those who were attempting to extend its practice!

The increased status of the UNFPA 1984 compared with ten years earlier, as well as a further element of routinization, was indicated by the appointment of Raphael Salas, the Director of UNFPA, as Secretary-General of the Conference itself. The existing responsible organization earned the major responsibility for the arrangement of the conference, and UNFPA, and Population Division officials, formed its Secretariat. Hence, there was evidence to suggest that the 1984 Conference had become less "special" than its 1974 precursor in that it had been attached more closely to the existing organizational structures of the United Nations.

This development was in part a consequence of adjustments in the institutional arrangements for dealing with population policies in the United Nations system, in particular the emergence of UNFPA since the 1970s. The two conferences certainly helped very considerably to expand that organization: on both occasions it was recommended formally that it should be expanded, and through the 1970s its level of finance increased faster than that of any other of the Funds and Programmes, with the exception of UNICEF. Contributions to it had grown from $42.6 million in 1973 to $132.4 million in 1980, compared with $71.3 million in 1973 and $278.7 million in 1980 for UNICEF, and $331.7 million and $705.2 million for the United Nations Development Programme.[82] Its level of finance in the 1980s – up to 1986 – did not increase, but it fared no worse in this respect than UNICEF or UNDP. The UNFPA clearly emerged as the United Nations lead organization for population policy during the 1970s and its Director, Raphael Salas, established a distinguished reputation for himself. He explained that "the main purposes of the UNFPA are [inter alia]: to help coordinate population programmes among various elements of the UN system . . . and to extend the capabilities of the relevant agencies", but "if a project . . . does not duplicate programmes being undertaken by the United Nations agencies . . . the fund would be willing to consider such a project for funding". The fund serves as the link between the policy-making bodies of the United Nations and the actual programme implementation within a single country. And that is, of course, what the fund is all about.[83]

The question naturally arises of why the client states had so strongly supported UNFPA, when they so firmly resisted the "activists" at Bucharest. Part of the answer lies in the character of Salas himself, who seems to be unusual amongst the heads of United Nations organizations in that he professes to have a vision of redundancy. In the third phase of population policy he aims to "phase out assistance or foreign experts as appropriate bodies at the country level are progressively taking over".[84] States are to be helped to dispense with UNFPA: but in the meantime country plans are explicitly stressed and national initiatives encouraged. "Considerable autonomy is to be allowed to national field staff" and they may choose an external organization outside the UN system, if the country wishes, as partners (as executing agency) . . . later more non-governmental agencies and governments themselves become the executing agency. This trend is encouraged by a move from small-scale to country programmes.[85]

Salas seemed to have succeeded in conveying the impression that UNFPA was essentially on the side of national governments, and was there to make itself dispensable. It fits in well with the "statist" approach, unlike so many of the Specialized Agencies which, intentionally or not, too often seem like mercenary armies in fifteenth-century Italy: once invited in they are hard to persuade to leave.

Indeed, UNFPA succeeded in asserting itself as the lead organization for population policies at the expense of a number of Specialized Agencies, particularly the World Health Organization. The eclipse of the agencies in this field is illustrated by the preparatory arrangements for the two conferences. The 1974 Preparatory Committee was established by the Secretary-General "in association with the executive heads of the specialized agencies concerned and nongovernmental organizations to assist in formulating the agenda and . . . necessary arrangements".[86] In 1984, however, the Preparatory Committee was made up of states' representatives in the Population Commission.[87] The ACC's contribution was an *ad hoc* task force intended to deal with the "substantive contributions of the regional commissions, the Specialized Agencies, and the other bodies of the UN system, to the monitoring of population trends and policies in this review and appraisal exercise".[88] The impression conveyed is that this was a somewhat wan effort to keep a foot in the door. On the one hand, therefore, the UNFPA's role was greatly expanded. The two conferences contributed significantly to this, and the Secretary-General's *Report* on its further expansion of 1986 recommended a further expansion of its role. On the other hand, the claims of the Specialized Agencies, particularly the WHO, to be the lead agency for population questions had been rebuffed. Institutional adjustment had taken place and the conferences contributed greatly to this.

The global population conferences both symbolized and promoted changes in attitudes towards active population policy. The underlying developments are relatively uncontentious: countries became generally more active in the area, and accepted that population control should not simply be left to be overtaken by the development process. It may be, of course, that a retreat from the more radical claims for a New International Economic Order between 1974 and the mid-1980s contributed to this, but it is hard to resist the conclusion that the Bucharest Conference pushed these changes along. But it is also clear that initially the approach of the population community was at variance with the "statist" inclinations of so many of the relatively new or recently constituted states: the Bucharest Conference had the curious consequence that it facilitated the general acceptance of the policy while rejecting a particular version of its presentation.

Population control is a global problem but it is striking that this has not meant that it has led to a supranational approach. There is a realization of global implications, but this has not been allowed to swamp state sovereignty. Indeed the evidence seems to suggest that cooperation, even with regard to such pressing, global problems as this, follows from the development, even strengthening, of the participating units. The problem did not release pressure which constrained the state, but rather created opportunities, at this stage, for its entrenchment. To use the jargon of the study of international organization, there has been harmonization, and some coordination but no supranationalism. There have also, certainly, been institutional adjustments, in that UNFPA has emerged as the lead organization in the area. But the UNFPA is not a specialized agency: its funding depends upon voluntary contributions and its very success has depended upon its omission of any claim to be a part of an international government. Indeed precisely the opposite is the case: it has self-consciously deployed itself on the side of state-building.

In this phase of international society, therefore, the collective good appears to be best served by a sharpening of the realization of self-interest. The two global conferences on population, but especially the one held in Bucharest in August 1974, have certainly contributed to this. Once more we return to the principle of symbiosis which, as has been argued at various points earlier in this book, is closely linked to the theory of consociation.

Notes

1. See Milos Macura, "The Significance of the United Nations International Population Conferences", in *Population Bulletin of the United Nations*, Nos. 19/20, 1986, New York: UN, 1987, pp. 14–26.
2. Quoted in Joint Inspection Unit, *Secretariat Organization and Procedures for Preparation of United Nations Special Conferences*, prepared by Mark E. Allen et al., JIU/REP/82/2, Geneva (February 1982) p. 2.
3. A/2361/(XII) 19 December 1967.
4. Halvor Gille in Rafael Salas, *International Population Assistance: the First Decade*, Oxford: Pergamon Press, 1979, p. 379.
5. Ibid., p. 379.
6. Jason L. Finkle and Barbara B. Crane, "Ideology and Politics at Mexico City: the United States at the 1984 International Conference on Population", *Population and Development Review*, Vol. 11 (March 1985) No. 1, p. 6.
7. Jason L. Finkle and Barbara B. Crane, "The World Health Organization and the Population Issue: Organizational Values in the United Nations", *Population and Development Review*, Vol. 2 (Sept./Dec. 1976) Nos. 3 and 4, p. 371.
8. United Nations, Economic and Social Council, *Population Commission*, E/CN.9/292/Rev.I/Add.I (7 February 1974) p. 4.
9. United Nations, Economic and Social Council, *Population Commission*, E/CN.9/243 (13 September 1971) p. 5.
10. Ibid., p. 6, para. 12.
11. Ibid., p. 7, para. 14.
12. United Nations, Economic and Social Council Population Commission, *Report of the Consultative Group of Experts on Questions Relating to the Holding of a Third World Population Conference held at Headquarters 14–16 April 1979*, E/CN.9/224/Add.I, 27 August 1969, p. 5, para. 13.
13. Ibid.

14. Reported in *Planet*, Bucharest, 19 August 1974.
15. Reference footnote (12), p. 3, para. 8.
16. Ibid., p. 7, para. 16.
17. Finkle and Crane, 1976, op. cit., p. 375.
18. Ibid., p. 375.
19. Finkle and Crane, 1975, op. cit., pp. 90–1.
20. Ibid., p. 90.
21. United Nations, Economic and Social Council, Population Commission, *Question of Holding a Third World Population Conference: Report of the Secretary-General*, E/CN.9/224 (6 October 1969) p. 2, para. 5.
22. Finkle and Crane, 1975, op. cit., pp. 90–1.
23. United Nations, Economic and Social Council, E.1484 (XLVIII) (June 1970) p. 4.
24. See E/CN.9/224, op. cit., p. 1.
25. Finkle and Crane, 1975, op. cit., p. 87.
26. E/CN.9/224/Add.I, op. cit., p. 2, para. I.
27. E/CN.9/224, op. cit., p. 2, para. 3.
28. *Planet*, Bucharest, 18 August 1974.
29. E/CN.9/224/Add.I, op. cit., p. 6, para. 13.
30. Ibid., p. 11, para. 30.
31. Ibid.
32. Reported in E/CN.9/287/Add.I (9 October 1973) passim.
33. *Planet*, Bucharest, 20 August 1974, p. 1.
34. E/CN.9/224/Add.I, op. cit., p. 4, para. 10.
35. Ibid., p. 5, para. 12.
36. E/CN.9/SR.287–306, p. 9.
37. Economic and Social Council, 1672B (L11) (2 June 1972) p. 2.
38. *Planet*, Bucharest, 18 August 1974, p. 5.
39. For a statement of financial implications of the conference see UN, Economic and Social Council, Population Commission, Fifteenth Session, *Statement of Administrative and Financial Implications . . . by the Secretary General . . .*, E/CN.9/224/Add.2 (3 November 1969) p. 2 for Secretariat expenses.
40. Finkle and Crane, 1976, op. cit., p. 381.
41. See Chapter 1 above.
42. *Planet*, Bucharest, 27 August, p. 1.
43. The following discussion of this issue is developed from the arguments of Finkle and Crane, 1975, op. cit. The author is pleased to acknowledge this debt.
44. Reproduced in full, *Population and Development Review*, Vol. 1 (September 1975) No. 1, pp. 163–82.
45. Finkle and Crane, 1975, op. cit., p. 89.
46. Reported in Paul Demeny, "Bucharest, Mexico City and Beyond", *Population and Development Review*, Vol. 11 (March 1985) No. 1, p. 99.
47. *Planet*, Bucharest, 19 August 1974, p. 6.
48. United Nations, Economic and Social Council, *Preparatory Committee for the World Population Conference 1974: Report of the First Session*, E/Conf.60/PC/1 (4 June 1971) p. 14, para. 32.
49. Draft World Population Plan of Action, Section C, para. 276, reproduced in *Population and Development Review*, Vol. 1 (September 1975) No. 1, pp. 163–82.
50. Ibid., Section C, para. 35.
51. Ibid., Section C, para. 17.
52. Ibid., Section C, para. 53.

53. Bernard Berelson, "The World Population Plan of Action: Where Now?", *Population and Development Review*, Vol. 1 (September 1975) No. 1, p. 143.
54. United Nations, Economic and Social Council, *Preparatory Committee for the World Population Conference 1974: Report of the Second Session*, E/Conf.60/PC/2 (20 August 1971) P. 3, Para. 5.
55. For the draft/final comparisons the author is grateful to Bernard Berelson, 1975, op. cit.; the interpretation here is, however, entirely the responsibility of the present writer.
56. Finkle and Crane, 1975, op. cit., p. 105.
57. See Parker Mauldin, Nazli Choucri, et al., "A Report on Bucharest", *Studies in Family Planning*, Vol. 5 (1975) No. 12 (whole volume).
58. Finkle and Crane, 1975, op. cit., pp. 102–03.
59. Joint Inspection Unit, *Some Reflections on Reform of the United Nations*, prepared by Maurice Bertrand, JIU./REP/85/9, Geneva, 1985.
60. See Finkle and Crane, 1975, op. cit., pp. 103–04.
61. Reported, ibid., p. 97.
62. Ibid., p. 96.
63. *Planet*, Bucharest, 21 August 1974.
64. Finkle and Crane, 1975, op. cit., p. 107.
65. United Nations, International Conference on Population, Mexico City, August, 1984, *Review and Appraisal of the World Population Plan of Action: Report of the Secretary-General*, E/Conf.76/4 (19 June 1984) p. 34, para. 130.
66. See UN, General Assembly, *Operational Actions for Development of the United Nations System*, A/38/258, Table 5, p. 35, which reported a decline of 1.5% 1979–81; and OECD, *1984 Review: Development Cooperation* (Paris: 1984) p. 100, which reported a decline in contributions to UNFPA of 0.5%, 1980–84.
67. E/Conf.76/4, op. cit., p. 132, para. 537.
68. E/Conf.76/4, op. cit., p. 34, para. 128.
69. Ibid., pp. 28–31, para. 117.
70. Data reported in *The Guardian*, 19 May 1992.
71. Ibid., pp. 31–3.
72. Ibid., p. 36, para. 132.
73. Ibid., p. 23, para. 96.
74. See Finkle and Crane, 1985, op. cit., especially pp. 16–20.
75. Written by Roger A. Brooks for *Backgrounder: A United Nations Assessment Project Study*, Washington DC: The Heritage Foundation, 14 January 1986.
76. Finkle and Crane, 1985, op. cit., p. 11.
77. United Nations, *Report of the International Conference on Population, Mexico City 6–14 August 1984*, E/Conf.76/19, 1984, p. 21.
78. Finkle and Crane, 1985, op. cit., p. 8.
79. In the final revised text the US was alone in entering a strongly worded dissenting view: it "strongly protested the inclusion of this issue, believing it politically disuasive and extraneous to the work of the conference". Documents, *The International Conference on Population 1984, Population and Development Review*, Vol. 10 (December 1984) No. 4, p. 771.
80. Paul Demeny, "Bucharest, Mexico City and Beyond", *Population and Development Review*, Vol. 11 (March 1985) No. 1, p. 101.
81. Documents, source cited in fn. 78, p. 780.
82. Figures from Table 5, A/38/258, op. cit., p. 35.
83. Rafael Salas, 1979, op. cit., pp. 149–51.
84. Ibid., p. 155.
85. Ibid., pp. 235–7.

86. E/Conf.60/P.C./I, op. cit., p. 4.
87. United Nations, Economic and Social Council, *Population Questions: Report of the Preparatory Committee for the International Conference on Population, 1984,* E/1984/28 (17 February 1984) p. 18.
88. United Nations, Economic and Social Council, Preparatory Committee . . ., *Preparations for the Conference* . . ., E/Conf.76/PC/5 (25 November 1983) p. 3, para. 6.

9 The role of the United Nations in global security in the early 1990s: how far forwards?*

Introduction[1]

The political climate in which the United Nations Secretary-General Javier Perez De Cuellar presented his Annual Report to the General Assembly in the autumn of 1982 was hardly propitious for the well-being of international peace and security. A bloody war had been fought over the Falkland/Malvinas Islands after Argentina had invaded the islands. The Argentinians were expelled by the British but the victors showed a remarkable inability to respond innovatively in a political manner to their military superiority: the international community, while it supported the British reversal of the Argentine invasion, was critical of British obduracy on the basic issues at stake. Elsewhere in the world an even bloodier war was being fought between Iraq and Iran. In this instance the Iraqi invasion appeared to have the tacit approval of the international community. For it was seen as one way of checking the revolutionary ambitions of the Islamic Republic of Iran.

Not only did Saddam Hussein escape effective sanction, but he received support from many Arab countries and also from Western Powers such as France as well as from the Soviet Union. But that support was not enough to enable him to get the upper hand militarily. The outsiders wished to see neither an Iraqi victory nor an Iranian victory, for, in either case, the long term consequences were feared not only by the Western Powers but also by many states in the region. Intervention was designed to prevent a situation in which either side could win. In neither of these two wars could the role of the United Nations be seen as crucial or glorious despite their obvious relevance for the institution's principal purpose – the promotion of international peace and security.

* The author wishes to thank Chatham House for permission to use the text in this chapter. It is a version of their Discussion Paper No. 38, published in February 1992, and written jointly by the author and A.J.R. Groom. The author also wishes to thank A.J.R. Groom for his kind permission to include in this discussion the parts of the text which he wrote. These are the Introduction to this chapter, and most of the discussion of Resolution 687.

At the global level, while the guns were silent between the North Atlantic Treaty Organization (NATO) and the Warsaw Treaty Organization (WTO), the second Cold War was in full flood. The two superpowers were on opposite sides in many regional conflicts, rhetoric of the "empire of evil" resounded around the debating chambers of the world – whether in the United Nations or in the Helsinki Review Conference in Madrid – and both superpowers demonstrated a proclivity to use their arms, the Soviets in Afghanistan and the US in a comical if tragic invasion of Grenada. To make matters worse, the superpowers were hardly talking to one another. There had been a continuous dialogue about the arms race, and, in particular, nuclear questions from the beginning of negotiations on the Nuclear Test Ban Treaty in the late 1950s until the early 1980s when first one and then the other superpower broke off the dialogue. Moreover, the arms race was continuing apace. The impetus that had been derived from the agreed document and plan of action as well as framework for negotiation, arrived at in the First United Nations General Assembly Special Session on Disarmament in 1978, had completely petered out by the time the Second Special Session was held in 1982.

In all of this the United Nations was on the sidelines and penniless – as it still was in 1992! Its vocation as a forum for pursuing international peace and security was being questioned increasingly and even in an area where it had undoubtedly been the instrument of a major improvement in international peace and security – that of the United Nations peacekeeping operations – it often proved impossible for it to act, as when the United States, France and Italy, joined later by Britain, sent a multinational force to Beirut.

There was, therefore, good reason for the Secretary-General to feel a sense of despair. He had neither the means nor the entrée to achieve the goals that had been thrust upon him. The United Nations framework itself had become dilapidated and in gross need of reform. In short, a great experiment was in danger of failure.

In this context the Secretary-General had nothing to lose by facing facts. The member states of the United Nations, especially those who are given, through the Charter, a prime responsibility for the maintenance of international peace and security, namely the permanent members of the Security Council, needed to accept their responsibilities. The Secretary-General therefore, called upon the Permanent Members either "to put up or shut up". Either the Security Council should be used in such a way as to enable it to play a useful role in the maintenance of international peace and security or the organization would become irrelevant to current world problems. The Secretary-General was candid:

Certainly we have strayed far from the Charter in recent years. Governments that believe they can win an international objective by force are often quite ready to do so, and domestic opinion not infrequently applauds such a course. The Security Council, the primary organ of the United Nations for the maintenance of international peace and security, all too often finds itself unable to take decisive action to resolve international conflicts and its resolutions are increasingly defied or ignored by those that feel themselves strong enough to do so. Too frequently the Council seems powerless to generate the support and influence to ensure that its decisions are respected, even when these are taken unanimously. Thus the process of peaceful settlement of disputes prescribed in the Charter is often brushed aside. Sterner measures for world peace were envisaged in Chapter VII of the Charter, which was conceived as a key element of the United Nations system of collective security, but the prospect of realizing such measures is now deemed almost impossible in our divided international community. We are perilously near to a new international anarchy.

I believe that we are at present embarked on an exceedingly dangerous course, one symptom of which is the crisis in the multilateral approach in international affairs and the concomitant erosion of the authority and status of world and regional intergovernmental institutions. Above all, this trend has adversely affected the United Nations, the instrument that was created specifically to prevent such a self-destructive course. Such a trend must be reversed before once again we bring upon ourselves a global catastrophe and find ourselves without institutions effective enough to prevent it. . .

Unfortunately there has been a tendency to avoid bringing critical problems to the Security Council, or to do so too late for the Council to have any serious influence on their development. It is essential to reverse this trend if the Council is to play its role as the primary world authority for international peace and security. I do not believe that it is necessarily wise or responsible of the Council to leave such matters to the judgement of the conflicting parties to the point where the Council's irrelevance to some ongoing wars becomes a matter of comment by world public opinion. . .

Adequate working relations between the permanent members of the Security Council are a *sine qua non* of the Council's effectiveness. Whatever their relations may be outside the United Nations, within the Council the permanent members, which have special rights and special responsibilities under the Charter, share a sacred trust that should not go by default owing to their bilateral difficulties. When this happens, the Council and therefore the United Nations are the losers, since the system of collective security envisaged by the Charter pre-supposes, at the minimum, a working relationship among the permanent members. I appeal to the members of the Council, especially its permanent members, to reassess their obligations in that regard and to fulfil them at the high level of responsibility indicated in the Charter.[2]

How different was the situation at the beginning of the 1990s in the final months of Mr Perez de Cuellar's tenure. The cold war that was raging in the early 1980s was now over. The face of Europe had changed dramatically, indeed, the changes would have been inconceivable in 1982. Moreover, the beginnings were already evident of a decolonization of the last great multinational empire that fought the First World War. Such changes altered the agenda, but they did not make the question of international peace and security any less acute, whether it be in the welling up of many traditional conflicts in Eastern Europe and the Balkans, or the brutal invasion of Kuwait by the very same Saddam Hussein who had at the beginning of the previous decade invaded Iran. But the context was now different for, although the Charter of Paris of November 1990 was to signify the end of the cold war, the winding down of the military machines on the ground had not yet taken place. Disarmament negotiations in a wide range of fields, both nuclear and conventional were continuing apace and indeed, unilateral disarmament was an increasing feature of the international landscape. But the powerful military machine built by the United States and its allies in the context of the cold war still existed though it was now without a role. Moreover, the five permanent members of the Security Council (P5) had slowly learnt to cooperate with one another, beginning with the Iran–Iraq conflict and continuing with Namibia, Afghanistan and Cambodia. They had developed procedures and above all trust and confidence in each other to begin to fulfil the role of permanent members as conceived by the founding fathers of the United Nations Charter.[3]

Thus the response of the international community through the United Nations to the challenge of Saddam Hussein in August 1990 was altogether different from the response of September 1980. Perhaps Saddam Hussein felt that the situation was not so different. After all, he had long had the tacit support of the Western Powers and of the Soviet Union, he had an arguable case in his differences with Kuwait, and the Kuwaiti regime was not one to elicit any great admiration, anymore than that of a number of other traditional regimes in the region. If the time was not yet ripe he had nevertheless a military machine that could make it right. It was not until his action had met with the almost unanimous disapproval of states, including the Middle Eastern countries, the members of the Non-aligned Movement, and the developed states alike, that he explicitly presented his actions as a bold attempt to seize an initiative which would enable him to put the question of Palestine at the top of the international agenda. But this option may have been in his mind from the beginning as a means of rallying support for the invasion.

In a sense he could throw all his cards in the air and wherever they came down they would be better for the Palestinians. If the name of the game was linkage then subsequent events showed that he succeeded, for the question of Kuwait and the question of Palestine were indeed linked. The Madrid Conference on the Middle East so mightily laboured for by the United States brought Israel to the negotiating table with the Palestinians, but the price for achieving this was horrendous for the people of Iraq and of Kuwait.

Yet the Iraqi annexation of Kuwait breached a fundamental principle that was dear to all states in the United Nations, not only because of its intrinsic worth, but also because if Iraq succeeded, then others might be tempted to follow its example. Moreover, if Iraq succeeded it would be a major independent action by a regional Power against the wishes of the superpowers. Others might likewise feel themselves free to act in a similar manner, and the ability of the superpowers and other world powers to manage the global system of international peace and security would be significantly debilitated.

In short, Saddam Hussein's action threatened small powers and it threatened the superpowers. There can be little surprise therefore that it engendered an overwhelming coalition. While Britain, in similar circumstances, had benefited from overwhelming support in the General Assembly in reversing the Argentine occupation of the Falkland/Malvinas, in the case of Kuwait that support was both military and financial. Significant military forces were provided by the United States, Britain, France, Egypt, Syria, Saudi Arabia and the Gulf states. Token contributions came from many other countries and massive financial support was provided by Germany and Japan. For all its peculiar features the response to the Iraqi invasion was as near a textbook case of collective security as we are likely to find, and it is to that response of the international community that we now turn.

From aggression to war

The invasion and annexation of Kuwait by Iraq on the 2nd of August 1990 was the clearest case of aggression by one state against another since the end of the Second World War, and the response of the United Nations was also in many ways its most immediate and effective. It took only a few hours to adopt Resolution 660 in the Security Council, agreed unanimously – except for the non-participation of Yemen, which condemned the invasion – and only four days later (6 August) mandatory sanctions were imposed by the Council against Iraq, acting under Chapter VII and Article 51 of the Charter, in Resolution 661. These were approved by a vote of 13 in favour, no negative votes, and only two abstentions, Cuba and Yemen. The overwhelming opposition of the international community to the Iraqi proposal to create a "comprehensive and eternal merger" with Kuwait was revealed in the unanimous approval of Resolution 662 on 9 August.

The Security Council approved 14 resolutions in connection with the Gulf war, up to the date of Iraq's surrender on 7 April 1991; a number of further resolutions were approved after the settlement. In addition to those already mentioned were three further resolutions which instigated major developments in the campaign against Iraq. Their precise wording was the result of complex negotiation, and the meaning is subject to interpretation which is explained below. They were:

> *Resolution 665* (25 August 1990), which authorized the "states cooperating with the Government of Kuwait" "to use such measures as may be necessary" to "ensure strict implementation" of the provisions "related to shipping" of Resolution 661. The implication was that this authorized the use of naval forces in the Gulf by the US and the UK to enforce sanctions.
> *Resolution 678* (29 November 1990), which was interpreted as authorizing the use of force to compel Iraq to withdraw from Kuwait, and which was the legal basis for the conduct of Desert Storm, which began 17 January 1991;[4] and
> *Resolution 687* (3 April 1991), which determined the terms of the settlement at the end of the war.

These resolutions were the focus of the major shifts in diplomacy in the United Nations concerning the crisis and form the main reference points of this chapter.

The focus here is on the diplomacy which led to the approval of these key resolutions; how did an adequate level of support emerge? In this context it should be recalled that on substantive issues the Charter permits any one of the five permanent members of the Security Council to apply a veto: to be approved a resolution must not be vetoed and must attract the support of four of the ten non-permanent members, but in cases of major importance, such as this, those supporting a positive response strongly prefer unanimity. It is, therefore, essential to examine not only the pattern of relations between the permanent members (P5), but also that between the P5 and the others, and that among the non-permanent members.

Three questions are relevant to understanding the terms of the resolutions, and were critical in the diplomacy leading to their adoption. First, what were the general intentions of the main activist states? This primarily concerns the intentions of the US, UK and French governments. Second, what were the reasons for the caution or hostility of the others? The main reluctant states were Cuba, Yemen, Columbia and Malaysia, which became known as the Gang of Four, but the USSR and China also had doubts about some aspects of some resolutions. Third, what were seen to be the specific constraints upon the ways of managing the proposed actions and how far in consequence did the precise wording of the resolutions reflect the Charter's stated principles and involve the organization's formal machinery?

A further important question concerns the lessons to be learned from the Gulf experience for the future role of the United Nations in the area of the maintenance of international peace and security. A key conclusion is that there is a downside to the considerable achievement of the organization in the Gulf: there is a need to rethink several aspects of its procedures, so that, it is argued, a fourth phase of the history of the United Nations as regards its security functions is entered. The Gulf experience may be judged to have been in many ways a triumph for the organization, but this should not lead to complacency about its existing machinery.

The main concerns of diplomacy through the period evolved from an early phase of broad consensus about the need for action, which is most clearly expressed in Resolutions 660 and 661, when agreement was determined largely by existing diplomatic circumstances and an instinctive reaction against the invasion of Kuwait; diplomacy in the United Nations at this point was relatively uncomplicated reflecting a consensus which emerged spontaneously. In a second phase, however – that leading up to Resolution 665 – the consensus was put under threat by a division between those states in the Security Council which wished to use the forms of the United Nations as outlined in the Charter, led by the Soviet Union, and those which were prepared if necessary to act outside the Charter framework strictly defined, relying particularly upon Article 51 which asserts an "inherent right of individual or collective self-defence if an armed attack occurs". The reference to Article 51 was in effect an assertion of a right, which they possessed anyway under international law regardless of the Charter, to defend themselves and if requested, as was the case with Kuwait, to come to the aid of others. But some authorities also argued that explicit reference to Article 51 in Resolution 661 made further resolutions to sanction the "interdiction" of goods moving to or from Iraq redundant.

This was followed by a period from September 1990 to the agreement of Resolution 678 in late November 1990 when, as they built up the level of their armaments in the Gulf, the main activist states, the United States and Britain, paradoxically became much more concerned to obtain the moral sanction of the international community for the use of force, which was clearly now in their minds, in the form of the overwhelming backing of the Security Council; it was now clear, however, that the command of the forces, and control of the conduct of the war, would be external to the United Nations in the hands of the United States. During the campaign itself, from 17 January until late February, the United Nations had very little direct impact either upon the conduct of the war or the terms on which it might be concluded. In a final phase, however, there was a swing back to the full involvement of the United Nations in order to negotiate the terms on which the war was to be ended and which were to be imposed upon the Iraqis. Under Resolution 687 the United Nations was to be the framework for managing the peace settlement, which in its scale of reference and implications for the role of an international organization at the end of a war, is without precedent. Indeed, as will be argued later, the implementation of 687 led to a functional though not a territorial invasion of Iraq.

The diplomacy concerning Resolutions 600 and 661

Resolution 660 contains a forthright condemnation of the Iraqi invasion of Kuwait and demands an immediate withdrawal of Iraqi forces to their position on 1 August 1990. Resolution 661 imposed comprehensive economic and financial sanctions against Iraq and established a Committee, made up of all members of the Security Council, to supervise their imposition. In both resolutions there is reference to the legal basis of the action in Chapter VII of the Charter, with Articles 39 and 40 being explicitly mentioned in 660 but not in 661 and, as already mentioned, Article 51 is invoked in 661. The immediate forthright condemnation and the rapid imposition of comprehensive sanctions were unique in the history of the United Nations; the only previous examples in the United Nations were those against Rhodesia in the 1960s and 1970s, and on exports of arms to South Africa, when action had only followed after much discussion and procrastination. In this case, however, the British played a key role in getting a rapid response. By chance Mrs Thatcher was in the United States at the time of the invasion, and allegedly vigorously urged President Bush to act, and the British representatives in New York strongly backed this effort with considerable energy and expertise.

At this stage, however, the British in particular were concerned that the resolution should not be formulated in such a way as to place restrictions on their freedom to act in conjunction with allies to protect their interests in the Middle East. At that stage, of course, they could not be sure about the future course of action of the Security Council. It should be recalled that up to that date the record of the UN regarding effective action was not very impressive, and the position of those who might be prepared to act had to be safeguarded. This explains the references to the "states cooperating with the Government of Kuwait" and the reference to Article 51; this would sanction further action by them outside the UN framework.

But the simple fact is that this rapid and decisive response was mainly due to the chance juxtaposition of a number of favourable circumstances in the developing positions of the main states involved, and less to any imaginative diplomacy within the United Nations. Indeed the Iraqi action was a masterpiece of bad timing as such highly favourable circumstances had emerged relatively recently. As Ambassador Pickering later pointed out, the contemptuous response of the Iraqi leader to the United Nations reflected his misunderstanding of the situation but also strengthened the resolve of its members. At this early stage even the build up of troops by the US and the UK in Saudi Arabia in the week immediately following 660 was seen as necessary primarily to prevent further moves by the Iraqis beyond Kuwait into Saudi Arabia, rather than as the first steps towards the use of force to get him to withdraw.

The United States policy under President Bush, who had himself been the United States Ambassador at the United Nations, had continued the trend towards a more favourable view of the organization which had begun in the later years of the term of office of his predecessor, Ronald Reagan. Bush, and his Secretary of State, James Baker, were from the United States East coast establishment and were inclined to a more liberal attitude towards international cooperation on the basis of multilateralism. There were for the US, as for the other Western states, practical interests such as the maintenance of stable and adequate supplies of oil. But a concern with the system and its future were also real and powerful considerations. The Soviet Union under Gorbachev had also chosen to work much more closely with the United Nations and this had been clearly indicated by Gorbachev's speech to the General Assembly in 1988 and his letter in Pravda of September 1987.[5] But Gorbachev also saw a more positive role in the United Nations as an extension of the principles of Perestroika and Glasnost within the Soviet Union. The internal reforms were to be a stage in a process of global reform within which the Soviet Union would play a leading role.

The Chinese were also well disposed towards cooperation with the four other permanent members at this time. They were anxious to reestablish their reputation after the disaster of Tiananmen Square, and were also keen to demonstrate that they were worthy of Western economic aid. They stressed that such cooperation and support for Kuwait served their national interests – they had developed good relations with the Gulf states – and were less prepared to express commitment to a new world order, or to other larger principles such as a stronger United Nations. But China's position was also conducive to a positive response on the part of the United Nations to the invasion of Kuwait.

These favourable developments in the attitudes of the major powers were built on by a British initiative when Sir John Thomson, British Ambassador to the United Nations, proposed in late 1986 regular meetings of the group of five permanent members (P5) to discuss current problems and coordinate their positions before meetings of the Security Council. By the time of the invasion there had emerged a habit of harmonizing policy in this framework among the five which had contributed to a number of significant successes for the organization, such as the ending of the Iran–Iraq war, moves towards ending the crisis over Cambodia, and the independence process in Namibia. There was also, however, a negative lesson; it was important not to repeat the mistake of September 1980 when the Security Council had mishandled the Iraqi attack on Iran. The organization can be said to have been on a learning curve! The dynamics of relations between the members of this group, and between them and the other members of the Security Council, are complex, and will be discussed more extensively in the next section. But at this point it is sufficient to point out that the initial response of the P5 to the Gulf crisis was in part a matter of carrying forwards a consensus that had emerged earlier. But, beyond that, in the late 1980s there had appeared a new positive sentiment among British and US leaders; that this was the dawn of a new era of liberal internationalism.

There was the feeling that if the United Nations failed to act effectively now, when a range of circumstances were so much in its favour, then the future of the organization would be seriously at risk, and the maintenance of international peace and security in jeopardy. The organization had rarely before been called upon to deal with such a clear case of aggression by one state against another, and the Security Council for the first time could rely on a significant measure of Great Power agreement, which was a principle of effective action upon which the founders had insisted.

The French government was anxious not to let the British make all the running among the European members of the Security Council and no doubt was thus motivated to keep itself in the vanguard of this new arrangement. Indeed it was the French who brought about the habit of rotating the chairmanship of the P5, though the way in which this happened and the order of rotation were rather peculiar. When the French said that they could not see why the British should remain permanently in the Chair, and would be prepared to take it over, the British response was to insist upon the rotation principle to involve all members. This meant, however, that in 1989 the French as the main claimants followed the British for the first time. But the successor to the French, if alphabetical order had been followed, the USSR, was unprepared for the role. The Chinese therefore took on the role, and the United States succeeded the Chinese, as the Soviet Union was still unready. The resulting order of chairmanship of the P5 which applied through the period of the crisis was, therefore: France, August–October 1990; China, November 1990–January 1991; United States, February–April 1991; USSR May–July 1991; and, United Kingdom, August–October 1991. (The succession of the Presidency of the Security Council is covered in the next section.)

The machinery of the P5 was also strengthened; an office was allocated and permanent officials appointed in early 1991. The commitment of the permanent members to the success of the coordination of the Five was therefore likely to be enhanced by their determination not to be excluded from its administrative arrangements, and by a realization that when they were acting as coordinator its failure would damage their individual diplomatic status – rather as in the European Community taking on the Presidency strengthens members' sense of responsibility for the common interest. Thus the practice of P5 was never to take an issue to the Security Council unless they had formed a consensus amongst themselves; during the period of the crisis the only exception to this rule was Resolution 678 when the Chinese abstained.

The Chinese, though somewhat less committed to the activities of the Five, and with some doubts about its implications for the developing states, nevertheless went along with the new arrangements. One motivation was certainly an unwillingness to be excluded from such an influential coalition. After Resolution 661 they were also faced with a tactical dilemma; that if they used their veto, the Americans and the British could act on the basis of Article 51. The Chinese were, however, the most active in preventing the Five from excluding the others from their insider consultations: they were instrumental in insisting that reports by the Five to the Security Council should not be introduced as having been agreed but only as items for discussion, and they attempted to prevent the individual members of the group from using the framework to pursue their own separate interests, as when the French attempted to mobilize the Five in support of French interests in the Lebanon.

The Iraqis misinterpreted the attitudes of the big states and failed to appreciate that the appearance of the P5 and its successes, and the general commitment of its members to making it work, had made a difference. Action was now much more likely than it would have been even two years earlier. But the non-permanent members were also inclined to support the active response of the United Nations – Finland and Canada and Austria had few problems with this, and, as a representative of the dissenting states sourly observed, the Côte d'Ivoire, Ethiopia, Zaire and Ecuador were in the pockets of one or other of the P5.

But Saddam also miscalculated the positions of states which were his erstwhile friends; after all the US, the USSR and the French had supported him against Iran, and the French had supplied him with arms. He also revealed a fundamental misunderstanding of the position of the Western states when he released the hostages taken by him allegedly to form a "human shield"; he seemed to think that this was all that was needed to meet their complaints, whereas the harsh reality was that it was incidental and in military terms he would have done better to keep them.

He also misinterpreted the position of the Arab countries; the Gulf Cooperation Council supported Kuwait, and the Egyptian government, which had long disliked him, and the Syrians were against him. Even his late appeal to the Arab world to stay united because of the Palestinian issue, and his somewhat sudden and public conversion to the practice of the faith, proved ineffective in attracting Arab support. This meant that there were only four states with real potential for dissent – Malaysia, Yemen, Cuba and Columbia; of these Malaysia had some problems because of a significant Muslim element in its population, but was usually "leant on" by the British; Columbia was anxious not to appear to be slavishly following the United States, but nevertheless was subject to US pressure at the end of the day. This left Cuba and Yemen as the member states of the Council outside P5 which were most likely to abstain or vote against resolutions on the Gulf.

In the event, however, the only dissent on the early resolutions came from the Yemen on Resolution 661. The Yemeni government was motivated in part by a dislike of outside intervention in the Arab world, in part by a dislike of Saudi Arabia, against whom it also had some territorial claims, by a group of pro-Iraqi advisers near to the President, and by the pressure of its own public opinion; it was the product of the peaceful union in 1990 of North and South Yemen and its government was proud of the fact that it was now allowing a wide range of opinions to be expressed: public opinion mattered. Later on these doubts were reinforced by what it saw as the UN's being taken over by the great powers and used by them for their own purposes. They were not following the rule of law as established in the Charter. Even the dissenting states were nevertheless clear at this early stage that firm action against Saddam Hussein was necessary.

The diplomacy of Resolutions 665 and 670

The period between the approval of Resolution 661 on 6 August and the approval of Resolution 665 on 25 August was one of much more intensive diplomacy within the United Nations than had been the case previously. Resolution 665 in effect sanctioned the use of US and UK naval vessels in the Gulf to intercept ships suspected of breaking the sanctions on trade with Iraq, though it should be stressed that the resolution legitimized a course of action which the British and Americans had already said they would follow. The Resolution also arguably represented a step towards acknowledging the legitimacy of using force for wider purposes than the interdiction of shipping, as it required all states to coordinate their actions through the Military Staff Committee to get Saddam out of Kuwait. All states were also requested to help the interdicting states. The resolution was approved with no negative votes and the two abstentions of Cuba and Yemen. But the wording was the subject of considerable and sometimes, it was reported, rather acrimonious diplomacy, as a course had to be steered between the differing positions of the member states – including the permanent members. In the key section the Security Council called

upon those Member States co-operating with the Government of Kuwait which are deploying maritime forces to the area to use such measures commensurate to the specific circumstances as may be necessary under the authority of the Security Council to halt all inward and outward maritime shipping in order to inspect and verify their cargoes and destinations and to ensure strict implementation of the provisions related to such shipping laid down in resolution 661.

In an earlier draft there had been reference to the possible use of minimum force, a formula which was preferred by the Americans and the

British; the use of the milder form of "such measures commensurate to the specific circumstances" was the condition of the approval of at least one of the P5 which would otherwise have abstained, namely the Chinese. Even the French, who were closer to the activist states said in this context that they were not ready to become a "co-belligerent" with the US, but the Chinese seemed to be the firmest in their opposition.

At this point it was the US and the UK which were the most active in their support of firm action. Although it is impossible to demarcate precisely the phases of UN involvement in the Gulf, there is some evidence to suggest that up until a date around late September, when Resolution 670 placed restrictions on air traffic to Iraq and further tightened the maritime blockade, the two front runners would if necessary do what had to be done in self-defence under Article 51. The approval of the UN for each new step was preferred, but they already had in Resolution 661 the minimum necessary mandate from the world body. There was, therefore, the danger that "Washington and London could move beyond the carefully constructed consensus that has marked council actions to date in the crisis,"[6] and one official pointed out that "if the Americans don't watch out there's a risk of a split Council."

Three major perspectives on how to proceed were now apparent. The British and the Americans were already acting on the basis of the assumption that the possibility of force should be spelled out to Saddam and that the control of this military action would remain with the states which contributed it. In fact the command and control arrangements which were preferred were versions of those developed in the NATO context over many years. A second group accepted that the use of force might be necessary but wanted it to be subject to a more direct form of control by the United Nations; in other words there was a dislike of the Anglo-American position which threatened to sideline the global organization as had happened in the Korean War of the early fifties. The Soviet Union was the main promoter of this position at this stage. Third, however, were states, like the Gang of Four, and the Chinese, which favoured a cautious approach to the use of military force and preferred to rely upon the use of sanctions short of force.

This group was determined, at this stage, to avoid giving the US and the British a direct UN mandate to use force. Hence although Resolution 665 went beyond Article 41 of the Charter, which permits the Security Council to introduce sanctions, it stopped short of Article 42 which includes explicit reference to military means. Indeed the joke was made that the Resolution was based on Article 41.[7] Resolution 665 was, therefore, the first of several occasions on which the strict letter of the Charter was reinterpreted in order to meet the needs of the moment.

In the diplomatic process the normal sequence was for the first drafts of proposed Council resolutions to be prepared primarily by the Americans or the British but usually the former. The British had the lead on a few occasions as with Resolution 661 and probably on Resolution 665, but always in very close consultation with the US. The French were then normally brought into the consultation process, and the view was that this was the crucial step in the development of consensus among the P5; if the French were prepared to agree the other members of the Five would probably follow. The importance of this should be stressed; there is a sense in which the French had the veto. It should also be stressed that Saddam made a catastrophic mistake in invading the French Embassy in Kuwait in early September. It stiffened French resolve to stay with the activist states. The French had the lead, however, on a small number of resolutions, discussed later. No instance of either the Russians or the Chinese having the lead on any Resolution can be identified.

It is undeniable that the special relationship between the British and the United States was of key importance in the management in the United Nations of the diplomatic process regarding the Gulf crisis. That this special relationship was real was something that seems to have become particularly evident to the Americans at this time: many of the processes of what international relations specialists call complex interdependence could be identified. The British Embassy in Washington was described as having been itself a participant in the internal US foreign policy-making process and regularly received documents of a higher level of security clearance than any other state including Canada. The mutual help of the two states in the area of intelligence was probably the key to this; after all the British had helped the Americans to set up the CIA! After the loss of documents by an RAF officer – they were stolen from his car, but returned by the thief! – the Americans were more cautious. Operational information was shared only 24 hours or less before action.

American officials also reported that outside Washington they frequently heard about the position of United States agencies such as the Pentagon from British officials. There were also occasions when, allegedly, the British and parts of the American system conspired together to persuade the State Department to change its mind. Not surprisingly specific illustrations of this were hard to come by, but that this had happened during the crisis was frequently reported.

There was also the strong impression that as British and American personnel and forces in the Gulf were built up the techniques for their management and coordination were increasingly taken from NATO. It should not be forgotten though that the Americans had been practising both troop deployments and bombing missions over the Gulf for at least ten years as part of the Carter doctrine, and the rapid deployment force to which it led later. The protection of the *status quo* in Saudi Arabia was a long standing US commitment. But from January on into the war NATO procedures were used by the coalition forces, and the alliance also approved the deployment and logistical support of the forces in Turkey. NATO also provided a convenient framework for consultation between the allies. "Everything", one official said, "slotted into place easily" because plans had already been developed and rehearsed in the other context.

The Gulf military command and control arrangements therefore emerge as largely a product of Anglo-American cooperation in the NATO context, again underlining the importance of the Anglo-American relationship at the heart of Gulf diplomacy. It is also likely that the strength of Britain's voice in this was much amplified by the special British training for desert warfare which is said to be "a part of British military lore."[8] The French, for their part, proved adaptable and made useful contributions to the war in the air, despite their being less involved on the ground in NATO arrangements.

The response of the Soviet Union to these developments was in some ways predictable. It was disinclined, because of internal troubles and the recent experience in Afghanistan, to become directly involved in the military arrangements. On the other hand it was from their point of view undesirable to allow what could become essentially a NATO operation to go ahead in the Middle East. On 14 August the Soviet Foreign Ministry issued a "surprisingly critical statement about US military deployments" there.[9] One way of countering this would be to place the United Nations at the centre of the control and command of the operation.

There is also evidence to suggest that the Soviet government also wished to do this because it would give the Soviet generals a role on the world stage which would divert their attention away from what could be regarded by them as rather uncongenial internal developments at home. It would also fit in with President Gorbachev's image of the future of the United Nations and the Soviet role therein. The Soviet policy was therefore to try to activate the mechanisms laid down in Chapter VII of the Charter regarding enforcement procedures, in particular Article 47 under which a Military Staff Committee was to be established in order

to advise and assist the Security Council on all questions relating to the Security Council's military requirements for the maintenance of international peace and security, the employment and command of forces placed at its disposal, and the regulation of armaments, and possible disarmament.

The Military Staff Committee was to be made up of the "Chiefs of Staff of the Permanent Members of the Security Council or their representatives" (Article 47.2), and was to be "responsible under the Security Council for the strategic direction of any armed forces placed at the disposal of the Security Council" (Article 47.4). In other words in the case of enforcement action under Chapter VII of the Charter, to which explicit reference was made in Resolution 665 as in the later 678, the text requires that the Military Staff Committee (MSC) be in charge. This explains the sensitivity of the issue of the explicit reference to the use of force; the activist states remained, however, firmly opposed both to giving the MSC any meaningful role in the crisis, and to acting on the basis of other articles of Chapter VII regarding the provision of forces which are discussed below. It was largely as a concession to the Soviet Union that states were enjoined to use "appropriate mechanisms of the Military Staff Committee" "to coordinate their actions in pursuit" of the naval blockade.

The efforts of the Soviet Union to give greater prominence to the Military Staff Committee nevertheless met with little success. It did meet once at senior level at the time of the negotiations on Resolution 665, to advise and be informed about the naval deployments in the Gulf, but, until October, its regular meetings were gestures by the West to mollify the USSR. The simple fact was that the main activist states saw little role for the MSC, thought that control and command should be in the hands of those which contributed the forces, and did not take Soviet intentions seriously.

The diplomacy about Resolution 678

Resolution 678 was perhaps the biggest single step taken by the United Nations during the crisis as it in effect sanctioned the engagement of Iraqi forces by the allied forces under American command on 17 January 1991. It was approved with two states voting against, Yemen and Cuba, and one abstention, China, on 29 November, on the eve of the Americans' handing over of the Presidency of the Security Council to their successors in that office, the Yemen. There is, however, evidence that the British took a leading role in brokering this resolution, and in circumventing proposals to forestall the military option. It is worth recording the succession of the Presidencies of the Council here as it has implications for the development of events. In August the position had been held by Romania, in September by the USSR, followed by the United Kingdom in October, then the Americans and the Yemenis. In 1991 the office holders were Zaire in January, Zambia in February, Austria in March, Belgium in April and China in May.

Resolution 678 recalled and reaffirmed all the previous resolutions, its sponsors affirmed that they were acting under Chapter VII of the Charter, and in Paragraph 2, authorized

member states cooperating with the Government of Kuwait, unless Iraq on or before 15 January 1991 fully implements, as set forth in paragraph 1 above, the foregoing resolutions, to use all necessary means to uphold and implement resolution 660 (1990) and all subsequent relevant resolutions and to restore international peace and security in the area;

and requested "all states to provide appropriate support for the actions undertaken in pursuance of paragraph 2 . . . ." Once more it will be noticed that there was in the Resolution no explicit reference to the use of force, though it may be understood as being implied among other available measures. This omission was of significance for a number of reasons.

Most importantly it permitted the Soviet Union to vote for the motion and the Chinese not to veto it and to abstain. It is clear that had there been explicit reference to the use of force the USSR would have abstained and the Chinese vetoed the resolution. Soviet Foreign Minister Shevardnadze made it clear that his government could not accept the first draft of the resolution as prepared by the Americans and the British for consultation with the others. The United States Secretary of State, James Baker had very much preferred to include in the resolution an explicit reference to the use of force to increase pressure upon Saddam, but eventually accepted somewhat reluctantly the compromise formula, which, it was reported, the Soviet government played a leading part in devising. The Americans did, however, insist upon making it clear in an oral statement immediately after the approval of the resolution that it meant the use of force. This was reminiscent of the procedure used by the Council at the end of the Iran–Iraq war when in Resolution 598 the parties to the dispute had been warned that unspecified consequences would follow unless they ceased fighting forthwith; the consequences were then spelled out orally as meaning complete economic sanctions.

The Soviet government also accepted that no specific requirement for a further meeting of the Security Council before the onset of hostilities should be built into the Resolution, and that therefore by implication they could commence on the present authority at the stated date. This element of automaticity was reported as being a British contribution. The Soviet Union presumably believed that this element was compensated for by the so-called *pause for peace*, as this would give time for sanctions, combined with new diplomatic initiatives to achieve a peaceful outcome. It represented a Sword of Damocles over the Iraqis to which the Russians thought they would respond positively. Nevertheless Mr Shevardnadze's acceptance of the automaticity element was thought to have been a serious mistake by his critics in the Soviet Union.

Towards the end of the pause for peace there were discussions among the P5 about holding a further meeting of the Council before hostilities actually broke out, but this was rejected. By this time the Presidency of the Council was held by Zaire and it may be surprising that no initiative to convene the Council in these circumstances was taken either by that country or by any of the other states outside the P5 which might have had doubts about the momentum of events. The Security Council's Provisional rules of procedure 1, 2, and 3, which still apply, allow the President to call a meeting of the Council at any time he deems necessary, or at the request of any member.[10] But although the President can exercise his influence he cannot insist upon a meeting to discuss a particular matter in the absence of a consensus that one should be held. In sum the consensus among the Five against a meeting, and their capacity to exercise pressures against the others, is a sufficient explanation.

The diplomacy which led up to the adoption of Resolution 678 does, however, reveal a certain pragmatism in the attitude of the activist states towards the procedures of the United Nations. The use of the words "all necessary means" meant that the strict form of the arrangements of Chapter VII could be more easily evaded since they did not necessarily mean the use of force. As Article 42, which concerns military sanctions, had not been mentioned in the resolution, arguments from the idealist states to invoke Articles 43 through 47 had much less force. The founders clearly intended, however, that once the Council had acted under Article 42 the provisions of the remainder of Chapter VII should then apply. Article 43 requires:

all members of the United Nations, in order to contribute to the maintenance of international peace and security, to undertake to make available to the Security Council, on its call and in accordance with a special agreement or agreements, armed forces, assistance and facilities, including rights of passage, necessary for the purpose of maintaining international peace and security . . .

and

Such agreement or agreements shall be negotiated as soon as possible on the initiative of the Security Council. They shall be concluded between the Security Council and Members or between the Security Council and Groups of Members and shall be subject to ratification by the signatory states in accordance with their respective constitutional processes.

The point does not need labouring that strict adherence to the procedures of Chapter VII entails a UN command structure under the Security Council – the Military Staff Committee – with all members involved in setting up and approving agreements about the forces to be allocated. The advantage of not mentioning Article 42, from the point of view of the states which did not want such close UN involvement, was that pressures in this direction were less. In this way the UN Charter proved flexible enough to be adapted to the Gulf crisis, which was so different from any circumstances envisaged by the founders.

It is ironic that the United States had supported an explicit reference to force in the first draft, and was only persuaded out of it by the USSR and, presumably, the British. Far from "carefully crafting" the resolution to avoid the involvement of the MSC and whole Council in the conduct of the war, as one commentator suggested, the main activist state had opposed the form of words which kept them on the right side of the Charter.[11] Such a cavalier approach reinforces the case of those who argue that the UN was used by the activist states; by this stage, although they very much wanted the approval of the world community, at the end of the day they were prepared to go it alone. But paradoxically this preparedness became a form of pressure on the others to stay in convoy.

At this point, therefore, a tension between two attitudes towards the United Nations in its enforcement role emerged particularly clearly. On the one side were those – the idealists – who stressed the importance of following the rules of the organization as laid out in the Charter, and seeking always to reconcile action with these principles and articles. Hence there were those, such as the Yemen – but their view was very widely represented in the smaller and middle ranking states, and in the view of the Secretary-General – that sanctions should be given much more time to have an effect upon Saddam, and that the stated procedures should be followed because they were what now existed, and the UN had to be seen to be acting within its own laws. The positive side of their objections is reflected in the comment on Resolution 678 – that it "authorized persons who were not named to pursue goals that were unclear by means that were unspecified!"[12] If the established rules about how to deal with aggression were inadequate then they should be altered, but not evaded. The case of Iraq should be used to build procedures which would have a general relevance for future action.

On the other hand were those – the realists – who were determined to deal with the current problem and regarded the existing procedures as malleable in the light of the overwhelming need to do what had to be done.

In this view there was a tendency to see Iraq as an exceptional case, one which went beyond the pale of normal lawlessness, where a particular demon had to be dealt with, so that various exceptions to the existing procedures, and contraventions of the principle that international authority in the long term should be strengthened, were permissible and necessary. Indeed this view appeared in the discussions about how to tackle the problem of Iraqi biological weapons in the Conference on Disarmament in Geneva in the late summer of 1991; the Americans saw the arrangements imposed upon the Iraqis as exceptional and not establishing any precedents regarding such matters as inspection, verification and disposal procedures, which could later have general applicability. Iraq was to be treated like Germany after the First World War.

The realist camp recognized that if there were to be effective action against Iraq it was necessary to use the command and control structures of the states contributing the forces – to work through the Military Staff Committee was impossible. This position was eloquently put by Sir Anthony Parsons shortly after the end of the war. He said

We are witnessing a military operation almost unprecedented in terms of logistical effort, conceptual and operational planning, meticulous co-ordination and unfettered command and control. The scale has been necessitated by massive arms supplies to Iraq over decades. . . . In these circumstances, it is frivolous to imagine the 15-member Security Council (which at present includes Cuba and the Yemen) making plans for the application of armed force. . . . There would never be agreement, still less a vestige of military security. . . . It is equally bizarre to believe that the five-member military staff committee (United States, Soviet Union, Britain, France and China) could have undertaken the strategic direction of any "armed forces placed at the disposal of the Security Council" (Article 47) with anything like the speed and efficiency displayed by General Colin Powell.[13]

This was very much the view of the main activist states, supported with spasmodic enthusiasm by the French, with the bemused cooperation of the Russians, and usually the reluctant tolerance of the Chinese.

What seems to have happened is that the lead states decided at some point in late September or early October that the best strategy was to assume that war to get Saddam out of Kuwait was the likeliest outcome and to begin planning now to win that war. This may have been immediately before 674 when Mr Primakov the Soviet envoy visited Baghdad to explore the prospects for a settlement: his report it may be assumed was depressing.[14] After that point a campaign was mounted around the United Nations which was intended to orchestrate increasing pressure upon Saddam and at the same time to gather as much support as possible from the Security Council, as preparations continued for making quite sure that the war could be won. A further significant build up of US forces in November indicated that war was now a real possibility, though of course ground troops had been prepared for war from much earlier in the event of Saddam's invading Saudi Arabia. The view that war was likely was translated fairly easily into the proposition that it should be fought at the earliest possible date in order to prevent Saddam's acquiring more powerful weaponry including atomic weapons.

Acting within the legal framework of the UN was secondary to this: it was judged in the light of its capacity to fulfil external goals rather than defended as a value in itself. Hence James Baker's comment, as the negotiations which led to the adoption of 678 were taking place, that until the UN delivers the resolution its "credibility is at stake".[15] One commentator writing on 28 November said that "the US and Britain . . . argue that they are still entitled to initiate military action against Iraq regardless of what the Security Council decides."[16]

There appeared a greater concern with controlling the pace of the campaign. As one official reported there seemed to be an anxiety on the part of the Americans not to interrupt the flow of the mounting crescendo of opposition to Iraq. A kind of self-fulfilling prophecy was then instigated in which the solidarity of the Council was reinforced by Saddam's uncanny knack for showing his contempt for each further UN action. As US Ambasssador to the UN Thomas Pickering put it:

It was the way in which he went about the aggression and then the way in which he dealt with the council or, in most cases, failed to deal with the council, that helped to bring people together in the absolute necessity to meet the aggression by action within the Security Council . . . and to move from one more difficult step to another.[17]

That the management of this process was regarded as being a delicate matter is shown by the American impatience at any attempt to put forward resolutions which could get in the way of this developing crescendo, or challenge the Anglo-American lead. For instance Resolution 667, which condemned Iraqi behaviour regarding the embassies in Kuwait, had been promoted by the French, but the Americans opposed its being put forward and refused even to sponsor it. They did, however, join in its unanimous approval by the Council on 16 September 1990 – including the favourable votes of Yemen and Cuba.

From late September through until 678 on 29 November there were Resolutions of mounting severity against Saddam, which included 670 of 25 September and 674 of 29 October 1990. The latter had been urged strongly by the British Prime Minister, Mrs Thatcher, and was intended to establish charges against Saddam personally, in addition to requiring reparations, by inviting states to collect information on Saddam's violations of the preceding resolutions, and of international conventions on the rules of war and diplomatic and consular relations. Indeed the tone of 674 reveals the personal imprint of the British Prime Minister. The drift to war was, however, by this stage also being fuelled by the logic of the situation: those who wanted only non-military sanctions nevertheless had to approve military and other threats to increase the credibility of those sanctions, but this tended to legitimize the military preparations. As is shown below, once these preparations were complete further pressures and incentives were created which encouraged the use of the available forces in an offensive campaign.

The main activist states were, however, prepared to make what use they could of the procedures of the United Nations in the cause of increasing the pressures against Saddam. Their attitude towards the Military Staff Committee in this period was different from that shown earlier. Towards the end of the French period as Coordinator of the P5 in October there were a number of meetings of the MSC at the French Mission in New York together with the Ambassadors of the member states. Unlike the meetings in August these were now seen as being of symbolic importance in the context of the campaign against Saddam. They were a further demonstration of the unity of the Five and their preparedness for action. Shortly after the approval of Resolution 674 on 29 October, there was a meeting of the MSC which according to an official communiqué, was at its highest level since 1947 with the Americans sending a three-star general, and the Russians, Colonel-General Bromislav Omelichev, First Deputy Chief of the Soviet General Staff.[18]

There is little evidence to suggest that the Americans and the British made much effort to involve the Secretary-General more closely in their campaign. Indeed the only occasion on which he was formally requested to use his good offices was in Section B, Paragraph 123 of 674. Even this reference was brief and was reported to have been a sop to the idealists in the specific shape of the Non-aligned Movement in what was otherwise an extremely hard-hitting resolution. Perhaps they were suspicious of his attitude as revealed in early August when he seemed to resent the actions of the lead states: "what we are seeing is that in agreement with the governments of Saudi Arabia and Kuwait, some decisions have been taken but not in the context of the UN Resolutions."[19] As time passed it looked increasingly as if they were happy that his absence in Peru at the time of the invasion had tarnished his public reputation.

When he visited Baghdad on 14 January in order to attempt mediation just before the expiry of the Pause for Peace he was continuing with an initiative that had been started by the French on 13 January 1991. The attitude of the US and the UK to the French initiative was described ironically as being "not very warm", again presumably because it got in the way of the crescendo, and the French decided not to pursue it in the absence of any commitment by Saddam to withdraw from Kuwait. Their text was, however, used by the Secretary-General as the basis for his late appeal to the Iraqis. The French effort enabled them to remain credible with the idealists – they had tried and got no movement from Saddam. Both efforts, in that they demonstrated Saddam's intransigence strengthened the idea that an offensive campaign against him would be justified: it would be a just war.

As Brian Urquhart has pointed out, one difficulty in using the Secretary-General until towards the end of the Pause for Peace was the way in which the institution's mechanisms had developed.

For over 40 years the Security Council largely operated under Chapter VI (Pacific Settlement of Disputes), relying increasingly on the Secretary-General's good offices and using processes of mediation, conciliation and peace-keeping (an ad hoc extension of Chapter VI), which tended to treat the parties to a conflict "even-handedly". Such a process was often indecisive in settling disputes.[20]

From the point of view of the activist states involving the Secretary-General looked like a commitment to mediation, which was excluded early on in the development of the crisis. It was only at the end that the Secretary-General's intervention, like those of the Russians and the French, *accidentally* proved to be very useful; it demonstrated that Saddam simply would not yield and that no deal was possible.

The central question which reemerges with clarity at this point is what were the underlying motivations of the states which acted as the pace-setters? They were, by the time of Resolution 678, clearly not acting merely as upholders of the literal rules of the global organization, though they may have been acting in the spirit of the Charter: a generous view would be that they adapted the Charter in order to promote its principles in the only way possible in the early 1990s. But the military action was not a Chapter VII operation, even though there were genuflections in that direction. It also seems clear that the states had become convinced before the agreement of 678 that they would have to use force, and in some ways by acting on the assumption that this was probable they made it more likely.

There was, it may be concluded, a further dimension, not yet covered, of the diplomacy of the lead states. This was that they both discovered through the autumn of 1990 the *will* to use force, and this will was not just the result of Saddam's efforts. From his point of view, though, his timing was particularly unfortunate, as it coincided with a unique set of circumstances. As an American official commented – even six months later that will might not have existed.[21] What were the circumstances which generated this will to act?

In the case of the US the early 1990s were a time when the massive increase in military expenditure under Ronald Reagan had begun to bear fruit. There was new equipment and a new resolve, and the feeling after a series of rather second rate military adventures that this was the time to prove something about American military capacity and the resolve to use it. Putting the point in the somewhat longer term – this was the occasion when the imperatives of military technology resulting from the superpower military relationship had reached their most advanced expression, and the developments in the Soviet sphere had not as yet had the consequence of scaling down US military capacity to any significant extent. Here was a highly skilled military machine, equipped with the most advanced military technology the world had ever seen, which appeared at the moment of its fullest development to be about to lose its main justification for existence. The "need to do" led to "can do" and in turn to "will and should do".

Reinforcing this was a reaction against the argument developed by a number of high profile academics, such as Paul Kennedy, that the United States was losing its ability to lead the world and would be sucked into a vortex of decline.[22] Americans had read the book but were not yet quite convinced. There was nevertheless a sense of imminent decline which made it likely that an opportunity to reestablish power and position would be seized. Saddam Hussein gave the Americans this opportunity.

Nothing could better illustrate the position of the Americans than the tendency for senior officials in the United States Administration to

juxtapose two arguments in their speeches after the war: that now was the
time for the establishment of a new world order, incorporating the traditional great principles of international society, the freedom and equality of
nations and the need for international cooperation and multilateral
arrangements;[23] and against this, the view that the Gulf crisis demonstrates
that the US was not in decline after all, and could still show the world the
way. President Bush pointed out on 13 April 1991 that: "Never before have
so many millions drawn hope from the American idea. Never before has the
world looked more to the American example."[24] And Robert Gates, the
Deputy National Security Advisor, told a meeting of the American
Newspaper Publisher's Association on 7 May 1991 that

if you believed many commentators, analysts and academicians in recent years, the
future holds in store decline for the United States – its leadership and influence
waning and resented, its policies undisciplined, unimaginative and lacking vision and
its economic decreasingly competitive. . . . Yet today, no one questions the reality
of only one superpower and its leadership. In all the usual measures of national
power – economic, military, cultural, political and even philosophical – we have no
challengers . . . too many have been left behind because they underestimated the
impact of American leadership, power, confident engagement, national will and
democratic example – from the Persian Gulf to a reunified Germany, to Eastern
Europe to Latin America.[25]

The Gulf crisis was met by the Americans with a potent mixture of capacity
and will which might not, however, endure.

There is less to say about the British side. Their views were likely to be
affected by those of the Americans as they moved towards "enthusiasm",
because they kept each other's company. But it is also significant that this
was moving towards the end of Mrs Thatcher's third administration which
had conducted a successful major military campaign nine years earlier, and
which had encouraged attitudes of not tolerating those who flouted the
standards of good behaviour. Mrs Thatcher was confident in her role as a
world stateswoman of stature, was close to the British Ambassador at the
United Nations at the time of the invasion, Sir Crispin Tickel, and actually
present in the US when it happened. She was, of course, struck by the
unique arrogance of Saddam's contravention of a sacred principle of international relations – the first outright annexation of another state since 1945
– and aware of the recent improvement in the role of the United Nations
to which Britain had contributed a great deal. Patience with opposition was
not her style, and this was a good time to be firm. In this matter, unlike
some others – most notably the issue of relations with the European
Community – the Foreign Office and herself were in complete agreement.

After the approval of Resolution 678 until the outbreak of war the main
disagreement among the member states of the Security Council was between
those who insisted that the onus to respond had now finally been placed
upon Saddam Hussein – everything had been said and it was for him to
withdraw or take the consequences – and those states which still thought
that there should be diplomatic efforts involving fresh approaches and
proposals to Iraq. As pointed out above, towards the end of the pause the

French almost broke ranks with the US and the British, and the Russians also tried a unilateral approach to Baghdad. The US and the British were beforehand highly critical of such moves, seeing them as presenting opportunities to Saddam to further extend the pause, and divide the coalition which opposed him. In the event, however, as pointed out, they confirmed his obduracy.

But the military imperatives had now become more pressing. The activist states became aware that the further extension of the period of sanctions posed serious problems for them. It meant that the delay might extend through the summer, when the climate would make action difficult. The intense heat would create unbearable conditions for soldiers prepared for a modern war, and the onset of Ramadan would create special difficulties. Saddam Hussein would also inevitably be given more opportunities to break the ranks of the coalition. Increasingly the arguments seemed tipped in favour of early action rather than further delay, as the window of opportunity would be closed.

The Group of Four nevertheless put forward proposals of their own at this late stage, with the advice of a group of what were described as "mad professors from Harvard", an effort which was much disparaged. On 3 December the Group produced a paper which recommended two stages in the peace process.[26] In a first stage Saddam would withdraw under the supervision of a peacekeeping force organized by the Secretary-General, and the Security Council would provide "an assurance that there shall not be any foreign intervention against Kuwait or Iraq". In a second stage, after Iraqi withdrawal from Kuwait, all foreign forces "should withdraw from the region immediately" and the Council "should lift all sanctions against Iraq enacted through its previous resolutions".[27] All financial claims between the parties to the dispute "which are not settled equitably through negotiations between them, shall be referred to the international Court of Justice or any other legal procedures, agreed to by the parties". On 14 January 1991 a similar set of proposals were again put forward by the Yemen and its allies.[28] There was also an attempt to mobilize the Non-aligned Movement in the cause of peace; the one visible expression of this, however, was an attempt by Yugoslavia in January to set up a meeting with Saddam. This proved abortive.

But the activist states were by this time simply not prepared to accept a link between their withdrawal and either Saddam's withdrawal from Kuwait, or any immediate withdrawal from the Middle East thereafter. And sanctions could not be lifted simply on compliance with Resolutions 660, 662 and 664, as was stated in the plan.[29] There was now also the question of reparations, the issues brought up in Resolution 674, and, though this had not as yet been formally indicated, the question of the destruction of the weapons of mass destruction. There was in other words, before the war began, an agenda of peace-making which went far beyond the kind of return to the *status quo ante* which was the basis of the plan of the Group of Four. Much more was now expected of Saddam than simply withdrawing from Kuwait – as if nothing had happened!

There was no further meeting of the Council to discuss the Gulf crisis before war broke out on 17 January. The decision to move then was taken by the Americans in consultation with the British, and there is no evidence to suggest that even the other members of the P5 were consulted before the act. Indeed there was some anxiety that the Americans were now prepared to act outside the mandate of the Security Council even with regard to the settlement at the end of the war, by deciding unilaterally who could and could not take part in the peace process.[30]

During the war the United Nations was not involved in any meaningful way. There were no reports to the Council, or to the Military Staff Committee, or to the Secretary-General. In February, however, discussions began among the P5 about the settlement at the end of the war. The UN organization was not consulted about the details of this settlement, which was largely put together by the US and the British with some French involvement. On 3 April this settlement was approved by the Security Council in the form of Resolution 687, with one negative vote, Cuba, and abstentions from Yemen and Ecuador. The Chinese supported the resolution, though it had been feared that they might abstain; the conventions of the P5 suggested that the Chinese would not use their veto. It was said that they supported the resolution because of a development which had not been noticed at the time by the West: a visit by the Foreign Minister of Kuwait to Beijing three days before the vote.

Resolution 687 – the "Mother of all Resolutions"

On 3 April 1991 the Security Council passed resolution 687 subsequently known as the "Mother of all Resolutions". It required a far more extensive involvement by an international organization in a settlement at the end of a war than had ever previously been seen, and was described by Ambassador Pickering as "quite unique". When it was approved it was clear that Iraq was about to surrender – offensive combat operations had been halted by the coalition forces on 28 February – and on 7 April the Iraqi government said that it had no choice but to accept the terms proposed. On the same day, however, the British Ambassador to the United Nations, Sir David Hannay – who had now succeeded Sir Crispin Tickel – met with the Secretary-General to discuss the possibility of establishing safe havens in Iraq to protect the Kurds, who were being brutally attacked by Saddam. The Kurdish problem became a further concern of the United Nations over and above the specific concerns of Resolution 687, in addition to the problems of other refugees and oppressed peoples in Iraq and the surrounding countries, which are discussed below.

The resolution was sponsored by Belgium, France, Romania, the United Kingdom, the United States and Zaire and it was adopted by 12 votes in favour with 1 against (Cuba) and 2 abstentions (Ecuador and Yemen). With a resolution of this scale it is not surprising that its preparation began well before the cease-fire. Indeed there is evidence that its discussion began before the onset of the land war against Iraq on 24 February 1991,[31] but after the opening of the war in the air. Its terms were Draconian and it constituted a diktat to the Iraqi government: the decision seems to have been taken well in advance of the peace that Iraq was to be severely punished for its transgression. Not only does it represent the absolute victory on the battlefield of the alliance, acting under the authorization of the United Nations, but its content seems to indicate a determination on the part of the United States and Britain to punish Iraq as a uniquely dangerous, criminal state, and not as a conventional malefactor in international society.

In this they were supported by the other permanent members of the Security Council and a significant international coalition including major regional powers such as Syria, Egypt and Saudi Arabia. In this case the non-specific wording of Resolution 678 had the advantage that it could be the basis of a mounting crescendo of measures against Saddam, not only to defeat him in war, but also to subject him to peace terms appropriate to his having been placed beyond the pale. He had to be deprived of the dangerous weapons which he had acquired, and subject to constraints which assumed a general criminal propensity.

All the member states except the Chinese contributed to the development of Resolution 687 so that it was not possible to identify a particular state as having the lead; the Kuwaitis and the Saudi Arabians also had an input. The British made significant contributions, however, in identifying the dominant purpose of the resolution, and they played a major role in formulating the terms on the identification of the boundary, and on locating and eliminating Saddam's biological, chemical and nuclear weapons. British Prime Minister John Major was closely involved in the latter, which a British official described as "one of our outstanding efforts".

Saddam Hussein had promised the coalition "The Mother of All Battles": not only did he reap the consequences of the massive onslaught of allied military power, but he also faced "The Mother of all Resolutions". We turn now to the operative parts of Resolution 687.

Boundaries

Firstly, the resolution:

> *Demands* that Iraq and Kuwait respect the inviolability of the international boundary and the allocation of islands set out in the "Agreed Minutes Between the State of Kuwait and the Republic of Iraq Regarding the Restoration of Friendly Relations, Recognition and Related Matters", signed by them in the exercise of their sovereignty at Baghdad on 4 October 1963. . .
> *Calls on* the Secretary-General to lend his assistance to make arrangements with Iraq and Kuwait to demarcate the boundary between Iraq and Kuwait. . .
> *Decides* to guarantee the inviolability of the above-mentioned international boundary and to take as appropriate all necessary measures to that end in accordance with the Charter. . .

It is perhaps important to stress the decision of the Council that it will take all necessary measures to guarantee the inviolability of the border. The phrase "all necessary measures" has, in the context of previous resolutions, acquired a political significance since the military action which began in mid-January fell under the same phrase. Since the passing of Resolution 687 a good deal of progress has been made in this matter so that now, after aerial surveys, maps are expected to be ready at the end of February 1992 for the actual demarcation of the border.

The UN force

The second area of activity that the resolution prescribes is the ". . . immediate deployment of a United Nations Observer Unit to monitor the Khor Abdullah and a demilitarized zone, which is hereby established, extending 10 kilometres into Iraq and 5 kilometres into Kuwait. . .". The Khor Abdullah waterway is some 40 kilometres long and the demilitarized zone on the border between Iraq and Kuwait is approximately 200 kilometres long. Only when the deployment of the Observer Unit was complete to the satisfaction of the Secretary-General would the member states cooperating with Kuwait bring their military presence in Iraq to an end. On 6 April 1991 the Secretary-General submitted his plan for a "United Nations Iraq–Kuwait Observation Mission" (UNIKOM) and on 9 April the Security Council approved the plan and decided to set up UNIKOM for an initial period of six months. UNIKOM functions "under the command of the United Nations, vested in the Secretary-General, under the authority of the Security Council". The plan for UNIKOM was that it would be comprised of both armed and unarmed military personnel and composed of a group of some 300 military observers and an infantry contingent of approximately 680 soldiers and officers. The maximum initial strength foreseen for UNIKOM would be approximately 1,440 all ranks. Its personnel include nationals of all five permanent members of the Security Council and its commander is Major-General Greindl of Austria who has had significant previous UN experience in Cyprus.

Resolution 689 of the 9 April 1991 was adopted unanimously. It deals with the further implementation of UNIKOM. It contains some interesting and awesome features for both of the host states. First, it is placed specifically under Chapter VII of the Charter of the United Nations and second, it states that termination will be by a decision of the Security Council which will review the question every six months. Thus UNIKOM was established as a stronger form of a peacekeeping force in the sense that it was not to be dependent upon the consent of the host countries; there are only a small number of previous instances of this. However, it is not an enforcement agency since its functions are to monitor the waterway and the land boundary agreed in 1963 and to deter violations of that boundary as well as to observe any hostile or potentially hostile action mounted from the territory of one state on the other. Nevertheless, the fact that it is not dependent upon the consent of the host countries and that it is situated under Chapter VII indicates quite clearly that it is an observation mission with teeth.

So far this mission has been successful. Indeed, its role in the Bubiyan Island incident on 28 August 1991 was particularly helpful. In this instance the Kuwaitis alleged that the Iraqis had been firing on the island which is part of Kuwait. Although the island is outside the demilitarized zone, nevertheless UNIKOM did investigate and it found no evidence of firing. However, both the demarcation of the boundary and the establishment of the observer mission are trivial in comparison with the demands of the Security Council on Iraq in regard to its present and future military capabilities.

Disarmament

The main resolution 687:

> *Invites* Iraq to reaffirm unconditionally its obligations under the Geneva Protocol for the Prohibition of the Use in War of Asphyxiating, Poisonous or Other Gases, and of Bacteriological Methods of Warfare, signed at Geneva on 17 June 1925, and to ratify the Convention on the Prohibition of the Development, Production and Stockpiling of Bacteriological (Biological) and Toxin Weapons and on their Destruction, of 10 April 1972;
>
> *Decides* that Iraq shall unconditionally accept the destruction, removal, or rendering harmless, under international supervision, of: a) all chemical and biological weapons and all stocks of agents and all related subsystems and components and all research, development, support and manufacturing facilities; b) all ballistic missiles with a range greater than 150 kilometres and related major parts, and repair and production facilities. . .

The Council went on to order Iraq to submit to the Secretary-General within 15 days a "declaration of the locations, amounts and types of all items specified . . . and agree to urgent, on-site inspection . . .". The Secretary-General was then enjoined in consultation with appropriate governments and others to develop and submit to the Security Council a plan for the completion of a number of functions. These included:

i)   the forming of a Special Commission, which shall carry out immediate on-site inspection of Iraq's biological, chemical and missile capabilities, based on Iraq's declarations and the designation of any additional locations by the Special Commission itself;
ii) the yielding by Iraq of possession to the Special Commission for destruction, removal or rendering harmless, taking into account the requirements of public safety, of all items specified . . . including items at the additional locations designated by the Special Commission . . . and the destruction by Iraq, under supervision of the Special Commission, of all its missile capabilities including launchers as specified. . .
iii) the provision by the Special Commission of the assistance and cooperation to the Director-General of the International Atomic Energy Agency (IAEA) required. . .

Ambassador Rolf Ekeus of Sweden was subsequently appointed as the head of the Special Commission. The Council then went on to decide that "Iraq shall unconditionally undertake not to use, develop, construct or acquire any of the items specified . . . above. . ." and it requested the Secretary-General in consultation with the Special Commission ". . . to develop a plan for the future ongoing monitoring and verification of Iraq's compliance. . .".

Not only was Iraq invited to reaffirm unconditionally its obligations under the Non-Proliferation Treaty, but the Council also decided that

Iraq shall unconditionally agree not to acquire or develop nuclear weapons or nuclear-weapons-usable material or any subsystems or components or any research, development, support or manufacturing facilities related to the above. . . .

Such existing weapons or material was to be revealed to the Secretary-General and the Director-General of the IAEA within 15 days as was the location, amount and type of such weapons or weapons-usable material. All of these were to be placed under the "exclusive control, for custody and removal, of the IAEA, with the assistance and cooperation of the Special Commission. . .". Iraq was obliged to accept "urgent on-site inspection and the destruction, removal or rendering harmless as appropriate of all items specified. . ." as well as to accept the plan for the future continuing monitoring and verification of its compliance with these undertakings.

The Director-General of IAEA, through the Secretary-General and with the assistance and cooperation of the Special Commission, was to carry out immediate on-site inspection of Iraq's nuclear capabilities based on Iraq's declarations and the designation of any additional locations by the Special Commission prior to the destruction, removal or rendering harmless as appropriate of all items. The destruction of weapons and the permanent system of verification were, and were intended to be, highly intrusive as subsequent events have demonstrated. They were a challenge to the sovereignty of Iraq.

The magnitude of the task facing the Special Commission and the IAEA teams can be judged by a UN report of 21 October 1991 that it would take at least two years to clear Iraq of chemical weapons. The physical danger to personnel was obvious in that they could be dealing with extremely dangerous weapons often in a very fragile condition. Moreover, Iraq has now been obliged to admit that it has a nuclear weapon programme and an IAEA report has said that it is "well advanced in the production of a nuclear weapon".[32]

Reinforcing the powers to inspect

As the investigating teams got to work they were buttressed by three subsequent Security Council resolutions. Resolution 669 was passed unanimously on the 17 June 1991 and it determined that Iraq was to pay the full cost for the destruction of the proscribed weapons. Resolution 700 was also unanimous and it approved the guidelines for the full implementation of the arms embargo. Resolution 715, passed unanimously on 11 October 1991, took the intrusive element further and in some regards it was a response to the foot dragging and deliberate obstruction on the part of the Iraqis. This obstruction led to the car park incident where inspectors were confined to a car park for several days in a face-to-face confrontation with Iraqi authorities because, in effect, the inspectors had penetrated the bureaucratic framework and obtained the documentation at the heart of the Iraqi nuclear programme. The leader of the particular inspection team, a US citizen, was, however, passing the information obtained directly to the United States without passing through either the UN in New York or the IAEA. For this contravention of his status he was severely reprimanded.

Resolution 715 contained two plans. The first was a plan of the Secretary-General for chemical and biological weapons and for missiles over 150 kilometres range, that is, it covered the area which the Special Commission had made its own. The second plan came from the IAEA and it dealt with nuclear arms, nuclear weapons material and attendant installations. The resolution stated that Iraq must allow UN and IAEA inspectors access to all civil and military installations which were suspected of an arms capacity, all laboratories and research projects, the scientists and technicians working there and it also instituted controls over imports and exports. Since the knowledge that Iraq has cannot be unlearned, it is significant that the access to individuals is also stipulated. The reaction of the Iraqi Ambassador at the United Nations to this Draconian intervention was that the Head of the Special Commission was now virtually, as in British mandate times, the High Commissioner for Iraq.[33] In short, as the Head of the Special Commission, Ambassador Ekeus commented verification procedures were "very stringent and very intrusive".[34] In order to accomplish this a variety of techniques are being used including high-altitude aerial surveys, helicopter sweeps and painstaking on-site inspections whether of installations or of the bureaucratic infrastructure and its attendant paperwork. In response the Iraqi authorities have wriggled, have threatened and have dodged but the relentless pressure of the verification teams and their skill appears slowly to be making substantial progress towards the unlocking of all Iraq's secrets in these areas.

By October 1991 sufficient progress had been made for David Kay, the Chief UN Inspector for Iraqi nuclear capabilities, to comment that the Iraqi programme was highly sophisticated even in comparison with those of Europe and the US. He acknowleged the excellence of Iraqi scientists of which there now existed a complete list. Moreover, Douglas England, the Head of the UN ballistic experts, was able to verify the destruction of the "supergun" with a range of 700 kilometres. Finally Hans Blix, Director of the IAEA, announced that many suppliers had delivered material to Iraq in defiance of IAEA controls, which would doubtless give rise to future embarrassment for such suppliers.

Reparations and compensation

The next part of Resolution 687 reaffirmed that Iraq

is liable under international law for any direct loss, damage, including environmental damage and the depletion of natural resources, or injury to foreign Governments, nationals and corporations, as a result of Iraq's unlawful invasion and occupation of Kuwait.

It also decided that Iraq could not repudiate its foreign debt and that it must "scrupulously adhere to all of its obligations concerning servicing and repayment of its foreign debt". The resolution called for the setting up of a fund to pay compensation for claims which would contain *inter alia*

mechanisms for determining the appropriate level of Iraq's contribution to the fund based on a percentage of the value of the exports of petroleum and petroleum products from Iraq . . . taking into account the requirements of the people of Iraq, Iraq's payment capacity as assessed in conjunction with the financial institutions taking into consideration external debt service, and the needs of the Iraqi economy. . .

Resolution 692 of 20 May 1991 voted, with Cuba abstaining, to establish the compensation fund. The percentage of the value of petroleum exports was fixed at 30% which was almost the equivalent to the Iraqi arms budget prior to the war. This part of the resolution also obliged Iraq to return Kuwaiti property and by September 1991 it was reported that the transfer of gold bricks, banknotes and coins back to Kuwait had been completed and that Iraq had begun to return valuable items which had been taken from Kuwait's National Library.[35]

Iraq, of course, had already been subject to effective economic sanctions and the "Mother of all Resolutions" allowed foodstuffs to be sold to Iraq in addition to medical and health supplies which had been available hitherto. These, however, had to be for "essential civilian needs" as agreed by the Sanctions Committee. Moreover, in general the sanctions would be reviewed every 60 days. It was envisaged that the sanctions will be lifted only when Iraq has complied with all the provisions on chemical and biological weapons, on nuclear materials, missiles and after an effective system of inspection and monitoring for future verification purposes has been established.

The suffering of the people of Iraq, both during the war and subsequent to it, has been immense. *Le Monde* of 26 October 1991 carries an Iraqi report that 68,000 child deaths are attributable to the embargo. UNICEF has suggested that 340,000 people are in danger of death. Yet, the Iraqi government appears to be restricting supplies. Nevertheless, the Security Council has been responsive to this human suffering to the extent that, as a result of Sadruddin Aga Khan's report to the Security Council and a UN inter-agency report after visiting Iraq, Resolution 706 was passed on 15 August 1991. This authorized the sale of 1.6 billion US dollars of petroleum products to pay for food imports and to service and repay debts.

Although Iraq did not make full use of this facility, nevertheless Resolution 712 of 19 September 1991 further confirmed the availability of $1.6 billion and allowed for the immediate release of one-third of this sum from the escrow account in order to meet Iraq's civilian needs. To the extent that it is not making abundant use of the facilities available to it for meeting the needs of its civilian population, it appears that Saddam Hussein is using their plight to play on the consciences of Western and other allied public opinion and also to inculcate or further enhance a sense of hatred by the Iraqi population of the coalition to whom their lamentable condition is attributed. This might be seen as a further refinement of the use of hostages by Saddam Hussein's government.

The final substantive part of the resolution concerned the repatriation through the International Committee of the Red Cross (ICRC) of all Kuwaiti and third country nationals in Iraq. Iraq is also required not to commit or support any act of international terrorism. It is not clear the extent to which all Kuwaiti or third country nationals have left Iraq. Kuwait has argued as late as 25 July 1991, that some 4,000 prisoners of war remain in Iraq without the ICRC being accorded access to them.[36]

For the most part the provisions of the "Mother of all Resolutions" have been implemented. The enduring parts of the resolution concern the identification and destruction of categories of military activity and weapon systems that pose an inordinate threat to other countries in the region and indeed, have a bearing upon state practice in warfare. The use of chemical and biological weapons and the sustained attempt to develop a military nuclear capability is a capacity that Iraq is being denied because of its past use of such weapons or the likelihood of their future use by Iraq. If Iraq uses chemical or biological weapons again and even more so, if it were to use nuclear weapons, then important taboos in the international system will have been broken. The first state to use nuclear weapons since 1945 will in effect alter the rules of international warfare and international diplomacy. It is for this reason that the leaders of the coalition are determined to destroy and eliminate, and keep eliminated, such capacity on the part of Iraq. Moreover, the delivery systems for such weapons are also being destroyed, so that Iraq cannot threaten its neighbours. Nevertheless Iraq will still maintain a substantial conventional military capability, although the degree to which it will be able to keep its existing weapon systems in good working order due to the arms embargo, and non-provision of spares, is a moot point. Clearly the Iraqi military no longer has an offensive capability but that does not mean to say that it cannot act brutally within the confines of its own country. It is therefore to the events which followed the "Mother of all Resolutions" that we now turn as a further chapter in a human tragedy which engulfed the peoples living in Iraq unfolded.

The humanitarian dimension

The losses in the military hostilities of the coalition forces were almost miraculously small. On the other hand the losses of the civilian population in Iraq, despite the considerable efforts of the coalition forces to spare the civilian population, were immense. The losses of the Iraqi armed forces were commensurate with the overwhelming nature of their defeat. Yet this was not to be the end of it.

Very substantial population movements occurred in four major areas in the course of the Kuwait crisis. Initially there was the movement of approaching a million people out of Iraq, mainly through Jordan, before hostilities occurred. After hostilities there was the incredible sight of the march of the Kurdish people in Iraq, in biblical proportions, to the Turkish border. Again, more than a million refugees left Iraq to seek safety in Iran. Lastly, and also within Iraq itself there were substantial movements of populations such as are to be found in almost any war theatre.

The refugees who moved into Jordan in August and September 1990 were mainly third party nationals moving from Kuwait via Iraq to return to their home countries. The camps that the Jordanians set up followed by those installed by the UN system and nongovernmental organizations cared for three-quarters of a million people, of whom none died for lack of care in the camps. Initially the flood of refugees was cared for by the Jordanian authorities, but they were gradually overwhelmed. They called in UNDRO (United Nations Disaster Relief Organization) on the 22nd August 1990 and UNDRO was made the lead agency for dealing with the problem. It called the first meeting of relief donors on the 24th August in Geneva. On the 12th September 1990 the Secretary-General appointed a personal representative for humanitarian assistance who was Prince Sadruddin Aga Khan. His brief was to concern himself with the political and diplomatic questions associated with the refugees, with raising funds and with cooperation with UNDRO.

As the flood of third country nationals slowed to a trickle, the relief organizations prepared themselves for the likelihood of a further need in case of hostilities breaking out. UNDRO made a plan for dealing with evacuees if war were to break out. This plan was formulated on the 19th October 1990 and updated on 11th January 1991. It assumed that 100,000 refugees would need care for 90 days in each of four host countries, namely Turkey, Jordan, Syria and Iran. In fact, there were few international refugees when hostilities did break out – just over 20,000 who mainly crossed the border from Iraq into Jordan.

The plan envisaged the following division of responsibilities. Camp management was to be provided by the UN High Commission for Refugees (UNHCR). Water, health sanitation and nutrition were assigned to the World Health Organization (WHO) and the UN International Children's Emergency Fund (UNICEF). The transportation of people was given to the International Organization of Migration which had played an important role in transferring the third country nationals to their home countries. Food was the province of the World Food Programme and the transportation of supplies was assigned to the World Food Programme (WFP) and the High Commission for Refugees. Other agencies also prepositioned resources, for example, the ICRC prepositioned camp material in Cyprus and Jordan for 60,000 people by the end of 1990. At the start of hostilities this was increased to material for 250,000 people with 50% being available along the Iran–Iraq border, 20% in Iraq in the Kurdish areas and 20% in Jordan.

As a result of the rising against Saddam Hussein by the Shi'ites in the south and the Kurds in the north and the brutal repression of this rising, there was a two-way flood of refugees. The Kurds trekked north through the barren mountains to the Turkish border where they were not allowed to pass and to seek asylum in Turkey. The UN agencies found it very difficult to approach the Turkish–Iraqi border from either side. Firstly the Turkish government did not wish to allow the High Commission for Refugees to operate in Turkey on any scale. Turkey was not ready to give the right of asylum to these refugees because it felt incapable of absorbing them economically, culturally and, above all, politically. As the crisis grew the coalition forces, especially the French, British and the European Community, followed by the United States, established a military presence on the border which began to provide assistance. This was acceptable to Turkey since it did not carry the same political and legal obligations as an operation by the HCR. Equally, the agencies found it very hard to get to the Iraqi side of the border, for this reason the early activity dealing with the Kurdish refugees was very much an allied affair.

This human problem, the scale of which defied the imagination, could not leave the Security Council unmoved and the response of the Council was Resolution 688 of 5 April 1991. This was sponsored by Belgium, France and the United Kingdom, and was the result of a French initiative. The French government had long supported moves to intervene in Iraq on humanitarian grounds. It was stated that the repression of Iraqi civilians, and especially the Kurds, by their own government had "consequences . . . which threatened international peace and security in the region". In other words Resolution 688 justified international intervention in Iraq to defend the Kurds in terms which were analagous to those used to justify intervention on behalf of Kuwait: it justified a breach of the principle of Iraq's right to exclusive domestic jurisdiction as enshrined in Article 2(7) of the Charter. Iraq was informed that it must cooperate with the Secretary-General and allow immediate access to the area by international humanitarian organizations. The Secretary-General was empowered to pursue this and Sadruddin Aga Khan was appointed the Executive Delegate for the "UN Inter-Agency Humanitarian Programme for Iraq, Kuwait and the Iraq/Turkey and Iraq/Iran border areas".

The Resolution caused some anxiety in that with Resolution 687 it could be seen as implementing what was in effect a functional occupation of Iraq. By functional occupation we mean that in certain domains and geographical areas Iraq was to be prevented from exercising its sovereignty under threat of fierce sanctions if it challenged UN resolutions in these matters.

The Memorandum of Understanding

With the backing of this resolution Sadruddin made a Memorandum Of Understanding with Iraq on the 18th April 1991 which led to the establishment of United Nations Humanitarian Centres (UNHUCs) to assist the population and to organize air lifts and relief convoys. As an annex to this MOU, on the 25th May, United Nations Guards were allowed into the region of Kurdistan up to a maximum of 500 men to ensure the security of the United Nations operations and to act as "a moral witness". Thus the UN took over the camps which had been originally set up by the British, Americans and French. By this time there was good cooperation between the HCR and allied troops as well as with Turkey. The UN agencies now had access to the zone and whereas in the past only the allied forces could cross the border, and the agencies could not stockpile as much material as they wanted to because of their lack of funds and their obligation to be reactive, they were now able to function in a more organized fashion. The ICRC and the NGOs had for some time been able to function with a greater degree of ease, but only because they could shelter under the framework of either the intervention of the allies or under the authority or wing of the United Nations. The number of relief operations rose to 25 organizations in Kurdistan, but there were only 5 in Southern Iraq because the presence of the agencies in the north acted as an inhibiting factor on the Iraqi government in a way that was not the case in the south.

The allied military ground forces withdrew from Northern Iraq in September 1991, although allied air forces continue to fly in Iraqi airspace as far south as the 36th parallel, that is south of Mosul, but north of Kirkur (*Le Monde*, 16 October 1991). But for a while in the autumn of 1991 there was anxiety because the Memorandum Of Understanding with the Iraqi government was due to run out at the end of the year. In the event, however, the Iraqis agreed to its renewal in December for a further six months. The question remained, however, of the adequacy of such ad hoc arrangements, and problems about how to cope with the harsh winter for the refugees remained very serious, especially after the departure of allied forces from Iraqi soil. It was also evident that there was an urgent need for an allied deterrent force in southern Turkey. The fundamental point was that it was essential to maintain the secure conditions in which UN agencies could operate; there was the further point that if UN agencies were forced to withdraw, so would the nongovernmental organizations which operate in the shadow of the UN agencies. The possibilities of another human catastrophe in Kurdistan were indeed real.

In the Western press the 1.3 million refugees who left Iraq for Iran were largely forgotten. The British government, as represented by Linda Chalker, were particulary concerned that the United Nations should be more active in the southern area of Iraq, and in this was strongly supported by Sadruddin. Happily, although precarious, the fate of those who crossed into Iran was somewhat better than those who traipsed to the Turkish border. The Iranian Red Crescent responded well in the circumstances and the ICRC had the capacity to help to a significant degree. In addition the UN agencies gradually came to play a rather greater role. However, despite some distinguished efforts they were no more than palliatives in face of an enormous movement of people.

A refugee, to receive international protection from UNHCR and other like bodies, must, among other things, cross an international border. However, in war it is frequent that there are large movements of populations within a country. While strictly speaking such people did not fall under the rubric of the UNHCR, in fact the High Commission for Refugees played a significant role in the aftermath of hostilities. Its rationale for doing so was that many of the refugees were in fact returning from Iran, particularly in the south. However, since there was no obvious criterion to determine whether or not objectively an individual had returned from Iran, HCR adopted a liberal interpretation and aided refugees who were, in essence, internal refugees despite their being strictly outside of its remit. The ICRC was also active in Iraq as it had been well established since the onset of the Iran–Iraq war. Likewise other agencies or organizations had a presence in the country which they were able to reactivate after hostilities. Moreover, the UN agencies such as the World Health Organization sent individuals or even missions to Iraq to estimate the needs of the people. Sadruddin Aga Khan also used his mission to try to deter the Iraqi military from the brutal repression of the Shi'ite population in the south by insisting on visiting the marsh areas where it was reported that the Iraqi army was about to undertake large scale punitive operations. In terms of need such efforts were puny, but it is a moot point whether the agencies could have done more in the circumstances and it is to this general framework for humanitarian aid of the UN system, that we now turn.

The humanitarian system at work

The United Nations Disaster Relief Organization (UNDRO) has been widely criticized, particularly by the British and United States governments, as being of poor quality. Indeed, other agencies do not find UNDRO to be credible because of its inexperience in relief operations and it is a widely held view that its top level staff are not of the highest quality. Moreover, UNDRO has not drawn a sharp line between operational and non-operational activities. With only 29 professionals it is hardly able to go operational and therefore, it needs to confine itself to the gathering of information, supply of expertise and the coordination of the activities of others. UNDRO's bad press may be in part justified but there is surely much unjust criticism of this and other UN agencies based on totally unrealistic expectations given the enormous demands being made in relation to the paucity of resources available and the practical restrictions on being proactive.

One feature of the Kuwait crisis was the lack of strong standing arrangements for coordination among the UN agencies. Indeed, there is a clear need for a standing inter-agency group for emergencies. In point of fact however, when called upon, UNDRO did act as the lead agency and did act quickly. The UN agencies can only operate when they are invited to do so and clearly they did not have an easy entrée into Turkey, Iraq or Iran, at least initially. When they were able to secure access they gave a good account of themselves but they were hamstrung for lack of resources. They tend to be reactive because they do not have the resources to be proactive and governments are unwilling to give them such resources.

Moreover, once they are in a reactive mode, they have to use what is available on the market, since frequently they require large amounts of goods which are simply not available and have to be ordered and manufactured. It was indeed fortunate that, in preparation for a need in Afghanistan, UNHCR had been able to acquire resources earlier, which were now available for the crisis in Kuwait. But these were rapidly being depleted.

The ICRC is in a unique position in that through its very nature and through its function it has access to the parties to a conflict. This access is buttressed by a long tradition of humanitarian work, but in order to preserve that access, the ICRC has to be scrupulous in not abusing its position as a neutral. What has been built up over a century of humanitarian work can be quickly dissipated if the ICRC begins to act in a consistent manner beyond the parameters that the parties to the conflict accept. The other NGOs have strengths and weaknesses. They are often able to call upon significant resources and they do not constitute such a threat to governments and therefore are able to have an easier access. But they, too, find coordination difficult since they must maintain their market niche, their image and the enthusiasm of their supporters and operatives. Their supporters, in particular, wish to be associated with a particular idea or type of action. If coordination means that this idea or type of action is diluted then the support may melt away. In short, NGOs need to justify themselves to their constituency otherwise their resources will dry up. Hence, it is not only "the barons" who run the major humanitarian agencies who have difficulties in coordinating their work, but also the NGO network.

Happily, a reasonable division of labour occurred, as we saw, in the division of responsibilities in the UNDRO plan prior to hostilities. A particular feature of the agency response, besides that of UNICEF, UNHCR and ICRC which although not a UN agency in some regards acts as one, was the emergence of UNDRO as a lead agency and the particular roles played by the International Organization for Migration and the World Food Programme. Indeed, the logistic base of the World Food Programme is such that the argument is being made that it should expand this role and become *de facto* the UN system's logistics agency. Of course, in any emergency logistics are crucial and the World Food Programme served the system well.

UNDRO, as coordinator, worked well and a system emerged which virtually brought order out of chaos. It was the SUNEM system (Senior United Nations Emergency Manager). A SUNEM was appointed in each of the four principal countries – Iran, Jordan, Syria and Turkey – where there were programmes and each SUNEM reported to UNDRO. The SUNEM acted as liaison officer for all UN work with the local government and also as liaison officer with the NGOs. The major bodies all combined with the system, namely UNHCR, UNDRO, WHO, WFP, UNICEF, FAO, ITU, ICRC, LRCS and NGOs. There was, therefore, no great failure to coordinate in the field or in Geneva, but the agencies felt strongly that the Secretary-General appointed too many special representatives – of whom there were six. These various missions caused an element of confusion. For example, the Secretary-General sent Under Secretary-General Martti Ahtisaari and former Under Secretary-General Abdulrahim Farah to Kuwait and Iraq on two separate missions to report on humanitarian needs. Prince Sadruddin Aga Khan was also active, as were Erik Suy and Ambassador Brunner. Of course, their functions were intended to be different but in a fast changing situation in the aftermath of war, with military activities still proceeding as Saddam Hussein pursued his internal enemies, the men and women in the field who had succeeded in establishing a working system of coordination thought that there was confusion and lack of direction in New York. Moreover, the position of the agencies was changing.

The cooperation between the five permanent members of the Security Council had a knock-on effect in the agencies, in the sense that the P5 had an unofficial veto, or at least the three Western members did, since they had the ability to put some money into the pot. Moreover, the association of UN agencies with the independent actions in Iraq by the three Western permanent members in some senses prejudiced the neutrality of HCR since the permanent members were also highly influential in the agencies. They can influence the agencies to work in parallel, indeed to cooperate with their independent actions in a way that they cannot do with the ICRC. Thus, while the ICRC was able to maintain its neutrality in regard to the parties, the agencies were not. In this case the association with the three permanent members acting independently facilitated their task, but it may undermine their credibility in the eyes of governments for future occasions. Moreover, the agencies themselves are getting into a position whereby they can thrust themselves into an emergency by threatening a host government to defer development work in that country if access is not given.

Implications of the UN role in Iraq for the development of the system

It appears, looking back on the Kuwait crisis, that the humanitarian part of the UN system is beginning to get that brain that Sir Robert Jackson could not find in his famous report two decades ago.[37] In short, the system is becoming less sub-system dominant and there is emerging a better and more rational system of coordination, whether it is the SUNEM system within countries or the specialization in various tasks with UNDRO acting as coordinator among the agencies. In addition to this, the Secretary-General came to Geneva on several occasions to meet jointly with agency heads, with donors, with client countries and with NGOs to deal with problems. These consultations began to take on a systemic element and it is interesting that they were functionally organized involving all actors. They therefore became a sort of parliament for the humanitarian aspects of the crisis. It will be interesting to see the extent to which a similar practice is followed in a future emergency of this sort.

Reflecting on what happened, in the debate in the General Assembly on International Humanitarian Aid, held on the 4th and 5th November 1991, the European Community proposed the creation of a post of Under Secretary-General of the United Nations charged with the coordination of humanitarian aid.[38] Clearly the experience of humanitarian intervention by the United Nations on behalf of the Kurdish population in Iraq, organized without the agreement of Baghdad, in large part, seems to have changed the nature of the debate on this issue giving it a clear political dimension. Many developing countries, and China, are fearful that the idea of reinforcing humanitarian aid through the nomination of a coordinator will be likely to increase the right of intervention in the internal affairs of sovereign states. The proposal of the EC, as well as a report from the Secretary-General, concentrates on three points, firstly the nomination of a coordinator for humanitarian actions at the rank of Under Secretary-General, secondly the creation of an emergency fund which will have permanently at its disposition $50,000,000 and finally, the creation of an emergency committee which would coordinate the network of specialized agencies and nongovernmental organizations who are concerned with humanitarian aid. The role of the coordinator will thus be to receive the first information about a catastrophe and to synthesize this information. The role is also to coordinate the action of the agencies and to launch an appeal to donor countries. The coordinator will be empowered to call upon the human and material resources of the UN agencies and enter into contact with the authorities of the country in which the catastrophe has taken place. However, speakers from the EC did underline that the principle of subsidiarity would be applied and thus the state within which the catastrophe had occurred would have the primary role in the provision of humanitarian assistance. Nevertheless, the idea of a coordinator who would epitomize international opinion and action in a particular catastrophe and whose activities might well lead to pressure for, or indeed, actual humanitarian intervention, is not one to recommend itself to some of the more repressive regimes of the globe. Moreover, some of the major agencies such as UNDRO, UNICEF and HCR are not particularly enamoured to see their work put under the control of some outside suzerain.

What the Kuwait crisis has done is, nevertheless, to give a fillip to the idea that state sovereignty will not always or necessarily prevail in the face of a need for humanitarian intervention, whether sanctioned by the United Nations in the form of a resolution, as in the case of the intervention by the Western Powers in northern Iraq, or legitimized by approval in some other context, such as in the communiqué of the Group of Seven in July 1991. Moreover, humanitarian aid frequently is concerned with human rights, either directly or implicitly. The moral witness of the agencies and NGOs in Iraq combined with the capacity and willingness of three of the permanent members to act with no explicit disapproval from the other two permanent members, will, if sustained in other cases, give rise to a new element in international politics. A precedent is on the verge of being made and whether or not it comes to fruition will depend substantially on the degree of cohesion on the matter among the five permanent members of the Security Council. Their influence permeates throughout the UN system and especially, as we have seen, in the area of humanitarian matters. It may serve to make the UN system more effective, but will it prejudice its acceptability? Given the willingness of the P5 to act, does this matter? It may be just as another UN agency, the IMF, has developed a powerful role in economic questions, particularly of developing countries, so, the UN system, particularly if an effective coordinator is appointed, may well develop a similar role in the area of humanitarian aid with the ability to twist arms on questions of human rights. The Kuwait crisis has led to a movement in that direction.

It seems therefore, that Iraq has been subjected to a functional occupation by the allied forces in the sense that in certain areas Iraq is subject to management by the coalition forces through the instruments of the UN system. In particular, this is the case as we have seen with the control of nuclear weapons, chemical weapons and biological weapons and it is also the case with humanitarian intervention through the Memorandum Of Understanding. The forcible disarmament of Iraq in certain areas has a permanent aspect, while that of humanitarian intervention does not. It will, therefore, be of significance to see whether, and in what form, the Memorandum Of Understanding giving the agencies the right to operate in Iraq, is renewed at the end of its next term in mid-1992. The aspect of moral witness includes a political threat and beyond that political threat lies the proved ability and willingness of the allies to intervene militarily.

A wider context must be seen to this: the United Nations is also embarking upon a number of other operations ranging from the supervision of elections, to a form of trusteeship or international control for a country as in the case of Cambodia. Many, if not all of these operations, are possible because of the concordance of the permanent five. But as the permanent five become more successful, they arouse suspicion and fear of others. The scale of operations is thus increasing, and while the degree of success is unlikely to be linear, the face of world politics may be in the process of changing in a fundamental way.

The United Nations was able to make Desert Storm a just war and as a consequence of that it was able to intervene in a humanitarian manner. While the motivation for allied action within the UN framework had many sources, nevertheless it was aggression that was the catalyst that brought the other factors into line. By themselves they were not strong enough to cause Western intervention, for example, because of oil, and it was the UN system which was best able to marshall this catalytic factor into effective action.

The United Nations is evermore into the business of global riot control. The Kuwait crisis accelerated the development of this capacity and proclivity for intervention. Whereas in the past the United Nations was hamstrung because of Article 2(7), this has now been, and is being, eroded, but it has not been eliminated and, while the breakthrough is important, it is likely to elicit adverse reactions. For many countries the actions of the P5 through the UN system were a lesser evil than the unbridled aggression of Saddam Hussein. But there is now a need to get the double standards on intervention right and here the question of Palestine is of great importance. Moreover, if the UN is to be seen as an acceptable institution for global riot control, it also has to reflect the agenda of all the major groups of actors and not just that of the P5 and especially its Western component. It is not sufficient to deal with disarmament, drugs, terrorism, immigration and the like, it is also necessary to deal with the agenda of others which is much more concerned with development issues. In this regard the humanitarian activities of the UN system can be a useful help, if only a palliative, alongside the more fundamental and structural need for change to engender real development. If the UN system is seen by many as the P5 and the IMF, it may be able to determine behaviour, but it will not be able to win hearts and minds and without that there can be no long term stability. The UN system has the capacity to respond to other needs, particularly in the humanitarian area. It also needs to be given the capacity to go beyond the sterilities of zero growth in real terms in its development work. Thus the Secretary-General repeated in his report to the General Assembly in September 1991, ". . . agreement among the permanent members must carry with it the willing support of a majority of nations if it is to facilitate movement towards a better and a saner world."

Implications for the future of UN arrangements for the maintenance of international peace and security

For many people, including the United States President, the experience of the United Nations in the Gulf represented a transition from a period of relative ineffectiveness in the area of international security, to one of solid achievement. The success in the Gulf should not be underestimated, but a sober assessment of the use made of the United Nations by the Great Powers reveals some grounds for concern. The New World Order should be accompanied by appropriate adjustments in the working arrangements of the world organization.

The underlying problem is that the Gulf crisis was a success for the powers but less so for the organization. Although the action then was legitimized through the organization, it was NOT based on Chapter VII procedures, and the war was managed outside the organization. Furthermore it depended very much on improvization by the Great Powers – finding ways of building from what the Charter said when this was impracticable in the much changed world of the 1990s compared with 1945. On the positive side it could be said that the Charter proved flexible enough to allow this development, and that it permitted the necessary adjustment in procedures. The worrying thing is that it depended on a chance coincidence of favourable circumstances in the positions of the permanent members of the Security Council; this means that there is little or no legacy of experience which can be built on for the future and which would make it more likely that the same firm response would be met by any state which contemplated aggression. Of course, it has happened once and could happen again, and that thought must in future be in the mind of the prospective malefactor; but a weakening of Great Power resolve would not be balanced by any countervailing enhancement of the inducements to act deriving from the institution's arrangements.

One problem is that the success of the P5 has led to changes in the pattern of work of the Security Council, and, indeed, of the General Assembly, which have caused the developing countries to fear that they are being excluded from the key decisions of the organization. The Security Council has changed from being a forum for discussion and negotiation, with, if anything, over protracted meetings, dominated by ideology and nit-picking, to being a ratifying chamber for decisions the major outlines of which have been agreed elsewhere. The sessions have become rather short and focused strictly upon getting through an agenda formed largely by the P5. The Resolution which ended the Iran–Iraq war took five months of negotiation outside the Council but only about 15 minutes to approve in it. There may well have been consultations with the non-permanent members before then but nevertheless the small and medium sized states have begun to fear that they are spectators at the world organization rather than participants. This is not just a view expressed by members of the Non-aligned Movement: the medium sized and smaller developed states have expressed it too.

It is necessary to find ways of mitigating this problem, without losing the very positive contributions of the emergence of P5 and of the Great Power consensus on which it is based. As John Thomson put it:

While still under the influence of a victorious Security Council operation, the international community needs to increase expectations of a repeat performance. To a great extent this depends upon the US playing as a member of the Security Council team rather than as its owner.[39]

Ways need to be found to bridge the gap between the Powers and the others.

For instance, a way of reconciling the practical requirement for effective command and control of forces acting in the name of the UN, and the need to involve the organization through the Council and such institutions as the Military Staff Committee, must be found. It is simply not acceptable to declare, as did one official, that the Military Staff Committee is "flaky", and that such involvement does not suit those who contribute the bulk of the forces. In any case there will be very few occasions on which the scale of force required in the Gulf will be necessary – or available.

A possible way to a satisfactory compromise between the need for effectiveness and the need for involvement is to go in precisely the opposite direction from that followed in the Gulf crisis with regard to activating Articles 43 to 47. That would involve the members of the Security Council together in concluding agreements for a United Nations force on a permanent basis, i.e. before the event, and setting up on this basis a small rapid deployment force under the control of a commander, and staff, appointed by the Military Staff Committee, and approved by the Security Council.[40] The Military Staff Committee would be the overseer of such an organization, being the body to which the commander would be answerable in the event of action, and would approve strategies and contingencies, and would in turn be answerable to the Security Council. It would not be responsible for the hands-on command of such a force, and details of the arrangement could be modified, for instance to give a more immediate role to the Security Council.

What is sought is an arrangement which would encourage full consultation with all the members of the Council in the event of a crisis, and a sense that the organization was fully engaged, but which would also allow a degree of initiative on the part of the Great Powers. It should be stressed again that success in the Gulf depended on the unique military power of the US, and that this is likely to be scaled down in the years to come. Indeed one US officer pointed out that had the crisis happened even a year later the response would probably not have been what it was. We need to find ways of enhancing the capacity of the organization as compensation for this decline.

This arrangement does not go beyond the present terms of the Charter, but rather returns to the original interpretation of it, in that it involves a permanent force. The Charter may also be interpreted as meaning that a force could be recreated whenever a crisis arises, which was the version rejected by the Powers in the Gulf crisis. It has the advantage of involving the non-permanent members of the Council in the negotiations required to establish the new force before it is required, and in determining the circumstances in which it might be used; they will feel that UN procedures are being used and that they are not excluded. Such a force could be identified in various ways; probably the most practical first step would be to earmark contingents of national forces, to train them for UN use, and to arrange exercises under the UN command. They would not, however, be under full time UN command: the model would be that of NATO in peacetime.

At the same time there is little or no risk for the permanent members, as they retain the veto, and the right to reject arrangements which look impossible. The existence of the force is however likely to increase the status of the non-permanent members of Council, as they will have a part in deciding about its use; it may also, by existing, create a self-fulfilling prophecy in making its use seem more acceptable. At the same time the option remains open for the P5 to act under Article 51 if they think it necessary, and establish cooperative arrangements with the UN force if it seems desirable.

But the point should be stressed that such a force would be part of a spectrum of military activity available to the United Nations; in this case it amounts to peacekeeping tending towards enforcement, which could act on the basis of Chapter VII. At another part of the spectrum is a requirement for a force which is concerned with traditional peacekeeping as it has developed in the United Nations. The present writers agree with Sir Anthony Parsons, when he wrote that "the traditional form of UN peacekeeping, namely lightly armed forces removable at the whim of the parties to the dispute, will not do."[41] But there is still a great need for interpositionary forces, which may be more lightly, or defensively armed, than those concerned with enforcement, though this may be the time to reduce the amount of "ad hocery" connected with them, and to professionalize further the institutions and arrangements on which they depend. This means agreements with states about the allocation of troops and equipment which involve a commitment for them to provide these as and

when necesssary. It has been said that the part of the Secretar
with peacekeeping forces should be more than "a corner gro
which implies a need for more involvement by high level mili
a permanent basis.

There is a need to go beyond the improvizational methods which were
seen by Dag Hammarskjold as the only way of arranging matters in view
of the tensions between the East and West. The end of the Cold War has
significantly increased the likelihood that peacekeeping forces will be used
in a wider range of disputes, and has made it easier to put firm and
relatively permanent arrangements in place. In this case too, however, the
Military Staff Committee could be involved in providing advice, and the
Security Council in providing a forum in which representatives of the
various groups of states could be involved.

These adjustments are, however, only aspects of what could be called a
fourth phase in the development of the role of global international organization in the area of international peace and security. In the first phase the
international organization, the League of Nations, acted as a fire brigade,
responding when war broke out. In the second, the organization was given
a more permanent watching mandate with the main institutions, such as the
Security Council, being permanent ones; the fire brigade was permanently
on stand by. In the third phase, the peacekeeping forces were developed,
which were based on what was described as Chapter 6½, being intended
not to settle a conflict but to stop the parties to it from trying to settle it
by force. In the fourth phase the organization could get much more actively
and closely involved in monitoring international developments, in surveying
troop movements on a day-to-day basis, acquiring information about any
development which could lead to the use of violence, including the setting
up of an arms transfer register. An extension of this would be the active
involvement of the Security Council in registering the movement and sales
of arms, and in establishing guidelines to regulate their distribution. Some
movement in this direction has already taken place in the section of the
Secretariat administered in the early 1990s by James Jonah, but this operation needs to be considerably expanded, particularly to include improved
facilities for analysing the information which comes in.

There are many ideas about how to increase the flow of information. Use
could be made of satellites, even of commercial satellites, and one suggestion was for the members of the United Nations to agree through a treaty
to a right of access to their territories for UN inspectors. The fourth phase
would be characterized by the Security Council's having much improved
access to information concerning security questions through an office under
the Secretary-General: there would be a kind of global security watch.

Before the Gulf crisis it was said that there were only two occasions in
the history of the United Nations when the Secretary-General and the
Council did not have very adequate knowledge of a developing crisis; the
Cyprus crisis of 1974, and the Falklands/Malvinas crisis of 1982. This may
or may not be the case but it misses the point. This is to combine a certainty
in the mind of a potential aggressor that whatever is contemplated is seen
clearly by the global organization, and that there is an instrument available

and working which could respond quickly. At the moment this middle level response is absent. The power of the Great Powers is needed, and their cooperation is essential. But most crises will not need the massive escalation which seemed necessary in the Gulf and in the routine of the organization's dealings with transgressors a lesser response may be all that is required.

Notes

1. The author is deeply grateful for the help given him in writing this chapter by a very large number of officials in the United Nations and in national missions in New York and in Geneva. Interviews were carried out mainly in September 1990 in New York and in July 1990 in Geneva. Any mistakes of fact or judgement are, of course, entirely those of the author.
2. Javier Perez de Cuellar, *Report of the Secretary-General on the Work of the Organization*, United Nations, New York, 7. 1X 82.
3. See A.J.R. Groom and Paul Taylor, "Britain and the United Nations", in John Trent and Gene Lyons (Editors), *National Attitudes towards the United Nations*, forthcoming, 1992.
4. Under international law the coalition states did not require the sanction of Chapter VII in order to seek the liberation of Kuwait. But such sanction was required for the specific form of the response.
5. See Mikhail Gorbachev, *Realities and Guarantees for a Secure World*, Novosti Press Agency Publishing House, Moscow, 1987, especially section V. P. 14.
6. Michael Littlejohns, "Security Council Plays Down Sanctions Differences", *Financial Times*, Wednesday, 15 August 1990.
7. Edward Mortimer, *Financial Times*, 18 September 1990.
8. David White, *Financial Times*, Wednesday, 15 August 1990.
9. *Financial Times*, 15 August 1990.
10. See Davidson Nicol, with Margaret Croke and Babatunde Adeniran, *The United Nations Security Council: Towards Greater Effectiveness*, UNITAR, New York, 1982, Chapter 2.
11. John Gittings, *The Guardian*, 28 November, 1990.
12. Interview with a Yemeni official, September, 1990.
13. Anthony Parsons, "World Peace Bites Back", *The Times*, 12 October 1990.
14. See *Financial Times*, 30 October 1990.
15. Quoted in Gittings, loc. cit.
16. Ibid.
17. Ambassador Pickering, quoted in United States Information Service, *European Wireless Alert*, 08 05 91, Pp. 3–4.
18. *Financial Times*, 30 October, 1990.
19. Quoted in Littlejohns, loc. cit.
20. Brian Urquhart, "The Role of the United Nations in the Iraq–Kuwait Conflict in 1990", in *SIPRI Yearbook 1991: World Armaments and Disarmament*, Stockholm, P. 621.
21. Interview in New York, September, 1991.
22. Paul Kennedy, *The Rise and Fall of the Great Powers*, Random House, New York, 1987.
23. See President Bush's speech to the Maxwell Air Force Base War College, 13 April 1991, in United States Department of State, Bureau of Public Affairs, *The New World Order: Documentation Collection No.2*, Washington DC.
24. Ibid., P. 3.
25. Address by Deputy National Security Advisor, Robert Gates to the American

Newspaper Publisher's Association, Vancouver, BC, 7 May 1991 reproduced in *New World Order: Documentation Collection*, loc. cit., No. 1.

26. In a document described as a Working Paper, under the title *Framework for Peace Situation between Iraq and Kuwait*, unpublished.
27. Ibid., P. 2, Para. (ii).
28. Document untitled and unpublished.
29. Loc. cit., Preamble.
30. For example, the letter from Brigadier Michael Harbottle, on the speech in early February 1991 by James Baker to the Senate Foreign Relations Committee, to *The Times*, 12 February 1991.
31. See the very useful account of the progress of the war in John Bullock, "Who Really Won?", *The Independent on Sunday: The Sunday Review*, December 1991, Pp. 10–15.
32. *UN News Summary*, London Office, 11 October 1991.
33. *Le Monde*, 14 October 1991.
34. *UN News Summary*, London Office, 1 August 1991.
35. UN London Office, *News Summary*, 16 September 1991.
36. UN London Office, *News Summary*, 25 July 1991.
37. Sir Robert Jackson, *Study of the Capacity of the United Nations System*, United Nations, Geneva, 1969.
38. *Le Monde*, 7 November 1991.
39. *The Guardian*, 28 February 1991.
40. See the leading article recommending this course of action in the *Financial Times*, 25 March 1991.
41. Sir Anthony Parsons, "A Need the UN can Meet", *The Times*, 9 August 1990. See also his "The United Nations after the Gulf War", *The Round Table*, 1991, 319, Pp. 265–273.
42. Interview with an American official, New York, September, 1990.

10 Conclusions

What conclusions may be drawn from the preceding discussion?

This book has taken a distinctive approach to the analysis of international organization in that it has concentrated primarily upon the development of international organization in international society, and its implications for the state, rather than upon international organization as a form of international public administration, where organization is seen as a set of procedures and rules about behaviour, the practical application of which to specific tasks is to be examined.

The reader will have gathered that the main components of the argument have already been set out in the Introductions to each of the book's four sections, and this brief chapter should be seen as a reconsideration and development of the main points discussed there. Together the Introductions and what follows can be read as a single chapter.

In many ways the state has been able to use the emergence of more pressing global problems to strengthen its protective clothing. The Gulf War demonstrated that international society was determined to resist the annexation of one of its members and one consequence was that the sanctity of the frontiers of states was reasserted. In some ways this was enshrined in Security Council resolutions more forcefully than had previously been the case, even to the point of asserting that any further violation of the frontiers of Kuwait would in itself be enough to activate the peace enforcement procedures. At the same time, however, and somewhat paradoxically, it was apparent that standards had emerged which governments thought should be generally maintained, for instance, regarding human rights, and, if these were transgressed, the international community had the right to take appropriate action even if this meant intervention within the miscreant's frontiers.

It is striking that developments in Europe and developments in the Gulf crisis are connected – an observation which, to borrow from the Heineken advert, only the student of international relations can reach. In both contexts, the state had been semi-detached from the performance of key tasks, the exclusive control of which used to be seen as a condition of its existence (this point is discussed further below). In Western Europe, of course, this is illustrated by the gradual acceptance of the view that a number of functions – since Maastricht including defence – could in some sense be carried out on behalf of the state by a regional organization. What is increasingly at issue is not whether national control should or should not be maintained, but the form of common management, and the retention of a capacity to pursue a national strategy with regard to allocating powers to non-exclusive decision-making structures. International organizations appeared in response to the perceived need to defend common values.

Of course the unusual powers of the United Nations in Iraq at the end of the Gulf War were a consequence of the dispensations of the victorious coalition, but in both the Gulf War and Western Europe, a shift in general views about what was essential to the sovereignty of the states was noticeable. The global pattern was of a general modification of the view about where the line was to be drawn between the exclusive jurisdiction of the state and the responsibility of the international community, though in the early 1990s this applied primarily to questions of human rights, and perhaps to certain aspects of security, such as the right to intervene to remove weapons of mass destruction from irresponsible hands. But this development may be seen as an early stage of a more general process of accepting a wider range of common management, which has gone much further than elsewhere in Western Europe.

If these developments are viewed from a realist perspective a number of problems immediately strike the eye. This is a world in which links are established between the internal arrangements of the state and international society, and, indeed, in which international society has legitimate access to those arrangments, so that, within limits, standards can be monitored and protected. This is a world in which attention is focused, not on the eternal verity of sovereignty, but upon the changes in the conditions under which it is exercised. Traditional realists have tended to resist the suggestion that such conditions are in any sense malleable. This is also a world in which the culture of international society is seen to be itself capable of development so that it begins to play a positive role in the process whereby the interests of states are defined. This is something which is implicit in regime theory, but the extent to which it marks a departure from the principles of traditional realism has perhaps not been appreciated.

Despite this, one of the themes of this book is that there is much about realism which remains relevant. In particular the key concepts of the state and of sovereignty remain central, and the interest of the existing states in their own survival is fundamental. Indeed what have been described as problems from the realist point of view may be better understood as amendments to that theory. But to concede this point is to accept a different vision of realism from the traditional one. Within broad limits – the acceptance of the state and sovereignty – it becomes a flexible, evolutionary theory, rather than an account of what are construed as the eternal verities of international society. In particular it excludes the inevitability of conflict, though it insists upon the pursuit of self-interest. But this is filtered through an international culture – a regime – and a set of procedures, which, at the regional as at the global level, encourage its redefinition in the light of that of the collectivity.

This supports the theme of *symbiosis*: on the one hand the assertion of a traditional principle of sovereignty, the sanctity of frontiers, but on the other, and as a corollary, the acceptance of a weakening of the right of exclusive domestic jurisdiction with regard to the legitimate actions of international organizations. This is the case at both the regional and the global level, and the reformed realist paradigm employed in this book allows the parallel developments at both levels to be identified. Community and the individual entities were each being developed in association with the other. There was a new synthesis of the two kinds of rights – those of the collectivity and those of the separate states. Despite this evolution, the state was not under threat.

For the student of international organization this argument is extremely important, as it envisages an increasing role for the collectivity of states based on a consensus about values, which was emerging slowly at the global level, and more rapidly in some regions. That there are departures and exceptions, as in the terrible wars in Eastern Europe in the early 1990s, does not invalidate this point. The instrument of the collectivity is, of course, international organization. At the same time though, the state is reinforced in many of its aspects, and hence the idea of a dialectical development in international society, one stage of which – the moment of the coexistence of thesis and antithesis – the idea of symbiosis, and, indeed, of consociation, captures effectively.

The idea of consociation also evades an ancient problem about the development of international organizations, which was discussed, amongst others, by Rousseau and Kant: that an international federalizing process was a contradiction in terms in that it was impossible to have a federal arrangement which was strong enough to defeat the aggresssive intentions of sovereign states. If a traditional view of federalism is adopted they were, of course, quite correct in this assumption; a federation of sovereign states as a means of maintaining international peace is contrary to the fundamental principles of international society as it assumes a hierarchy of sovereigns. Consociation suggests, however, that the strength of one might be positively related – not negatively, as argued by Rousseau – to the strength of the other. There is a parallel evolution of powers, which are mutually sustaining, rather than a transcending of one by the other, which inevitably removes the sovereignty of the lesser power, and thus destroys the system of states which it was intended to preserve.

The general pattern seemed to be comparable at the regional level, even in the most advanced example, with that at the global level. In neither case, despite the apparent movement towards regional federalism, was the state under threat, despite the blatherings of the members of the Bruges group in Britain in the early 1990s: even in the European Community what was happening was that the conditions of sovereignty were changing rather than that sovereignty was under threat. At the global level, however, the interaction between the two drives, towards national autonomy and towards collective responsibility, was often the opposite of that at the regional level, with the need for collective action being used to strengthen the state. For instance population control seemed to involve an issue of massive importance for the survival of the planet. But the states still bartered their separate national interests for the collective one, a fact which refuted the prejudice that there was any self-evident hierarchy among the issues on the global agenda. At the time of writing in April 1992 a similar pattern was detectable in the bargaining preceding the Global Environmental Conference in Brazil, scheduled for June 1992. What was observed was the use of the issue to further strengthen the states, whilst at the same time making "soft" concessions to the general need – in this case that of controlling the rate of population growth or limiting environmental damage.

This was not just a matter of different hierarchies of interest, though these were certainly evident, with development aid being bargained for population or environmental controls; it was also a question of defending the right of national institutions to decide on their own account what to do about these matters, and, beyond that, to harness the issue to the task of state-building, in defiance of the supranational ambitions of the planners.

These various conclusions at the regional and at the global level are easier to understand and to reconcile with each other in the context of the kind of modified realism developed in the Introduction to Section 1. This is not intended to be a frontal attack on liberal pluralism, but simply an assertion of the usefulness of a particular theoretical framework for the task attempted in this volume. The task of reconciling the contradictions which emerge, when liberal pluralism is applied at the regional and the global levels, must wait for a different occasion, but it was not intended to show that this was impossible. In any case, theorizing is a dialectal process, and this volume is part of the process of theory-building, and no claim is made that it is the end of the road.

The question arises of how far the European Community's experience is relevant to the rest of the world. There were, of course, in the early 1990s many differences between the pattern of regionalism in Europe and elsewhere, but, as was argued in Chapter 2, there are reasons for supposing that there were general pressures in the same direction. The European experience has to be considered because attempts were made to emulate it elsewhere and because lessons learned from what happened in the European Community could be applied in other regional contexts. It is important to have the right lessons!

In Chapters 1 and 2 the pressures towards regionalism were discussed and three phases of the process were indicated. In an early phase contiguous states established common forums in which they could discuss policies and cooperate in a minimum way. In this phase the collectivity is a product of the attempts by the separate states to extend their influence over the others. In a second phase there was a much stronger sense of work to be done together in the regions, though the methods involved unanimity, primitive intergovernmentalism, and not much sense of any need for overall coordination; this was described as a phase of local sectoralism. In a third phase, there was a realization of the need for systems of common management and for the allocation of competences to joint institutions. The first and second phases occurred in Europe before the Second World War, and the third phase began in the post-war period. By the 1990s, however, Western Europe was well into the third phase, beyond local sectoralism, and towards a more sophisticated regionalism. In other parts of the world, of course, only the second phase at most had been attained.

There was one respect in which Western Europe was ahead of the rest which should be stressed. A change was evident in the way in which the idea of national self-determination was understood, which signified a major shift in thinking about the conditions of sovereignty. Indeed in that small region a new version of the idea of national self-determination had begun to emerge by the early 1990s, which was not evident as yet in other regions. What had happened was that the utilitarian aspects of sovereignty had been semi-detached from the principle of national self-determination.

It was now possible in Western Europe to allow crucial tasks to be managed at the larger level, without this being seen as a challenge to the principle of national autonomy. For example by the early 1990s the Scottish nationalists had come to see the European Community as a support for their claim for national autonomy: autonomy had become a way of relating to the outside world, whereas in earlier years claims for autonomy amounted to a means of withdrawal into an introspective concern with national issues, and a form of detachment from the larger entity. But this was only one case of a general tendency to accept that within the territory of the European Community tasks should be performed at the most appropiate level determined in the light of technical criteria rather than exclusive nationalism. Even foreign policy and defence, previously judged to be at the heart of sovereignty, seemed amenable to this semi-detachment from the principle of national autonomy. What remedied the situation, of course, was that the states could be said to have pooled their sovereignty rather than abandoned it, and they sought increasingly sophisticated ways of managing their common enterprise to protect this principle.

In Eastern Europe, after the ending of the Cold War, however, there was a much more primitive version of the principle of national self-determination. There was still an insistence upon keeping a wider range of essential tasks firmly attached to the emerging nations: they wished to establish national currencies, armies, economic policies and the like, when there were signs that the countries in Western Europe had begun to feel that exclusive controls over these were not part of the necessary condition of sovereignty. In her view of this Mrs Thatcher was again wrong; what she had interpreted as a regrettable tendency towards centralization in Western Europe, precisely when the Soviet system was collapsing, was in fact a move towards a more modern view of national self-determination in the West precisely when Eastern Europe was returning to a more primitive nationalism.

Again the long cycle is interesting: Western Europe was the homeland of the principle of national self-determination and the connection between retaining control of key tasks and national autonomy used to be stressed there; perhaps Western Europe was once more ahead of the pack in the early 1990s, in demonstrating that national autonomy did not necessarily involve an exclusive utilitarianism. It could become a way of relating rather than of excluding.

A further major conclusion concerns the pattern of growth of the regional and global international organizations. There were many reasons to suppose that global international organization had reached a plateau in the early 1980s as defined by the input of financial resources, but that the level of regional organization continued to increase at a rapid rate through the

1980s into the early 1990s – the time of writing. In other words international society was becoming increasingly regionalized; this was in part a question of special factors encouraging regionalism, and in part a product of the special character of the development of international organization at the global level. The latter was lacking in the dynamics deriving from utilitarian functionalism (weak links between task areas), the fear of marginalization (no equivalent of being relegated to the second tier, as in the European Community), and a weaker sense of common culture.

But the point should be stressed once more that this pattern of development was not likely to reduce the number of states in the world, but was likely to alter the way in which they related to each other in the long term. Even the most advanced grouping of states, the European Community, was saved from federalism by a consociational structure and a pattern of symbiotic relationships between the separate states and the collectivity. There was an increasing habit of relating together to the outside world, but no prohibition on individual states doing this if they were so minded. What should be stressed again is that success with regional federalism merely recreates traditional international society; success with a consociational process transforms it.

A major claim of the book is that regionalization represents a radical transformation of international society in so far as it can be reconciled with the survival of existing states. As was argued in the Introduction to Section 1, visions of regionalization which tend to federalism are not radical at the international level; they merely recreate an international society which is readily understood from the perspective of traditional realism. Viewing regionalization as a federalizing process also creates a major problem in the theory of international relations; the need to reconcile an idealist view of regionalism with a realist view of general international society. It creates discontinuities of theory.

At least consociationalism points to the possibility of new patterns of relations emerging between groupings of states, which are consistent with changing patterns of relations between those states, or the groups of which they are members, at the international level. This is in accordance with the modified version of Hobbesian realism which was discussed in the Introduction to Section 1.

Index

abortion 197
Ad Hoc Committee for Institutional Affairs
  56, 78
ad hoc conferences 126, 130, 133, 146
Adoninno Committee 54
Advisory Committee on Administrative and
  Budgetary Questions (ACABQ) 143,
  149–51, 153–4
Africa 27, 43–4, 196
Africa South of the Sahara 27, 28, 31
aggregation 134, 137–8
Agricultural Fund (EC) 103
agricultural intervention scheme 67
aid
  humanitarian 239–44
  regional 65
Aitken, J. 58
alliances 38, 39
Allison, G.T. 124
Almond, G. 82, 91
ambitions, statesmen's 31
Ameri, H. 126
America 27
  see also United States (US)
anti-internationalism 163–4
area dimension 15–16
Asia 27, 43–4, 196
Athens Summit (1983) 50
autonomy 87, 254

Baker, J. 212, 219, 223
banking 61
bankruptcy 71
banks, regional development 30
Beitz, C. 123
Benedick, D. 196–7
Bertrand, M. 11–12, 12–13, 18, 40, 124,
  126
Bertrand Reports
  on information supply (1984) 147
  on institutional arrangements (1985) 11,
    133–6, 147, 193
Birch, A.H. 92
blacks, in US 121
Blix, H. 233
boundaries and frontiers 62, 229–30, 250
Brandt Report (1983) 30, 116

British Aerospace 89–90
Brittan, L. 89–90, 92, 94
Bruges Group 80, 252
Bruges Speech (Thatcher 1988) 50, 75–6, 77
Brussels
  European Council Meeting (1984) 54
  Summit Agreement (1988) 65
Bubiyan Island 231
Buckley, J. 197
budgetary discipline
  in EC 65, 69–70
  in UN 70–3
Burton, J.W. 13
Bush, G. 211–12, 226
Butler, Sir M. 58

Calude, I.L. Jr.
'can-do' mentality 122
capital movements 61
capitalism, international 34
Carillo-Flores, A. 187, 193–4
Chalker, L. 238
chemical weapons 232, 233, 235
Cheysson, C. 51
China 196, 212, 214
Chirac, J. 69
citizenship rights 103
Claude, I. 42
co-decision-making 60
coalitions 38–9, 73–4, 93, 179–80
Coate, R.A. and Puchala, D.J. 164
cobweb analogy 40–2
Cold War 206
collectivity of states 252, 253
colonialism 32
Columbia 215
commerce 5
Committee of Eighteen Report (1986)
  147–52, 152–4, 154–6
Committee on Programme and Coordination
  (CPC) 127, 130, 135, 143–4
  budget decisions 163
  meetings (1987) 156–7
  role strengthening 152–3
  and UN budget reform 149–51,
    154–5
Committee of Regions 101, 106

Common Agricultural Policy (CAP) 50, 53, 66-7
Common Market 35
compensation 234-5
concessions
  Mrs Thatcher's 65-70
  on budgetary discipline 69-70
  on community budget 74
  on visible agenda 66-8
Conciliation Committee 100, 101
conferences
  environmental 123, 252-3
  on International Economic Cooperation (1976) 29
  population 181, 182, 184-95, 196-200
  see also special conferences
consensus voting 38, 82, 107, 156-7, 252
  building 88
  in CPC 155, 157
  in Gulf War 210
  over UN budget 163
consociationalism 3, 48, 81-4, 108, 252
  and federalism 84-92
  and symbiosis 92, 114-15
Consultative Committee on Substantive Questions (CCSQ) 134
consumer standards 122
contiguity 17-18
contributions 160-7, 175
  see also individual organizations
cooperation 94
  functional 84
  global pressures 113
  limits 116
  regional 11
  Security Council 174
Cooperative Procedure 99
coordination
  decisions 107
  organizations' work 15-16
Corbett, R. 60
costs 44
Cox, R.W. 8, 22
Crane, B.B. and Finkle, J.L. 193, 194
Cresson, E. 106
critical theory 22
Cross Operational Programme Analyses (COPAs) 130, 137, 146
cultural values 17, 41
currency 104

Dahrendorf, R. 81
debt crisis 29-30
decision-making 60
  about management and coordination 107
  about policy 107
  by consensus in CPC 155, 157, 163
  central lack in UN 144

and consociation 48, 87-9
Council of Ministers 57
and EC institutions 99-100
defence 38, 39
  economic 32-3
  policy 101
Delors, J. 76-7
Delors Plan 107
democracies, Anglo-American 82, 88, 91
dependency theory 11, 123
Desert Storm 243
detachment, national 92
Deutsch, K.D. 37
developing states, and population policy 191-2, 196
Development and International Economic Cooperation, Director-General appointment 127-8, 135, 142, 146
diplomacy 210-11
  British 50-5, 65-6, 66-7
  French 54
  Resolution 600 and 661 211-15
  Resolution 665 and 670 215-19
  Resolution 678 219-28
  Resolution 687 228-44
disarmament
  of Iraq 231-2, 243
  superpower 207-8
Dooge Committee 56, 64
duplication 134, 135, 136
Dutch Parliament 86

economic development, and fertility control 192-3
economic integration theory (Meade, Viner et al) 19-20
Economic and Social Council (ECOSOC) 126-7, 134-5, 136, 139
  reform 128-30, 146-7
  review 154
  see also Committee on Programme and Coordination (CPC)
economic union, and sovereignty 103-5
Ekeus, R. 232, 233
elites 3, 9-10, 33
  behaviour 83-4
  cartel of 48, 81-3, 85-6, 87-8, 93, 114
emissions control 63
emulation 30-1
England, D. 233
enterprise 76
environment 63-4, 103, 121-3
  conferences 123, 252-3
equalization 38
Europe 24-7, 75
Europe:The Future 51
Europe, Eastern 254
Europe without Frontiers 45, 57, 60

European Central Bank 77
European Coal and Steel Community (ECSC)
    21, 107
European Communities Act (1972) 96
European Community (EC) 17, 72, 80, 94
    advanced federalism 1
    budget 53
        British contributions 49–55
        imbalance 69, 71
    budgetary discipline 65, 69–70
    Commission 87–90
        Completing the Internal Market 57
    common defence idea 38
    constitutional arrangements 94, 95–9
    diplomatic agenda 65
    Directives non-compliance 100
    expansion 37
    integration 2–3, 5–6, 35–7
        in 1980s and early 1990s 49–79
    legal arrangements 94
    periphery states 14
    relevance to world 253–5
    sovereignty changes 252
    as trade freeing model 30
    two-tier system 35, 49, 55–6, 58, 63, 93
    see also Maastricht Agreement (1991)
European Council 88
    and foreign policy 100
    meetings 65
        Brussels (1984) 51, 54, 57–8, 65
        Fontainebleu (1984) 51
        Milan (1985) 57–8
European Court of Justice (ECJ) 96
European Monetary System (EMS) 63, 105
European Parliament 99–101, 105–6
European Space Agency 64
European Union 99
    Treaty 54, 55
external policy 43
external relations 101–2

Falklands War (1982) 205
family planning programmes 183
farm spending 65
Faure, M. 56
federalism 80, 84, 252, 255
    advanced 1
    and consociationalism 84–92
    definition 90
    and regionalism 108
    risks 93–4
fertility control 192–3
financial envelope 153–4
Finkle, J.L. and Crane, B.B. 193, 194
Fontainebleu, European Council Meeting
    (1984) 51
Food and Agriculture Organization (FAO)
    144, 159

financial crisis 166, 170–1, 172, 173–4
    reform 165, 170
food problems 123
foreign policy 93, 99, 100
fragmentation 134, 136–7
France 53, 54, 213
frontiers see boundaries and frontiers
functionalism 8, 15, 20–1, 40, 84
    cobweb analogy 40–2

Gahli, B.B. 128
Gang of Four 210
Gates, R. 226
Gaulle, C. de 106
Gille, H. 182
Gilpin, R. 34
Global Environment Conference (Brazil
    1992) 252–3
global organizations
    development 113–18
    growth 254–5
Gonzales, F. 67
Gorbachev, M. 212, 218
Gramm-Rudman Balanced Budget Act (1985)
    144, 164
Great Britain 8, 35, 74
    budgetary contributions to EC 49–55
    diplomacy 50–5, 65–6, 66–7
Green Parties 122
Group of 77 29, 30, 38
Group of Experts 125
    Report (1975) 146
Group of Four 227
Guardian, The 69
Gulf War (1991) 208–9, 209–48, 250–1

Haas, E.B. 9–10
Hammarskjold, D. 247
Hannay, Sir D. 228
Hazzard, S. 152
Heritage Foundation (US) 145, 163–4, 177,
    197
Hill, M. 127
Hobbes, T. 3–5, 180
Horizon 2000 project 64
Howe, Sir G. 58
humanitarian system 235–7, 239–41
Hurd, D. 62, 74–5
Hussein, S. 205, 208–9, 214, 229
    see also Gulf War

industry 64, 103
influence, sphere of 38
Inglehart, R. 122
institutions
    arrangements 106–7
        see also Bertrand Reports
    and decision-making 99–100

global 40
reform proposals 56-7
insurance services 61
integration 9
EC
in 1980s and early 1990s 49-79
increasing pressure 35-6
economic 19-20
regional 2-3, 5-6, 80-111
interdependence 2
interest group politics 121
intergovernmental organizations 27
International Atomic Energy Agency (IAEA) 231-2
International Committee of the Red Cross (ICRC) 240, 241
International Labour Organization (ILO) 143, 144, 156, 159
financial crisis 166, 168-70, 171-2, 173, 174
Governing Body 168, 169
Programme, Financial and Administrative Committee (PFAC) 168-9
International Monetary Fund (IMF) 29-30
International Organization of Migration 236, 240
International Population Conference (Mexico City 1984) 181, 182, 196-200
International Sea Authority 116
Iran-Iraq War 205
Iraq 208-9, 209-51
isolation, British 8, 74

Jackson Report (1969) 146
Jackson, Sir R. 241
Jacobson, H.K. 167-8
Jervis, R. 122
Joint Inspection Unit 120, 131, 133
Jonah, J. 247
judicial arrangements 100

Kassebaum Amendment (1985) 70, 144-5, 155-6, 159
Kassebaum, N. 144
Kay, D. 233
Kennedy, P. 225
Khan, Prince S. Aga 234, 237-8, 239, 241
Khor Abdullah waterway 230
knowledge-forming 124
Kohl, H. 49, 52-5, 54-5, 58-9
Kothari, R. 11
Krasner, S.D. 16, 31-2
Kurdish problem 228, 237, 242
Kuwait, Iraqi annexation of 208-9
Kuznets, S. 31

Labour Party 75
Latin America 196

law primacy, Community 95
Law of the Sea Convention 116
Le Monde 183, 234
League of Nations 247
Least Developed Countries (LDCs) 129
Lebanon 82
legislation 99-101
liberal pluralism 2, 253
Lijphart, A. 81, 82, 84, 90
Lipset, S.M. 84
Luard, E. 144
Lustick, I. 83
Luxembourg Accords (1966) 57, 88, 91, 97, 98, 107

Maastricht Agreement (1991) 40, 94, 95-9, 105-8
adjustments introduced in 99-101
common defence idea 38
constitutional implications 101-3
sovereignty and economic and monetary union 103-5
and subsidiarity 87
mad cow disease 88, 110
Major, J. 229
majority voting 82, 88, 91, 96-8
Malaysia 214-15
maldistribution 123
Maldive Islands 32
management 107
marginalization 114
markets, regional 31
Marks and Spencer syndrome 32-3, 44-5
Marshall Aid programme (1948-52) 33
Masters, R. 13, 39, 43
Meade, J. et al 31
Medium Term Plans (UN) 148, 153, 155, 167, 169, 172
Milan, European Council meeting (1985) 57-8
milieu goals 31-2
Military Staff Committee 218-19, 221, 222, 224, 245, 247
minorities 86, 87, 92
Mitrany, D. 8, 40, 41, 109, 125
ECSC support 21
Mitterand, F. 49-55, 56, 58-9, 77, 106
see also European Community (EC), two-tier system
monetary union 107
and sovereignty 103-5
multi-bloc model 13, 39, 42
Myrdal, G. 127

nation
definition 110
states 75-6
National Assemblies 96

nationalism 7, 92
neofunctionalism 9, 77, 84, 108
New Agenda 139
New International Economic Order (NIEO)
     189, 192–3, 200
   creation attempt (1974) 29
New World Order 244
Nichol, W. 69
1969 Group of Experts 183–4, 185–6
nongovernmental organizations 10
North Atlantic Treaty Organization (NATO)
     39, 217
Northern Ireland 86
nuclear energy 124
nuclear weapons 232, 233, 235
Nye, J.S. 10–11, 28, 31, 33, 34

Olson, M. 43
Ombudsman 101
Omelichev, Col-Gen. B. 224
one-world doctrine 7
operational world 123
organizations, international, total and
     regional memberships 24–7
Oubouzar, M. 193

P5 213, 213–14, 220, 244–5
parliaments, national 100
Parsons, Sir A. 222, 246
peace 244–8
peacekeeping force 230, 246–7
Pérez de Cuéllar, J. 205
performance criterion 20
personnel policies 151–2, 154
Peterson, M.J. 38
Pickering, T. 223
policy 43, 94, 102
   common 101
   decisions 107
   defence 101
   economic and monetary 105
   environment 103
   foreign 92, 99, 100
   payments 165
   personnel 151–2, 154
   population 181, 182–3, 187–8, 190–2,
     196–7, 200
   social 102–3
Political Union see Maastricht Agreement
     (1991)
population
   activities 182, 183
   control 181–204, 252
   movements 236–7, 238
   politization 198–95
   see also policy, population
post-acquisitive society (Inglehart) 122
power 4, 106

reserve 97, 98, 102
prediction 11–12
prescription 11–12
problem-solving 8, 22
problems
   global 123–4
     statist approach 179–80
productivity criteria 19
programmes 14–15
   and difficulties created 128–9
   integrated 16, 18
projects 14–15
proportionality 82
Puchala, D.J. and Coate, R.A. 164
puppeteer analogy 84

racial equality 121
rational process 15
Reagan, R. 145
realism 3–4, 6, 251
rebate, budget 69
refugees 236–7, 238–9
regime theory 2–3, 16–17, 34, 113–14
Regional Fund 103
regional organizations 10, 28–9, 31, 33
   growth 24–8, 43–4, 254–5
   nongovernmental 30
regionalism 1–2, 108, 253, 255
   concept 7–22
   definition 7–8
   encouragement pressures 33
   global 5–6
   practice 24–46
   separate islands of 34–5
   unfashionability 33–4
regionalization 255
relationship
   Anglo-American 217
   Franco-British 53
relief operations 238
reparations 234–5
repatriation 235
research and technology 102–3
reservation of functions 134, 135
Resolution 687 228–44
   Memorandum of Understanding 237–9,
     243
   reinforcing powers to inspect 232–3
resources
   own 67–8, 69
   in UN 143
revenue-raising 65
Rifkind, M. 56
rights, individual 101
riot control, global 243
Rocard, M. 106
Russett, B. 9, 10, 13–14

Salas, R. 184, 199–200
sanctions 215, 234
Sarkesian, S.C. 31, 32
satellites 247
Sauvy, A. 189
scales analogy 84
Scottish Nationalists 254
sectoralism 7–8, 21, 33, 193
    local 11, 29–33, 34, 253
security 3–5, 13, 32–3, 209
    economic 37–8
    future arrangement 244–8
    global 205–49
self-determination, national 91–2, 254
Senior United Nations Emergency Manager
    (SUNEM) 240
sensitivity 38
set-aide programme 67
Shevardnadze, E. 219–20
Shi'ite population 237, 239
Shultz, G. 175–6
Single European Act (1985) 72, 94, 97, 107
    character of 55
    and Cooperative Procedure 99
    negociations 58–65
Social Charter 85–6
Social Fund 103
Social Policy 102–3
social provision 86
sovereignty 1, 38, 80, 92, 94, 252
    changes in 251, 254
    and economic and monetary union 103–5
    and humanitarian intervention 242–3
    and Maastricht Agreement 95–6, 103–5
    protection 117
    and World Population Plan 189–90
Soviet Union, and Kuwait invasion 218–20
space, regional, dimensions of 14, 16,
    17–21, 19, 42
special conferences 119–25, 128, 130–2,
    138–9
    ad hoc conferences 126, 130, 133, 146
    advantages and disadvantages 132–3
    definition 120
    location 129–30
    population 181–4, 188
    reasons for calling 121–5
    special sessions 126, 132, 146
    in UN reform process 146
Specialized Agencies 8, 12, 16, 117, 118,
    124–5
    Administrative Committee for
        Coordination (ACC) 126–7, 134–5
    budget-making 167–71
    new 115
    problems in 115–16
    reforms 16, 156
'spill over' 35, 36

stability 82, 83
staffing 89, 172–4
standards 107, 132
    consumer 122
state
    -building 2, 6, 80, 108–9
    apparatus as umpire 88–9
    dissolution 2
Structural Funds 67–8, 86, 103, 110
subsidiarity 87, 98
superpowers 32, 206, 207–8
supranationalism 74, 190, 192
Switzerland 82
symbiosis 3, 50, 81, 108, 251–2
    and consociationalism 92, 114–15
    at global level 114
    state and region 36, 38, 50

Tarbah, L. 183, 190, 193
technology and research 102–3
Tennessee Valley Authority 21, 41
tensions 82, 87
territory dimensions 18–21
terrorism 62, 235
Thatcher, M. 50–5, 72, 73, 211
    Bruges speech 50, 75–6, 77
    image of Europe 75–6
    and Kuwait invasion 211, 223, 226
    negociations on SEA 58–77
    place in cartel 93
    rhetoric about EC partners 110
    social charter opposition 85–6
    see also concessions
Third World 29–30, 38
Thomson, Sir J. 212–13, 245
Thorne, C. 110
Tickel, Sir C. 226
Times, The 54, 58, 68
town and country planning 103
trade 30–1, 31
transport policy 102
Treaty of Friendship, Franco-German (1963)
    55
Treaty of Rome (1957) 94, 95, 106–7
Turkey 237

unanimity of votes 103, 107, 210
UNCTAD 29, 129, 135, 136
United Nations Development Programme
    (UNDP) 118, 134, 137, 146, 184, 188
United Nations Disaster Relief Organization
    (UNDRO) 236, 239–41
United Nations Fund For Population
    Activities (UNFPA) 184, 198–200, 201
United Nations High Commission for
    Refugees (UNHCR) 236
United Nations Humanitarian Centres
    (UNHUCs) 238–9

United Nations International Children's
    Emergency Fund (UNICEF) 236
United Nations Iraq–Kuwait Observation
    Mission (UNIKOM) 230–1
United Nations (UN)
    budget 142–3, 143–5, 163
        arrangements weaknesses 143, 148–52
        contributions
            scale reduction case 175–6
            shortfall 159–67
            voluntary 174–5
        expansion 144
        reform 149–51, 154–5
    budgetary discipline 70–3
    central arrangements 116
    development 12, 118
    financial pressures 159–78
    Funds and Programmes 115, 117, 118,
        128–9
    General Assembly 144
        Fifth Committee 155
    peace and security arrangements 144–8
    polycentric system 126, 131, 146–7
    Population Commission 185, 187
    and population questions 184
    reform 133, 142–58
        process 119–41, 146–8
    reorganization need 12–13
    Resolution 35/10C 131
    role
        in global security 205–49
        in Iraq implications 241–4
    Security Council 40, 114, 174
        change in work of 244–5
        EC external relations with 101–2
        Resolutions in Gulf War 209, 210,
            211–35, 237
        role 206–7, 208
        and sanctions against Iraq 215
    social and economic system 137–8, 139,
        152
    system failures 133–4
    voting power/financial power discrepancy
        142, 144–5, 156
    weaknesses 125–32
    see also diplomacy; Economic and Social
        Council (ECOSOC); Gulf War;
        Resolution 687; special conferences;
        Specialized Agencies
United States (US)
    at 1984 population conference 196–8
    blacks in 121
    budgetary deficit 164–5
    and budgetary discipline 70
    contributions
        to international organizations 160–7
        to UN 142–3, 163
            scale reduction case 175–6
            shortfall 144–5, 157, 159, 163
    intervention policy 32
    and Kuwait invasion 45, 221, 225
    reform strategy for UN 159–67
    see also Heritage Foundation; Kassebaum
        Amendment
Urquhart, B. 224

VAT 51–2, 62–3
veto action 82, 100
    decisions 87–8
    and majority voting 96–7
Viner, J. et al 31
visas, entry 103
vulnerability 38, 91

Wallace, W. 57
weighted voting 144–5
West European Union 38
Whitehead, J.C. 164
Williamson, R.S. 165, 167
World Bank 134
World Food Programme (WFP) 236, 239
World Health Organization (WHO) 144,
    159, 236
    effects of financial crisis 166, 167–8,
        171–2, 173, 174
    and population activities 184, 188
    Programme Committee 167–8
World Population Conference (Bucharest
    1974) 181, 184–95, 200
    achievements 195–6
World Population Plan of Action (WPPA)
    181, 188–96, 197–8
    Review and Appraisal 195

Yearbook of International Organizations 24,
    27
Yemen 215
Young, H. 65–6, 74
Young, O. 11

NOTTINGHAM UNIVERSITY LIBRARY